Lecture Notes in Computer Science 3283

Commenced Publication in 1973
Founding and Former Series Editors:
Gerhard Goos, Juris Hartmanis, and Jan van Leeuwen

Finn Arve Aagesen   Chutiporn Anutariya
Vilas Wuwongse (Eds.)

Intelligence in Communication Systems

IFIP International Conference, INTELLCOMM 2004
Bangkok, Thailand, November 23-26, 2004
Proceedings

 Springer

Volume Editors

Finn Arve Aagesen
Norwegian University of Science and Technology
Department of Telematics
7034 Trondheim-NTNU, Norway
E-mail: finnarve@item.ntnu.no

Chutiporn Anutariya
Shinawatra University
School of Information and Communication Technology
Computer Science Program
99 Moo 10, Bantoey, Samkok, Pathumthani 12160, Thailand
E-mail: chutiporn@shinawatra.ac.th

Vilas Wuwongse
Asian Institute of Technology
School of Advanced Technologies
Computer Science and Information Management Program
P.O. Box 4, Klong Luang, Pathumthani 12120, Thailand
E-mail: vw@cs.ait.ac.th

Library of Congress Control Number: 2004115151

CR Subject Classification (1998): H.4, H.5.1, H.3, C.2, I.2

ISSN 0302-9743
ISBN 3-540-23893-X Springer Berlin Heidelberg New York

Springer is a part of Springer Science+Business Media

springeronline.com

© 2004 IFIP International Federation for Information Processing, Hofstrasse 3, A-2361 Laxenburg, Austria
Printed in Germany

Typesetting: Camera-ready by author, data conversion by Scientific Publishing Services, Chennai, India
Printed on acid-free paper   SPIN: 11354406   06/3142   5 4 3 2 1 0

Preface

The 2004 IFIP International Conference on Intelligence in Communication Systems (INTELLCOMM 2004), held in Bangkok, Thailand, 23–26 November 2004, was the successor and an expansion of SMARTNET, a series of annual conferences on intelligence in networks held during 1995–2003 under the auspices of IFIP TC6's Working Group 6.7. The Internet and Web provide more connection facilities, hence the man-man, man-machine and machine-machine interactions will increase and communication will have an important role in modern systems. In order to obtain effective and efficient communication, artistic, social and technical issues have to be tackled in a holistic and integrated manner. However, communication techniques, concepts and solutions which have been developed so far treat these issues separately, so that there arises a need for communication researchers and practitioners in different fields (engineering, science and arts) to meet, share their experience and explore all possibilities of developing integrated and advanced solutions which incorporate ideas from such disciplines as communication arts, art design, linguistics, Web technologies, computer system architecture and protocols, computer science and artificial intelligence.

INTELLCOMM 2004 was jointly sponsored by IFIP WG 6.7: Smart Networks and WG 6.4: Internet Applications Engineering and aimed to provide an international forum which brings academia, researchers, practitioners and service providers together. The discussion areas covered the latest research topics and advanced technological solutions in the area of intelligence in communication systems, ranging from architectures for adaptable networks/services and Semantic Web/Web services technologies to intelligent service application interface and intelligent human interaction.

INTELLCOMM 2004 received 112 paper submissions from 28 countries. From these, 24 were accepted, and are included in this proceedings. There were also 3 papers accepted for poster presentation, published separately. The technical program comprised one day of tutorials, followed by keynote speech, paper and poster sessions.

The tutorial sessions were arranged with the topics: "Intelligence in Communication Systems: Evolution, Trends and Business Opportunities," "Open Mobile Services," "QoS and Security in the Embedded Internet," "Metadata Development" and "Ontology Engineering".

The speakers and topics of the five keynote sessions were: Dr. Reda Reda from Siemens AG in Germany: "Intelligence in Communication Systems, the Business Point of View," Prof. Toyoaki Nishida from the University of Tokyo in Japan: "Conversational Knowledge Process for Social Intelligence Design," Prof. Guy Pujolle from the University of Paris in France: "Smart Router and Intelligent Protocol," Prof. Dieter Fensel from the University of Innsbruck in Austria: "Triple-Space Computing: Semantic Web Services Based on Persistent Publication of Information," and Prof. Lill Kristiansen from the Norwegian University of Science and Technologies in Norway: "Mobility and Intelligence in Telecom: How and Where to Handle It?" The materials of the keynote speeches are also included in this volume.

The eight technical paper sessions were arranged on: "QoS and Security," "Intelligent Communication Systems with NLP," "QoS," "Location and Context-Aware Services," "Protocol and Application Architecture," "Semantic Web and Service Architecture," "Adaptability Architecture" and "Network and Mobility Management."

Many people contributed to the organization of this conference. We thank the members of the Program Committee for their continuous advice and help in reviewing and selecting papers. We would also like to thank IFIP TC6 and the corporate patrons for their support of this conference. Finally, we would like to express our gratitude to the Organizing Committee Advisor Dr. Manoo Ordeedolchest and the Organizing Committee for their excellent work.

November 2004

Finn Arve Aagesen
Chutiporn Anutariya
Vilas Wuwongse

Organization

Program Committee Co-chair

Finn Arve Aagesen (Norwegian University of Science and Technology, Norway)
Chutiporn Anutariya (Shinawatra University, Thailand)
Vilas Wuwongse (Asian Institute of Technology, Thailand)

Program Committee

Sebastian Abeck (University of Karlsruhe, Germany)
Kiyoshi Akama (Hokkaido University, Japan)
Harold Boley (National Research Council of Canada, Canada)
Raouf Boutaba (Waterloo University, Canada)
Tru Hoang Cao (Ho Chi Minh City University of Technology, Vietnam)
Nigel Collier (National Institue of Informatics, Japan)
Phan Minh Dung (Asian Institute of Technology, Thailand)
Tapio Erke (Asian Institute of Technology, Thailand)
Dieter Fensel (University of Innsbruck, Austria)
Dominique Gaïti (Technical University of Troyes, France)
Arun Iyengar (IBM Research, USA)
Guy Leduc (University of Liège, Belgium)
Olli Martikainen (University of Oulu, Finland)
Lorne G. Mason (McGill University, Canada)
Riichiro Mizoguchi (Osaka University, Japan)
Elie Najm (ENST Paris, France)
Ekawit Nantajeewarawat (Thamasat University, Thailand)
Bernhard Plattner (ETH Zürich, Switzerland)
Ana Pont-Sanjuan (Polytechnic University of Valencia, Spain)
Aiko Pras (University of Twente, The Netherlands)
Guy Pujolle (Laboratoire LIP6, France)
Reda Reda (Siemens AG, Austria)
Ramakoti Sadananda (Asian Institute of Technology, Thailand)
Tadao Saito (University of Tokyo, Japan)
Awnashilal B. Sharma (Asian Institute of Technology, Thailand)
Marcin Solarski (Fraunhofer FOKUS, Germany)
Virach Sornlertlamvanich (NECTEC, Thailand)
Otto Spaniol (RWTH Aachen University, Germany)
James P.G. Sterbenz (BBN Technologies, USA)
Said Tabet (Nisus Inc., USA)
Do van Thanh (NTNU, Norway)
Samir Tohme (ENST Paris, France)

Anne-Marie Vercoustre (CSIRO Mathematical and Information Sciences, Australia)
Naoki Wakamiya (Osaka University, Japan)

Additional Reviewers

Thomas Becker (Fraunhofer Institute FOKUS, Germany)
Elisa Boschi (Fraunhofer Institute FOKUS, Germany)
Ranganai Chaparadza (GMD FOKUS, Germany)
Jose Gil-Salinas (Polytechnic University of Valencia, Spain)
Bjanre E. Helvik (NTNU, Norway)
Jan Henke (University of Innsbruck, Austria)
Michael Kleis (Fraunhofer Institute FOKUS, Germany)
Svein Knapskog (NTNU, Norway)
Jacek Kopecky (Digital Enterprise Research Institute, Austria)
Stig Frode Mjoelsnes (NTNU, Norway)
Livia Predoiu (Digital Enterprise Research Institute, Austria)
Mario Schuster (Fraunhofer FOKUS, Germany)
Norvald Stol (NTNU, Norway)
Amund Tveit (NTNU, Norway)
Otto Wittner (NTNU, Norway)

Organizing Committee Advisor

Manoo Ordeedolchest (Software Industry Promotion Agency, Thailand)

Organizing Committee Chair

Vilas Wuwongse (Asian Institute of Technology, Thailand)

Organizing Committee

Chindakorn Tuchinda (Ericsson, Thailand)
Pojanan Ratanajaipan (Shinawatra University, Thailand)
Rachanee Ungrangsi (Shinawatra University, Thailand)

Sponsors

IFIP WG 6.7: Smart Networks
IFIP WG 6.4: Internet Applications Engineering

Corporate Patrons

Platinum

- TOT Corporation Public Company Limited, Thailand

Gold

- CAT Telecom Public Company Limited, Thailand
- Ericsson (Thailand) Ltd.
- National Electronics and Computer Technology Center (NECTEC), Thailand

Silver

- Advance Info Service Public Company Limited (AIS), Thailand
- Hewlett-Packard (Thailand) Ltd., Thailand
- Software Industry Promotion Agency (SIPA), Thailand
- Thai Airways International Public Company Limited, Thailand
- Total Access Communication Public Company Limited (DTAC), Thailand

Platinum Corporate Patron

Gold Corporate Patrons

Silver Corporate Patrons

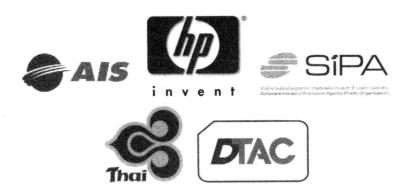

Table of Contents

Keynote Speech

QoS and Security

Intelligent Communication System with NLP

QoS

Location and Context Aware Services

Protocol and Application Architecture

Semantic Web and Service Architecture

Adaptability Architecture

Network and Mobility Management

Intelligence in Communication Systems
Evolution, Trends and Business Opportunities

Reda Reda

Information Communication Networks ICN
Marketing, Siemens AG, Germany
Tel. +43 676 4915503
reda.reda@siemens.com

Abstract. This paper reports the findings of recent studies on the impact of intelligence in modern/future-oriented telecom networks. The ICT/ telecommunication market evolution and future trends are presented. Subsequently, the business opportunities are also discussed. The main drivers for the evolution as well as market success are mobility, security, and intelligence in the network.

Though the global economy is still far from recovery, analysts expect the world telecom market in 2004 to exceed 1,000 billion Euros, with an impressive annual growth rate of between 3% and 4%

Current security threats and security fiascos reveal the fact that, in spite all innovative and advanced security solutions offered by renowned companies, the security market is still quite promising. There are big business opportunities for mature solutions involving intrusion detection systems, fire walls, antivirus systems, encryption and secure mobility.

The evolution towards mobility is currently passing from third-generation to fourth-generation, milli-wave lAN and HAPS solutions in the next decade. Considering the technological evolution and the current trends, the telecommunication market will present excellent opportunities for intelligent solutions and products that provide maximum bandwidth with optimal mobility, convergence between mobile and fixed networks, connectivity on demand, and finally build, transfer, optimize, manage and operate the network.

1 Introduction

The ICT market represents almost 39% of the total world electronics market. 55% of which are generated by the telecommunication industry. Thus the telecom business is the main driving force for progress of the electronics industry and subsequently for the global economical and technological progress. This paper will report on the impact of intelligence in modern/future-oriented telecom networks, and technological trends, subsequently, the business opportunities are discussed.

A. Aagesen et al. (Eds.): INTELLCOMM 2004, LNCS 3283, pp. 1–15, 2004.

2 ICT Market

The development and growth of the Information and Communication Technology (ICT) market over the recent years has been exceptional, perhaps even unique in the history of industrial change, despite the global economical disaster, and despite the political instability.

While the markets in Europe are still struggling with the aftermath of the global economic downturn, the US economy is showing strong signs of recovery.

2.1 Development of the ICT World Market

The ICT world market in 2003 exceeded the magic 2.000 Billion-Euro mark, with a quite impressing unexpected annual growth rate of 1.4 % as follows:

+ 1.2 % for Europe,
    0 % for USA,
− 0.8 % for Japan and
+ 4.8 % for Rest of the World (RoW).

For 2004, the annual growth rate of ICT world market is expected even to exceed the value of 3%. (3%-4%).

Considering the split out of the ICT market, the telecom market resembles more than 55% of the ICT market, whereas the IT is less than 45% (see Fig. 1).

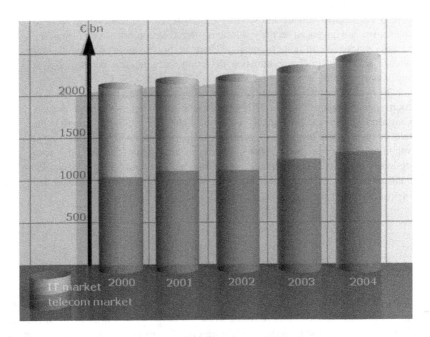

Fig. 1. Worldwide ICT Market. Growth (2000–2004)

2.2 World Telecommunication Market by Region

The current analysis considered the breakdown approach Europe, USA, Japan and RoW to take into account the mutual influence of the €, $, and the Yen.

In 2003, the worldwide communication market showed the following breakdown:

Europe	29.2 %
USA	24.5 %
Japan	12.3 %
RoW	34 %

The expected growth rates in 2004 are:

Europe	3.0 % (promising because it include eastern Europe)
USA	–0.6 %
Japan	–1.1 %
RoW	5.9 % (very promising)
Total average growth rate	2.5 %

This analysis gives a good impression, where to have a good business opportunity in the telecom world.

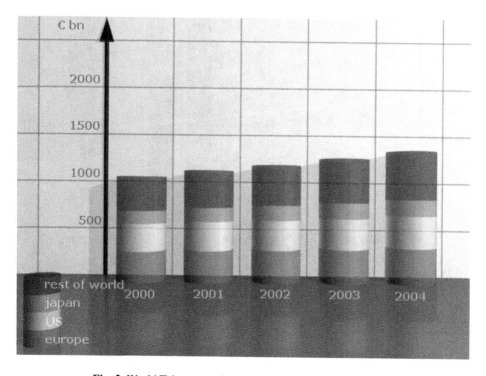

Fig. 2. World Telecommunication Market by Region (2000–2004)

2.3 ICT Market in Selected European Countries

The following table displays the total national Telecom Market achieved in 2003 for some selected European countries. The annual growth rate was within the range 1.5 in Greece and 3.2 % in the UK. (see in Figure 3).

Austria: € 7.3 B
Belgium: € 9 2 B
France: € 39.5 B
Italy: € 41.1 B
Denmark: € 5.8 B
Greece: € 5.6 B
Netherlands: € 15 B
Switzerland: € 9.1B
Sweden: € 9.9 B
United Kingdom: € 57.4 B

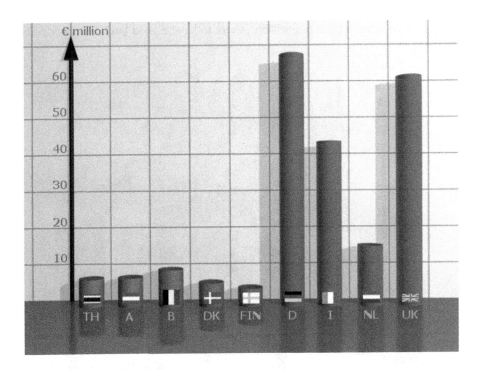

Fig. 3. ICT Market in Selected European Countries (2003) together with the conference host

2.4 Telecommunication Market in Thailand

Asia is the world's largest ICT market as well as boasting the world's fastest growing economy. Thailand, the host of INTELLCOM o4 has one of the most promising markets in Asia. Thailand's ICT market in 2003 was about $1.4 billion and is expected to grow by 12-15% over the near term. Fast-changing technology, competitive prices and the entry of new strong financial players have intensified the competition in Thailand's telecommunications market. The growth rate of fixed line telephones is relatively slow at 5-7 percent due to high acquisition costs. On the other hand, the mobile phone growth rate is incredible. The penetration rate expanded from 18 percent in early 2002 to 22 percent, or 18.5 million subscribers at the end of the year. Monthly fee cutting and value-added services such as higher data speed technologies, multimedia capabilities and short-message-services are the most important of today's sales strategies. Even though Thailand is not leading in implementing new technologies, the country has followed developed market trends on wireless technologies from analog to digital, then WAP to broadband.

Thailand's Internet usage has grown tremendously, by approximately 20-30% year-on-year, with 3.5 million users at the end of 2002. Wireless Hot Spots are a new trend and are increasingly being deployed in business areas, commercial buildings, shopping malls, and airports. Although the opportunity for ICT equipment and services shows solid growth, the barrier for new entrants is the delay in the establishment of independent regulators in the form of a National Telecommunication Commission (NTC) and National Broadcasting Commission (NBC), as licensing and spectrum allocation is on hold until this is completed. Once established, however, these two agencies will play an important role in Thailand's communication and broadcasting sector. Best prospects for Thailand's ICT market include 2.5-3G services, high-speed Internet, wireless hot spots, e-procurement, e-government, and e-education systems.

The following table presents the highlight parameters for Thailand in a comparison with Austria.

Table 1. Thailand and Austria at a Glance (2003)

	Population (Million)	Area (Million sq. Km.)	GDP (Billion $)	Tel. Main Lines (Millions)	Tel. Mobile (Millions)	Internet Users (Millions)
Austria	8	84	245	4	6.4	3.3
Thailand	65	514	476	4.5	16	4.8

3 Security

3.1 ICT Security Market

Inspite all innovative and advanced security solutions offered by renowned companies, security disasters at the international level are no more controllable. The current security threats and security fiascos get no end, from the famous worm "Sassa" to intrusion of the NASA, Visa, Microsoft, FBI, NSA and Pentagon servers, to discard whole telecommunication networks .

Thus security issue is getting more and more importance in every business aspect, especially telecommunication. With the growing use of voice and data communication to transfer sensitive corporate information, and global use of the Internet as a data and information highway, it is now essential for companies, organizations and public authorities to realize security strategies. In all considerations about security, it is essential to take into account the magic CIA triad – Confidentiality, Integrity and Availability – the key factors of each security solution.

Though the ever-lasting global economical disaster, a continuous increase in the ICT market is expected. From one side the current security threats act as motivation to spend and increase security budget, from the other side, ICT industry, especially communication companies, will do everything to avoid more security fiascos, which would mean, end of business.

An illustrative example is security market in Western Europe. In 2002, ICT security spending was some € 9.6 billion. This number increased rapidly to € 12.1 billion, and expected to exceed € 15 billion this year (2004). Almost 34 % is spent internally and the remaining is spent externally.

With the increasing awareness and pressure to introduce and improve ICT security, total European ICT security spending is expected to rise to around € 19 billion by 2005 with external spending growing to around € 12.5 billion.

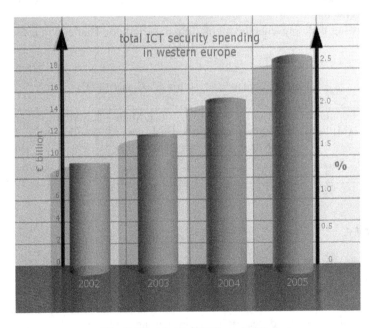

Fig. 4. Worldwide ICT Security Market

3.2 ICT Security Solutions Spending

The strong desire for the base level of protection that firewall and anti-virus solutions provide means that penetration rates of these technologies are high end users. Also recognize that intrusion detection and vulnerability assessment solutions can increase the protection levels offered by firewalls and anti-virus and have also looked to solutions that increase employee productivity and free up valuable bandwidth, such as URL filtering.

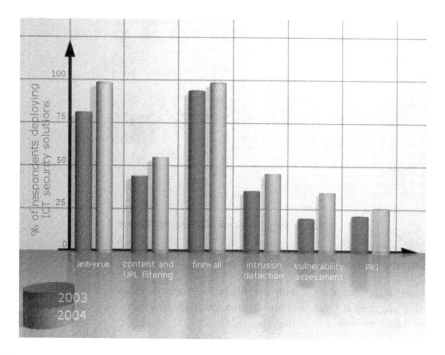

Fig. 5. Percentage of respondents deploying ICT security solutions worldwide. Comparing these percentages in 2002 & 2003 respectively, it is clear that the anti-virus detection solutions, firewall and intrusion detection solutions are gaining a continuous increasing value

3.3 Key Facts in ICT Security Market

In 2002, the ICT industry in Western Europe spent over € 3.7 billion on leading security solutions. The main categories were firewall, antivirus and ID management for wire-line and wireless networks.

In 2003, this number increased with 30%, and it is expected to increase to € 7.7 billion in 2005.

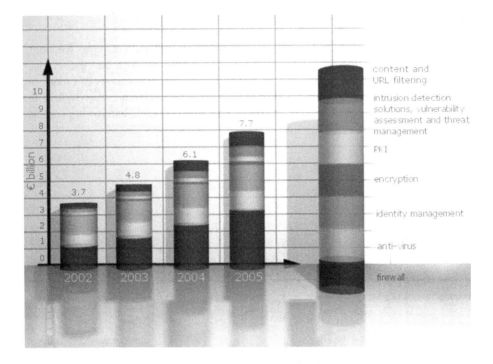

Fig. 6. Split-Out of the ICT Security Market

3.4 Driving Potentials and Security Trends

The main factors acting as driving potentials for security market and its technological evolution are: Legacy, national and international security from one side, and hacker, cracker, black hat world from the other side.

The most technological evolution progress is detected within the following sectors:

Physical Security which deals with controlling access to the most sensitive system resources, such as administration computers, servers, and routers. If unauthorized people access critical resources, all additional software and hardware security procedures are useless. Smart Card is e very good example.

Intrusion Detection Systems (IDS) are commonly implemented as distributed systems. A set of detection devices is positioned in critical points of the private network and a central device collects reports from detection devices and signals possible attacks to the administrators.

Encryption: Two basic types of encryption systems are defined depending on how keys are managed, that is, the private-key and the public-key systems. Recently, security companies presented "new" techniques in Cryptography. Here are two examples:

- Quantum cryptography provides a way to communicate with complete security over an insecure channel such as an unguarded optical fiber. The security is guaranteed by the fundamental quantum properties of light rather than by computational complexity or physical barriers to interception
- Hardware supported encryption. (Already available commercially) there are components, especially designed for online applications that allow IPsec (Internet Protocol Security) for VPN Connections and SSL (Secure Sockets Layer) transactions.

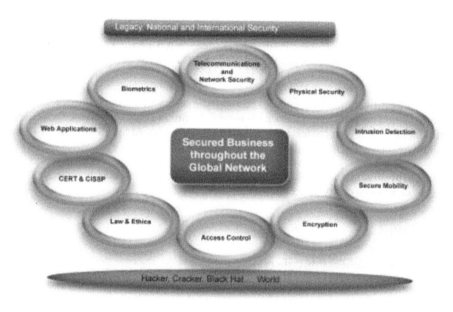

Fig. 7. Driving Potentials and Security Technological Trends

Biometrics are security techniques for recognizing a person based on a physiological or behavioral characteristic. Some of the features measured: face, fingerprints, hand geometry, handwriting, iris, retinal, vein, and voice. Biometric technologies are becoming the foundation of an extensive array of highly secure identification and personal verification solutions. As the level of security breaches and transaction fraud increases, the need for highly secure identification and personal verification technologies is becoming apparent. Several companies are providing advanced biometrics-based solutions like ID Mouse, ID Center and ID Modules solutions.

Telecommunications and Network Security: This is one of the key issues for the success of a Next Generation Network. The business trend will be more and more advanced security solutions to support emerging web applications like e-commerce, m-business, multimedia entertainment/ edutainment, emergency and critical ad-hoc networking applications and. location based application and services. IP tunneling and IPSec are expected to play big roles: IP tunneling achieves this objective by encapsulating, at the boundary between the private and the public Network. IPSec establishes a logical connection, between source and destination. The Security Association (SA), specifies security parameters configuring authentication and encryption. Several types of encryption can be selected through IPSec, such as Triple DES, RC5, IDEA, CAST and Blowfish. IPSec can work in tunnel mode and, therefore, can be used to build virtual private networks over the public internet. Considering the current global political instabilities, it is expected that a product or solution providing reliable administration and execution of Lawful Interception in the network. Note that in many national and upcoming international laws, providers of telecommunication networks are obliged to allow or perform lawful interception.

CERT ® Coordination Center is an American research and development centre of Internet security expertise, federally funded. CERT (www.cert.org) offers a wide range of valuable information related to Internet security.

CISSP ® Certification is designed to recognize mastery of an international standard for information security and understanding of a Common Body of Knowledge (CBK). Certification enhances a professional's career and provides added IS credibility to the company/team. (www.isc2.org).

Secure Mobility including innovative solutions for wireless end to end security, W-LAN security, security of mobile devices, etc.

4 Mobility

4.1 Market of Mobile Subscribers

The mobility of the global personal communications and the increasing demand of seamless coverage and multimedia integrated services is getting more and more urgent and important, on one hand, wideband/broadband wireless communications have very bright business perspective, on the other hand, world's huge market potential should be the source- driving force for the technical evolution and advance of this sector.

Mobility is the magic formula for every successful ICT future business. This fact is demonstrated by the development of number of GSM subscribers worldwide. It exceeded the one billion mark already in 2002, and still growing up. Fig. 8 displays the progress and forecast of the worldwide mobile subscribers from 2002 through 2007. Based on strong growth in Asia and Latin America this number will exceed even the 2 billion mark In 3 years.

Overall, it is estimated that there will be 1.6 billion mobile communications subscribers around the globe by year-end 2004, of which nearly 750 million, or 44% of the total, will be in the Asia Pacific Region. Between 2004 and 2009, we expect total mobile subscribers to increase at a compound annual growth rate (CAGR) of 8.5%, topping 2.5 billion subscribers by year-end 2009. The number of mobile subscribers will top the 2 billion mark sometime in the latter half of 2005.

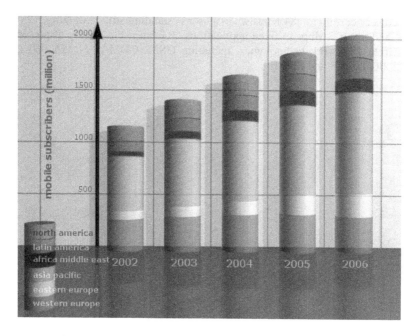

Fig. 8. Development of the Global Mobile Subscribers (2002–2006)

From the business point of view, this reveals the fact that mobility is a fruitful future business with promising business opportunities.

4.2 Technological Evolution of Mobility

The two main factors governing the telecommunication business are: the never ending demand on more and more bandwidth and the increasing demand on more mobility. These two factors are inversely affecting each other i.e. the more mobility, the less bandwidth. The evolution of the wireless technology can be summarized as follows:

Mobility evolution is currently going through third generation towards fourth generation, Milli-wave lAN and HAPS solutions next 2 decades. Telecommunication market will present excellent opportunities to intelligent solutions and products that provide maximum bandwidth with optimal mobility, convergence between mobile and fixed networks, Networks on demand, and finally build transfer, optimize, manage and operate the network.

The evolution began with 1G (Analogue cellular), This was followed by 2G (also known as (PCS) Personal Communications Services) which converts voice to digital data for transmission over the air and then back to voice. Subsequent technology is the 2.5G networks with GPRS or 1xRTT which changed existing wireless networks to a packet-switched service, thus increasing data transmission speeds. Most carriers moved to this wireless technology before making the upgrade to 3G. Finally came the 3G which combines high-speed mobile access with Internet Protocol

(IP) based services, up to 384 Kbps when a user is standing still or walking, 128 Kbps in a car, and up to 2 Mbps in fixed applications. 3G can use a variety of present and future wireless network technologies, including GSM, CDMA, TDMA, WCDMA, CDMA2000, UMTS and EDGE.

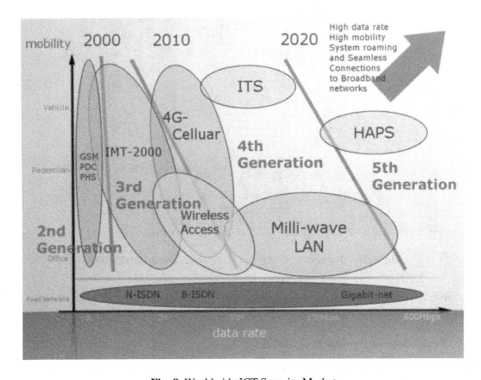

Fig. 9. Worldwide ICT Security Market

The **4G** is expected to come next decade with the following motivations:

- Support interactive multimedia services: teleconferencing, wireless Internet, etc.
- Wider bandwidths, higher bit rates.
- Global mobility and service portability.
- Low cost.
- Scalability of mobile networks and
- Back to Top.

Expected characteristics of 4G are:

- Entirely packet-switched networks.
- All network elements are digital.
- Higher bandwidths to provide multimedia services at lower cost (up to 100Mbps).

5 Technological Trends and Business Opportunities

The development and growth of the Information and Communication Technology market over the recent years has been exceptional, perhaps even unique in the history of industrial change, despite the global economical disaster, and despite the political instability. While the markets in Europe are still struggling with the aftermath of the global economic downturn, the US economy is showing strong signs of recovery.

Despite the instability of the financial markets and despite the global political instability, every single day we get successes stories of telecom industries in the headlines:

Some of the recent headlines:

xx1 networks to buy xx2 for £255M .

xx3 to rename itself xx4- Communications once deal (1,4 B $) completed.

xx5 Telco expresses interest in partnering with xx6 PTT .

Global wireless users set to exceed 1.75Bn in 2007 – xx7:number of users worldwide set to grow 9% by 2007.

xx8 buys xx9 for $800M IN Stock .

Profits at xx10, beat forecasts.

(xx: stays for name of different companies)

The Big Question is now is: who still has money?, who is still ready to spend, and what for?

According to recent studies, the market in a number of regions, still offer business opportunities to the telecom industry These regions include: Eastern Europe, Far east, especially China and some of the third world countries.

The enlargement of the European Union is expected to have an important impact on the European ICT markets. ICT investment in the Acceding Countries is still below the EU average, and it will take some years to reach the IT penetration and spending levels characteristic for most countries in Western Europe. However, From the business/technological point of view, innovation is without doubt the main success driver. Innovation is seen as "the creation of new products or services which impact the Return On Investment (ROI) at a short range base. Thus we consider the possible areas where innovation is still required, or themes, which are not jet mature enough, these are (globally): Security, Performance, Mobility, Bandwidth and Consumer Oriented Web-Applications e.g.

- Advanced technique to allow for high performance delivering VoD. Service and huge data streams multicast.
- Providing precise timing and location information, think about a higher speed physical layer.
- Dynamic and efficient service systems taking into account. On the one hand, the continuous varying availability of the resources, on the other hand the fact that the resources are increasingly configurable, extendable, and replaceable.
- Employing artificial intelligence to resolve and handle complex problems and optimising performance dynamics of the telecommunication networks.
- Interface control and management of mobile ad hoc networks.
- Mobile computing and the architecture of mobile distributed virtual memory.

- Platform for web-based architecture providing common services for mobile as well as stationary access.
- Emerging technology concerning service-oriented database management system (DBMS) that provides a flexible and loosely-coupled model for distributed computing.
- Bandwidth research.
- Active/ad hoc networks.
- Intelligent human interaction.
- Smart, flexible and easy to configure web services.

6 Conclusion

The Information and Communication Technology is slowly recovering, however, the Telecommunication world provide a market full of opportunities. This paper reported on the impact of intelligence in modern/future-oriented telecom networks. The ICT/Telecommunication market evolution and future trends were presented. Subsequently, the business opportunities were discussed. The main drivers for the evolution as well as market success are mobility, security, and intelligence in the network.

References

Literature

[1] European Information Technology Observatory, 2004.
[2] Pictures of the Future, , ISSN 1618.5498 , Siemens AG, Spring 2004.
[3] Innovationen Versprechen an die Zukunft, Thomas Ganswindet, Hofmann Undcampe Verlag, ISBN 3-455-09451-1, 2004 (in German)
[4] Quantum Cryptography, Brendan, University of Cape, Town, Department of Computer Science, 21 March 2004 (http://people.cs.uct.ac.za/~bfry/Work/Security/ BFRY_Security _Essay.pdf)
[5] "Quantum   Theory,"   Microsoft®   Encarta®   Online   Encyclopedia   2004 (http://encarta.msn.com © 2004 Microsoft Corporation. All Rights Reserved)
[6] The Innovation Dilemma, When New Technologies Cause Great Firms to Fail Clayton M. Christensen, Michael E. Raynor today! Publisher: Harvard Business School Press, ISBN: 75845851)

Internet References

3GPP home page: http://www.3GPP.org
Datamonitor: http://www.datamonitor.com/
European Information Technology Observatory: http://www.eito.com/
Financial Times: http://news.ft.com/
Forester Communications: http://www.forester.net/
Gartner Group http://www4.gartner.com/
Global Internet Project: http://www.gip.org/
IEEE: http://www.ieee.org/

IEEE Communications Society: http://www.comsoc.org/
International Data Corporation: http://www.idc.com/
International Engineering Society: http://www.iec.org/
International Softswitch Consortium: http://www.softswitch.org/
Internet Society: http://www.isoc.org/
Internet Surveys: http://www.nua.com/
InterPlanetary Network Special Interest Group: http://ipnsig.org/
Mobile Wireless Internet Forum (MWIF), http://www.mwif.org/
Next Generation Internet: http://www.ngi.gov/
OVUM: http://www.ovum.com/
Smau Italy: http://www.smau.it/
The CIA World Fact Book: http://www.odci.gov/cia/publications/factbook/

Intelligent Routers and Smart Protocols

Guy Pujolle[1] and Dominique Gaïti[2]

[1] LIP6, University of Paris 6, 75015 Paris, France
Guy.Pujolle@lip6.fr
[2] UTT, 12 rue Marie Curie, 10000 Troyes, France
Dominique.Gaiti@utt.fr

Abstract. IP networks are now well established. However, control, management and optimization schemes are provided in a static and basic way. Network control and management with intelligent software agents offers a new way to master quality of service, security and mobility management. This new paradigm allows a dynamic and intelligent control of the equipment in a local manner, a global network control in a cooperative manner, a more autonomous network management, and a better guaranty of all important functionalities like end to end quality of service and security. In this paper we provide an illustration of such a paradigm through a testbed of an architecture based on intelligent routers and smart protocols. This Goal-Based Networking (GBN) architecture, using adaptable protocols named STP/SP (Smart Transport Protocol/Smart Protocol), is able to optimize the communications through the networks. Finally, we discuss the pros and cons of this new architecture.

1 Introduction

The popularity of the Internet has caused the traffic on the Internet to grow drastically every year for the last several years. It has also spurred the emergence of the quality of service (QoS) for Internet Protocol (IP) to support multimedia application like ToIP. To sustain growth, the IP world needs to provide new technologies for guarantying quality of service. Integrated services and differentiated services have been normalized to support multimedia applications. The routers in the IP networks play a critical role in providing these services. The demand of QOS on private enterprise networks has also been growing rapidly. These networks face significant bandwidth challenges as new application types, especially desktop applications uniting voice, video, and data traffic need to be delivered on the network infrastructure. This growth in IP traffic is beginning to stress the traditional software and hardware-based design of current-day routers and as a result has created new challenges for router design.

To achieve high-throughput and quality of service, high-performance software and hardware together with large memories were required. Fortunately, many changes in technology (both networking and silicon) have changed the landscape for implementing high-speed routers. However, scalability problems were discovered with InterServ technologies and statistical problems with DiffServ. Moreover, these technologies are rather complicated to size and we assist to important configuration problems that need specialized engineers.

A. Aagesen et al. (Eds.): INTELLCOMM 2004, LNCS 3283, pp. 16–27, 2004.
© IFIP International Federation for Information Processing 2004

This paper proposes a new paradigm for providing a smart networking technique allowing a real time network configuration. Indeed, we propose to introduce intelligent routers able to configure themselves depending on the state of the network and to define a new generation of smart protocols.

The rest of the paper is organized as follows. First we introduce the smart networking paradigm and the implication on the routers. Then, we introduce a new protocol stack, the STP/SP model, followed by the description of the smart architecture (Goal Based Networking architecture) to support the deployment of the intelligent routers and the STP/SP model. Finally, we present an analysis of this architecture and we conclude this work.

2 Smart Networking and Intelligent Routers

As user needs are becoming increasingly various, demanding and customized, IP networks and more generally telecommunication networks have to evolve in order to satisfy these requirements. That is, a network has to integrate more quality of service, mobility, dynamicity, service adaptation, etc. This evolution will make users satisfied, but it will surely create more complexity in the network generating difficulties in the control process.

Since there is no control mechanism which gives optimal performance whatever the network conditions are, we argue that an adaptive and dynamic selection of control mechanisms, taking into account the current traffic situation, is able to optimize the network resources uses and to come up to a more important number of user expectations associated with QoS. To realize such functionalities, it is necessary to be able to configure automatically the network in real time. Therefore, all the routers must be able to react to any kind of change in the network. Different techniques could be applied but as the most difficult moment is congestion, the technique has to be autonomic and routers have to turn into intelligent routers.

Due to these different issues, a multi-agent approach is the solution. In fact, agents own some features like autonomy, proactivity, cooperation, etc. predisposing them to operate actively in a dynamic environment like IP networks. Agents, by consulting their local knowledge and by taking into consideration the limited available information they possess about their neighbors, select the most relevant management mechanisms to the current situation.

A multi-agent system is composed of a set of agents which solve problems that are beyond their individual capabilities [1]. Multi-agent systems have proven their reliability when being used in numerous areas like: (1) the road traffic control ([2], [3]); (2) biologic phenomena simulation like the study of eco-systems [4] or the study of ant-colonies [5], for example; (3) social phenomena simulation like the study of consumer behaviors in a competitive market [6]; (4) industrial applications like the control of electrical power distribution systems, the negotiation of brands, etc. By its nature, multi-agent approach is well suited to control distributed systems. IP networks are good examples of such distributed systems. This explains partly the considerable contribution of agent technology when introduced in this area. The aim was mainly to solve a particular problem or a set of problems in networks like: the discovery of topology in a dynamic network by mobile agents ([7], [8]), the optimization of routing process in a constellation of satellites [9], the fault location by ant agents [10], and even the maximization of channel assignment in a cellular network [11].

Our approach consists in integrating agents in the different routers. These agents optimize the network QoS parameters (delay, jitter, loss percentage of a class of traffic, etc.), by adapting the activated control mechanisms in order to better fit the traffic nature and volume, and the user profiles. Agents may be reactive, cognitive or hybrid [1], [4], [12]. Reactive agents are suitable for situations where we need less treatment and faster actions. Cognitive agents, on the other side, allow making decisions and planning based on deliberations taking into account the knowledge of the agent about itself and the others. A hybrid agent is composed of several concurrent layers. In INTERRAP [13], for example, three layers are present: a reactive layer, a local planning layer, and a cooperative layer. The approach we propose is different. In fact, every node has one cognitive agent that supervises, monitors, and manages a set of reactive agents. Each reactive agent has a specific functioning realizing a given task (queue control, scheduling, dropping, metering, etc.) and aiming to optimize some QoS parameters. The cognitive agent (we call it Master Agent) is responsible for the control mechanisms selection of the different reactive agents, regarding the current situation and the occurring events. By using such an architecture, we aim to take advantage of both the reactive and cognitive approaches and avoid shortcomings of the hybrid approach (coordination between the different layers, for instance).

To get the agent-based smart networking approach, we propose to select the appropriate control mechanisms among:

- Adaptive: the agent adapts its actions according to the incoming events and to its vision of the current system state. The approach we propose is adaptive as the agent adapts the current control mechanisms and the actions undertaken when a certain event occurs. The actions the control mechanism executes may become no longer valid and must therefore be replaced by other actions. These new actions are, indeed, more suitable to the current observed state;

- Distributed: each agent is responsible for a local control. There is no centralization of the information collected by the different agents, and the decisions the agent performs are in no way based on global parameters. This feature is very important as it avoids having bottlenecks around a central control entity;

- Local: the agent executes actions on the elements of the node it belongs to. These actions depend on local parameters. However, the agent can use information sent by its neighbors to adapt the activated control mechanisms;

- Scalable: our approach is scalable because it is based on a multi-agent system which scales well with the growing size of the controlled network. In order to adaptively control a new node, one has to integrate an agent (or a group of agents) in this node to perform the control.

Our model relies on two kinds of agents: (1) Master agent: which supervises the other agents in addition to what is happening in the node; (2) the other agents: which are responsible for a specific management task within the node. We can distinguish the two following levels of decision within a node:

At level 0, we find the different control mechanisms of the node, which are currently activated. Each control mechanism is characterized by its own parameters, conditions and actions, which can be monitored and modified by the Master Agent. Some of the proposed management mechanisms are inspired from known algorithms but have been agentified in order to get better performance and better cooperation between agents.

Different agents belong to this level (Scheduler Agent, Queue Control Agent, Admission Controller Agent, Routing Agent, Dropping Agent, Metering Agent, Classifying Agent, etc.). Each of these agents is responsible for a specific task within the node. So each agent responds to a limited set of events and performs actions ignoring the treatments handled by other agents lying on the same node or on the neighborhood. This allows to the agents of this level to remain simple and fast. More complex treatments are indeed left to the Master Agent.

At level 1, is lying a Master Agent responsible for monitoring, managing, and controlling the entities of level 0 in addition to the different interactions with the other nodes like cooperation, negotiation, messages processing, etc. This agent owns a model of its local environment (its neighbors) that helps him to take its own decisions. The Master Agent chooses the actions to undertake by consulting the current state of the system (neighbors nodes state, percentage of local loss, percentage of its queue load, etc.) and the meta-rules at its disposal in order to have only the most relevant control mechanisms activated with the appropriate parameters. The node, thanks to the two decision levels, responds to internal events (loss percentage for a class of traffic, load percentage of a queue, etc.) and to external ones (message sent by a neighbor node, reception of a new packet, etc.).

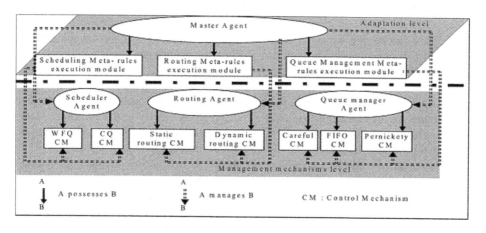

Fig. 1. Two levels of decision within the node

The Master Agent owns a set of meta-rules allowing it to decide on actions to perform relating to the different node tasks like queue management, scheduling, etc. (Figure 1). These meta-rules permit the selection of the appropriate control mechanisms to activate the best actions to execute. They respond to a set of events and trigger actions affecting the control mechanisms supervised by that Master Agent. Their role is to control a set of mechanisms in order to provide the best functioning of the node and to avoid incoherent decisions within the same node. These meta-rules give the node the means to guarantee that the set of actions executed, at every moment by its agents, are coherent in addition to be the most relevant to the current situation.

The actions of the routers have local consequences in that they modify some aspects of the functioning of the router (its control mechanisms) and some parameters of the control mechanisms (queue load, loss percentage, etc.). They may, however, influence the decisions of other nodes. In fact, by sending messages bringing new information on the state of the sender node, a Master Agent meta-rule on the receiver node may fire. This can involve a change within the receiver node (the inhibition of an activated control mechanism, or the activation of another one, etc.). This change may have repercussions on other nodes, and so forth until the entire network becomes affected.

This dynamic process aims to adapt the network to new conditions and to take advantage of the agent abilities to alleviate the global system. We argue that these agents will achieve an optimal adaptive control process because of the following two points: (1) each agent holds different processes (control mechanisms and adaptive selection of these mechanisms) allowing to take the most relevant decision at every moment; (2) the agents are implicitly cooperative in the sense that they own meta-rules that take into account the state of the neighbors in the process of control mechanisms selection. In fact, when having to decide on control mechanisms to adopt, the node takes into consideration the information received from other nodes.

3   A New Smart Architecture STP/SP

In the previous section we introduced intelligent routers. In this section we are interested in discussing the opportunity to link the intelligent routers using smart protocols adapted to the environment and the type of traffic.

TCP/IP architecture was created for the interconnection of networks running with different architectures. Then, the TCP/IP architecture was chosen as the unique architecture for all communications. The advantage is clearly to permit a universal interconnection scheme of any kind of machines. However, TCP/IP is only a trade-off and we wonder if specific architectures IP compatible or not could not be a better solution to optimize the communications. It was shown in paper [14] that TCP/IP is not the optimum protocol as soon as some constraints have to be realized. For example, TCP/IP is a rather bad protocol for energy consumption and not at all adapted to sensor networks.

The idea is to propose a Smart Protocol (SP) that can adapt to the environment, for optimizing battery or optimizing reliability or optimizing QoS or any other interesting functionality. The design of a Smart Protocol at the network layer that is aware of the upper and the lower layers and adapts their communication to a set of parameters is obviously the ultimate communication architecture that can support current and emerging wireless networks. This new context-aware architecture that we named STP/SP Smart Transport Protocol/Smart Protocol could be compatible with IP.

Indeed, the SP protocol is a set of protocols SP1, SP2, ...SPn that could be either derived from the IP protocol or could be adapted to specific environments. In the same way the STP protocol is a set of protocol that could be derived from the TCP protocol or from independent protocols. In this paper, we are interested in the compatibility of STP/SP with the TCP/IP architecture. Indeed, the TCP/IP functionalities are rich enough to cope with the different situations.

All the different architectures are easily interconnected through a classical TCP/IP protocol. For instance, a sensor network will deploy its STP/SP protocol stack that support the requirements of the application set up over the sensor network. This sensor network will be interconnected through a classical TCP/IP gateway to another network that deploys another STP/SP protocol stack which supports the requirements of this other network. This might sound as going back to the period where the networks deploy their proprietary protocols. Then, IP was designed to interconnect these networks. Next IP was generalized and today reached the point where this protocol cannot cope with all types of environment such as wireless environments. The difference between the STP/SP approach and the former proprietary solutions is that STP/SP will basically use the TCP/IP concepts and functionalities, but in a smart way. In fact, rather than deploying TCP/IP in the same way in any environment without being aware of the requirements of this environment, STP/SP will offer a smart TCP/IP like environment. This will keep the simplicity and efficiency of TCP/IP, but will add a smart process that is totally absent in TCP/IP. This smart process will be deployed using a new architecture in the network guided by a set of objectives named Goals.

We describe this global architecture in Figure 2. The objective of this architecture is to implement the smart process of selecting the sub-protocol of the STP/SP protocol that fulfils the requirements of the concerned network. This is a goal-based networking architecture and the control is a goal-based control.

4 A Goal-Based Networking Architecture

The goal-based architecture is composed of mainly two mechanisms: The smart mechanism to select the STP/SP protocol and its parameters, and the enforcement mechanism to enforce the decisions of the smart mechanism. For that we use the agent-based scheme described in the previous section, and we use some concepts of the policy based networking [15] such as the enforcement procedures to implement the mechanism.

An agent-based platform permits a meta-control structure such as the platform described in [16]. Assuming that for each network node we associate one or several agents, the network can be seen as a multi-agent system. The main goal of this system is to decide about the control to use for optimizing a given functionality described in the goal distributed by the Master Agent.

Intelligent agents are able to acquire and to process information about situations that are "not here and not now", i.e., spatially and temporally remote. By doing so, an agent may have a chance to avoid future problems or at least to reduce the effects. These capabilities allow agents to adapt their behavior according to the traffic flows going through the node.

It is important to note that other works has proposed a decision mechanism in the network to enforce decision or policies in the network. This typical architecture named Policy-based Networking (PBN) enforces high level decisions without unfortunately considering the problem optimization of parameters related to lower levels of the network. It's only a top down approach. In our proposed architecture, we intend to use the enforcement procedure of policy-based networking architecture that is an interesting concept for automating the enforcement of the smart mechanism decisions. The Goal-based architecture considers the optimizing problem related to the higher but also the lower layers of the network, and enforces the most suitable STP/SP protocols and parameters for the given network and application.

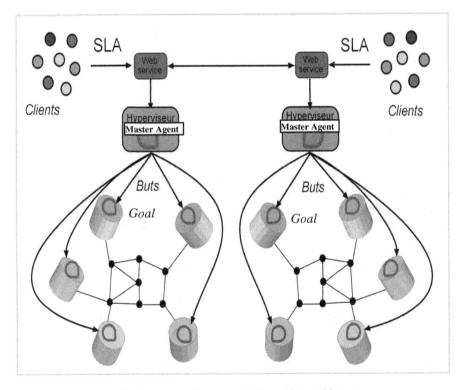

Fig. 2. The global Goal-based Networking architecture

Figure 2 depicts the global Goal-based Networking architecture (GBN) and Figure 3 depicts the GBN and STP/SP reference model.

First, users can enter their SLA through a Web service scheme for example. The manager of the network can also enter the network configurations corresponding to the goals of the network. A Master Agent in layer 1 is able to decide about the global goal of the network. This Master Agent is supported by any kind of centralized servers if any. As soon as defined, the goal is distributed to the different routers that could be named Goal Enforcement Point (GEP). Knowing the goal, the different nodes have to apply policies and define the control mechanisms. A configuration of the routers is provided to reach the goal. The configuration affects the software, the hardware and the protocol stack.

The agents in the GEP are forming the multi-agent system of level 0 described in the previous section.

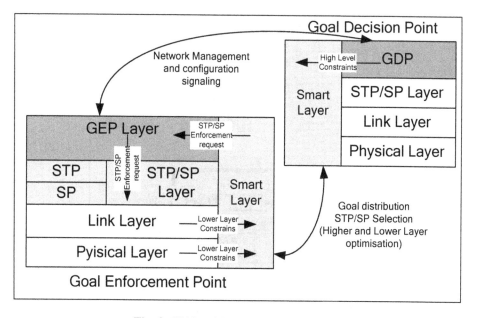

Fig. 3. GBN and STP/SP reference Model

The Smart Layer is in charge of collecting the different constraints from the layers 0 but also from the higher layer (layer 1), then specify and update the goal of the network which is about what to optimise in the network and what to be offered by the network. Note that the classical approaches consider only, what to be offered by the network. After specifying the network goal, the smart layer selects the STP/SP protocols and parameters that will optimize the specified goal. The smart layer will keep updating the goal of the network based on the current state of the network or on a new policies introduced by the Goal Decision Point.

The choice of the protocol can be seen at two levels: the local (level 0) and the global level (level 1). One specific agent in each node (Smart Layer) may be defined for deciding the local protocol in cooperation with the other similar agent of the multi-agent system. Each agent has to perform a specific procedure, which is triggered according to the state of the node, to the QoS required, and to any other reason. This constitutes a local level for the decision. Moreover, agents can periodically interact to exchange their knowledge and ask to other agents if they need information they do not have. This constitutes the global level.

The smart layer interacts with the Goal Enforcement point (GEP) in order to enforce the STP/SP selected protocol that realizes the global goal. This implies also the definition of the algorithms to manage the CPU, the sensor, the radio or any parameter of the traffic conditioner as shown in section 3.

Indeed, the traffic conditioner is replaced by an extended traffic conditioner (XTC) where different algorithms can be supported. The GEP is in charge to decide the value of the parameters and to decide about the protocol to be used. Within the entities that can be configured, classical control mechanisms as droppers, meters, schedulers, markers, etc. may be found but also resource of the battery, availability, security parameters, radio parameters, etc. This XTC is shown in Figure 4.

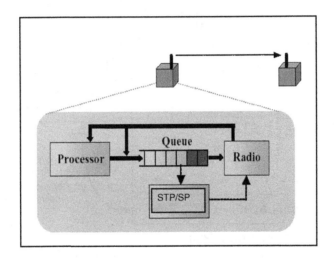

Fig. 4. The Extended Traffic Conditioner XTC

5   Simulation and Testbed Results

In this section, we are interested in a performance evaluation of a simple tesbed to understand the pros and the cons of the new architecture with intelligent routers and s smart protocol stack.

For the STP/SP architecture we chose only two states for the SP protocol: a protocol using packets as long as possible and a protocol with only short packets (100 bytes). Two kinds of clients were defined:

- Telephony which induces an IP packet payload of 16 bits and a throughput of 8 Kbps per call. The IP packet may be either padded to reach 100 bytes or can group several available payloads. In this case the waiting time cannot exceed 48 ms (namely three payloads can be encapsulated in the same IP packet). The response time of the end to end delay cannot be greater than 200 ms and only 1 percent of packets may arrive in late (they are dropped at the arrival but the quality of the voice is maintained).

- File transfer with 1 million bytes per file. When available packet get a 10 000 bytes length and in the other case the file is segmented to produce 100 bytes packet length.

The arrival process of telephone calls is exponentially distributed. The length of telephone calls is 3 minutes on the average and exponentially distributed. The arrival process of the files transfers is exponentially distributed and the average length is 1 million bytes at a constant rate of 2 Mbps. Traffics introduced by these two applications are identical and equal to 1 Mbps. Namely, idle period and busy period for the file transfer are 0.5. On the average 125 telephone calls are running.

Two goals were defined: minimizing the energy consumption in the global network and optimizing the number of successful telephone calls.

The model is a tandem queuing system composed of five nodes in series. The first queue receives the arriving packets and the queues are FIFO. The service process is dependent on the length of the packets with a rate of 2.5 Mbps.

Results of our simulation show that the lifetime of the networks is more than twice when the length of the packets is as long as possible but 20% of the telephone calls are loosing more than 1 percent of packets so are dropped. The energy consumption is divided by more than two. On the contrary, when using 100 bytes length packets, all the telephone calls are running correctly but the lifetime is divided by 2.

The previous example does not take into account the possibility to add intelligent routers in the network. To analyze the performance of intelligent routers we developed a simulation package that includes a simulation of networks elements as routers, switches, terminal equipment and so on and the real agent-based software with the Master Agent and the real time agents at the layer 0. Today a large number of results are available in different papers   showing the efficiency of the method.

The main drawback of this solution is the fact to add a large number of software agents in the network and increase the complexity of the routers. Indeed, this complexity is quite easy to handle with the new generation of routers offering a JVM through a standard interface. All the mechanisms described are now under industrial development via a start-up depending on Paris 6 University and the University of Technology of Troyes.

6 Conclusion

This paper introduced a new communication architecture to better support QoS and new functionalities using intelligent routers and smart protocols. Intelligent routers are self configurable using an agent-based control scheme. STP/SP (Smart Transport Protocol/Smart Protocol) is a smart communication model that will use different transport and network protocols adapted to the current environment. This architecture and these protocols consider not only the policies provided by the business plan but also the constraints of the lower layers of the network. A Goal-based architecture is proposed to provide the selection of control mechanisms to optimize the configuration of the routers and of the protocols. This architecture interacts with thenetwork equipment and protocols in order to configure the network with the selected protocols and parameters. An analysis of our architecture shows that a real time configuration of routers and a smart selection of the communication protocols bring an important improvement of the performance.

References

1. Ferber J. Multi-Agent Systems: An Introduction to Distributed Artificial Intelligence. Addison Wesley Longman, 1999.
2. Bazzan A.L.C., Wahle J. and Klügl F. Agents in Traffic Modelling - From Reactive to Social Behaviour. KI'99, Bonn, Germany, LNAI 1701, pp 303-307 September 1999.
3. Moukas A., Chandrinos K. and Maes P. Trafficopter: A Distributed Collection System for Traffic Information. CIA'98, Paris, France, LNAI 1435 pp 34-43, July 1998.
4. Doran J. Agent-Based Modelling of EcoSystems for Sustainable Resource Management. 3rd EASSS'01, Prague, Czech Republic, LNAI 2086, pp 383-403, July 2001.
5. Drogoul A., Corbara B. ad Fresneau D. MANTA: New experimental results on the emergence of (artificial) ant societies".in Artificial Societies: the computer simulation of social life, Nigel Gilbert & R. Conte (Eds), UCL Press, London, 1995.
6. Bensaid L., Drogoul A., and Bouron T. Agent-Based Interaction Analysis of Consumer Behavior. AAMAS'2002, Bologna, Italy, July 2002.
7. Minar N., Kramer K.H. and Maes P. Cooperating Mobile Agents for Dynamic Network Routing. in "Software Agents for Future Communication Systems", Chapter 12, Springer Verlag, pp 287-304, 1999.
8. Roychoudhuri R., et al. Topology discovery in ad hoc Wireless Networks Using Mobile Agents. MATA'2000, Paris, France. LNAI 1931, pp 1-15. September 2000.
9. Sigel E., et al. Application of Ant Colony Optimization to Adaptive Routing in LEO Telecommunications Satellite Network. Annals of Telecommunications, vol.57, no.5-6, pp 520-539, May-June 2002.
10. White T. et al. Distributed Fault Location in Networks using Learning Mobile Agents. PRIMA'99, Kyoto, Japan. LNAI 1733, pp 182-196. December 1999.
11. Bodanese E.L. and Cuthbert L.G. A Multi-Agent Channel Allocation Scheme for Cellular Mobile Networks. ICMAS'2000, USA. IEEE Computer Society press, pp 63-70, July 2000.
12. Wooldridge M. Intelligent Agents. In « Multiagent Systems : a Modern Approach to Distributed Artificial Intelligence » Weiss G. Press, pp 27-77, 1999.
13. Müller J.P and Pischel M. Modelling Reactive Behaviour in Vertically Layered Agent Architecture. ECAI'94, Amsterdam, Netherlands. John Wiley & Sons, pp 709-713, 1994.
14. Pujolle G., Chaouchi H., Gaïti D., Beyond TCP/IP : A Context Aware Architecture, Kluwer Publisher, Net-Con 2004, Palma, Spain, 2004.
15. D. C.Verma, Simplifying Network administration using policy-based management, IEEE Network **16**(2), 2002.
16. Merghem L., Gaïti D. and Pujolle G. On Using Agents in End to End Adaptive Monitoring. E2EMon Workshop, in conjunction with MMNS'2003, Belfast, Northern Ireland, LNCS 2839, pp 422-435, September 2003.

17. D. Gaïti, and G. Pujolle, Performance management issues in ATM networks: traffic and congestion control, IEEE/ACM Transactions on Networking, 4(2), 1996.
18. Gaïti D. and Merghem L.: Network modeling and simulation: a behavioral approach, Smartnet conference, Kluwer Academic Publishers, pp. 19-36, Finland, April 2002.
19. Merghem L. and Gaïti D.: Behavioural Multi-agent simulation of an Active Telecommunication Network, STAIRS 2002, France. IOS Press, pp 217-226, July 2002.

Conversational Knowledge Process
for Social Intelligence Design

Toyoaki Nishida

Dept. of Intelligence Science and Technology,
Graduate School of Informatics, Kyoto University,
Yoshida-Honmachi, Sakyo-ku, Kyoto 606-8501, Japan
nishida@i.kyoto-u.ac.jp
http://www.ii.ist.i.kyoto-u.ac.jp/~nishida/

Abstract. The Internet and ubiquitous network technologies have succeeded in connecting people and knowledge over space and time. The next step is to realize knowledgeable communities on the ubiquitous network. Social Intelligence Design is a field of research on harmonizing people and artifacts by focusing on social intelligence, defined as the ability of actors and agents to learn and to solve problems as a function of social structure and to manage their relationships with each other. In this paper, I present a computational approach to understanding and augmenting the conversational knowledge process that is a collective activity for knowledge creation, management, and application where conversational communications are used as a primary means of interaction among participating agents. The key idea is conversation quantization, a technique of approximating a continuous flow of conversation by a series of conversation quanta that represent points of the discourse. Conversation quantization enables to implement a rather robust conversational system by basing it on a large amount of conversational quanta collected from the real world. I survey major results concerning acquisition, annotation, adaptation, and understanding of conversation quanta.

1 Introduction

The Internet and ubiquitous network technologies have succeeded in connecting people and knowledge over space and time. In order for networked people and knowledge to be creative, proper communication functions for supporting the community knowledge process need to be implemented, for communities play a central role in knowledge creation.

Social Intelligence Design is a field of research on harmonizing people and artifacts by focusing on social intelligence, defined as the ability of actors and agents to learn and to solve problems as a function of social structure and to manage their relationships with each other [1].

Social Intelligence Design aims to integrate understanding and designing social intelligence. Engineering aspects of Social Intelligence Design involve design and implementation of systems and environments, ranging from group collaboration support systems that facilitate common ground building, goal-oriented interaction

A. Aagesen et al. (Eds.): INTELLCOMM 2004, LNCS 3283, pp. 28–42, 2004.

among participants, to community support systems that support a large-scale online discussions. Scientific aspects involve cognitive and social psychological understanding of social intelligence, attempting to provide a means for predicting and evaluating the effect of a given communication medium on the nature of discussions, interaction dynamics, and conclusions.

Our approach places a particular emphasis on the use of conversational communications in the knowledge process, for conversation is the most natural and effective means for people to manifest their social intelligence such as heuristically producing stories from different points of view, making tacit-explicit knowledge conversion, and entraining participants to the subject.

In this paper, I present a computational approach to understanding and augmenting the conversational knowledge process that is a collective activity for knowledge creation, management, and application where conversational communications are used as a primary means of interaction among participating agents.

The key idea is conversation quantization, a technique of approximating a continuous flow of conversation by a series of conversation quanta that represent points of the discourse. Conversation quantization enables to implement a rather robust conversational system by basing it on a large amount of conversation quanta collected from the real world. I survey major results concerning acquisition, annotation, adaptation, and understanding of conversation quanta.

2 Conversation Quantization

Conversation Quantization is a technique of articulating a continuous flow of conversation by a series of objects called conversation quanta each of which represents a point of the discourse. Conceptually, it consists of extraction, accumulation, processing, and application of conversation quanta (Fig. 1). The extraction of conversation quantum results from identification and encoding of coherent segments of interactions in a conversational situation. The extracted conversation quanta are accumulated in a server, processed whenever necessary, and applied to other conversational situations. The application of a conversation quantum in a target situation involves production of conversational sequence or other form of presenting the content of information stored in the conversation quantum.

Conversation quantization allows for implementing a conversation system by reusing a collection of conversation quanta gathered from real/hypothetical conversation situations. Given a conversational situation, a conversation quantum that best matches it will be sought from the collection of conversation quanta, and one role of the participants of the retrieved conversation quantum can be replayed by an embodied conversational agent, and other roles will be mapped to the participants in the given conversational situation. Such an algorithm is relatively easy to implement and rather robust in nature.

The granularity and size of conversation quanta essentially depend on the context and background knowledge of the observer. Although the detailed investigation of the nature of conversation quantization is left for future, we conjecture, based on experiments made so far, that each conversation quantum roughly corresponds to a small talk often identified in the discourse of daily conversations.

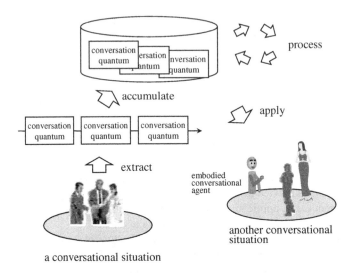

Fig. 1. Conversation quantization -- the concept

The implementation of conversation quantization depends on the data structure for representing conversation quanta. One could use plain video clips as representation but its utility in retrieving and processing would be quite limited and a large cost would be required in retrieving, editing, and applying conversation quanta. Alternatively, a deep semantic representation using logical formulas or case frames would not be ideal due to the expense and their limited capability of representing nonverbal information. A reasonable implementation appears to use annotated videos and images to represent a conversation quantum.

The current focus of our research is on acquisition, annotation, adaptation, and understanding of conversation quanta (Fig. 2). The simplest method of acquiring conversation quanta is manual input by an external observer. Alternatively, a more sophisticated method of extraction may involve automatic identification of a coherent segments of interactions from a conversational situation, and automatic annotation to the objects and events. Conversation quanta may well be generated from other media such as written documents using natural language processing techniques.

There are generally two methods of presenting the content of a conversation quantum. One is temporal expansion that generates a temporal sequence of information presentation actions. By dynamically switching among multiple conversation quanta upon the other participants' utterances, we can give the system an interactive flavor. An alternative one is spatial expansion that generates information landscape which is a spatial representation of the content of conversation quantum. An information landscape enables the user to visually grasp the global nature of knowledge, explore the information space, and accommodate new information at an appropriate place.

It is critical for us to establish a means for evaluating the effect of information tools in the user community. Social Intelligence Quantity (SIQ) is a measure of intelligence collectively possessed by a group of people. With a proper characterization of SIQ,

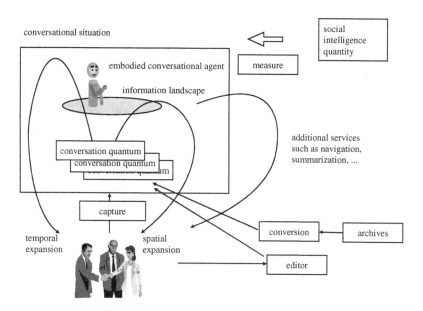

Fig. 2. A general architecture of a conversational system based on conversation quantization

the effect of a given information tool can be measured as a difference of the SIQ of the users for before and after the information tool is applied.

In the following sections, I overview the systems implemented the idea of based on conversation quantization.

3 EgoChat

EgoChat is a system for enabling an asynchronous conversational communication among community members [2,3]. EgoChat implements both temporal and spatial expansion of conversation quanta (Fig.3).

In EgoChat, a simple implementation of conversation quantization using data structures called knowledge cards, stories and knowledge channel was employed. A knowledge card is relatively self-contained package of tacit and explicit knowledge, enabling one to implement a rather robust conversational system without introducing a complex discourse generation algorithm (Fig.4). A story is a sequence of knowledge cards, representing a complete story based on a plot. In a story, preceding and succeeding knowledge cards give a discourse to each knowledge card.

EgoChat is based on the talking-virtualized-egos metaphor. A virtualized ego is a conversational agent that talks on behalf of the user. Each virtualized ego stores and maintains the user's personal memory as a collection of knowledge cards and presents them on behalf of the user. It helps the user not only develop her/his personal memory but also better understand other members' interest, belief, opinion, knowledge, and way of thinking, which is valuable for building mutual understanding. We use a powerful dialogue engine that permits a virtualized ego to answer questions by search-

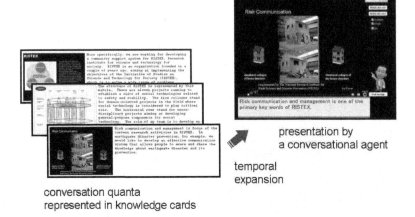

presentation by
a conversational agent

temporal
expansion

conversation quanta
represented in knowledge cards

Fig. 3. Implementation of conversation quantization theory in EgoChat

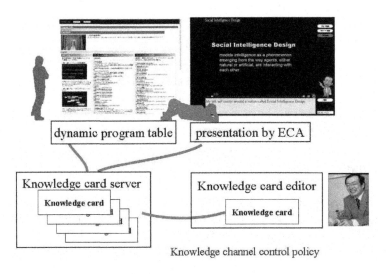

dynamic program table   presentation by ECA

Knowledge card server

Knowledge card

Knowledge card editor

Knowledge card

Knowledge channel control policy

Fig. 4. The architecture of the EgoChat system

ing for the best match from a potentially large list of question-answering pairs prepared in advance.

EgoChat provides a couple of unique features. First, it integrates personal and interpersonal knowledge life cycles. At earlier stages of the lifecycle when knowledge is not well captured, the user might want to describe her/his idea as one or more knowledge card and have the virtualized ego present them for personal review. After a while when the knowledge becomes clear and evident to the user, s/he might want to delegate her/his virtualized ego to her/his colleagues to present the idea and ask for critiques. The automatic question answering facility of EgoChat will encourage the audience to ask questions or give comments. The virtualized ego can reproduce the question-answering session with the audience so the owner can review the interactions. It will highly motivate the owner to supply more knowledge or improve existing knowledge for better competence.

Second, EgoChat allows for specifying a channel policy that is used to define the control strategies of the sender and the receiver. Four types of strategies are identified depending on whether the strategy is about the order of programs in a single program stream or about the way multiple program streams are mixed, and whether the program scheduling is static or dynamic. The skeleton of the actual flow structure of knowledge cards for a given pair of the sender and receiver is determined by resolving constraints of their channel policies. It can be visually presented to the user by a dynamic program table.

4 The Sustainable Knowledge Globe

A persistent memory system is an approach to spatio-temporal expansion of conversation quanta. By establishing a long-term relationship with a persistent memory that can coevolves with the user's biological memory, the user, as we believe, will be able to find easily an appropriate place to accommodate new information and make it ready for later use.

We are developing a system called the Sustainable Knowledge Globe (SKG) that permits the user to build her/his own customizable intellectual world by spatially arranging information (Fig. 5) [4].

The user can move around on the surface of the globe in search for interesting items and create/reconfigure landmarks consisting of a visual image and a text for later reference.

Presentation by an embodied conversational agent is a temporal representation of knowledge in the sense that the major axis behind the representation is a temporal evolution of a story. In contrast, the configuration of knowledge items on the surface

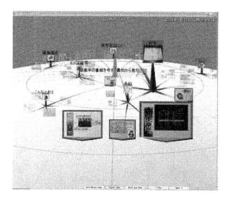

Fig. 5. Screenshots of Sustainable Knowledge Globe (SKG). A quarter view of the globe on the left, and the first person view on the right

of the globe is a spatial representation. SKG allows the user to switch between temporal representation that allows for in-depth causal understanding of the issue and spatial representation that facilitates global and geometric understanding of the subjects.

5 Capturing Conversation Scenes by Multiple Sensors

A sophisticated method of capturing conversation quanta in the real world environment is proposed by Sumi et al [5]. They implemented a smart room environment where conversational activities can be captured by environment sensors (such as video cameras, trackers and microphones ubiquitously set up around the room) and wearable sensors (such as video cameras, trackers, microphones, and physiological sensors). In order to supplement the limited capability of sensors, LED tags (ID tags with an infrared LED) and IR tracker (infrared signal tracking devices) are used to annotate the audio/video data with the positional information. Significant intervals or moments of activities are defined as interaction primitives called "events". Currently, five event types are recognized, including "stay", "coexist", "gaze", "attention", and "facing" (Fig.6). Events are captured by the behavior of IR trackers and LED tags in the room. For example, a temporal interval will be identified as a (joint) attention event when an LED tag attached to an object is simultaneously captured by IR trackers worn by two users, and the object in focus will be marked as a socially important object during the interval.

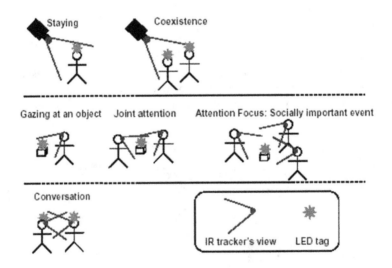

Fig. 6. Interactive Primitives [5]

They also invented a novel method of spatially displaying captured video clips called Spatio-Temporal Video Collage. A virtual 3D space is used as a medium for re-experiencing the conversations in the environment captured from multiple view-

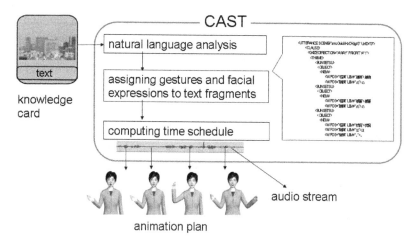

Fig. 7. Generating Animation by CAST

points videos that capture a particular scene. Visual objects standing for persons or exhibits that attracted attentions are placed in the virtual space with the arrangement depending on the structure of social attention. It reflects the perceived world of participants rather than the objective view.

6 SPOC

SPOC (Stream-oriented Public Opinion Channel) is a web-based multimedia environment that enables novice users to embody a story as multimedia content and distribute it on the Internet [6,7]. A sophisticated presentation generation from the plain-text representation of conversation quanta specifying utterances of participants in the conversation is addressed. The system produces both digital camera work and agent animations according to linguistic information in a given natural language text (Fig. 7).

We have collected and analyzed presentations by seven people and identified nine features as factors of predicting gesture occurrence. The analysis is reflected in the set of rules for determining the gestures of an embodied conversational agent. For example, one rule specifies that if an enhancement is encountered, a "beat gesture" (a simple flick of the hand or fingers up and down) will be generated.

The animation generator called CAST implements the mechanism for determining appropriate agent behaviors according to the linguistic information contained in Japanese text as. CAST consists of the Agent Behavior Selection Module (ABS), the Language Tagging Module (LTM), a Text-to-Speech engine (TTS), and a Flash-based character animation system RISA (RIStex animated Agent system). When CAST receives a text input, it will forward it to the ABS. The ABS selects appropriate gestures and facial expressions according to linguistic information calculated by the LTM. The ABS calculates a time schedule for the set of agent actions based on the timing in formation obtained by accessing the TTS. The output from the ABS is a set of animation instructions that can be interpreted and executed by the RISA animation system.

As an optional function in CAST, we have also built a component called the Enhancement Generator that automatically adds highlighting animations to agent gesture animations after the gestures are determined by the ABS. Two types of highlighting methods are incorporated to emphasize synchronization between verbal (speech) and nonverbal (gesture) behaviors.

One is superimposition with beat gesture. Beat gestures simply emphasize one part of an utterance without representing the meaning of a word. To visualize synchronization between the emphasized words and a beat gesture, the Enhancement Generator adds a superimposition of the emphasized words to the agent's beat gesture animation.

The other is illustrative animation with metaphoric gesture. When a specific shape of gesture is assigned to a metaphoric gesture, it will be emphasized by illustrative animations, such as an arrow and a line. If the emphasized concept implies motion or movement, such as "increase" or "decrease," the direction of the movement will be illustrated by an arrow animation. If the emphasized concept expresses a static state, a motionless picture will be used to emphasize the gesture. For example, when the agent is performing a "long" gesture, a rectangle shape is shown near the agent's hands to emphasize the length.

7 IPOC

IPOC (Immersive Public Opinion Channel) [8,9] is a successor of SPOC. IPOC allows for expanding conversation quanta in a virtual immersive environment. Users can interact with conversational agents in a story-space, which is a panoramic picture background and stories are embedded in the background (Fig.8). The embedded stories are presented on demand by the user or spontaneously according to the discourse. Stories are used to represent a discourse structure consisting of more than one conversation quantum.

In order to generate a more complex set of nonverbal behaviors in an immersive environment, theories of nonverbal communication are extensively studied and incorporated in the agent behavior generation system. Sidner proposed conversation management, collaboration behavior, and engagement behaviors as communicative capabilities required for collaborative robots [10]. Conversation management includes abilities of turn taking, interpreting the intentions of participants in the conversation, and updating the state of the conversation. Collaboration behavior determines agent's next action in order to accomplish the goal for the conversation and the collaboration with the user. Engagement behaviors consist of initiating a collaborative interaction, maintaining the interaction, and disengaging from the interaction.

The Interaction Control Component (ICC) of the IPOC system interprets inputs from a speech recognizer and a sensor system, and generates verbal and nonverbal behaviors performed by conversational agents. The major components of ICC are the Conversation Manager (CM) that maintains the history and the current state of the conversation, the Collaboration Behavior Generation Module (CBG) that selects the next Card to be read and determines agents' behaviors in telling a story, and Engage-

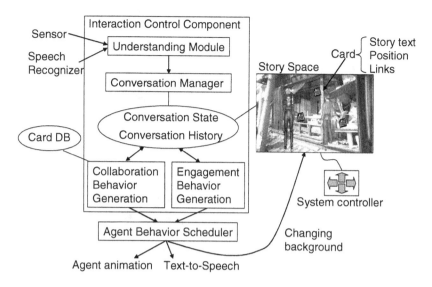

Fig. 8. The architecture of IPOC [9]

ment behavior generation (EBG) that determines appropriate engagement behaviors according to the state of the conversation.

8 Weblog Analyzer

Fukuhara develops a Weblog analyzer for understanding the social concern using Weblog articles [11]. The technique might be applied to extracting trends from a large collection of dynamically changing conversation quanta.

The Weblog analyzer automatically collects Weblog articles and displays the recent trends of social concern as a temporal transition pattern of the number of Weblog articles that co-occur with representative keywords. The Weblog analyzer consists of a database, an httpd server, and several Perl scripts for collecting and retrieving Weblog articles. The Weblog analyzer collects RSS (RDF Site Summary[1]) files of Weblog sites. An RSS file contains the title, the summary, the date of publish, the author, and the category of articles. The current system is programmed to collect RSS files every 10 minutes, from personal Weblog sites, news sites, and governmental Web sites. The current Weblog analyzer started to collect articles from 18 March 2004, and acquired more than a million articles by July 12, 2004.

The temporal behaviors of the observed social concern can be classified into five categories: periodic (several peals appear periodically), gradual increase (a peak appears gradually), sensitive (has a keen peak), trailing (the social concern persists after one or several matters occur), and others (Fig.9).

---

[1] http://web.resource.org/rss/1.0/spec

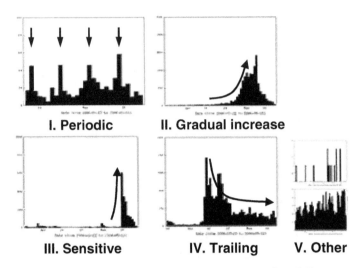

Fig. 9. Patterns of social concern transition over time [11]

9 Social Intelligence Quantity

Social Intelligence Quantity (SIQ) is a framework of standardized quantitative measurement of social intelligence [12]. Our approach combines the qualitative evaluation consisting of questionnaire and protocol analysis, and the quantitative evaluation consisting of the network log analysis, the factorial experiment and the standardized psychological scale. SIQ was first introduced as a means for evaluating communication tools. SIQ consists of SIQ-Personal and SIQ-Collective.

SIQ-Personal specifies the individual's personal attitudes to the society. SIQ-Personal is measured with the individual's information desire and intention to participate in the community. Matsumura investigated in detail the information desire and identified that the information acquisition desire consists of the interpersonal relation desire, the trend information acquisition desire, the information publication desire, the information monopoly desire, and the information acquisition desire [13].

Matsumura also investigated the structure of the individual's intention to participate in the community, in terms of the estimate of the community, the evaluation of tools, and the intention. He introduced seven factors (i.e., the intention of active participation, the intention of continuous participation, the benefits of using tools, the interest in the tool, the clarity of others' idea, the contribution to their community, and the understanding of the community's status) and proposed a causal model based on the statistic analysis of the test users' subjective evaluation (Fig. 10).

These results indicated that the intention to participate in a community was influenced by the benefit received by using a communication tool. The benefit was affected by factors associated with understanding the state of a community. The individual's subjective contribution had a strong effect on the benefits of using a tool. The individual's subjective contribution depends on the understanding of the state of a community and the clarity of others' opinion.   Thus, in order to evaluate a communication tool for supporting a community, we should examine not only users' subjective evaluation of a communication tool but also their subjective evaluation of a community.

SIQ-Collective represents the community's status of information and knowledge sharing or knowledge creation. SIQ-Collective is measured with the amount of information in the community, and the objective indices such as the diversity and the convergence of information.

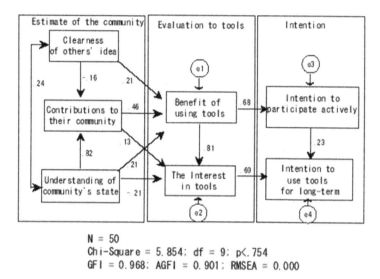

N = 50
Chi-Square = 5.854: df = 9: p<.754
GFI = 0.968: AGFI = 0.901: RMSEA = 0.000

Fig. 10. A causal model concerning the intention of participating in a community and using a tool [13]

10   Discussion and Future Perspectives

I propose to take a data-driven approach by introducing a conceptual framework based on conversation quantization, rather than resorting to an algorithmic-centric framework. I believe a conceptual framework is suitable for capturing different approaches employing different computational frameworks with the same orientation. By basing the entire framework on a vague notion of quantization, it is possible to organize pieces of research into a rather comprehensive framework of conversation systems even though the author of each piece does not have an explicit image of the whole. In the previous sections, I have surveyed representative work on acquisition, annotation, adaptation, and understanding of conversation quanta, in attempt to integrate a vast varieties of attempts regarding conversational systems in a coherent framework.

There are many interesting work left for the future research. Among others, we need to build a more detailed and elegant theory of conversation quantization. We have already obtained an empirical characterization of conversation quanta, but we do not have a systematic and theoretical account of conversation quanta. A more sophisticated theory of conversation quanta will permit us to better design the representation and basic operation for conversation quanta. It may well enable us to predict the cost and effect of building a conversation system based on conversation quantization.

Another big concern is automatic capture of conversation quanta. In addition to the work described so far in this paper, there are a number of interesting work. Minoh and Kakusho developed a robust method for automatically recognizing communicative events in a real class room by integrating audio and visual information processing [14]. Rutkowski studied a method for monitoring and estimating efficiency of the human-human communication based on recorded audio and video by computing correlation between sender activities and receiver responses [15]. Taniguchi and Arita used computer vision techniques to realize the notion of real time human proxy to virtually create a classroom for distributed learning environments [16]. Kurohashi and Shibata integrate robust natural language processing techniques and computer vision to automatically annotate videos with closed caption [17]. Nakamura developed an intelligent video production system that can compute the best matching between the given index-scenario and video stream captured by camera to produce an annotated video [18]. Those work should be incorporated into the theory of conversation quantization.

11 Conclusion

In this paper, I have presented a computational approach to understanding and augmenting the conversational knowledge process that is a collective activity for knowledge creation, management, and application where conversational communications are used as a primary means of interaction among participating agents. I have introduced the notion of conversation quantization, a technique of approximating a continuous flow of conversation by a series of conversation quanta that represent points of the discourse. Conversation quantization enables to implement a rather robust conversational system by basing the conversational system the large amount of conversational quanta collected from the real world. I have surveyed major results concerning acquisition, annotation, adaptation, and understanding of conversational quanta.

References

1. B T. Nishida. Social Intelligence Design for Web Intelligence, Special Issue on Web Intelligence, IEEE Computer, Vol. 35, No. 11, pp. 37-41, November, 2002.
2. H. Kubota, T. Nishida: Channel Design for Strategic Knowledge Interaction, in Proceedings KES 2003, pp. 1037-1043, 2003.
3. Hidekazu Kubota, Jaewon Hur, and Toyoaki Nishida: Agent-based Content Management System, in Proceedings of the 3rd Workshop on Social Intelligence Deisgn (SID 2004), CTIT Workshop Proceedings, pp. 77-84, 2004.

4. Toyoaki Nishida, Yasuyuki Sumi, Hidekazu Kubota, Hung-Hsuan Huang: A Computational Model Of Conversational Knowledge Process, to be presented at 1st International Workshop on "Intelligent Media Technology for Communicative Intelligence", affiliated with 4th National Conference on Multimedia and Network Information Systems, Szklarska Poreba, Poland, September 16-17, 2004.
5. Yasuyuki Sumi, Kenji Mase, Christof Mueller, Shoichiro Iwasawa, Sadanori Ito, Masashi Takahashi, Ken Kumagai, Yusuke Otaka: Collage of Video and Sound for Raising the Awareness of Situated Conversations, to be presented at International Workshop on Intelligent Media Technology for Communicative Intelligence in Warsaw, Poland September 13-14, 2004
6. Nakano, Y. I., Murayama, T., and Nishida, T.: Multimodal Story-based Communication: Integrating a Movie and a Conversational Agent. Vol.E87-D No.6 pp.1338-1346 2004/6.
7. Q. Li, Y. Nakano, M. Okamoto, and T. Nishida: Highlighting Multimodal Synchronization for Embodied Conversational Agent, the 2nd International Conference on Information Technology for Application (ICITA 2004), 2004.
8. Yukiko I. Nakano, Masashi Okamoto, and Toyoaki Nishida: Enriching agent animation with Gestures and Highlighting Effects, to be presented at International Workshop on Intelligent Media Technology for Communicative Intelligence in Warsaw, Poland September 13-14, 2004
9. Yukiko I. Nakano, Toshiyasu Murayama, and Toyoaki Nishida: Engagement in Situated Communication By Conversational Agents, to be presented at 1st International Workshop on "Intelligent Media Technology for Communicative Intelligence", affiliated with 4th National Conference on Multimedia and Network Information Systems, Szklarska Poreba, Poland, September 16-17, 2004.
10. Sidner, C. L., C. Lee, and N. Lesh: Engagement Rules for Human-Robot Collaborative Interactions, in Proc. IEEE International Conference on Systems, Man & Cybernetics (CSMC), Vol. 4, pp. 3957-3962, 2003
11. Tomohiro Fukuhara and Toshihiro Murayama: An Analysis Tool for Understanding Social Concerns using Weblog articles, to be presented at 1st International Workshop on "Intelligent Media Technology for Communicative Intelligence", affiliated with 4th National Conference on Multimedia and Network Information Systems, Szklarska Poreba, Poland, September 16-17, 2004.
12. Koji Yamashita and Toyoaki Nishida: SIQ (Social Intelligence Quantity): Evaluation Package for Network Communication Tools, APCHI 2002 -- 5th Asia Pacific Conference on Computer Human Interaction - Beijing, China, 1-4 November 2002.
13. Ken'ichi Matsumura: The Measures for the Evaluation of Communication Tools: the Causality between the Intention and Users' Subjective Estimation of Community, in Proceedings of the 3rd Workshop on Social Intelligence Deisgn (SID 2004), CTIT Workshop Proceedings, pp. 85-90, 2004.
14. Minoh, S.Nishiguchi:"Environmental Media - In the Case of Lecture Archiving System," Proc. Int. Conf. Knowledge-Based Intelligent Information & Engineering Systems (KES2003), Vol.II, pp.1070-1076 (2003).
15. Rutkowski, M., Seki, S., Yamakata, Y., Kakusho, K., and Minoh, M.: "Toward the Human Communication Efficiendy Monitoring from Captured Audio and Video Media in Real Environment," Proc. Int. Conf. Knowledge-Based Intelligent Information & Engineering Systems (KES2003), Vol.II, pp.1093-1100 (2003).

16. Arita, D. and Taniguchi, R.: Non-verbal Human Communication Using Avatars in a Virtual Space, in Proc. Int. Conf. Knowledge-Based Intelligent Information & Engineering Systems (KES2003), pp. 1077-1084, Sep. 2003.
17. Shibata, T., Kawahara, D., Okamoto, M., Kurohashi, S., and Nishida, T.: Structural Analy-sis of Instruction Utterances, in Proceedings KES 2003, pp. 1054-1061, 2003.
18. Ozeki, M., Izuno, H., Itoh, M., Nakamura, Y., and Ohta, Y.: Object Tracking and Task Rec-ognition for Producing Intaractive Video Content --- Semi-automatic indexing for QUEVICO, in Proc. Int. Conf. Knowledge-Based Intelligent Information & Engineering Systems (KES2003), pp.1044-1053, 2003

Triple-Space Computing: Semantic Web Services Based on Persistent Publication of Information

Dieter Fensel

Digital Enterprise Research Institute (DERI),
DERI Innsbruck, Leopold-Franzens Universität Innsbruck, Austria
DERI Galway, National University of Ireland, Galway
dieter.fensel@deri.org

Abstract. This paper discusses possible routes to moving the web from a collection of human readable pieces of information connecting humans, to a webthat connects computing devices based on machine-processable semantics of dataand distributed computing. The current shortcomings of web service technologyare analyzed and a new paradigm for fully enabled semantic web services isproposed which is called **triple-based** or triple-space computing.

1 Introduction

The web is a tremendous success story. Starting as an in-house solution for exchangingscientific information it has become, in slightly more than a decade, a world wide usedmedia for information dissemination and access. In many respects, it has become themajor means for publishing and accessing information. Its scalability and the comfortand speed in disseminating information is unprecedented. However, it is solely a webfor humans. Computers do not have access to the provided information and in return donot provide any support in processing this information. Two complementary trends areabout to change this transformation of the web, from being for humans only, into a webthat interweaves computers to provide support for human interactions at a much higherlevel than is available with current web technology.

- The semantic web is about adding machine-processable semantics to data. The computer can "understand" the information and therefore process it on behalf of the human user (cf. [Fensel, 2003]).
- Web services try to employ the web as a global infrastructure for distributed computation, for integrating various applications, and for the automatization of business processes (cf. [Alonso et al., 2003]). The web will not only be the place where human readable information is published but the place where global computing is realized.

Eventually, semantic web services promise the combination of semantic web with webservice technology. A fully mechanized web for computer interaction would become anew infrastructure on which humans organize their cooperations and businessrelationships (cf. [Fensel & Bussler, 2002]).

These trends promise to provide the holy grail of computer science. The semantic web promises to make information understandable to a computer and web

A. Aagesen et al. (Eds.): INTELLCOMM 2004, LNCS 3283, pp. 43–53, 2004.

services promise to provide smooth and painless integration of disparate applications. Web services offer a new level of automatization in eWork and eCommerce, where fully open and flexible cooperation can be achieved, on the fly, with low programming costs. However, the current implementations of web service technology are still far from reaching these goals. There are a couple of obvious reasons for this. Integrating heterogeneous and dynamically changing applications is a tremendous task. Currently, a bizarre flow of standards and pseudo-standards are published to achieve this goal. We are still far away from the point where we can ensure that there is emerging consensus around some proposals and from deciding on whether these proposals deliver what they are promising. Also many of the existing proposals cover the required functionality at a very low level, only. Spoken in layman term's, remote procedure calls over HTTP may not be the right level of functionality to align business processes in a smooth and scalable fashion. Established standards in the pre-web eCommerce area such as EDI/ EDIFACT[1] provides a much higher level of support for mechanizing business transactions.

These obstacles may eventually be overcome, however these may also be an indication of a deeper problem around web services. Actually as we show in this paper, web services do not have much in common with the web. They are based on message exchange rather than on addressable and persistent publication, which is a key principle underlying the web. Thus, they have to deal with all the issues around message exchange and how to implement reference-, time-, and space-decoupled interactions. Actually web services are not sufficiently advanced to use the web as a means of information publishing and access.

Investigating true web services, that are based on the web paradigm for exchanging information, is at the core of this paper. We will investigate the potential of tuple- or space-based computing and the necessity to combine it with semantics. We will call this proposal triple-based computing and we show how this naturally fits into the vision of a semantic web. In a nutshell, realizing services on top of the semantic web may be a more realistic pathway to achieving semantic web services rather than trying to enrich web services with semantic annotations.

The contents of this paper are organized as follows. Section 2 discusses the web, the semantic web, web services, and eventually semantic web services as the web of machines that may evolve from the web primarily for humans. Section 3 analyzes web services and questions whether they actually have much to do with the web. Section 4 provides a vision on what actual web services could look like. They would use the web as a global tuplespace and the required extension of this tuplespace into a triplespace naturally adds semantics and the semantic web to them. Section 5 concludes the paper.

2   Elements and Directions in Achieving Semantic Web Services

We split the discussion of elements and directions in achieving semantic web services into two parts. Section 2.1 discusses the major elements the future web may be based on. We start the discussion with the web itself and continues with discussing the semantic web, web services, and their combination in semantic web services. Section 2.2 follows up the discussion by investigating two different paths that may eventually lead from the current web to semantic web services.

---

[1] http://www.unece.org/trade/untdid/welcome.htm

2.1   Four Dimensions Describing the Future of the Web

Figure 1 illustrates four major stages in the development of the web: (1) the web as a collection of information accessible to the human reader; (2) the semantic web that adds machine-processable semantics and mechanized information processing; (3) web services that employ the web as a platform for distributed computing; and (4) semantic web services that combine both in providing mechanized service discovery, parametrization, composition, and execution. We will briefly elaborate on all four stages.

The **World Wide Web** is a big and impressive success story, both in terms of the amount of available information and of the growth rate of human users. It has started to penetrate most areas of our daily lives and business. This success is based on it's simplicity. The restrictiveness of HTTP and HTML allowed software developers, information providers, and users to gain easy access to this new media, helping it to reach a critical mass. However, this simplicity may hamper the further development of the Web. Or in other words: What we see currently is the very first version of the web and the next version will probably be even bigger and much more powerful compared to what we have now. It started as an in-house solution for a small group of users. Soon, it established itself as a world-wide communication media for hundreds of millions of people. In a small number of years it will interweave one billion people and will penetrate many more types of devices than just computers.

It is also clear that the current state of web technology is generating serious obstacles for it's further growth. The bottlenecks of current web technology create problems in searching information, problems in extracting information, problems in maintaining information, and problems in generating information. All these problems are caused by the simplicity of current web technology. Computers are used as devices to post and render information. However, they do not have any access to the actual content and therefore can provide only very limited support in accessing and processing this information. In consequence, the main burden in accessing, extracting, interpreting, and processing information is left to the human user.

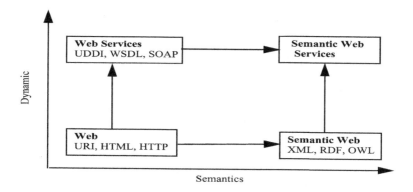

Fig. 1. The four major stages in the development of the Web

Tim Berners-Lee created the vision of a **Semantic Web** that provides automated information access based on machine-processable semantics of data and heuristics that make use of these meta data. The explicit representation of the semantics of data accompanied with domain theories (i.e., ontologies) will enable a web that provides a qualitatively new level of service. New recommendations[2] such as XML, RDF, and OWL allow the adding of machine-processable semantics to the information present on the web. The semantic web will weave together an incredibly large network of human knowledge, with complementary machine processability. Various automated services will support the user in achieving goals via accessing and providing information in a machine-understandable form. This process may ultimately lead to extremely knowledgeable systems with various specialized reasoning services that may support us in nearly all aspects of our daily life, becoming as necessary for us as access to electric power.

The current web is mainly a collection of information but does not yet provide support in processing this information, i.e., in using the computer as a computational device. Recent efforts around UDDI[3], WSDL[4], and SOAP[5] have tried to lift the web to a new level of service. Software applications can be accessed and executed via the web based on the idea of **Web services**. Web services can significantly increase the web architecture's potential, by providing a way of automating program communication. Therefore, they are the focus of much interest from various software development companies. Web services connect computers and devices with each other using the Internet to exchange data and combine data in new ways. The key to web services is on-the-fly software composition through the use of loosely coupled, reusable software components. This has fundamental implications in both technical and business terms. Software can be delivered and paid for as fluid streams of services as opposed to packaged products. It is possible to achieve automatic, ad hoc interoperability between systems to accomplish organizational tasks. Examples include both business application, such as automated procurement and supply chain management, and non-commercial applications, which include military applications. Web services can be completely decentralized and distributed over the Internet and accessed by a wide variety of communications devices. Organizations can be released from the burden of complex, slow and expensive software integration and instead focus on the value of their offerings and mission critical tasks. The dynamic enterprise and dynamic value chains would become achievable and may be even mandatory for competitive advantage.

Still, more work needs to be done before the web service infrastructure can make this vision come true. Current web service technology provides limited support in mechanizing service recognition, service configuration and combination (i.e., realizing complex workflows and business logics with web services), service comparison and automated negotiation. In a business environment, the vision of flexible and autonomous web service translates into automatic cooperation between enterprise services. Any enterprise requiring a business interaction with another enterprise can automatically discover and select the appropriate optimal web services relying on selection policies. This can be achieved by adding machine-processable semantics to the description of web services based on semantic web technology. **Semantic web services** can be invoked automatically and payment processes can be

---

[2] http://www.w3c.org/
[3] http://www.uddi.org/
[4] http://www.w3.org/TR/wsdl
[5] http://www.w3.org/TR/soap12-part1/

initiated.[6] Any necessary mediation would be applied based on data and process ontologies and the automatic translation and semantic interoperation. An example would be supply chain relationships where an enterprise manufacturing short-lived goods must frequently seek suppliers as well as buyers dynamically. Instead of employees constantly searching for suppliers and buyers, the web service infrastructure does it automatically within the defined constraints. Other applications areas for this technology are Enterprise-Application Integration (EAI), eWork, and Knowledge Management.

2.2 Two Ways to Heaven

When taking a closer look at Figure 1 it turns out that *two potential paths* in achieving semantic web services are implicitly present there. You can move to semantic web services via the web service track or via the semantic web track (see Figure 2)[7]

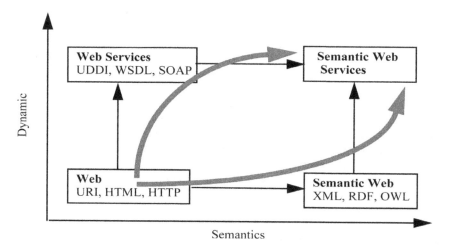

Fig. 2. The two major footpaths in developing the Web

Projects such as DERI[8] and DIP[9] follow the first path. The current web service stack is taken as a starting point and semantic annotations are designed to complement these elements. Semantics should be added to WSDL interface descriptions and choreography and orchestration elements. A strong mediation service is developed to cope with all the various miss-matches in data, protocol and process specifications.

In fact, this is not the only possible road to semantic web services. Alternatively one could directly focus on further developing the semantic web. By putting more and

---

[6] See for initiatives in this area OWL-S (http://www.daml.org/services/), IRS-II (http:// kmi.open.ac.uk/projects/irs/), and WSMO (http://www.wsmo.org/).
[7] This section results from personal communication with Tim Berners-Lee and Eric Miller.
[8] http://www.deri.org/
[9] http://dip.semanticweb.org/

more ontologies and semantically annotated data on the web, services will evolve naturally that make use of these descriptions. In practical terms, one could ontologize existing standards such as EDI and EDIFACT and invite new business partners to make use of these public descriptions for implementing their trading relationships. Instead of deploying standards for service descriptions (and there is already a frightening number of pseudo standards in the arena) one could provide more and more reusable formalized descriptions on the web of services that can be exploited to achieve their functionality. This idea will be discussed further in the next section when we discuss the severe shortcomings of the current web service infrastructure.

3 Are Web Services Really Web Services? – No!

Besides their name, *web* services do not have much to do with the web. Let's illustrate this briefly by assuming a time machine would bring us back to the pre-web time. What was a very common way, back then, of accessing a research paper? One was posting an email kindly asking for the paper and a friendly colleague posting it as an attachment. Dissemination of information was based on message exchange. The communication overhead in publishing and accessing information was high and dissemination was therefore quite limited and slow. Then the web came into being and changed the situation significantly. The author had to publish the paper once by putting it on his web page. After this, he could forget about it and focus on writing new papers. New services such as citeseer[10] even ensure durability of this publication beyond the life time of a web page (i.e., they disable the delete operation on the information space). All the potential readers could get instant access to the paper without requiring a two-stage message-exchange process. This tremendously scaled and speeded up the dissemination process of information. When comparing web services with this essential web principle it becomes quite obvious that web services are **not** about the web.

Web services require close coupling of applications they integrate. Applications communicate via message exchange requiring strong coupling in terms of reference and time. The communication has to be directed to the web service addressed and the communication must be synchronous. If both parties do not implement and jointly agree on the specific way this mechanism is implemented, then the applications must support asynchronous communication. The web is strongly based on the opposite principles. Information is published in a persistent and widely accessible manner.[11] Any other application can access this information at any point in time without having to request the publishing process to directly refer to it as a receiver of it's information. It is true that web services uses the internet as a transport media (relying on protocols such as FTP, SMTP, or HTTP), however that is all they have in common with the web.

Given this obvious evidence it is surprising that many more authors already have not complained about the erroneous naming of web services, that could be likened to the situation in the emperor's new clothes. Actually, the criticisms of the REST community (cf. [Fielding, 2000]) back up this argument and the position of this paper. Their two major criticisms around web services are about improper usage of URIs and

---

[10] http://citeseer.ist.psu.edu/cs
[11] For privacy issues, protected sub-fragments of the web can be defined.

messing up the state-less architecture of the web (cf. [Fielding & Taylor, 2002], [zur Muehlen et al., 2004]).

When sending and receiving SOAP messages, the content of the information is hidden in the body and *not addressed as an explicit web resource* with it's own URI. Therefore, all web machinery involving caching or security checks is disabled since its use would require the parsing and understanding of all possible XML dialects that can be used to write a SOAP message. Referring to the content via an explicit URI in an HTTP request would allow the content of a message to be treated like any other web resource.

The web service stack can be used to model state-full resources. However, one of the basic design principle of the web and REST architectures is not to provide state-full protocols and resources explicitly. Thus, application integration and servers for this architecture are easy to build. Every HTTP request for a URI should retrieve the same contents independently of what has happened before in other sessions or in a history of the current session. This allows thin servers to be used, that do not need to store, manage and retrieve the earlier session history, for the current session.[12] When a stateful conversation is required this should be explicitly modelled by different URIs. In consequence, *there should not be one URI for a web service and hidden ways to model and exchange state information* but each potential state of a web service should be explicitly addressable by a different URI. This conforms to the web and REST's way of modelling a stateful conversation for a state-less protocol and adhers to their architecture.

These criticisms of the REST community reinforces this paper's arguments. Web services do not rely on the central principles of the web: publication of information based on a global and persistent URI, instead, stateful conversations based on the hidden content of messages are established. The next section explores what web services would look like that are fully based on the web and it's underlying principles that made it such a success.

4 Triple-Spaced Computing

This section will discuss what a service paradigm that conforms with the basic principles of the web could look like. We start by discussing tuple-spaced computing as a paradigm to exchange data between applications. Then we introduce the concept of semantic self-description of information, which naturally lead us into a discussion of the triple space.

4.1 Tuple-Spaced Computing

Tuple-based computing has been introduced in parallel programming languages, such as Linda, to implement communication between parallel processes (cf. [Gerlernter, 1992]). Instead of sending messages backward and forward a simple means of

---

[12] Actually cookies are a work-around of this principle, however they break when a client is run on different machines.

communication is provided. Processes can write, delete[13], and read tuples from a global persistent space.[14] A tuple is a set of ordered typed fields, each of which either contains a value or is undefined and a tuplespace is an abstract space containing all tuples and visible to all processes. The API for this is extremely simple and all complexity in message processing disappears (actually it is hidden in the middleware that implements the tuplespace). This tuplespace is similar to a blackboard in expert systems, where rules do not send messages to all other rules when they derive a fact. Rather, this is published by adding it to the publicly-visible board.

Tuple or space-based computing has one very strong advantage: It de-couples three orthogonal dimensions involved in information exchange (cf. Figure 3): reference, time, and space.

- Processes communicating with each other do not need to explicitly know each other. They exchange information by writing and reading tuples from the tuplespace, however, they do not need to set up an explicit connection channel, i.e., *reference-wise the processes are completely de-couple*d.
- Communication can be completely asynchronous since the tuplespace guarantees persistent storage of data, i.e., *time-wise the processes are completely de-couple*d.
- The processes can run in completely different computational environments as long as both can access the same tuplespace, i.e., *space-wise the processes are completely de-couple*d.

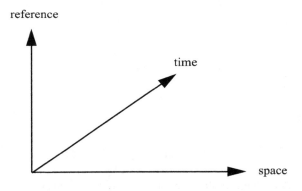

Fig. 3. Three separate dimensions of cooperation, taken from [Angerer, 2002]

This strong decoupling in all three relevant dimensions has obvious design advantages for defining reusable, distributed, heterogeneous, and quickly changing applications like those promised by web service technology. Also, complex APIs of current web service technology are replaced by simple read and write operations in a tuplespace. Notice that a service paradigm based on the tuple paradigm also revisits the web paradigm: information is persistently written to a global place where other processes can smoothly access it without starting a cascade of message exchanges.

---

[13] Actually, deleting tuples may not really be necessary in an exponentially growing space such as the web.
[14] *Global* in the *local* framework of an application that is decomposed by parallel processes.

Johanson and Fox [Johanson & Fox, 2004] describe the application of tuplespaces for coordination in interactive work spaces, focussing on providing software infrastructure for the dynamic interaction of heterogeneous and ad hoc collections of new and legacy devices, applications, and operating systems. The reasons why they refer to tuplespaces as the underlying communications model resembles all the requirements for web services that should enable fully flexible and open eWork and eCommerce. The following is a list of some of the requirements mentioned by Johanson and Fox [Johanson & Fox, 2004]: limited temporal decoupling, referential decoupling, extensibility, expressiveness, simple and portable APIs, easy debugging, scalability, and failure tolerance and recovery.

In side remarks [Johanson & Fox, 2004] also report shortcomings of current tuplespace models. They lack the means to name spaces, semantics, and structure in describing the information content of the tuples. The tuplespace provides a flat and simple data model that does not provide nesting, therefore, tuples with the same number of fields and field order, but different semantics, cannot be distinguished. Instead of following their ad-hoc repairs we propose a simple and promising solution for this. We propose to refine the tuplespace into a *triple space, where <subject, predicate, object> describe content and semantics of information*. The object can become a subject in a new triple thus defining a *graph structure* capturing structural information.

Fortunately with RDF[15] (cf. [Klyne & Carroll, 2004]) this space already exists and provides a natural link from the space-based computing paradigm into the semantic web. Notice that the semantic web is not made unnecessary based on the tuple-spaced paradigm. The global space can help to overcome heterogeneity in communication and cooperation, however, it does not provide any answer to data and information heterogeneity. In fact, this aspect is what the semantic web is all about.

4.2 Triple-Spaced Computing

The web and the tuplespace have many things in common. They are both global information spaces for persistent publication. Therefore, they share many of the same underlying principles. They differ in their application context. The web is a world wide information space for the human reader and the tuplespace is a local space for parallel processes in an application. Thus, the web adds some features that are currently lacking in the tuplespace.

First, with URIs the web provides a well-defined *reference mechanism* that has world-wide scalability to address chunks of information. Tuplespaces lack this mechanism since they were designed mostly for closed and local environments. Johanson and Fox [Johanson & Fox, 2004] already reported this as a bottleneck when applied in their setting of heterogeneity and dynamic change.

Second, the namespace mechanism of the web allows different applications to use the same vocabulary without blurring their communications. Namespaces help to keep the intended information coverage of identifiers separate even if they are named equally. Namespaces provides a well-defined *separation mechanism* that scales on a world-wide scale to distinguish chunks of information.

---

[15] http://www.w3.org/RDF/

Third, the web is an information space for humans and the tuplespace is an information space for computers, however, the *semantic* web is for machines too. It provides standards to represent machine-processable semantics of data. We already mentioned RDF that provides nested triples as a data model to represent data and their formal semantics on the web. This enables applications to publish and to access information in a machine processable manner. RDF Schema [Brickley & Guha, 2004] defines classes, properties, domain and range restrictions, and hierarchies of classes and properties on top of RDF. Thus, a richer data model than nested triples can be used to model and retrieve information. This gets even further extended by OWL [McGuinness & van Harmelen, 2004], a data modeling language based on description logic.

Therefore, the semantic web has the true potential to become the global space for application integration, like the tuplespace became a means for the local integration of parallel processes. It provides the means for global integration with the inherent complexity stemming from information heterogeneity and dynamic changes. As with tuplespace, it makes problems with protocol and process heterogeneity transparent, by it's uniform and simple means for accessing and retrieving information. Complex message exchange is replaced by simple read and write operations in a global space.

Having said this, it is also clear that this is not the end but just the beginning of an exercise. No application can quickly check the entire semantic web to find an interesting triple. Conversely, no application would simply publish a triple and then wait forever until another application picks it up. Clever middleware is required that provides a virtual global triplespace without requesting each application either to download or to search through the entire semantic web.[16] The triplespace needs to be divided up to provide security and privacy features as well as scalability. However, none of these requirements are really new. They apply to any application that deals with the web on a global scale.

5 Conclusions

Johanson and Fox [Johanson & Fox, 2004] expect ubiquitous computing as the "killer app" for tuple-space based computing because of the model's portability, extensibility, flexibility, and ability to deal with heterogeneous environments. Actually, truly web-service enabled eWork and eCommerce shares many, if not all of the features of ubiquitous computing. In fact, we think that a tuplespace-based communication model is close in spirit to the web and may help to bring web services to their full potential. It requires moving from a message-oriented communications model into a web where information is published (broadcast) based on a global and persistent URI.

The tuplespace helps to overcome many problems around heterogeneity in information distribution and information access. Since applications are decoupled in reference, time, and space, many issues in protocol and process alignment disappear because they are provided by the underlying middleware that implements the tuplespace. Still, the tuplespace does not contribute anything to the solution of data and information heterogeneity. In fact, there are already ad hoc proposals to add semantics to the data represented in it. Alternatively, this paper proposed a straightforward

---

[16] See for example the work of the company Tecco, http://www.tecco.at/en/index.html

approach using semantic web technology to provide a well established mechanism for that. It will transfer the tuplespace into an RDF-based triplespace. This triplespace provides the web with the means to exchange data between applications based on machine-processable semantics. Therefore, this triplespace may become the web for machines as the web, based on HTML, became the web for humans.

Acknowledgement

The paper is simply a synthesis of discussions I had with Tim Berners-Lee and Eva Kühn. It reflects only the private opinion of the author and not the official policy of DERI.

References

[Alonso et al., 2003]   G. Alonso, F. Casati, H. Kuno, and V. Machiraju: *Web Services*, Springer, 2003.

[Angerer, 2002]   B. Angerer: Space Based Computing: J2EE bekommt Konkurrenz aus dem eigenen Lager, *Datacom*, no 4, 2002.

[Brickley & Guha, 2004]   D. Brickley and R.V. Guha (eds.): RDF Vocabulary Description Language 1.0: RDF Schema, W3C Recommendation, February 2004, http://www.w3c.org/TR/ rdf-schema/

[Fensel, 2003]   D. Fensel: *Ontologies: Silverbullet for Knowledge Mana-gement and Electronic Commerce*, 2nd edition, Springer, 2003.

[Fensel & Bussler, 2002]   D. Fensel and C. Bussler: The Web Service Modeling Framework WSMF, *Electronic Commerce Research and Applications*, 1(2), 2002.

[Fielding, 2000]   R. T. Fielding: Architectural styles and the design of network-based software architectures, PhD Thesis, University of California, Irvine, 2000.

[Fielding & Taylor, 2002]   R. T. Fielding and R. N. Taylor: Principled Design of the Modern Web Architecture, *ACM Transactions on Internet Technology (TOIT)*, 2(2), May 2002:115-150.

[Gerlernter, 1992]   D. Gerlernter: *Mirrorworlds*, Oxford University Press, 1992.

[Johanson & Fox, 2004]   B. Johanson and A. Fox: Extending Tuplespaces for Coordi-nation in Interactive Workspaces, *Journal of Systems and Software*, 69(3), January 2004:243-266.

[Klyne & Carroll, 2004]   G. Klyne and J. J. Carroll (eds.): Resource Description Framework (RDF): Concepts and Abstract Syntax, W3C Recommendation, February 2004, http:// www.w3.org/TR/rdf-concepts/

[McGuinness & van Harmelen, 2004]   D L. McGuinness and F. van Harmelen (eds.): OWL Web Ontology Language: Overview, W3C Recommendation, February 2004, http://www.w3c.org/ TR/owl-features/

[zur Muehlen et al., 2004]   M. zur Muehlen, J. V. Nickerson, and K. D. Swenson: *Developing Web Services Choreography Standards -- The Case of REST vs. SOAP*, Decision Support Systems, 37, 2004.

Mobility and Intelligence in Telecom: How and Where to Handle It?

Lill Kristiansen

Dept. of Telematics, NTNU,
Norwegian University of Science and Technology,
O.S. Bragstads Plass 2A, NO-7491Trondheim, Norway
lill.kristiansen@item.ntnu.no
http://www.item.ntnu.no/~lillk

Abstract. We will look into handling of mobility and intelligence in new mobile systems. Our aim is to build telecom system(s) enabling many types of mobility, as well as many different types of 'rich' or 'intelligent' applications. We will look into 'beyond 3G systems' based on middleware. We will look back to the design of the 3GPP system UMTS IMS. We analyze different choices and solution in IMS with an eye to the needed *co-operation* (standardization) vs. the possibilities for *competitiveness*. I.e., we investigate the possibility to deploy services that shall not be standardized. Based on this we introduce some new refined mobility definitions aimed at middleware based systems. We also identify some further research issues to be solved before middleware can be fully introduced in new 'intelligent' telecom systems.

1 Introduction

Several research projects aiming at 'beyond 3G' plan to use middleware or some sort of platform for mobile code. We find it relevant to revisit TINA, but this time with a close eye also on the real time requirements from the telecom domain. TINA's slogan was: "A co-operative solution for a competitive world" [1]. This aim is still valid. Competition between operators and between operators and content provider etc. are becoming more important. We also revisit the design of the UMTS IMS system [2], because that design had some focus on competitive services.

TINA was based on the use of modern middleware platform. Based on Open Distributed Processing (ODP) TINA defined a Distributed Processing Environment (DPE). A well known ODP compliant architecture is CORBA, Common Object Request Broker Architecture, with its Object Request Broker (ORB) implementation TINA service architecture [3] introduced the notion of BAD (Business Administrative Domain) and related this to the DPE.

The paper is organized as follows: First we look at some trends relating to convergence and we look carefully into some mobility and middleware definitions in the context of this convergence. Then we 'make a step back' looking into the design of UMTS IMS (from around 1999). We identify important issues discussed during the design and standardization of that system. We then return to middleware, looking into

A. Aagesen et al. (Eds.): INTELLCOMM 2004, LNCS 3283, pp. 54–69, 2004.
© IFIP International Federation for Information Processing 2004

TINA, in the light of IMS. At the end we introduce some refined mobility definitions for middleware, and identify some related issues for further research in order to use middleware 'all over' in a modern telecom system.

2 Convergence

With convergence and the introduction of IP into telecom systems we also introduce some new separations. This means: Things that we former thought of as one thing, has now became several different entities. The user and terminal are now separated[1].We may illustrate the old systems and new convergent system as in Fig. 1.

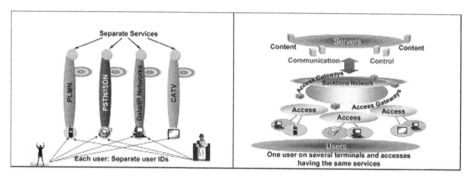

Fig. 1. Evolution: From several monolithic systems (left) towards an access agnostic system with user mobility. The left part illustrates *today's situation* where the user has several different identities, and several rather similar services. The similar services may be either *messaging service* with its variants (Email, SMS, Instant Messaging (IM),…) or *voice telephony service* with its variants: (GSM voice telephony with call forwarding to mobile-voicemail, PSTN voice telephony with fixed-line-voicemail etc). The right part illustrates a *new situation*, where user and terminal is separated, and the same services may be accessed from several devices with the same user id. Figure is modified from Ericsson, see e.g. [4]

Another aspect of convergence is the combination of GSM / GPRS / UMTS technology (with its continuous handover) with more discrete and nomadic services on PCs and PDAs via IP and WLAN (e.g. web, with email and chat etc.). We may note that discrete terminal mobility may be supported also in fixed networks. We may also note that the separation of *discrete* and *continuous* terminal mobility corresponds to the well known separation of *call-related* and *non-call-related* (see more details in section 2.2).

---

[1] We have all seen drawings of the 'ultimate communication device' having clock, screen, loud speakers, printer etc. all build in. But specialized devices like phone, clock, etc. will still be around. One may also foresee that PCs will continue to exist as separate entity despite of devices like 'chat boards' attached to mobile phones and PDAs. Thus we will still have a multitude of terminal types, and it is important to handle that one user can use several of these devices, inside one common system.

2.1 The New Separation of User and Terminal

When we are separating the user and the terminal, we need to take care then we talk about terminal mobility and user mobility. We will return to this in section 3.2.

IMS is 'access antagonistic', and this means that also fixed accesses should fit in. See Fig. 1 again. We will list some issues that must be looked into when designing such a system:

Where/on which terminal(s) do you want your call to be delivered? How/where to handle other special call treatment? End-point or network? What if the only available terminal and network is a 2G network (e.g. PSTN)? How to have access to your address book and more at all times and from all devices? How to treat hand-over and call transfer between different networks which may vary in both network capabilities and costs? Should A or B pay for B's mobility? [2]

Some of this issues are mostly related to the fact that one user is moving between several terminals, while others are mostly dealing with the relations between the home network domain, the visited (or access) network (and the endpoint). We will return to some of these questions later (e.g. in section 4).

2.2 Some Session Definitions Relating to Real Time

We have already indicated that log-on procedures to fixed line terminals should be possible within a future mobile system. Hence we have discrete and continuous mobility in our system. In telecom we traditionally have the following concepts:

- Call session and the so-called *call related services*. This is related to the normal telecom concept of 'soft real time'. A typical example is execution of call forwarding or call transfer. (Handover of call falls into the same category)
- Registration procedures and other *non-call-related services*. This is related to an interactive process involving the user and will have some timing requirement. Turning on the mobile and activating call forwarding are typical examples
- For the sake of completeness we should also mention *management services*. These services may be interactive or may even be run as a batch job.

TINA however ignored these differences in their modeling, and did not separate session data from persistent data. This might have caused some problems when implementing a services like 'multimedia call' in a real time and scalable way.

---

[2] In GSM the caller (A) pays for a national mobile call (i.e. A pays for some of B's mobility). This is possible because A knows that he calls a mobile number with a specific tariff. B pays for the roaming leg in case he is moved to abroad, since this is unknown to caller A. In US mobile systems, no separate number range was allocated for mobile calls, so in all cases the called party B paid. This resulted in a situation where many customers did not give out the mobile number, because of fear for the extra cost. This was partly a reason for the slow take up of mobile systems in the US. Note also that fixed telephony has different charging models in Europe and US, and this influence usage patterns.

3 Some Definitions Relating to Mobility and Middleware

We must be careful with our definitions. They may come from several sources, and implicitly have different contexts and assumptions surrounding them.

There are many notions of middleware. The GSM system may be seen as supporting location and migration transparencies to the applications in the GSM terminals. This view might work for some distributed applications, (typically those using socket programming). However, for building new distributed applications in general we may need to look more closely into the call setup procedures (sometimes called session control).

3.1 Initial Remark: Data and Code

In a von Neumann architecture we separate data and code. However, data may in fact be code. The 'classical example' is a Universal Turing machine taking a description of another Turing machine as input. A less abstract example is a compiler taking code as input.

We still find it useful to separate between *code* and *data*, not the least for performance reasons. Thus we may have *.exe* files and *.dat* files as well as (small or big) (control) data being communicated ('moved') over the network and we find it sometimes useful to distinguish them.

Code and *data* are just two ways of looking at the same thing. A relevant analogy is in physics where we can consider light either as *waves* or as *particles*. We can chose the one or the other approach depending on what properties we are aiming at. Reasoning about real time and performance are best done when code and data are seen as different entities.

However, other properties may easiest be deduced by playing with the 'code=data' concept. E.g. some properties of service interaction problems can be shown to be unsolvable by using these techniques and relating it to the halting problem results of Universal Turing machines. (See Gaarder and Audestad [5]).

3.2 Mobility Definitions

We start this section with definitions of terminal mobility and user mobility in a way that support the separations described in section 2.1.

Terminal Mobility is the ability of a terminal to change physical location. This includes terminals which can continue to support services while moving, and those that cannot. (From TINA [6])

Similar definitions are given in standardization documents describing currently existing mobile systems. The process of changing network access point is called a handover (or handoff) in the continuously case.

User mobility is defined as the ability for a user to connect to, or use, different terminals or terminal types for the purpose of communication. (From Ericsson [7])

This definition does not specify exactly the phrase 'for the sake of communication', nor does it specify exactly what communication services we are talking about. The next definition talks about all services (subscribed to by the user), and is hence somewhat more specific, as well as more difficult to fulfill.

Personal Mobility is the ability of a user to access [all[3]] services from any terminal and any location, (including invitations[4] to join sessions). This ability may be restricted due to contract agreements between the Consumer and Retailer, and due to user system capabilities. (From TINA [6])

This definition is pretty close to 3GPPs definition of Virtual Home Environment (VHE) defined in 3GPP [8]. It is also what we illustrate in Fig. 1 (right part).

Both these TINA definitions and the VHE definition of 3GPP are definitions of abstract concepts, not saying anything about how they should be implemented. (In fact TINA and 3GPP chose to implement them differently).

3.3 Agent Definitions

From Nwana [9] we have the following definitions:

- Agents may be classified by their mobility, i.e. by their ability to move around some network. This yields the classes of *static agent* or *mobile agent*.
- Secondly, they may be classed as either *deliberative agent* or *reactive agent*. Deliberative agents derive from the deliberative thinking paradigm: the agents possess an internal symbolic, reasoning model and they engage in planning and negotiation in order to achieve coordination with other agents.

We may also note that so far nothing is said about the communication aspects of these agents. In the light of the remarks in 3.1 we see that the definition of *static* and *mobile* may depend on how you choose to look at the system. Objects communicating via data exchange, may sometimes be seen as moving objects between them.

Much work on agents is based on deliberations and artificial intelligence (AI) technology. We will not go into that here. We will however illustrate some technology for mobile agents that do *not* use AI technology, as well as one well known static approach.

3.3.1 TACOMA Mobile Agents

We quote from [10]: An *agent* in TACOMA is a piece of code that can be installed and executed on a remote computer. Such an agent may explicitly migrate to other hosts in the network during execution. The TACOMA project focuses on operating system support for agents and how agents can be used to solve problems traditionally addressed by other distributed computing paradigms, e.g. the client/server model.

The TACOMA concept was used in the StormCast project [11] for reporting e.g. weather conditions from the fishing boats in the Artic Sea via satellite to the mainland Norway. Due to bad satellite links, (especially in bad weather, when the most needed), the code was sent from the mainland, and executed locally, and then the results were return to the mainland. We will return briefly to StormCast in Fig. 7.3).

3.3.2 SDL Processes as Static, Reactive Agents

It is a long tradition in telecom for modeling in SDL. SDL uses *static reactive agents* according to the definitions above. We may note that in telecom we are almost

---

[3] All is added here for clarity.

[4] 'Invitation to join sessions' are the TINA term corresponding to SIP INVITE (or a call setup).

always using the asynchronous communication scheme. We may also note that static agents can implement a mobile system. (GSM is a prime example).

3.4 ODP and Middleware Definitions

A simple picture of an ORB and the CORBA concepts is given in Fig. 2.1). The objects at the top are 'mobile', e.g. they can be accessed independently of their physical location. The object services, common facilities and the ORB itself will locate the object and perform the binding. Then the communication between the objects can take place. A TINA view of the DPE is given in Fig. 2.2).

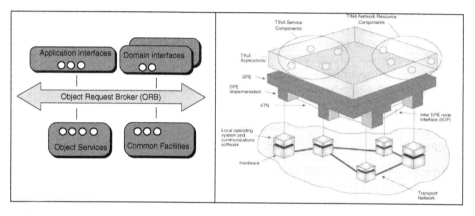

Fig. 2. Illustration of two different views of midleware. From a computer science view the network is often not shown (left). Quite naturally coming from the telecom side, TINA shows the networks: Transport Network (TN) and kernel TN (kTN). 2.1) Left: OMG-like from [12]. 2.2) Right: TINA-like, see e.g. [13]

We have the following important ODP transparencies. They will be offered by the middleware platform (the ORB/DPE and below).

Table 1. Some important ODP transparencies (from [14])

Access transparency	Hides the heterogeneity of the implementation language (by using Interface Definition Language IDL)
Location transparency	Hides the details of the location (node) of one object from the communicating other objects
Migration transparency	Hides the details of a migration function from the application objects

CORBA offers object services as well, such as Life cycle service, Naming service, Trading service, Notification service, etc.

There is a separation between migration and relocation in ODP. We will quote from Gavras [14]: 'The relocation function facilitates an uninterrupted client-server interaction during system changes'. Whether 'uninterrupted client-service interaction' means for real time in a telecom sense or 'just' for RPC over TCP is a bit unclear. Migration need not offer uninterrupted service.

We see that CORBA separates 2 types of timing constraints. They most probably correspond to the distinction between *non-call-related* and *management* in 2.2. Call related services (with stronger real time requirements) are most likely not covered by the ODP relocation concept.

4   Lessons Learnt from Designing the IMS System

Consider the question *'Where to place the 'intelligence'?* First we must define what we mean by 'intelligence'. In this paper we do not mean 'artificial intelligence', rather plain, simple functionality, like a call forwarding service, or a no-reply-functionality. We do however foresee new variants of call forwarding, or no-reply, using more complex information.

The old call forwarding services are simple in two ways: The treat all callers the same way, and they are based no simple call states such as:

- CFU Call Forwarding Unconditional
- CFBS Call Forwarding Busy Subscriber
- CFNR Call Forwarding No Reply

Now we foresee that presence and status information from an IM system may be used, as well as information from a calendar service. Some new possibilities of such services are given in [15].

We want to build new 'advanced' services. We are now ready to revisit the question *'Where to place the 'intelligence'?'.* We will do so by looking into related issues in IMS and how they were solved.

4.1   Issues in the Design of IMS

In IETF, SIP [16] is chosen as the standard for session initiation (and hence for call setup in multi media IP telephony). 3GPP has chosen SIP as well for their IMS system [2], but with some deviations in the system architecture and the business model. IMS is an access antagonistic system aiming at a convergent system, as illustrated in the right part of Fig. 1.

4.1.1   Real Time and Availability Issues

The telecom companies seems to prefer a layered approach to services, i.e. to build APIs from the call layer to a separate service layer. This is advocated in 3GPP [8] . IETF advocated an other approach with extensions, some of that history is documented on the web page [17].

One reason why the telecom companies wants an API might be that in this way the call layer may be more stable, and less affected by new features and value added services. Some real time protocols may be reused, (as in IN). Business aspects may affect the choice as well. We will not study this in more detail in this paper.

IMS is not based on mobile code. This again has something to do with the telecom requirements. It is simply much harder to guarantee the real time aspects if new foreign code starts running on your machine! It will also be much harder to guarantee 'the 5 nines' of service operation. Today we expect to be able to pick up the phone to the IT department when the computer network is down. This tell us something about the wanted availability of a modern phone system (also when it is based on IP!).

We may note that IMS is in some aspects a 'traditional' telecom system. It is based on proven technology (no mobile code), as well as the use of 'call flows'(MSCs). SDL may well be used in the internal design (though that is not formalized).

4.1.2 Issues Relating to Competition and Standardization

In the design of the IMS system some major questions were: I. Should the intelligence be in the endpoint or in the network? II. Should the intelligence be in the visited domain or in the home domain? One important issue before determining solutions to these questions was: III. What will enable us to deliver new advanced services to the market in a fast way, and at the same time obtain interoperability as well as possibilities for new competitive services?

The answer to III in UMTS IMS was: Keep the Serving call server (S-CSCF or S-CS for short) in the home domain. This allow for a 'minimal' need of standardizing the basic capabilities and features in a call setup. The wish was to avoid the standardization of value added services. Instead each domains can develop non-standard services via e.g. OSA or a separate service layer.

In such a traditional telecom system without mobile code we may place the functional entities ('boxes') in a matrix according to the layer and the domain they are in. Each of the 12 'boxes' are both software and hardware run by the same domain. This principle is illustrated by Fig. 3:

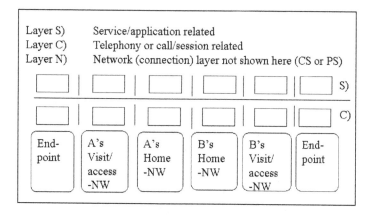

Fig. 3. Reference figure. Such a figure may be used to analyze business relations in a system. It can also be used to compare the architecture of GSM and IMS. (For more details, see [18])

Here we place IMS according to this reference figure.

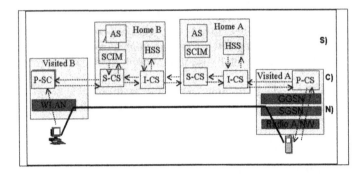

Fig. 4. IMS placed according to Fig. 3. For a similar figure of GSM and OSA, see [18]

4.2   Relating the IMS Architecture to Its 'Predecessor' IPT from Ericsson

Ericsson introduced some refinements of the H.323 system. These refinements were implemented in IPT II product in 1999-2000. Some of them were adopted as a formal standard (H.323 Annex K [19]). Others were proposed to ETSI Tiphon [20] but not accepted at that time (spring 1999). We may however say that even though the splitting was not accepted by Tiphon, the architecture and thinking behind the proposal was in the end accepted by 3GPP. (See also Ericsson press release [21]). The similarity with the 3GPP architecture is explained below:

   Fig. 5 shows the H.323 compliant system IPT II from Ericsson. We see that the gatekeeper (GK) has been split in 2 parts, the N-GK and the U-GK. This was in accordance with the proposal [20]. These two gatekeeper components correspond roughly to the IMS Call State Control Functions in IMS depicted in Fig. 4. The correspondence is as follows:

- N-GK corresponds roughly to Proxy-CSFC in IMS
- U-GK corresponds roughly to Serving-CSCF in IMS (and partly to HSS)

   In the 'classical' case of a PC to PSTN call, the called user (on the plain phone) would be treated by the PSTN system only. Here this is not the case. Instead the terminating half call is handled by the new IPT system, and the called party is an IPT-user. The IPT system supports the user mobility in an access antagonistic way, just like IMS. Fig. 5 shows how a PSTN user (B) will execute the new web-based services, and deliver the information to the calling user (A).

   Since the access is this case is fixed, continuous terminal mobility will not be supported. However, if user B later registers on a wireless terminal (WLAN or UTRAN access), then both terminal and user mobility will be supported.

   As in IMS the network centric solution with a 'user representative' in the home network enables personal mobility as well. The 'user representative' (S-CSCF and U-GK respectively) corresponds roughly to TINA's User Agent. In IPT as well as in IMS the main reason to place this 'user representative' in the home domain, was that the visiting domain(s) may be competitor(s) of the home domain.

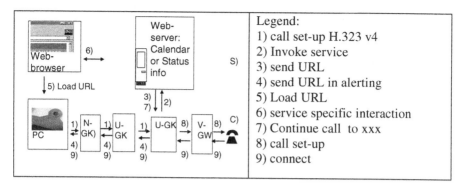

Fig. 5. Multimedia features in a Multi Media over IP system (based on Ericsson [22]). The entities are placed in accordance with Fig. 3

4.3 Concluding Remarks on the IMS System

We may notice that the system architecture in IMS is different from the GSM system architecture. Fig. 3 is useful when doing this comparison. In GSM the user profile (treating the supplementary services) is moved (as data) during registration from the home domain to the VLR/MSC in the visiting domain. Also the Camel API in GSM is different from the API approach proposed in IMS, as explained in [18]. When GSM was designed there was not much competition between the operators, in fact each operator was mainly national. We may notice that today the GSM operators are competitors. E.g. today Telia (Sweden) owns the 2nd largest GSM operator in Norway. This user profile transfer may thus reveal important user information to a competitor.

The solution in GSM requires that all the supplementary services (like CFU, CFNR etc.) are *fully standardized*. In that way the VLR / MSC would be able to treat the user profile data, and use it during its own execution of its (static) code. (Look back to section 3.1 for more on mobile data versus mobile code)

We will now return to TINA service architecture and middleware. Based on the experiences from IMS, we will revisit TINA and have an even closer look at TINA's slogan: "A co-operative solution for a competitive world". In particular we will look at business administrative domains. They will act as competitors. They will also use middleware from competing vendors. These middleware platform must co-operate, but they may also add extra functionality.

5   TINA Service Architecture

We will first give some basics of TINA. TINA Service Architecture was developed in several versions, the latest being [3] from 1997. TINA Consortium was a combination of telecom and computer (IT) companies. TINA was based on the use of a Distributed Processing Environment (DPE) and heavily influenced by ODP / CORBA.

In Fig. 2.2 we see a middleware platform where all objects 'float' freely around at the top. However, in the TINA Service Architecture we illustrate which domain each of the objects belongs. In Fig. 6 we see a typical example of domain boarders.

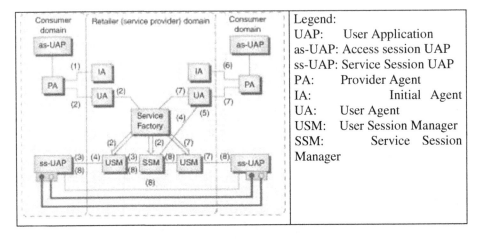

Fig. 6. TINA service session initiation with domains and multimedia streams shown. Figure from [12]. The numbers are referring to method invocations explained in TINA [3]

TINA chose to build the service session control in the applications *instead* of using the build in ORB and the common facilities. In this way we *may* obtain more control of the real time aspects, and make it easier to build call-related value added services. However TINA did not separate between call related services and management services. TINA did not separate between 'states' and persistent objects at the modeling level neither.

In general we may say that still today there are few telecom properties in most ORBs. Inside one domain (or one server farm), we may however use a telecom-enabled version of an ORB, such as e.g. TelORB [23]. But we are still far away from a situation where we have ORBs 'all over'.

In Fig. 6 the domain boarders are illustrated at the (application) object level. However, the details of how these objects maps to nodes are not shown, but it is obvious that the consumer domain is at the terminal (endpoint).

As we see in Fig. 6 TINA did not have a separate access provider. In order to support personal mobility (virtual home environment) it would be natural to place the User Agent in the home domain. But there was something missing in the TINA definitions: The end user was supposed to log on to his home domain User Agent. There were some discussions on how this binding should take place ([24]), since it actually involved the DPE of 2 (or 3) domains. See also Kristiansen [4], for some more on this issue. We may, however, note that several research projects working with TINA and mobility in the 90'ties actually introduced an 'access network' is some form, (see e.g. Thanh [25]). For newer information (2004) on CORBA and mobile endpoints, access network and home network, see OMG [26].

Today we have global operators (e.g. of the size of Vodafone). We can imagine one such operator which we call *worldwideltel.net* that offer wireless and fixed accesses. We may have the case that *Worldwideltel.net* is present both in the subscriber's home country, and in the visiting country. The User Agent (UA) may thus be migrated to a node in the visited country, but still be in the same company.

In fact maybe *worldwideltel.net* in UK and *worldwideltel.net* in US are (legally) separate entities, but still with much cooperation between them. (Much more cooperation than between real competitors). We may e.g. assume that they have the middleware in common and use their own internal network between their ORB nodes. To move objects between nodes is part of the job of an ORB. In this case we may see this as being done within one business administrative domain (BAD).

Another question is if it really matters to move the UA to a more local node. In a global world distance is of less importance, though is may of course reduce the latency somewhat to use a local node. We may note that in any case this can be one during registration phase (non-call related). To move objects during call setup phase is far more demanding, as indicated in section 2.2.

When we move object between domains we must take care. In particular, mobility between the endpoint and network needs a special type of care. This is because the sending of data over e.g. GPRS (even best effort) is not for free. Thus it is important to control when data are sent locally between objects (applications) inside the node (terminal) and when data is sent over the (billable) network.

6 Refinements of the DPE: New Types of Mobility

In this section we will use DPE instead of ORB, since ORB is often related more directly to existing CORBA compliant products.

TINA in 1997 introduced *business administrative domains* (here we use *BAD* for short). Though not formally defined in TINA [3], it was assumed that each BAD will have responsibility for the needed middleware (DPE) within its own domain.

From TINA [3] we quote: 'The overall objective of the service architecture is to support the most general case of business administrative domains, interacting with one another over a DPE, in order to offer business objects or applications for commercial gain'. We may note that the term 'a DPE' in this quote makes this statement somewhat unclear.

The intention was that each BAD should have software objects running on a DPE that suited their own needs. Then we need to distinguish between the following meanings:

- 'A DPE' meaning 'one common DPE used by all BADs.'
- 'Several DPEs' meaning 'each BAD choosing a DPE that suits their own requirements and with some basic interworking between the DPEs to ensure interoperability).'

TINA chose the interpretation given in second bullet. We may notice that also within one BAD there may be a need for several types of DPE, some supporting high availability and real time, and others that do so to a lesser degree. This is illustrated in Fig. 7.2) Between the domains we will need protocols and Service Level Agreements (SLAs).

Fig. 7.3 may be an illustration of the StormCast project as described briefly in section 3.2. In this case the server on the mainland and the satellite phones may be regarded as belonging to *one* domain[5]. Hence we call this concept for IntraDomain mobility, since the mobility is only internal to one (business) domain. In Fig. 7.2 and Fig. 7.3) there is one business domain, and 2 DPE technology domains.

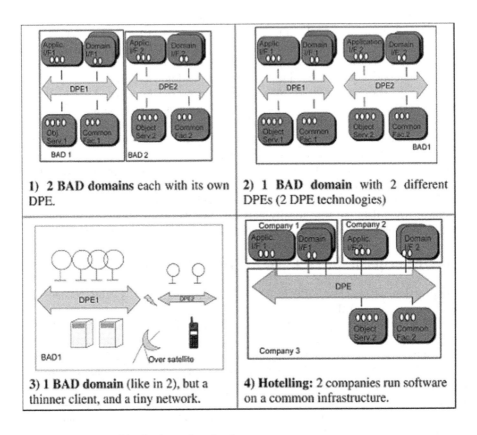

1) 2 BAD domains each with its own DPE.

2) 1 BAD domain with 2 different DPEs (2 DPE technologies)

3) 1 BAD domain (like in 2), but a thinner client, and a tiny network.

4) Hotelling: 2 companies run software on a common infrastructure.

Fig. 7. Refinements taking business domains into account

If we look into mobility across these domain boarders a refinement will be needed. Then we will have two domains like in Fig. 7.1), but the mobility will now be across the business domains. We will call this case InterDomain mobility.

Fig. 7.4 illustrates a case where Company 3 acts as a *hotel host* or *infrastructure provider* for Company1. The TINA concept of BAD is not valid any more because we are breaking the assumption of relations between DPE and BAD. To handle this case we will need even more refined definitions. The case of course gets further complicated by the fact that Company1 and Company2 share the same DPE. To formulate Service Level Agreements (SLAs) in this complex setting is for further study.

---

[5] In a general telecom setting we will regard the endpoint as a separate domain, like in Fig. 6.

We will now introduce several refined notions of mobility support of objects (or code), i.e. extending beyond the definitions of the transparencies in section 3.4 and Table 1. We will first look into the 'vertical' approach illustrated in Fig. 7.1. This corresponds to TINA's notion of BAD in the simplest case. This figure could also be refined with the notion of kTN provider and TN provider (i.e. like in Fig. 2.2).The new definitions will now be given. They all assume that each DPE is located inside one BAD, as explained earlier.

IntraDPE Mobility (DPE Mobility): Mobility of objects between nodes in one DPE domain. This definition is illustrated in Fig. 7.1) and Fig. 7.2). In this case the mobility of the objects are within DPE1 or within DPE2, but not across the DPE boarders. Implicitly this means that the objects stay inside one BAD.

IntraDomain Mobility (IntraBAD Mobility): Mobility of objects (between possibly different DPEs) within the same BAD. This definition is illustrated in Fig. 7.2) and Fig. 7.3). To support such mobility, the concept of *design portability* from TINA [6] may be needed.

InterDomain Mobility (InterBAD Mobility): Mobility of objects between business administrative domains. This corresponds to Fig. 7.1) when we allow full mobility. The issue of 'foreign code' will now pop up. (See 4.1.1)

We may also refine these 3 definitions with the real time concepts from section 2.2. Thus we may have objects that are mobile between different DPEs in the same BAD domain, but not in real time. This may e.g. correspond to a *planned* software upgrade or a planned migration of code, and this is different from handling the mobility in real time. This has similarities with the two ODP concepts migration and relocation. However, as we saw in 3.4, the ODP concepts may not distinguish between call related services demanding real time, and other services requiring some 'reasonable' response times.

7 Identification of Future Research Issues

We have seen that many of the requirements in telecom related to real time. A CORBA based middleware may be OK to use inside one domain. Here products like TelORB [23] is relevant. Across domains there are still some problems with such platform concepts and real time applications.

We will now look back to Fig. 2 and Fig. 7 and revisit the question: *Where should we place the ('intelligent') functionality?* In this case the question refines to: In the platform? In the DPE kernel? As common facilities? As object services? Or should we make the intelligence explicitly as a distributed application?

We will not answer these questions in detail here. We may however conclude briefly as follows: The more 'intelligence' or functionality we place down in the platform, the more we need to standardize (and the more time it takes).

There are also several other aspects to the questions above. To place something inside the DPE or below the DPE may be seen as a way of choosing the level of abstraction. Will this require that the domains agree on a common abstraction of their modeling? This question is again related to the design portability definition from TINA [6].

Some service creation methodologies assume that the same (design) methodology is used 'all over'. This is not realistic. Inside each domain the business itself should be able to use what they conceive as the best tools available to move from service creation, and down to running code. We need to allow for plain protocol interworking between domains.

8 Conclusion

We have studied the notions of platform and mobility. In particular we separate between sessions and objects that are mobile *in real time* (call related) and *not in real time*. We also separate objects being mobile *within* a business domain or *between* business domains. We separate object mobility *within* a DPE technology domain and *between* DPE technologies as well.

Questions like: *Where to place the intelligence?*, may have several answers. Based on the experienced from the design of the new multimedia IMS system in UMTS, we find it useful to consider this along two axes:

- A horizontal axis: from endpoint, via access network to core network.
- A vertical axis: from application layer to call layer to middleware layer.

We have given some new some definitions of mobility in a DPE setting. We have also identified some new research issues that needs to be answered.

It is important to analyze the need for standardization versus the need for competitive services and a quick time to market. It is also important to take the real time and other telecom requirements into account.

Acknowledgments

The author wants to thank several former co-workers in TINA core-team and in Ericsson (in Norway, Sweden, the Netherlands and elsewhere). Børge Nilsen then at Ericsson IPT (Norway) should be mentioned in particular.

References

[1] TINA Consortium web site: www.tinac.com (Accessed July 2004)
[2] 3GPP, IP Multimedia Subsystem (IMS); Stage 2 (release 5), TS 23.228
[3] TINA, Service Architecture Version 5.0, Baseline document, (1997)
[4] Kristiansen, L.: A 'user centric' appraoch to multi media services, TINA Conference, Paris, (2000) http://www.tinac.com/conference/Paris2000_14.htm
[5] Gaarder, K. and Audestad, J. A.: Feature Interaction Policies and the undecidability of a General Feature Interaction Problem, TINA Workshop, L'Aquila, Italy, (1993)
[6] TINA-C Glossary of Terms Version: 2.0, (1997)
[7] Ericsson, L.M.: Mobility and roaming technologies, ETSI Tiphon contribution 12TD088, (1999) http://www.item.ntnu.no/~lillk/docs/12td088.doc
[8] 3GPP, Virtual Home Environment/Open Service Access, Doc. no. TS 23.127
[9] Nwana, H. S.: Software Agents: An Overview, Knowledge Engineering Review, Vol. 11, No 3, (1996) 1-40, http://agents.umbc.edu/introduction/ao/
[10] TACOMA, http://www.tacoma.cs.uit.no/overview.html (Accessed April 2004)
[11] StormCast http://www.cs.uit.no/forskning/DOS/StormCast/ (Accessed April 2004)

[12] Braek, R.: Middleware lecture, tttm4160, NTNU ((Accessed April 2004)
http://www.item.ntnu.no/fag/ttm4160/Middleware/Middleware.pdf

[13] Handegaard, T. and Kristiansen, L.: The TINA Architecture, Telektronikk Vol. 94 No.1, ISSN 0085-7130, (1998), 95-106,

[14] Gavras, A.: Distributed Platforms for Telecom Applications, Telektronikk Vol.96, 4 ISSN 0085-7130, (2000) 137-145

[15] Bolstad, K.: Personalized options on no answer conditions; introducing HTTP based menus into IP multimedia telephony, M.Sc. thesis, Ifi, Univ. of Oslo, May 2001. Available http://www.item.ntnu.no/~lillk/docs/NoReply.pdf (Accessed July 2004)

[16] IETF Network Working Group, SIP: Session Initiation Protocol, RFC: 3261 http://www.ietf.org/rfc/rfc3261.txt

[17] Schulzrinne, H.: SIP Drafts: Extensions to Base Specification, web-page http://www.cs.columbia.edu/sip/drafts_base.html (Accessed July 2004)

[18] Kristiansen, L.: An Open Service Architecture With Location Aware Calls And Services, Proceeding of WOCN conference, Oman, (2004)

[19] ITU-T, H.323 Ver.4, Annex K

[20] L.M. Ericsson, Splitting the Gatekeeper, and some reasons to do so, ETSI Tiphon contribution 13TD104, (1999)

[21] L.M. Ericsson, IPT II press release, June 2000 http://www.ericsson.com/press/archive/2000Q2/20000607-0099.html

[22] Ericsson, L.M.: Services in H.323, Protocol Update, Presentation at VoN, Atlanta, Nov. 1999, http://www.item.ntnu.no/~lillk/presentations/Von-99-atlantawernerE.ppt

[23] Telorb, web page http://www.telorb.com (Accessed July 2004)

[24] TINA, Internal discussions on mobility with Hans Hegermann, core team member, 1996

[25] Thanh, D.V.: Mobility as an Open Distributed Processing transparency, Dr. Scient Thesis, Ifi, Univ.of Oslo, ISBN 82-7368-162-9, (1997)

[26] OMG, Wireless Access and Terminal Mobility in CORBA, Version 1.1, (2004)

Trust Negotiation with Nonmonotonic Access Policies

Phan Minh Dung and Phan Minh Thang

Department of Computer Science, Asian Institute of Technology,
GPO Box 4, Klong Luang, Pathumthani 12120, Thailand
{dung, thangphm}@cs.ait.ac.th

Abstract. We study the structure of nonmonotonic access policies for internet-based resources. We argue that such policies could be divided into two parts: the locally designed policies and imported policies. Imported policies should always be monotonic while the local policies could be nonmonotonic. We develop a safe proof procedure for nonmonotonic trust negotiation where safety means that access to a resource is granted only if its access policy is satisfied.

1   Introduction

Blaze, Feigenbaum and Lacy [1] introduced trust management (TM) as a new approach to decentralized authorization. An access decision in TM is based on two sources of information obtained from the credentials submitted by the clients and from local databases of collected credentials and observations. An example is an access policy of an auction site stating that a client with a valid digital credit card and no record of cheating is allowed to participate in its auction service. Such rule could be represented using Horn clauses as follows:

Believe(S,TrustWorthy(Auction),C) ← Believe(S,HaveFund,C),
                                    not Believe(S,Fraudster,C)

stating that server S believes that client C is trustworthy for access to the auction if S believes that C has sufficient fund and S has no evidence to believe that C is a fraudster where a valid credit card is a convincing proof for S that the client has sufficient fund.

It has been recognized in the literature that one of the key requirements for TM access policies is that it should be monotonic with respect to the client's submitted credentials but could be nonmonotonic with respect to the site's local information about the client [12]. This requirement is designed to avoid situations in which the client has been given access to some services, but later when he submits new credentials for other services, and the disclosure of the new credentials may terminate the access to those services granted to him before. The question of what kind of structure access policies should have to satisfy this requirement is still open.

A. Aagesen et al. (Eds.): INTELLCOMM 2004, LNCS 3283, pp. 70–84, 2004.
© IFIP International Federation for Information Processing 2004

A key aspect in TM is delegation. Delegation allows a principal to transfer authority over some resources to other principals. Delegation hence divides a principal's access policies into two parts: The principal's own policies and other components that are imported. Consider for example the policies of a book store that offered discount to its preferred customer [10]. Students from a nearby university U are its preferred customers. The book store policy also states that any preferred customer of an E-organization is also its preferred customer. The access policy hence consists of two parts: the book store local regulation that directly identifies who gets discount, and the imported regulation of the E-organization about its preferred customers.

Imported policies are rules to determine the beliefs of those who issued them. Therefore imported policies should be monotonic as otherwise, to evaluate them, an agent would need to have access to the entire information base (often including sensitive information) of the issuers of such policies. However in practice, agents are unlikely to let other agents having access to their sensitive local information. Hence, it is natural to expect imported policies to be monotonic.

Herzberg et all [6] has discussed nomonotonicity for access policies without imported rules. The monotonicity with respect to the client submitted credentials was not discussed in [6]. Though a proof procedure for nonmonotonic access policies has been given in [6], it is not clear what kind of declarative semantics this procedure has and especially how it is related to the semantics of nonmonotonic reasoning.

Trust negotiation is a process of exchanging certificates and policy statements that allows one party to establish sufficient trust on the other party to allow it access to some resource.

Logic programming has been shown to be an appropriate framework for studying trust management [10]. It is also well-known that the mechanism of negation as failure in logic programming provides a powerful tool for nonmonotonic reasoning [4, 5].

In this paper we study the structure of nonmonotonic access policies and develop a procedure for trust negotiation with nonmonotonic access policies. Our procedure is based on the sldnf procedure in logic programming. We then show that the proposed procedure produces safe negotiation in the sense that access to a resource is granted only if its access policy is satisfied.

2 Preliminaries: Logic Programming and Stable Model Semantics

A *program clause* is of the form $a \leftarrow a_1, \ldots, a_n, not\, b_1, \ldots, not\, b_m$ where a, $a_1, \ldots, a_n, b_1, \ldots, b_m$ are atoms. The clause is called *definite if $m = 0$*. A *logic program* is a set of program clauses.

Let P be a logic program and G be the set of all the ground instances of clauses in P. A *stable model* of P is defined as a set of ground atoms M such that M is the least Herbrand model of P_M where P_M is obtained from G as follows:

Delete every clause C from G whose body contains a negative literal $not\,A$ such that $A \in M$.

Delete all negative literals from the remaining clauses.

We write $P \models A$ for a ground atom A if A belongs to all stable models of P. More about semantics of logic programs could be found in [4, 5].

3   Structure of Nonmonotonic Access Policies

We assume an alphabet consisting of the following components:

- A set $\mathcal{R}$ of role (also called attribute) names
- A set of principal identifiers PI
- A set RE of resource identifiers.
- A distinct unary attribute symbol $Trustworthy$ (often abbreviated as TW)
- A ternary predicate $Bel(x,R,y)$ stating that x believes that y has attribute R.
- A binary predicate symbol $Hold(R,x)$ stating that x has attribute R.

A *principal term* is either a principal identifier from PI or a PI-variable where a PI-variable is a variable that could be instantiated with values from PI only.

A *certificate* is of the form Cert(A,R,B) where A,B are principal identifiers from PI and R is an attribute term. The purpose of a certificate is to certify that A believes that B has the attribute R. In practice, certificates have more complex structures. We restrict ourself on a simple form of certificates as we are focused on the study of nonmonotonic access policies. Certificates represent an important kind of resources that are different from those resources represented by resource identifiers from RE. We define a *resource term* either as a resource identifier, or a certificate.

A *attribute term* has the form $R(t_1, \ldots, t_n)$ where R is an n-ary attribute symbol from $\mathcal{R}$ and $t_1, \ldots, t_n$ are resource terms.

An *atom* is either of the form Bel(p,T,q) or Hold(T,p) where p,q are principal terms and T is an attribute term. q is called the *subject* of the atom while p is its *issuer*. A literal is an atom or the negation of an atom. The subject or issuer of a literal is the subject or issuer of its atom respectively.

Let $\mathcal{S}$ be a set of belief atoms and x,y be two principal terms appearing in some atoms in S. We say that there is a **flow of trust** from x to y in $\mathcal{S}$ if there are principal terms $p_1, \ldots, p_m$ and attribute terms $T_1, \ldots, T_{m-1}$ such that $Bel(p_i, T_i, p_{i+1}) \in \mathcal{S}$ and x = p_1 and $y = p_m$.

A *policy clause* of a principal A is of the form:

$$Bel(A, T, p) \leftarrow \alpha_1, \ldots, \alpha_n, not\, \alpha_{n+1}, \ldots, not\, \alpha_{n+k}$$

where A is a principal identifier, p is a principal term, T is a attribute term and $\alpha_1, \ldots, \alpha_{n+k}$ are atoms such that every variable except p appears as the subject of some positive literal in the body of the clause. The intuition behind this condition is that there is a flow of trust from some well-known principals, represented as principal identifiers in the clause, to any principal that could possibly appear in A's policy. A is called the *issuer* of the clause.

A principal term p is said to be *redundant* in a policy clause if there exists no flow of trust from p to the subject of the head of the clause in the set of positive literals of the clause body. A policy clause is said to be *nonredundant* if there is no redundant principal terms in its body.

It is not difficult to see that credentials defined in the languages RT_0, RT_1, RT_2 in the RT family [10] could be represented either as a certificate or as a policy clause in our framework.

An *access policy* of an principal A is defined as a a pair $APL = (LPL, IPL)$ where

- LPL is a finite set of local nonredundant policy clauses of A.
- IPL is a finite set of imported nonredundant policy clauses whose issuers are not A.

Consider the access policies of the book store (BS) example in the introduction. The policy clauses of BS are the following:

$$Bel(BS, TW(Discount), x) \leftarrow Bel(BS, PreferredCustomer, x)$$
$$Bel(BS, PreferredCustomer, x) \leftarrow Bel(U, Student, x)$$
$$Bel(BS, PreferredCustomer, x) \leftarrow Bel(EOrg, PreferredCustomer, x)$$

while the imported clauses are those determining who are the preferred customers of EOrg.

Imported policies are rules to determine the beliefs of those who issued them. Therefore imported policies should be monotonic as otherwise, to evaluate them, an agent would need to have access to the entire information base (often including sensitive information) of the issuers of such policies. However in practice, agents are unlikely to let other agents having access to their sensitive local information. Hence, it is natural to expect imported policies to be monotonic.

The *attribute dependency graph* of a access policy P is a directed graph whose nodes are the attributes appearing in P, and there is a positive (resp. negative) edge from α to β if α appears in the head of a clause in P and β appears in positive (resp. negative) literal in its body.

A path in the attribute dependency graph of P is said to be *positive* (resp *negative*) if all (resp. some) edges on this path are positive (resp. negative).

Now we can define formally the notion of a trust management system.

Definition 1. *Let A be a principal identifier. A Trust Management System (TMS) for A is represented as a quadruple $\langle APL, DBO, DBC, CA \rangle$ consisting of*

1. *An access policy $APL = (LPL, IPL)$ of A such that all imported clauses in it are definite.*
2. *a set DBO of ground atoms of the form Hold(R,B) where R is a ground attribute term and B is a principal identifier. Atoms in DBO represent information A has collected locally about other principals.*
3. *a set of certificates DBC that are in A's possession.*

4. *a set of client attributes $CA \subseteq \mathcal{R}$ that the A expects the client to satisfy. CA is hence required to satisfy the following conditions:*

   (a) *For each $T \in CA$, T does not appear in the head of each of the clauses of APL.*
   (b) *All paths leading to attributes in CA in the attribute dependency graph of P are positive.*
      As we will see shortly this condition ensures that the access policy is monotonic with respect to the client's submitted credentials.

From definition 1, it follows immediately that there is no path linking an attribute that appears in a negative literal in the body of some clause of APL to an attribute in CA in the attribute dependency graph of APL. This condition guarantees that when a server checks a negative condition, it does not require the client to send extra information.

Example 1. Consider the trust management system $\langle APL, DBO, DBC, CA \rangle$ of an agent S who oversees the access to sensitive documents in a hospital. The policy states that only doctors who could present a credential from a recognized hospital and are not known to have a careless conviction from recognized hospitals, have access to the documents. A recognized hospitals is either known locally or certified by other recognized hospitals [6]. The hospital access policies could be expressed as follows:

$$Bel(S, TrustWorthy(R), x) \leftarrow not\ Bel(S, Convicted, x),\ Bel(y, Doctor, x),$$
$$Bel(S, RecognizedHospital, y)$$
$$Bel(S, RecognizedHospital, x) \leftarrow Hold(RecognizedHospital, x)$$
$$Bel(S, RecognizedHospital, x) \leftarrow Bel(S, RecognizedHospital, y),$$
$$Bel(y, RecognizedHospital, x)$$
$$Bel(S, Convicted, x) \leftarrow Bel(S, RecognizedHospital, y), Bel(y, Convicted, x),$$

where R denotes the sensitive documents.

The local certificate database DBC consists of certificates Cert(S,Recognized Hospital,H), Cert(H,RecognizedHospital,K) and Cert(H,Convicted,P). The local database DBO contains the fact Hold(RecognizedHospital,H). The set of client attributes CA is defined by $CA = \{Doctor\}$.

Definition 2. *Let C be a principal identifier and $\mathcal{A} = \langle APL, DBO, DBC, CA \rangle$ be a TMS. A set SC of basic credentials of the form Cert(B,T,C) with $T \in CA$ is said to be a guarantee for C to get access to a resource R wrt $\mathcal{A}$ if*

$$APL \cup DBO \cup Th \models Bel(A, TrustWorthy(R), C)$$

where $Th = \{Bel(B, S, D) \mid Cert(B, S, D) \in DBC \cup SC\}$

The monotonicity with respect to the client submitted credentials is stated in the theorem below.

Theorem 1. *Let $\mathcal{A} = \langle APL, DBO, DBC, CA \rangle$ be a TMS of A, C be principal identifiers, SC be a guarantee for C to get access to R wrt $\mathcal{A}$ and SC' be a set of credentials of the form Cert(B,T,C) with $T \in CA$ such that $SC \subseteq SC'$. Then SC' is also a guarantee for C to get access to R wrt $\mathcal{A}$.*

Proof. Let $P = APL \cup DBO \cup \{Bel(B,S,D) \,|\, Cert(B,S,D) \in DBC \cup SC\}$ and $P' = APL \cup DBO \cup \{Bel(B,S,D) \,|\, Cert(B,S,D) \in DBC \cup SC'\}$. Further let $SC_0 = SC' \setminus SC$. Further let M' be stable models of P'. It is not difficult to see that $P'_{M'} = P_{M'} \cup \{Bel(B,S,D) \,|\, Cert(B,S,D) \in SC_0\}$. Let M be the least Herbrand model of $P_{M'}$. Hence $M \subseteq M'$. It is not difficult to see that for each atom $\alpha \in M' \setminus M$, there is a positive path from the attribute of α to an attribute of a certificate in SC_0 in the attribute dependency graph of APL. From the structure of trust management system (definition 1), it follows that α does not appear as a ground instance of a negative literals in any of the policy clauses. Hence $P_M = P_{M'}$. Hence M is a stable model of P. From the assumption that SC be a guarantee for C to get access to R wrt $\mathcal{A}$, it follows immmediately $Bel(A, TW(R), C) \in M'$. The theorem is proved.

4   Trust Negotiation with Nonmonotonic Access Policies

When a principal A wants to access a resource R controlled by B, A sends a request to B. B will consult its local policy to check whether A is trustworthy enough to be given access to R. During this process, B may ask A to send over some certificates to certify certain attributes of A. If the checking process is successful, B will send A a message informing it that its request for access to R has been granted. On the other hand, when A gets requests from B for A's certificates, A consults its own local policy to check whether B should be given access to the requested certificates. A may ask B to send over some certificates before sending B the requested certificates. An example is a scenario in which a client of a E-business orders some good. The business may ask the client for a credit card. Before sending the credit card to the business, the client may ask for a Better Business Bureau certificate from the business. In the following, we will model these processes.

There are many possible strategies on how trust negotiation could be conducted. Consider an example of a policy governing access to sensitive documents of a top secret project where only members of partner projects are allowed to access the documents.

$$Bel(S, TrustWorthy, x) \leftarrow Hold(Partner, y), Bel(y, Member, x),$$

An agent could work on many projects and is reluctant on its part to disclose its associations to these projects.

When getting a access request, S could reveal the partner projects and asks the client to prove its association to one of them. This would reveal sensitive information about identity of the partner projects and hence unacceptable to S. S could on the other hand ask the client to identify the projects he works in.

If one of them is a partner project of S, access is granted for the client. This would force the client to reveal its association to projects that it may consider to be sensitive. Which one is preferred could hardly be determined without considering the real context of such applications. The example indicates that there may be no conceptually best access policies evaluation strategy for all participants involved. The evaluation proof procedure we are going to present shortly may be an appropriate one in one context and less so in others. But anyway it represents an option that needs to be taken into consideration when a method is designed for access policy evaluation in an application.

The negotiation strategy developed in this paper is biased toward the manager of a resource. In the above example, when getting a access request, the server asks the client for credentials certifying its association to projects he works in. In this way, the server could protect its data but the client may have to expose more sensitive information than it loves to.

There are two kinds of requests that principals may send to each other:

- Original requests that start a negotiation process:

$$A \text{ to } B : Bel(B, TW(R), A)$$

  stating intuitively that A (the sender) asks B (the receiver) to check whether A is trustworthy for access to R.
- Requests that are sent in response to an earlier request:

$$A \text{ to } B : Bel(x, T, B)$$

  stating intuitively that A asks B for certificates certifying that B has attribute T.

Negotiation results are sent in messages of the following form:

$$A \text{ to } B : \textbf{success(R)}$$
$$A \text{ to } B : fail$$

in which A informs B that the negotiation for access to R has succeeded or failed respectively.

During a trust negotiation, the sets of certificates collected by participants change as the principals involved may have to send to the other side a number of certificates. We define a *state* of a principal B during a negotiation as a pair (sc,ss) where sc represents the set of certificates it has collected so far in his database of certificates and ss represents the set of certificates it has sent to the other side from the start of the current negotiation until now.

A negotiation is characterized by state change caused by sending and receiving requests. We use the notation $(sc, ss) \xrightarrow{M?;N!}_B (sc', ss')$ (resp. $(sc, ss) \xrightarrow{M!;N?}_B (sc', ss')$) to denote that when B receives (resp. sends) a request M, B will start its part in a negotiation process to satisfy M and B ends the negotiation when B sends out (resp. receives) message N containing the result of the negotiation. At the end of the negotiation, sc" is the set of credentials B has collected so far and ss" is the set of credentials B has sent over to A.

Definition 3. *Suppose principals A,B are in a state $st = (sc, ss)$, $st' = (sc', ss')$.
A state transition is triggered when a request M is sent or received.*

1. *Let M be of the form*

$$A \text{ to } B : Bel(B, TW(R), A)$$

   *where R is a resource but not a certificate. A negotiation is initiated when
   M is sent from A to B. It follows that $ss = ss' = \emptyset$. When B receives M,
   B checks its access policy to see whether A is trustworthy for access to R.
   Formally B constructs a local derivation (to be defined shortly) of the form*

$$Ld = (G_0, sc, \emptyset), \ldots, (G, sc", ss")$$

   and $G_0 = Bel(B, TW(R), A)$.
   (a) *If Ld is a successful local derivation wrt B (to be defined shortly) then
   following transition happens*

$$(sc, \emptyset) \xrightarrow{M?;N!}_B (sc", ss")$$

$$(sc', \emptyset) \xrightarrow{M!;N?}_A (sc' \cup ss", sc" \setminus sc)$$

   where N has the form

$$B \text{ to } A : \quad success(R)$$

   (b) *If Ld is a failed local derivation wrt B (to be defined shortly) then following transition happens*

$$(sc, \emptyset) \xrightarrow{M?;N!}_B (sc", ss")$$

$$(sc', \emptyset) \xrightarrow{M!;N?}_A (sc' \cup ss", sc" \setminus sc)$$

   where N has the form

$$B \text{ to } A : \quad fail$$

2. *Let M be of the form*

$$A \text{ to } B : Bel(p, T, B)$$

   *stating that A needs access to some certificate certifying that B has prop-
   erty T. Note that p is a principle term. Upon receiving M, B will check for
   those certificates of the form $Cert(C, T, B)$ in its pool of certificate DBC_B.
   B selects one of them and consults its local policy to check whether A could
   be given access to it. If the check is successful, the certificate will be sent to
   A If the check fails another certificate of the form $Cert(C, T, B)$ is selected
   and check whether it could be sent to A. The process continues until either
   B finds a certificate to send to A or B breaks the negotiation by sending a
   fail message to A. This process is formalized as follows:*

   *Let $SC = \{C_1, \ldots, C_m\}$, $m \geq 0$ be the set of certificates in SC of the
   form $Cert(C_i, T, B)$ such that p, C_i are unifiable.*

(a) If $SC = \emptyset$ then following transition happens:

$$(sc, ss) \xrightarrow{M?;N!}_B (sc, ss)$$

$$(sc', ss') \xrightarrow{M!;N?}_A (sc', ss')$$

where N has the form

$$B \text{ to } A : \; fail$$

(b) Let $SC \neq \emptyset$. Let $G_0 = K_1 \vee \ldots \vee K_m$ where $K_i = Bel(B, TW(C_i), A)$. There are two cases:

   i. There is a successful local derivation wrt B of the form

$$(G_0, sc, ss), \ldots, (H, sc", ss")$$

with $H = nil \vee K_{i+1} \vee \ldots \vee K_m$. Then following transition happens

$$(sc, ss) \xrightarrow{M?;N!}_B (sc", ss" \cup \{C_i\})$$

$$(sc', ss') \xrightarrow{M!;N?}_A (sc' \cup (ss" \setminus ss) \cup \{C_i\}, ss' \cup (sc" \setminus sc))$$

where N has the form

$$B \text{ to } A : \; success(C_i)$$

We will see later, a successful local derivation $(G, sc, ss), \ldots, (H, sc', ss')$ wrt B means that B has successively check that A could be given access to some of the certificate in SC. From $H = nil \vee K_{i+1} \vee \ldots \vee K_m$, this certificate is identified as C_i.

   ii. There is a failed local derivation wrt B of the form

$$(G_0, sc, ss), \ldots, (\emptyset, sc", ss")$$

then

$$(sc, ss) \xrightarrow{M?;N!}_B (sc", ss")$$

$$(sc', ss') \xrightarrow{M!;N?}_A (sc' \cup (ss" \setminus ss), ss' \cup (sc" \setminus sc))$$

where N has the form

$$B \text{ to } A : \; fail$$

We introduce now the notion of local derivation. First we define a *goal* as a disjunction $K_1 \vee \ldots \vee K_n$ where each K_i is a conjunction of literals.

Intuitively a local derivation from a goal G wrt B is a sequence of goals whose first element is G. Each step in the derivation corresponds to the application of some inference rule which replaces one of the conjunctions by a goal. In this paper, we use a depth-first strategy by always selecting the leftmost conjunction for expansion. A derivation is successful if one of the conjunction is an empty one. A derivation is failed if the last goal is the empty disjunction[1]. In the following, we give a formal definition of the inference steps involved.

---

[1] Note that empty conjunction denotes true while empty disjunction denotes false.

Let $B = \langle APl_B, DBO_B, DBC_B, CA_B \rangle$. Formally, a local derivation wrt B from a goal G is a sequence of pairs $(G_0, st_0), \ldots, (G_n, st_n)$ where G_i are goals, $G_0 = G$, $st_i = (sc_i, ss_i)$ are states of B. Each G_i in the sequence is obtained from the previous one using an inference rule given below. We employ depth-first search strategy by always selecting the leftmost literal in the leftmost conjunction for expansion.

For the purpose of simple reference, we call an atom of the form $Bel(x, T, A)$ where $T \in CA_B$ an *input atom* of B as A is expected to provide a certificate to certify it.

Definition 4. *Let L be the selected atom in G_i and suppose that G_i has the form $K_1 \vee \ldots \vee K_m$, where each K_i is a conjunction of literals. Let $K_1 = LK_1'$[2]. $(G_{i+1}, sc_{i+1}, ss_{i+1})$ is obtained from (G_i, sc_i, ss_i) by applying one of the following steps:*

1. *(Unfolding). L is a positive literal that is not an input atom[3]. Let $Cl = \{cl_1, \ldots, cl_k\}$ be the set of clauses in*

$$APl_B \cup DBO_B \cup \{Bel(D, S, E) \leftarrow | Cert(D, S, E) \in sc_i\}$$

   such that the heads of these clauses are unifiable with L and for each i, θ_i is the most general unifier (mgu) of L and the head of cl_i. There are two cases:
   (a) Cl is empty. Then

$$G_{i+1} = K_2 \vee \ldots \vee K_m$$

$$(sc_{i+1}, ss_{i+1}) = (sc_i, ss_i)$$

   (b) Cl is not empty. Let bd_i be the body of cl_i

$$G_{i+1} = (bd_1 K_1')\theta_1 \vee \ldots \vee (bd_k K_1')\theta_k \vee K_2 \vee \ldots \vee K_n$$

$$(sc_{i+1}, ss_{i+1}) = (sc_i, ss_i)$$

2. *(Negation As Failure). L is a negative literal. There are two cases:*
   (a) L is not ground. Then

$$G_{i+1} = K_2 \vee \ldots \vee K_m$$

$$(sc_{i+1}, ss_{i+1}) = (sc_i, ss_i)$$

   (b) L is ground. There are two cases:

---

[2] For simplicity, a conjunction is written as a sequence of its conjuncts.
[3] i.e. L has the form $Bel(p, T, C)$ such that $T \notin CR_B$.

i. $L = not\,Bel(B, T, D)$.

If there is a failed local derivation wrt B from $(Bel(B, T, D), sc_i, ss_i)$ then

$$G_{i+1} = K_1' \vee K_2 \vee \ldots \vee K_m$$

$$(sc_{i+1}, ss_{i+1}) = (sc_i, ss_i)^4$$

If there is successful local derivation wrt B from $(Bel(B, T, D), sc_i, ss_i)$ then

$$G_{i+1} = K_2 \vee \ldots \vee K_m$$

$$(sc_{i+1}, ss_{i+1}) = (sc_i, ss_i)$$

ii. $L = not\,Hold(T, C)$.

If $Hold(T, C) \notin DBO_B$ then

$$G_{i+1} = K_1' \vee K_2 \vee \ldots \vee K_m$$

$$(sc_{i+1}, ss_{i+1}) = (sc_i, ss_i)$$

If $Hold(T, C) \in DBO_B$ then

$$G_{i+1} = K_2 \vee \ldots \vee K_m$$

$$(sc_{i+1}, ss_{i+1}) = (sc_i, ss_i)$$

3. (Asking for Credential). L is a positive input literal, i.e L has the form $Bel(p, T, A)$ with $T \in CA_B$ and p a (possibly nonground) principal term.

Let $SC = \{C_1, \ldots, C_k\}$, $m \geq 0$ be the set of credentials in sc_i of the form $Cert(C_i, T, A)$ and θ_i be the substitution $\{p/C_i\}$ assigning C_i to p. There are two cases:

(a) $SC \neq \emptyset$. Then

$$G_{i+1} = K_{1,1} \vee \ldots \vee K_{1,k} \vee K_2 \vee \ldots \vee K_m$$

$$(sc_{i+1}, ss_{i+1}) = (sc_i, ss_i)$$

where $K_{1,j} = K_1' \theta_j$

---

[4] Note that due to lemma 1, the sets sc_i, ss_i do not change in any local derivation of Bel(B,T,D).

(b) $SC = \emptyset$, i.e. B can not find any certificate in its pool that certifies the belief L. B then starts a negotiation by sending A a request M of the form

$$B \text{ to } A : Bel(p, T, A)$$

If there is a successful negotiation of B with A represented by a transition $(sc_i, ss_i) \xrightarrow{M!;N?}_B (sc, ss)$ where N is a success message of the form "A to B: success(C)", then

$$G_{i+1} = K'_1\theta \vee K_2 \vee \ldots \vee K_k$$

if p is a variable and θ is the substitution $\{p/D\}$ assigning D to p and $C = Cert(D, T, A)$. Otherwise

$$G_{i+1} = K_1 \vee K_2 \vee \ldots \vee K_k$$

In both cases

$$(sc_{i+1}, ss_{i+1}) = (sc, ss)$$

If there is a failed negotiation of B with A represented by $(sc_i, ss_i) \xrightarrow{M!;N?}_B (sc, ss)$ where N is a fail message of the form A to B: fail, then

$$G_{i+1} = K_2 \vee \ldots \vee K_k$$

$$(sc_{i+1}, ss_{i+1}) = (sc, ss)$$

A local derivation $(G_0, sc_0, ss_0), \ldots, (G_n, sc_n, ss_n)$ of B is *successful* if G_n is of the form $nil \vee \mathcal{D}$. It *fails* if G_n is an empty disjunction.

Lemma 1. *Let $B = \langle APl_B, DBO_B, DBC_B, CR_B \rangle$, and $sc_0 = DBC_B$. Let $(G_0, sc_0, ss_0), \ldots, (G_n, sc_n, ss_n)$ be a local derivation wrt B with $G_0 = L$ such that $notL$ is a negative literal appearing in an ground instance of a policy clause in APL_B. Then there are no asking-for-credential-steps in the derivation and $sc_n = sc_0$ and $ss_n = ss_0$.*

Proof. Obvious from the fact that there is no path from a attribute occuring in a negative literal to an attribute in CA_B in the attribute dependency graph.

Example 2. Consider the hospital example 1. Suppose that P wants to access the sensitive documents. P has a certificate C = Cert(H,Doctor,P) issued by hospital H. P is willing to show every body his certificate, i.e. APL_P consists of the only clause

$$Bel(P, TW(C), x) \leftarrow$$

P starts a negotiation with S by sending S a request M of the form "P to S: Bel(S,TW(R),P)". After receiving M, S starts a local derivation as follows

$$Ld = (G_0, sc_0, ss_0), (G_1, sc_0, ss_0), (G_2, sc_0, ss_0)$$

to check whether P is trustworthy for access to the documents where

$G_0 = Bel(S, TW(R), P)$
$G_1 = not\ Bel(S, Convicted, P), Bel(y, Doctor, P),$
$\qquad Bel(S, RecognizedHospital, y)$
$G_2 = \emptyset$ and
$sc_0 = DBC, ss_0 = \emptyset.$

Note that the selected subgoal in G_1 is $not\ Bel(S, Convicted, P)$. As there is a successful local derivation from $(Bel(S, Convicted, P), sc_0, \emptyset)$ to $(nil, sc_0, \emptyset)$, we have $G_2 = \emptyset$.

S hence informs P that his request is rejected. We have

$$(sc_0, \emptyset) \xrightarrow{M?;N!}_S (sc_0, \emptyset)$$
$$(\{C\}, \emptyset) \xrightarrow{M!;N?}_P (\{C\}, \emptyset)$$

where N is of the form "S **to** P: fail".

The following theorem shows that the negotiation defined in this chapter is safe in the sense that access to a resource is granted to a client only if it has produces a guarantee to establish its trustworthiness.

Theorem 2. *(Safe Negotiation)*
Let $B = \langle APl_B, DBO_B, DBC_B, CR_B \rangle$, *and* $sc_0 = DBC_B$.

1. *Let* $(G_0, sc_0, ss_0), \ldots, (G_n, sc_n, ss_n)$ *be a local derivation wrt B with* $G_0 = \{Bel(B, TW(R), A)\}$. *Then* $sc_n \backslash sc_0$ *is a guarantee of* $Bel(B, TrustWorthy(C), A)$ *for each certificate* $C \in ss_n \backslash ss_0$.
   If the derivation is successful then $sc_n \backslash sc_0$ *is a guarantee of* $Bel(B, TrustWorthy$
   (R),A)
2. *Suppose that*

$$(sc, ss) \xrightarrow{M?;N!}_B (sc', ss')$$

   or

$$(sc, ss) \xrightarrow{M!;N?}_B (sc', ss')$$

   where $sc = DBC_B$. *Then for each* $C \in ss' \backslash ss$, $sc' \backslash sc$ *is a guarantee for* $Bel(B, TW(C),A)$ *wrt B where A is the other party in the negotiation.*

Proof (Sketch). Assertion 2 follows immediately from assertion 1. Assertion 1 is proved by induction on the depth of the nested negotiation invoked in asking-for-credential-steps. The full proof is tedious and long and the readers are referred to the full version of this paper.

5   Conclusion and Related Works

We have studied the structure of nonmonotonic access policies and provided a general sufficient condition that guarantees the monotonicity wrt the client submitted credentials. We also have argued that only locally defined policy clauses should be nonmonotonic. The semantics of our policy language is based on the stable semantics of logic programming. We have also given a procedure for trust negotiation within our framework and showed its safety.

A weakness of our negotiation procedure is that the negotiation parties do not know whether they have submitted enough credentials for access to a resource until access is granted. This problem could be avoided by sending partially evaluated policies instead of requests for certificates like in [3, 13]. We also do not consider the privacy of local data and policies. In the future works, the procedure should be extended to deal with these problems.

Our work is based and inspired by a large body of works on trust management and negotiation [1, 3, 6, 9, 10] though with the exception of Herberg et all [6], no author has studied problems related to nonmonotonic access policies.

Bonatti and Saramanti [3] present a framework for regulating access control and information release. Access policies are monotonic and are represented by condition-action rules. The credentials are complex and represented by terms.

Trust negotiation and strategies have been studied extensively in [9, 13]. Several criteria for trust negotiation have been proposed in [13]. It would be interesting to see how these criteria could be incorporated into our framework.

Our framework is very much inspired by the RT frameworks proposed by Li, Mitchell and Winsborough [10]. Both systems are based on logic programming. While the RT framework is proposed to combine the strengths of role-based access control and trust management, our is focused on the nonmonotonicity of access policies.

References

1. M. Blaze, J. Feigenbaum, J. Lacy Decentralized Trust Management. In *Proc of the 17th IEEE Symposium on Security and Privacy, Oakland, CA, May 1996*
2. M. Blaze, J. Feigenbaum, M. Strauss Compliance Checking in the PolicyMaker Trust management System. In *Proc. of Financial Cryptography '98, LNCS 1465, 1998*
3. P. A. Bonatti, P. Samarati A Uniform Framework for Regulating Service Access and Information Release on the Web. In Conference on Computer and Communication Security, Athens, Greece, 2000
4. P. M. Dung. Negation as hypothesis: an argument-based foundation for logic programming. Journal of Logic Programming, 1994
5. M. Gelfond, V. Lifschitz, The stable model semantics for logic programming. iclp5thWashington, Seattle1988K. Bowen and R. A. Kowalski, eds 1070–1080
6. A. Herzberg, I. Golan, O. Omer, Y. Mass. An efficient algorithm for establishing trust in strangers *http://www.cs.biu.ac.il/ herzbea/Papers/PKI/ec01-paper.pdf*

7. A. Hess, B. Smith, J. Jacobson, K. E. Seamons, M. Winslett, L. Yu, T. Yu. Negotiating Trust on the Web, In *IEEE Internet Computing*, pages 30-37. IEEE Press. November 2002.

8. N. Li, W. H. Winsborough, Towards Practial Automated Trust Negotiation. In *IEEE 3rd Intl. Workshop on Policies for Distributed Systems and Networks (Policy 2002)*. IEEE Press, June 2002.

9. X. Ma, M. Winslett, T. Yu. Prunes: An Efficient and Complete Strategy for Automated Trust Negotiation over the Internet. In *Proceeding of Seventh ACM Conference on Computer and Communications Security*(CCS-7), pages 210-219. ACM Press, November 2000.

10. N. Li, J. C. Mitchell, W. H. Winsborough. Design of a Role-based Trust-management Framework. In *Proceedings of the 2002 IEEE Symposium on Security and Privacy, May 2002*.

11. J. C. Mitchell, N. Li, W. H. Winsborough, Distributed Credential Chain Discovery in Trust Management. In *Proceeding of Eighth ACM Conference on Computer and Communications Security*(CCS-8), pages 156-165. ACM Press, November 2001.

12. K. E. Seamons, M. Winslett, T. Yu, B. Smith, E. Child, J. Jacobson, H. Mills, L. Yu. Requirements for Policy Languages for Trust Negotiation. In 3rd International Workshop on Policies for Distributed Systems and Networks, June 2002

13. T. Yu, M. Winslett. An Unified Scheme for Resource Protection in Automated Trust Negotiation. In IEEE Symposium on Security and Privacy, May 2003

Secure Many-to-One Transmission of q-ary Symbols*

Antoni Martínez-Ballesté, Francesc Sebé, and Josep Domingo-Ferrer

Universitat Rovira i Virgili - Tarragona, Catalonia, Spain
{anmartin, fsebe, jdomingo}@etse.urv.es

Abstract. There is a number of applications requiring a community of many senders to transmit some real-time information to a single receiver. Using unicast connections to send this traffic can result in data implosion and swamp the receiver. In [Domi04], a mechanism was proposed for secure bit transmission in large-scale many-to-one communications; we propose here an extension for securely sending q-ary symbols.

Keywords: Multicasting, Active network application, Network security.

1 Introduction

Several applications require a large group of senders to transmit some real-time information to a single receiver (many-to-one communication). A network of sensors sending status information to a control center is one example of such applications.

Many-to-one communication entails inherent scaling problems. Too many simultaneous senders transmitting data to the receiver may overwhelm or swamp the latter, a problem usually known as implosion. In addition to requiring solutions to implosion, some many-to-one applications require secure and real-time transmission. Security usually means that transmission from each sender to the receiver should be confidential and authentic.

1.1 Previous Work

The best way to avoid the implosion problem is that intermediate nodes aggregate the information sent from the large set of senders to the unique receiver. A few contributions about aggregation of data streams in many-to-one communications can be found in the literature. In [Wolf03], a technique called aggregated hierarchical multicast is presented, whereby packets are aggregated in multicast nodes. This technique, similar to Concast is introduced as an aggregation mechanism that basically suppresses duplicate packets. It must be noticed that large

---

* This work has been partly supported by the Spanish Ministry of Science and Technology and the European FEDER fund under project TIC2001-0633-C03-01 "STREAMOBILE".

A. Aagesen et al. (Eds.): INTELLCOMM 2004, LNCS 3283, pp. 85–91, 2004.

data packets can be output from inner nodes, depending on the information sent and the number of senders attached to a node. However, the network layer seems to be the natural place to carry out the aggregation of information. According to this, as stated in [Wolf03], the aggregation operation of data packets inside the network requires the support of the network infrastructure in terms of processing resources. The scheme described in our paper also requires the support of an *active network* [Psou99].

1.2   Contribution and Plan of This Paper

In this paper, a scalable protocol for many-to-one communication is presented. The scheme proposed consists of a set-up protocol to be run before any transmissions are started, and a transmission protocol to be run for each symbol transmission. From now on, the *senders* are the leaves in the routing tree, whereas the final *receiver* is the root of the tree. Our aim is to dramatically reduce the number of connections to the receiver, sending securely fixed-length aggregated packets.

The operation of the protocol can be summarized as follows: i) in order to receive the symbols from the senders U_i, a challenge message is multicast by the receiver to all senders, via the routing tree; ii) routers in the tree aggregate encoded messages M_i received from their child nodes/senders and send aggregated information up to their parent nodes; iii) the active node closest to the receiver, produces a final message containing all symbols σ_i transmitted by the senders. iv) the receiver is finally able to decode the aggregated symbols from the final message. In practice, a mapping between the application-level language and the symbol-level language is likely to be used, whereby sending a single word in the application-level language may require sending two or more symbols. This high-level mapping is out of the scope of this paper. The proposed protocols are described in detail in Section 2. Section 3 deals with the security of the proposed scheme, whereas performance issues are examined in Section 4. Finally, Section 5 contains some conclusions.

2   Secure Aggregated Symbol Transmission

Our proposal is based on super-increasing sequences [Merk78] and probabilistic additive public-key privacy homomorphisms (PH, [Okam98]). The knapsack problem over a superincreasing sequence is used for symbol extraction from the aggregated message. On the other hand, *privacy homomorphisms* (PHs) are encryption transformations mapping a set of operations on cleartext to another set of operations on ciphertext. A PH is called *additive* when its set of cleartext operations contains addition. A PH is called *probabilistic* if the encryption algorithm involves some random mechanism that chooses the ciphertext corresponding to a given cleartext from a set of possible ciphertexts. Privacy homomorphisms that will be used in our proposal below must be additive, probabilistic and public-key. The Okamoto-Uchiyama [Okam98] probabilistic public-key cryptosystem (OUPH) has an additive homomorphic property.

2.1   Construction

Protocol 1 (Set-Up).

1. The receiver chooses parameters l, u, where l will be used below and u is the number of senders. Let t be the bit length of each symbol to be transmitted.
2. The receiver computes tu intervals as follows:

$$\mathbf{I}_j = [I_j^{min}, I_j^{max}] = [(2^j - 2)2^l - 2^{j-1} + 2, (2^j - 1)2^l - 2^{j-1} + 1]$$

for $j = 1$ to tu. Each sender is assigned t intervals among the above; specifically $\mathbf{I}_{(i-1)t+1}$ to $\mathbf{I}_{it}$ correspond to the i-th sender.
3. The receiver generates a secret value k_i for each sender i, for $i = 1$ to u.
4. The receiver generates a key pair for a probabilistic additive public-key privacy homomorphism such that its cleartext space is $CT = \{0, 1, 2, \cdots, p-1\}$ where p should be larger than $2I_{tu}^{max}$. After some manipulation, it can be checked that the lower bound on p is

$$p > (2^{tu} - 1)2^{l+1} - 2^{tu} + 2 \tag{1}$$

5. The receiver multicasts the public key PK of the PH and I_j^{min} for $j{=}1$ to tu. In addition, the receiver secretly sends k_i to each sender U_i, who should keep it confidential (storing it in a tamper-resistant device such as a smart card would seem appropriate).

Protocol 2 (Real-Time Symbol Transmission).

1. *Transmission Request.* A challenge message is multicast by the receiver to all senders. This challenge contains a random value v.
2. *Message Generation.*
   (a) When a sender U_i receives the challenge message, she computes her own t values:

$$S_{ti-t+j} = I_{ti-t+j}^{min} + \mathcal{H}(v + j - 1 \| k_i) \tag{2}$$

   for $j{=}1$ to t where $\mathcal{H}$ is a one-way collision-free hash function yielding an l-bit integer as output. This condition on the output of $\mathcal{H}$ ensures that $S_{ti-t+j} \in \mathbf{I}_{ti-t+j}$, which in turn guarantees that the *entire sequence* $\mathcal{S} = \{S_j\}$ for $j = 1, \cdots, tu$ is *super-increasing*. Note that, since v and the parameters in Protocol 1 were chosen by the receiver, the latter can readily compute the subset of $\mathcal{S}$ corresponding to any sender. On the other hand, Condition (1) ensures that no overflow in CT will occur when adding encrypted terms of the super-increasing sequence over the ciphertext space CT'. Now, U_i can transmit $2^t - 1$ different symbols by sending the encrypted sum of a subset chosen among the $2^t - 1$ non-empty subsets of $\{S_{ti-t+1}, \cdots, S_{ti}\}$[1]. For instance, if the symbol σ is mapped to

---

[1] Note that the encrypted sum of the empty subset cannot be used to encode a value because anyone can send it or guess it.

the sum of values S_{ti-t+1} and S_{ti-t+3}, sender U_i computes the following message:

$$M_i = E_{PK}(S_{ti-t+1} + S_{ti-t+3})$$

where E_{PK} stands for the encryption function of the probabilistic additive public-key privacy homomorphism used.

(b) Finally U_i sends M_i up to her parent node. The size of M_i is discussed in Section 4.

3. *Message Aggregation.* Intermediate nodes receive messages from their child nodes/senders and do the following:
   (a) Once all expected messages $\{M_i\}_i$ have been received, the node aggregates them as $M = \sum_i' M_i$, where $\sum'$ stands for the ciphertext operation of the privacy homomorphism corresponding to cleartext addition.
   (b) The node sends M up to its parent node. The size of M is discussed in Section 4.

4. *Symbol Extraction.* When the previous process completes, the receiver finally receives an aggregated message M, from which the transmitted symbols are extracted as follows:
   (a) The receiver constructs the entire super-increasing sequence $\mathcal{S} = \{S_j\}$ for $j = 1$ to tu using, for each sender U_i, Equation (2).
   (b) The receiver decrypts M using its private key of the PH to recover a value T which is used to solve the super-increasing knapsack problem and obtain the sequence $\mathcal{S}' = \{S_1, S_2, \ldots\}$ that yields the values sent by the senders. From these values, the symbol σ_i sent by every sender U_i is easily retrieved, solving the knapsack problem [Merk78].

3   Security

A basic assumption when analyzing security is correctness in protocol execution, *i.e.* that Protocol 2 is followed by all senders without deviations. If one or more senders deviate, symbol extraction at the reception might fail. Correctness in execution can be enforced if senders are forced to using a computing device trusted by the receiver (*e.g.* a smart card). The receiver can use Protocol 1 to force senders, by refusing to give the secret keys k_i to anyone except sender smart cards issued or trusted by the receiver.

Property 1 (Confidentiality). If a secure probabilistic additive public-key PH is used in which *there is a negligible probability of obtaining the same ciphertext as a result of two independent encryptions of the same cleartext*, then an intruder cannot determine the symbol transmitted by a sender in Protocol 2.

Proof: Now, assume that the intruder captures a message M sent by U_i during Protocol 2. Decryption of M is not possible because the PH is secure and the intruder does not have access to the private key. Exhaustive search of the cleartext carried out by M will not be succeed, because of the assumption on PH. □

Property 2 (Authentication). If a secure public-key PH and a one-way collision-free hash function with l-bit output are used, the following holds: i) the probability of successfully impersonating another sender when sending a bit value to the receiver is 2^{-l};

ii) substituting a false message M' for a legitimate message $M \neq M'$ in the current transmission is at least as difficult as impersonation; iii) substituting a message M' for a legitimate message $M \neq M'$ in future transmissions using information from the current transmission is infeasible.

Proof: In the impersonation attack, an intruder who wants to impersonate a sender, needs to guess at least one of the values from $\mathcal{S}$ assigned to the sender so as to generate a *valid* message. These symbols are computed using a one-way collision-free hash function (see Equation (2)), thus the probability of the intruder randomly hitting the correct symbol is at most 2^{-l}.

A substitution attack can be mounted in the current transmission or in future transmissions:

- In the current transmission, assume the intruder wants to substitute a false message M' for an authentic message M sent by U_i, with $M' \neq M$. Without loss of generality, let $M = E_{PK}(S_a)$; for example, the intruder wants to transform M into the encrypted sum of any of the other values from $\mathcal{S}$ assigned to U_i. This requires the following steps: i) recover S_a from M, which is difficult; ii) compute any other symbol with knowledge of S_a, which is as difficult as mounting a successful impersonation attack (see above); iii) compute M'.
- A second possibility is for an internal intruder to use information derived from a current transmission of a message by U_i to alter future messages sent by U_i. But this is infeasible, because in subsequent executions of Protocol 2, a different super-increasing sequence will be used to encode the messages which does not depend on the current super-increasing sequence (see Equation (2)). □

4 Performance

Before presenting the performance comparison below, some preliminary remarks are required:

- The performance criterion considered is the bandwidth required by the aggregated traffic.
- We will consider an alternative system based on unicast transmissions from each sender to the receiver. Like in our system, the unicast transmissions in the benchmark system will be symbol-wise. We assume that the communication is real-time, so that symbols are transmitted as they are generated.
- We will require that each symbol transmission has the same security properties as transmissions in our system.
- For the sake of concreteness, we will use OUPH as a privacy homomorphism in this section.

In order to avoid the need for public-key encryption for a sender to send a confidential and authenticated symbol, we must assume that each sender U_i shares with the receiver a key k_i corresponding to a block cipher (*e.g.* AES). The message M containing the symbol σ will thus look like

$$M = E_{k_i}(\sigma\|ts\|ck), U_i$$

where $E_{k_i}(\cdot)$ stands for the encryption function of the block cipher, ts is a time-stamp, ck is a checksum and U_i is the identity of sender U_i. Integrity is ensured by ck and ts (the time-stamp prevents replacing future transmissions with past transmissions).

When u senders simultaneously send their encrypted symbols with the benchmark unicast system, $u(B + \log_2 u)$ bits are received by the receiver, assuming that B is the block bitlength of the block cipher and $\log_2 u$ is the bitlength of the sender identifier U_i. We assume also that the bitlength of $\sigma\|ts\|ck$ is less than or equal to B. For a block cipher such as AES, at least one has $B = 128$, so the previous assumption is reasonable. When u senders send their encrypted symbols with our system, all symbol transmissions are eventually aggregated into a single message

$$M = \prod_i M_i \pmod{n}$$

which is the only one reaching the receiver. M can be at most n, so its length is $\log_2 n$. Equivalently, the bitlength of M is

$$|M| = \log_2 n = \log_2(p^2 p') = 2\log_2 p + \log_2 p' = 3\log_2 p$$

where we have used that, in OUPH, $n = p^2 p'$ with $|p| = |p'|$. Now, already for a moderate number u of senders, p can be chosen close to its lower bound (1) while remaining large enough for factoring of $n = p^2 p'$ to stay hard, as required by OUPH. Therefore, if we use the generalized bound (1) we have

$$|M| \approx 3\log_2[(2^{tu} - 1)2^{l+1} - 2^{tu} + 2] \qquad (3)$$

It can be seen that Expression (3) is dominated by $3tu$ as the number of senders grows. Therefore, if the number u of senders is moderate to large and if the symbol bitlength is $t < (B + \log_2 u)/3$, the bandwidth $3tu$ required by our scheme is *less* than the bandwidth $u(B + \log_2 u)$ required by the benchmark unicast system. Since typical block sizes are as large as $B = 64, 128, 192$ or 256, the previous assumption on the symbol bitlength is reasonable. Besides, our proposal only requires one incoming connection to the receiver, whereas the unicast alternative requires u connections to the receiver, which calls for allocation of additional overhead bandwidth not included in the above comparison. Finally, it must be noticed that bandwidth reduction is achieved without increasing the computational burden at the receiver. Symbol extraction during Protocol 2 requires the receiver to build tu terms of a super-increasing sequence and to solve a super-increasing knapsack problem. The computational cost of doing this is similar to the cost of the u block decryptions required by the unicast benchmark.

5   Conclusions

The thrust behind the design of the scheme in this paper is the need for large-scale secure real-time many-to-one communication, that is, transmission of information whose symbols should not be buffered but be securely sent as they are generated. Our scheme can be applied whenever a large number of sending devices must communicate in real-time with a single node and there is a risk that the incoming bandwidth available at the receiving node may be a bottleneck. In the special case where the Okamoto-Uchiyama PH is used, the required incoming bandwidth at the receiver for u senders approximates $3tu$ bits when each sender securely transmits one q-ary symbol at a time, with $q = 2^t - 1$. This is not so far from the $u \log_2 q \approx tu$ bits required for *insecure* transmission of u q-ary symbols. Achieving the same security properties using unicast transmissions would typically need Bu bits split in u sender-receiver connections, where B is the block size of a block cipher.

References

[Domi04]   J. Domingo-Ferrer, A. Martínez-Ballesté, F. Sebé, "Secure reverse communication in a multicast tree", *3rd IFIP-TC6 Networking*, LNCS 3042, pp.807-816, Springer-Verlag, 2004.

[Merk78]   R. C. Merkle and M. Hellman, "Hiding information and signatures in trap-door knapsacks", *IEEE Transactions on Information Theory*, vol. 24, no. 5, pp. 525-530, 1978.

[Okam98]   T. Okamoto and S. Uchiyama, "A new public-key cryptosystem as secure as factoring", in *Advances in Cryptology - EUROCRYPT'98*, ed. K. Nyberg, LNCS 1403, Berlin: Springer-Verlag, pp. 308-318, 1998.

[Psou99]   K. Psounis, "Active networks: Applications, security, safety and architectures", *IEEE Communication Surveys*, vol. 2, no. 1, pp. 1-16, 1999.

[Wolf03]   T. Wolf and S. Y. Choi, "Aggregated hierarchical multicast - A many-to-many communication paradigm using programmable networks", *IEEE Transactions on Systems, Man and Cybernetics - C*, vol. 33, no. 3, pp. 358-369, Aug. 2003.

Efficiency Evaluation for Key Distribution Models in Satellite Terminals[*]

Taeshik Shon[1], Jongsub Moon[1], and HongMin Choi[2]

[1] Center for Information Security Technologies, Korea University, Seoul, Korea
{743zh2k,jsmoon}@korea.ac.kr
[2] Information Security Technology Institute, Secuve Co.Ltd., Seoul, Korea
partout@secuve.com

Abstract. With the increasing use of satellite communications, there is growing concern, regarding security problems. These problems are caused by characteristics such as providing world wide coverage with distance-insensitive cost, large transmission bandwidth, and so on. In this paper we propose four kinds of key distribution models to achieve information security between satellite terminals. Also, through performance analysis of proposed models, we verify their suitability to satellite environments.

Keywords: key distribution, satellite security, performance evaluation.

1 Introduction

With the development of communication technology, users want excellent information communication services provided at high speed, wide bandwidth, multimedia capability and mobility. Satellite communication can be used to fulfill such requirements. Thus, it is important to establish a secure communication channel among satellite terminals according to the rising demand of satellite communication. In this paper, we propose four kinds of key distribution models, and verify them. The paper is composed as follows: Section 1 introduces the overview of satellite security. Section 2 studies the considerations of key distribution models with push/pull scheme. Section 3 proposes four kinds of key distribution models in satellite environments. Section 4 verifies performance in these environment. Finally, Section 5 concludes this paper.

2 Previous Work

Key distribution procedure can be classified into the Push and Pull models in accordance with how to get a secret key. In the Push-typed model(as illustrated

---

[*] This work was supported (in part) by the Ministry of Information&Communications, Korea, under the Information Technology Research Center (ITRC) Support Program.

A. Aagesen et al. (Eds.): INTELLCOMM 2004, LNCS 3283, pp. 92–99, 2004.

in Figure 1), user A generates the secret key for secure channel establishment between users, and then transfers the generated secret key to a corresponding B after the authentication process of the security server. Such a Push model needs three times message exchanges for the secret key distribution as follows: User A requests authentication to the security server (i), the security server sends user A a encrypted message used between server and user B as a session key(ii), and finally A distributes the message to B. In the Pull typed key distribution model, User A requests authentication and key distribution to the security server, and then the security server distributes the secret key to each user. In such a Pull model, twice message exchanges are enough for the secret key distribution because this scheme transfers the secret key to each user from security server at the same time [1–4].

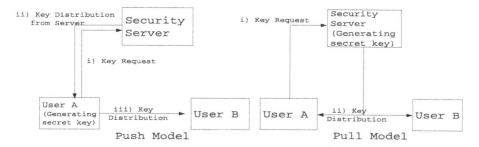

Fig. 1. Push and Pull-typed Key Distribution Models

3   Four Types of Key Distribution Models

Because satellite networks is affected by propagation delay caused by environmental characteristic, key distribution models must consider round trip delay (max:278msec, min:238msec). Thus, we must satisfy the requirement that simplifies key distribution procedure among terminals. Also, we must consider the processing speed of algorithm used to accomplish authentication, encryption and minimization of message sizes which is transmitted to other terminals.

Table 1. Combining between key distributions models and Encryption algorithms

Encryption Algorithm / Key Distribution Model	Symmetric Key Encryption	Public Key Encryption
Push	Case 1	Case 2
Pull	Case 3	Case 4

3.1   Push Typed Key Distribution Models (Case 1, Case2)

Push Typed Model with Symmetric Key Encryption (Case 1):

1. TA sends own ID_A and encrypted message including ID_B, Timestamp and the secret key between A and B to SS
2. If TA is authenticated, SS sends encrypted message including ID_A, Timestamp and the secret key to TA.
3. TA sends encrypted message including ID_A and the secret key to B.
    1. $TA \rightarrow SS : ID_A || E_{AS}[ID_B || K_{AB} || T]$
    2. $SS \rightarrow TA : E_{BS}[ID_A || K_{AB} || T]$
    3. $TA \rightarrow TB : E_{BS}[ID_A || K_{AB}]$

Table 2. Notations of Symmetric key algorithm

Notations	Description
SS	Satellite Security Server
TA, TB	Terminal A, Terminal B
K_{AB}	Secret key between A and B
E_{AB}	Encryption using secret key between A and B
E_{KUx}/E_{KRx}	Public key and Private key of X
$Sign_{KRx}()$	Sign value with private key of x
T	Timestamp
ID_X	Identification of Terminal X

Push Typed Model with Public Key Encryption algorithm (Case 2):

1. TA requests communication to SS through satellite. And, TA sends encrypted message with ID of Terminal A, B and the secret key to SS. In this time, the secret key is generated by TA.
2. SS sends encrypted message to TA. This message comprised as follows: Encrypted with public key of TB together with signature to message (m_2) which is comprised with identity of TA, secret key between TA and TB, and timestamp.
3. TA sends this encrypted message to TB.
    1. $TA \rightarrow SS : E_{KUss}[m_1 || Sign_{KUa}(m_1)]$
    2. $SS \rightarrow TA : E_{KUb}[m_2 || Sign_{KRss}(m_2)]$
    3. $TA \rightarrow TB : E_{KUb}[m_2 || Sign_{KRss}(m_2)]$
    $*m_1 = (ID_A || ID_B || K_{AB}), m_2 = (ID_B || K_{AB} || T)$

3.2   Pull Typed Key Distribution Models (Case 3, Case4)

Pull Typed Model Using Symmetric Key Encryption Algorithm (Case 3):

1. TA sends own ID_A and encrypted message including ID_B and timestamp to SS.

2. If TA is authenticated, SS sends encrypted message including ID_B and the secret key to TA. Also, SS sends encrypted message including ID_A, timestamp and the secret key to TB. In this procedure, the secret key for secure channel is generated by SS.
   1. $TA \rightarrow SS : E_{AS}[ID_A || ID_B || T]$
   2. $SS \rightarrow TA : E_{AS}[ID_B || K_{AB} || T]$
      $SS \rightarrow TB : E_{BS}[ID_A || K_{AB} || T]$

Pull Typed Model Using Public Key Encryption Algorithm (Case 4):
   1. TA requests communication to SS through satellite. At this time, TA sends encrypted message with ID of Terminal A, B to SS.
   2. SS sends encrypted message to TA. This message comprised as follows: Encrypted with public key of A together with signature to message (m_2) which is comprised with identity of A, secret key between TA and TB, and timestamp. Also SS sends encrypted message(m_3) to TB. In this procedure, the secret key for secure channel is generated by SS.
      1. $TA \rightarrow SS : E_{KUa}[m_1 || Sign_{KUa}(m_1)]$
      2. $SS \rightarrow TA : E_{KUa}[m_2 || Sign_{KRss}(m_2)]$
         $SS \rightarrow TB : E_{KUb}[m_3 || Sign_{KRss}(m_3)]$
         $*m_1 = (ID_A || ID_B), m_2 = (ID_A || K_{AB} || T), m_3 = (ID_B || K_{AB} || T)$

4 Performance Analysis

4.1 Experimental Methods

This section analyzes suitability of the proposed four kinds of key distribution models for satellite networks. To analyze suitability of proposed models, we calculate the sum of delay time related to some parameters such as encryption algorithm, distributed key length. We make model of satellite communication systems, as illustrated in Figure 2. It consists of satellite(SAT), satellite mobile terminals(MT) and satellite security server(SS). Our model of satellite systems referred to the security service modeling of normal data communication and included the characteristic of satellite networks[5, 6, 7, 8]. Table 3 indicates each parameters of model for satellite systems. We assume that packets arrive according to poisson distribution with arrival rate λ and service times have constant values such as μ_1, μ_2 and μ_3. Even if we consider additional information securityservices to each system such as encryption, decryption, signature and verifica-

Fig. 2. Modeling of satellite communication systems

Table 3. Notations of Modeling of Satellite Communication Systems

Notations	Description
ρ_i	Efficiency of normal systems
ρ_i'	Efficiency of information security systems
μ_i	Service rate of normal systems
μ_i'	Service rate of Information security systems
λ	Arrival rate
d_i	Differentiation between service rate of normal systems and service rate of information security systems
T	Total Delay
L_d	Delay time of satellite link

tion, arrival rate is maintained equally, but service rate is added by μ_1', μ_2' and μ_3' respectively. The best efficiency of this systems is $\mu_b' = max(1/\mu_i')$,i=1,2,3, that is, it is determined by system which has the longest service time. The average delay time of system is same as the sum of the spent time in each system queue. In modeling satellite systems, because we assume additionally the information security service to normal satellite systems, the service time of each system has additional deterministic service time (information security service). As according to the addition of information security service, the service time of each system also increases deterministically. Thus, among the queuing models, we made modeled satellite systems which provide information security service with an M/D/1 queuing model and derived an equation to calculate the delay time of total systems as follows.

$$\rho_i = \lambda/\mu_i, \ d_i = \mu_i/\mu_i'(\mu_i' = \mu_i/d_i) \tag{1}$$

$$\rho_i' = \lambda/\mu_i' = \lambda * d_i/\mu_i = d_i * \lambda/\mu_i = d_i * \rho_i \tag{2}$$

In equation (3), T is total delay and we can find it from w(M/D/1 queue's average delay time $\mu^{-1} + \rho\mu^{-1}/2(1-\rho)$) plus all systems delay time($\sum_{i=1,i\neq b}^{3} \frac{1}{\mu_i'}$) plus satellite propagation delay(ld*2).

$$T = w + \sum_{i=1,i\neq b}^{3} \frac{1}{\mu_i'} + (ld * 2), (\mu_b' = max[1/\mu_i'],_{i=1,2,3}) \tag{3}$$

$$= (1/\mu_b' + \rho_b'\mu_b^{-1}/2(1 - \rho_b')) + \sum_{i=1,i\neq b}^{3} \frac{1}{\mu_i'} + (ld * 2) \tag{4}$$

$$= \rho_b'\mu_b^{-1}/2(1 - \rho_b') + \sum_{i=1}^{3} \frac{1}{\mu_i'} + (ld * 2) \tag{5}$$

$$= \lambda/2\mu_b'(\mu_b' - \lambda) + \sum_{i=1}^{3} \frac{1}{\mu_i'} + (ld * 2) \tag{6}$$

In equation (6), we derived the total delay time of satellite systems.

All encryption algorithms were coded in C++ or ported to C++ from C implementations, compiled with Microsoft Visual C++ 6.0 SP4 (optimize for speed, blend code generation), and ran on a Celeron 850MHz processor under Windows 2000 SP 1(As illustrated Table 4, Table 5)[9]. Also we assumed that basic delay time of satellite communication systems and other systems is 0.01msec, round trip delay time between satellite and terminals is 250msec(that is, ld=125msec) and arrival rate is 10 packets/slot.

4.2   Experiment Results

In figure 3, we analyzed delay time considering basic round trip time of proposed Push and Pull-typed model with symmetric key encryption algorithms and its distributed key length. In this performance simulation, we used DES-EDE and DES as a symmetric key algorithm. We can see that proposed push typed model has about 750msec of delay time and pull typed model has about 500msec of delay time(As illustrated Fig. 3.) In the figure 4, we analyzed the delay time considering the basic round trip time of proposed Push and Pull-typed model with the public key algorithms and its distributed key length. In this performance simulation, we used RSA and ElGamal as a public key algorithm. If the proposed models distribute the secret key more than 2048bits of key length, we see that, on average, the delay between ElGamal and RSA, is about 914msec for the push model and about 664msec pull model(As illustrated Fig. 4.).

In the result of performance analysis, we can know that Pull typed model using symmetric algorithm (Case 3) has the shortest delay among the proposed four cases. Also, though there was basically 250msec of delay time difference between proposed Push and Pull models, if key distribution method with Pull scheme employs public key algorithm which has more than the key size of 2048bits(Case 4) and if key distribution method with Push scheme employs symmetric encryption algorithm (Case 1), the difference of entire delay time between the models decreases to 87msec. Thus, the propagation delay of satellite networks is the biggest factor to affect communication delay between the terminals. In other words, when we consider the propagation delay of satellite environments, the encryption algorithm processing speed of various key distribution models

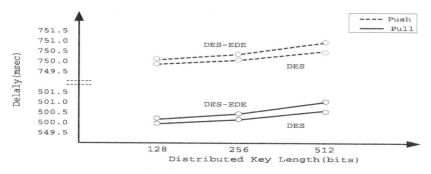

Fig. 3. Delay Comparison using Symmetric key encryption algorithms (Case1, Case3)

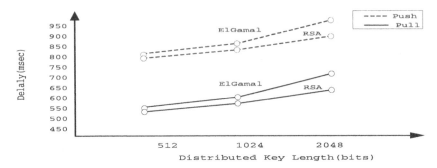

Fig. 4. Delay Comparison using Public key encryption algorithms (Case2, Case4)

doesn't influence the total delay of satellite communication much, so we need appropriate choice according to its application purposes.

5   Conclusion

In this paper, we have studied the security threats in satellite communication environments, their considerations and various key distribution models. After that, we proposed four kinds of key distribution models such as Push typed key distribution model using symmetric key encryption algorithm and public key encryption algorithm, Pull typed key distribution model using symmetric key algorithm and public key encryption algorithm as a method of information security in satellite networks, and made modeled of satellite communication system in accordance with its characteristic.

Through the performance analysis of proposed key distribution models using our simulation equations, we can see that, if the Pull typed key distribution model using public key algorithm distributes more than the key size of 2048bits, the difference of delay time between the four models is decreased below 87msec. Thus, through the performance analysis of the proposed four key distribution model, we can see the possibility of application of them to satellite networks, though they use different encryption algorithm and key distribution schemes.

Potential future work will include additional effectiveness testing with various key distribution models and encryption algorithms.

References

1. ANSI, *X9.17 Financial Institution Key Management Standard*, X9-Secretarait Banker Association, 1985
2. National Institute of Standards Technology, *Framework for National Information Infrastructure Services*, NISTR 5478 (Gaithersburg, MD: NIST, July 1994).
3. Bruce Schneier, *Applied Cryptography*, Wiley, pp53 64, 1996
4. Alfred J. Menezes, *Handbook of Cryptography*, pp497 514, CRC Press, 1997
5. S.W.Kim, *Frequency-Hopped Spread-Spectrum Random Access with Retransmission Cutoff and Code Rate Adjustment*, IEEE, Vol.10, No.2, Feb 1992

6. Hyoun K., *Traffic Control and Congestion Control in ATM over Satellite Networks*, IEEK, Vol.4, No.1, Nov 1998
7. Jerry Banks, *Discrete-Event System Simulation*, Prentice-Hall, pp264-265, 1996
8. Kyung Hyune Rhee, *Delay Analysis on Secure Data Communication*, KIISC, Vol.7, No.12, Dec 1997
9. William Stallings, *Cryptography and Network Security*, Prentice-Hall, pp 292-293

Appendix

Table 4. Symmetric Encryption Algorithm Processing Time

Algorithm	Bytes Processed	Time Taken	Mbps
DES	134217728	9.945	102.968
DES-EDE	33554432	6.740	37.984
RC5	536870912	12.988	315.368
Blowfish	134217728	7.091	144.408
MD5-MAC	1073741824	12.078	678.256

Table 5. Public key Encryption Algorithm Processing Time(msec/operation)

Algorithm	Encryption	Decryption	Signature	Verification
RSA 512	0.14	1.93	1.92	0.13
RSA 1024	0.32	10.23	10.29	0.30
RSA 2048	0.89	64.13	64.13	0.85
ElGamal 512	2.62	1.37	-	-
ElGamal 1024	11.03	5.77	-	-
ElGamal 2048	49.19	25.35	-	-

Speed Compensation for Improving Thai Spelling Recognition with a Continuous Speech Corpus

Chutima Pisarn and Thanaruk Theeramunkong

Sirindhorn International Institute of Technology,
131 Moo 5 Tiwanont Rd., Bangkadi, Muang, Phathumthani 12000, Thailand
{chutimap, thanaruk}@siit.tu.ac.th

Abstract. Spelling recognition is an approach to enhance a speech recognizer to cope with incorrectly recognized words and out-of-vocabulary words. This paper presents a general framework for Thai speech recognition, enhanced with spelling recognition. To implement Thai spelling recognition, Thai alphabets and their spelling methods are analyzed. Based on hidden Markov models, we propose a method to construct a Thai spelling recognition system using an existing continuous speech corpus. To compensate for speed differences between spelling utterances and continuous speech utterances, the adjustment of utterance speed is taken into account. Our system achieves up to 87.37% correctness and 87.18% accuracy with the mix-type language model.

1 Introduction

Currently several works on automatic speech recognition (ASR) for continuous speech are undergoing development, for systems that rely on dictionaries and those that can recognize out-of-vocabulary circumstances. In the situation of misrecognition and out-of-vocabulary words, a practical and efficient solution to assist the ASR is to equip a system with a spelling recognition subsystem, in which users can spell out a word, letter by letter. Spelling recognition is a challenging task with high interest for directory assistance services, or other applications where a large number of proper names or addresses are handled. Many works that focused on spelling recognition were widely developed in several languages, for instance, English, Spanish, Portuguese and German. In [1], hypothesis-verification Spanish continuous spelled proper name recognition over the telephone was proposed. Several feature sets were investigated in models of neural networks. In their succeeding work [2], three different recognition architectures, including the two-level architecture, the integrated architecture and the hypothesis-verification architecture, are analyzed and compared. In [3], a Portuguese subject-independent system for recognizing an isolated letter was introduced. The system is simulated to recognize speech utterances over a telephone line using the Hidden Markov Model (HMM). A number of experiments were made over four different perplexity language models. In [4], Mitchell and Setlur proposed a fast list matcher to select a name from the name list that was created from an n-best letter recognizer on spelling over the telephone line recognition task. In [5], an

A. Aagesen et al. (Eds.): INTELLCOMM 2004, LNCS 3283, pp. 100–111, 2004.

integration approach was proposed to combine word recognition with spelling recognition in a user-friendly manner as a fall-back strategy. As a German city name recognizer, the system was applied to directory assistance services.

Unlike other languages, spelling in Thai has several styles. One of them is similar to spelling in the English language, i.e., /h-@@4//m-@@0//z-aa0/ of "หมา" corresponding to /d-ii0//z-oo0// g-ii0/ for "dog". There are three additional methods in Thai spelling, where some syllables are inserted to make it more clear for the hearer. One method is to spell out a letter followed by its representative word's utterance. Another method is to mix between the former two types. The third method is to spell out a set of letters that form a syllable followed by its corresponding pronunciation. Thus far spelling recognition for Thai language has not been explored. One of main reasons is that there is no standard corpus for this purpose. Creating a corpus of spelled utterances is a time consuming task. Fortunately we have a normal speech corpus. In this work, we use the NECTEC-ATR Thai Speech Corpus, a standard continuous Thai speech corpus, for our spelling recognition system. Another objective of this work is to examine how a spelling system can be implemented using a normal Thai continuous speech corpus. That is, as the preliminary stage, we investigate the performance of spelling recognition using such an existing corpus.

This paper is organized as follows. In section 2, language characteristics in Thai are introduced. Section 3 presents our recognition framework. Four spelling styles for Thai words are discussed in section 4. The experimental results and their analysis are shown in section 5. Finally, a conclusion and our future works are given in section 6.

2   Thai Language Characteristics

2.1   Thai Alphabets

Theoretically, the Thai language has 69 alphabet symbols which can be grouped into three classes of phone expression; consonant, vowel and tone. There are 44, 21, and 4 alphabet symbols for consonants, vowels, and tones, respectively. Some Thai consonant symbols share the same phonetic sound. Because of this, there are only 21 phones for Thai consonants. On the other hand, some vowels can be combined with other vowels, resulting in 32 possible phones. However, in practice, only 18 alphabet symbols in the vowel class are used. There are 5 tones in Thai, including one without an alphabet symbol. Concludingly, there are 66 practical alphabet symbols as shown in Table 1.

Table 1. Thai alphabets: consonants, vowels and tones

Basic Classes	Alphabets in each class
Consonant	ก,ข,ฃ,ค,ฅ,ฆ,ง,จ,ฉ,ช,ซ,ฌ,ญ,ฎ,ฏ,ฐ,ฑ,ฒ,ณ,ด,ต,ถ,ท,ธ,น,บ,ป,ผ,ฝ,พ,ฟ,ภ,ม,ย,ร,ล,ว,ศ,ษ,ส,ห,ฬ,อ,ฮ
Vowel	อ, อะ, อิ, อา, อิ, อี, อื, อึ, อุ, อู, เอ, แอ, โอ, อำ, ไอ, ใอ, ฤ, อ
Tone	อ่, อ้, อ๊, อ๋

2.2 Thai Syllable Characteristics and Phonetic Representation

In the Thai language, a syllable can be separated into three parts; (1) initial consonant, (2) vowel and (3) final consonant. The phonetic representation of one syllable can be expressed in the form of $/C_i\text{-}V^T\text{-}C_f/$, where C_i is an initial consonant, V is a vowel, C_f is a final consonant and T is a tone which is phonetically attached to the vowel part. Following the concept presented in [6], there are 76 phonetic symbols and 5 tone symbols applied in this work as shown in Table 2.

Table 2. Phonetic symbols grouped as initial consonants, vowels, final consonants and tones

Initial Consonant (C_i)		Vowel (V)	Final Consonant (C_f)	Tone (T)
Base	Cluster			
$p,t,c,k,z,ph,$ $th,ch,k,h,b,$ $br,bl,d,dr,m,$ $n,ng,r,f,fr,fl,$ s,h,w,j	pr,phr,pl,phl $,tr,thr,kr,khr,$ $kl,khl,kw,$ khw	$a,aa,i,ii,v,vv,u,$ $uu,e,ee,x,xx,o,$ $oo,@,@@,q,$ $qq,ia,iia,va,$ vva,ua,uua	$p^\wedge,t^\wedge,k^\wedge,n^\wedge,m^\wedge,n^\wedge,$ $g^\wedge,j^\wedge,w^\wedge,f^\wedge,l^\wedge,s^\wedge,$ $ch^\wedge,jf^\wedge,ts^\wedge$	0 Mid 1 Low 2 Falling 3 High 4 Rising

Some initial consonants are cluster consonants. Each of them has a phone similar to that of a corresponding base consonant. For example, *pr*, *phr*, *pl*, and *phl* are similar to *p*. Naturally phones, especially those in the vowel class, are various in their duration. In Thai language, most vowels have their pairs: a short phone and its corresponding long phone. For example, the vowel pair *a* and *aa* have a similar phone but different durations. The other vowel pairs are *i-ii, v-vv, u-uu, e-ee, x-xx, o-oo, @-@@, q-qq, ia-iia, va-vva,* and *ua-uua*.

3 Our Framework

Figure 1 presents our recognition framework designed for a Thai continuous speech recognition system that incorporates a conventional recognizer with a spelling recognition subsystem. The whole process can be divided into two modules; (1) training module and (2) recognition module.

In the training module, waveforms of continuous speech utterances in a corpus are transformed to feature vectors by a signal quantization technique. The derived feature vectors are used for training a set of acoustic models. In the system, two language models are equipped; one model stands for traditional word recognition whereas the other is used for spelling recognition. The traditional language model is trained by transcriptions in the text corpus while the spelling language model is trained by sequences of letters in a proper name corpus.

In the recognition module, the two well-trained models, the acoustic model and the traditional language model, together with a pronunciation dictionary are applied to recognize a new utterance yielding a set of hypothesis results. Each hypothesis candidate is then checked to determine whether this hypotheis is valid or not. If all hypothesse are invalid, the system will turn to the spelling recognition subsystem.

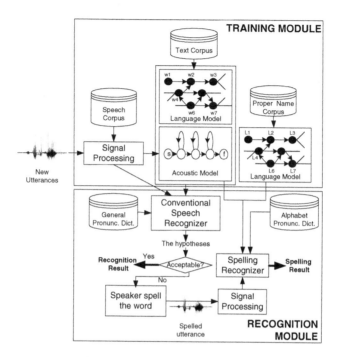

Fig. 1. Our Recognition framework

At this stage, the user is asked to spell the word letter-by-letter. The utterance of spelling is then fed to the signal-processing module to convert the waveform to feature vectors. In this work, as our preliminary stage, we focus on the spelling recognition subsystem. We use the acoustic models trained by normal continuous speech utterances because we lack a spelling corpus. Incorporating the acquired acoustic models with a trained spelling language model and an alphabetic pronunciation dictionary, spelling results can be obtained.

4 Spelling Styles for Thai Words

4.1 Basic Pronunciation of Thai Alphabets

As referred in section 2.1, there are three basic classes of Thai alphabet symbols. Pronouncing Thai alphabet symbols in different classes results in different styles. The consonant class alphabet symbols can be uttered in either of the following two styles. The first style is simply pronouncing the core sound of a consonant. For example, for the alphabet symbol 'ก', its core sound can be represented as the syllable phonetic

/k-@@0/. Normally, some consonants share the same core sound such as 'ค', 'ค', 'ฆ' have the same phonetic sound /kh-@@0/. In such a case, the hearer may encounter alphabet ambiguity. To solve this issue, the second style is generally applied by uttering a core sound of the consonant followed by the representative word of that consonant. Every consonant has its representative word. For example, the representative word of 'ก' is "ไก" (meaning: "chicken", sound. /k-a1 j^/), and that of 'ข' is "ไข" (meaning: egg, sound: /kh-a1-j^/). To express the alphabet 'ก' using this style, the sound /k-@@0/+/k-a1-j^/ is uttered.

Expressing symbol in the vowel class is quite different from that of the consonant class. There are two types of vowels. First-type vowels can be pronounced in two ways. One way is to pronounce the word "สระ" (meaning: "vowel", sound: /s-a1/ /r-a1/), followed by the core sound of the vowel. The other way is to simply pronounce the core sound of the vowel. For second-type vowels, they are uttered by calling their names. The vowel symbols of each type are listed in Table 3. As the last class, tone symbols can be pronounced by calling their names.

Table 3. Two types of vowels

Type	Vowels
The first-type	อะ, อา, อิ, อี, อึ, อื, อุ, อู, เอ, แอ, โอ, อำ, ไอ, ใอ
The second-type	อิ, อี, อ์, ฤ

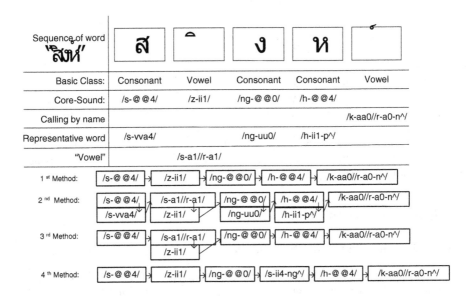

Fig. 2. Four Spelling Methods for the word "สิงห์"

4.2 Thai Word Spelling Methods

Spelling a word is done by uttering alphabet symbols in the word one by one in order. We can refer spelling to a combination of the pronunciation of each alphabet symbol in the word. Only four Thai commonly used spelling methods are addressed. For all methods, the second-type vowels and tones are pronounced by calling their names. The differences are taken place in spelling consonants and the first-type vowels. For the first spelling method, consonants are spelled by using only their core sounds, and first-type vowels are pronounced by their core sound without the word "สระ" (/s-a1/ /r-a1/). This spelling method is similar to spelling approach in English language.

For the second method, the representative word of each consonant is pronounced, after its core sound while pronouncing a first-type vowel is to utter the word "สระ" and then its core sound. In the third method, the way to pronounce a consonant and a vowel are varied. For instance, the word can be spelled by spelling a consonant using only its core sound but spelling a vowel by pronouncing "สระ"(/s-a1//r-a1/) with the vowel's core sound. The last method is to spell out a set of letters that form a syllable and then followed by its corresponding pronunciations. The spelling sequence of alphabets in each syllable starts with initial consonant, vowel, and followed by final consonant (if any) and tone (if any), and then, the sound of that syllable is inserted at the end of this sequence. The examples of these methods in spelling the word "สงห" are depicted in Figure 2. Because the second method is the prevalant spelling method in Thai, we concentrate an effort on this method.

5 Experimental Results and Analysis

5.1 Experimental Environment

As mentioned, unfortunately, the corpus for spelling recognition is not available at this time. Therefore, this work applies the NECTEC-ATR Thai Speech Corpus, constructed by NECTEC (National Electronics and Computer Technology Center) incorporated with ATR Spoken Language Translation Laboratories. In Thai language speech recognition, this corpus is often used for continuous speech recognition. This speech corpus is used as the training set for our spelling recognition system. The corpus contains 390 sentences gathered by assigning 42 subjects (21 males and 21 females) to read all sentences for one trial. Thus, there are 16,380 read utterances in total.

At the first place, by the reason of computation time, only utterances of 5 males and 5 females, are used, i.e., totally 3,900 trained utterances. In this work, the performance of spelling recognition using a normal continuous training corpus is investigated. Even when the training corpus has quite different characteristics compared to test utterances, we can expect a reasonable result. For the test utterances, we record 136 spelled proper names pronounced by six other subjects. These 136 proper names are shop names, company names, family names and first names.

The speech signals were digitized by 16-bit A/D converter of 16 kHz. A feature vector used in our experiment is a 39-feature vector, consisting of 12 PLP coefficients and the 0th coefficient, as well as their first and second order derivatives. Therefore, there are 39 elements in total.

There are three bigram language models used in this task; LM1, LM2 and LM3. LM1 is a close-type language model trained using 136 proper names from the test transcription. LM3 is an open-type language model trained using 5,971 Thai province, district, and sub district names. Since LM2 is a mix-type language model, a mixture of the two models, where both 146 proper names and 5,971 location names are used. In this work, we will focus on LM2.

A phone-based HMM is applied as the recognition system. The acoustic units used in this experiment are defined in the same manner as in [6]. All experiments, including automatic transcription labeling, are performed using the HTK toolkit [7]. We evaluate the recognition performance in the terms of correctness and accuracy. The word correctness is the ratio of the number of correct words to the total number of words while the word accuracy is the ratio of the number of correct words subtracted by the number of word insertion errors, to the total number of words. For detail of correct and accuracy, see [7].

5.2 Setting a Baseline

In the first experiment, we investigate the spelling results using the original training and testing data as they are. Using the phone-based HMM, all experiments are performed with context independent considerations. Context-independent means that the recognition of a certain phone does not depend on the phone's preceding or following phones. In this initial stage, for LM2, we can gain 83.38% correctness and 73.28% accuracy, respectively. The low accuracy indicates that there are a large number of insertion errors. We also analyzed the errors and found that many spelling results violated the applied language model (bigram model). Because of this, the weight ratio between the acoustic model and the language model is set to be a low value, forcing the language model more to be important than the acoustic model. The results in the cases that the weight is set to 0.1 and 0.2 gain the highest recognition. However, the weight ratio of 0.1 gains more recognition rate than that of 0.2 in most case. As a result, 85.71% correctness and 85.26% accuracy derived from the LM2 language model with the weight ratio of 0.1 becomes our baseline through this work. The results of various weight ratios are shown in Table 4.

Table 4. The recognition results of the baseline with various weight ratios

Weight ratio		1.0	0.2	0.1	0.05
LM1	Correctness	83.47	90.70	93.08	90.04
	Accuracy	73.87	88.86	92.89	88.35
LM2	Correctness	83.38	86.22	85.71	74.38
	Accuracy	73.28	84.17	85.26	73.92
LM3	Correctness	83.32	85.74	84.03	73.63
	Accuracy	72.79	83.06	83.33	73.07

5.3 Adjusting the Duration

The major difference between the training and the test sets is the duration of the utterances. The speeds of training and test utterances are measured in the form of the number of phones per second. The result indicates the speed of the test set is approximately 1.5 times slower than that of training utterances. To compensate for this duration difference between the training utterance and the test utterance, the time-stretching method [8], [9], [10], a method to stretch a speech signal, by preserving pitch and auditory features of the original signal, is applied in our signal preprocessing. Stretching the training utterances is performed using various scaling factors in order to investigate the effectiveness. Table 5 shows the recognition results of stretched training utterances with various scaling factors. Here, the original test utterances are used.

For all scaling factors, LM1 gains the highest recognition rate while LM3 obtains the lowest one. In principle, stretching training utterances causes the original utterances to be distorted. The more the utterances are stretched, the more distorted utterances we obtain. As a result, stretching train utterances to be 1.25 times of the original one yields the highest recognition rate while stretching them with 1.43 and 1.67 scaling factor causes the recognition rate to drop. The results show that 1.25Train gains higher correctness and accuracy for every language model. The recognition rate of LM2 are 87.37% correctness and 87.18% accuracy, which are improvements of 1.66% and 1.92%, respectively, compared to the baseline.

Table 5. Recognition results of stretched training utterances with various scaling factors

Model		1.25Train	1.43Train	1.67Train
LM1	Correctness	93.92	91.79	84.39
	Accuracy	93.76	91.65	84.01
LM2	Correctness	87.37	85.37	77.47
	Accuracy	87.18	85.19	76.94
LM3	Correctness	85.75	83.84	76.03
	Accuracy	85.41	83.38	75.37

5.4 Each Subject Test Utterance

The recognition results shown in Table 5 are performed using all six subjects' test utterances. We also investigate the recognition rate of an individual subject. The recognition result and the spelling speed of each subject are shown in Table 6. Note that the test utterances of different subjects have different speeds.

From Table 6, correctness and accuracy of all subjects are not very different. However, the spelling speech affects recognition performance. We observe that FS3 has the slowest spelling speed and we can obtain the lowest accuracy from FS3's experiment. This is caused by a relatively high difference between FS3's spelling speed and the average speed of the training utterances. To handle this issue, the two experiments are performed; (1) using stretched training utterances and 2) shrinking the test utterances to investigate the appropriate scaling factor of this subject. Table 7 and Table 8 indicate the recognition rate of FS3's test utterances in the environments of stretching training utterances experiment and shrinking test utterances.

In the case of using various scaling factors to stretch the training utterances, stretching train utterances to be 1.25, 1.43 and 1.67 times of the original utterances of FS3 outperforms the FS3's baseline for all language models. The 1.43Train achieves the highest recognition rate while stretching with the 1.67 scaling factor causes the recognition drop down. The results show that 1.43Train with LM2 gain 87.33% correctness and 86.70% accuracy, which results in correctness and accuracy gain of 5.98% and 12.60%, respectively, compared to the FS3's baseline results.

Table 6. The baseline results of each subject's test utterances and their spelling speeds

Subject	LM1		LM2		LM3		Speed
	Corr	Acc	Corr	Acc	Corr	Acc	(Phones/Sec.)
FS1	94.51	94.44	87.12	86.84	85.50	85.15	6.72
FS2	94.23	94.09	86.00	85.86	84.45	84.17	6.87
FS3	87.84	86.77	81.98	80.23	80.93	78.54	5.07
MS1	93.67	93.67	85.57	85.22	84.52	84.24	6.51
MS2	93.31	93.24	86.14	86.60	83.74	83.32	5.59
MS3	95.29	95.14	87.47	87.40	85.01	84.59	6.45

Table 7. Recognition of FS3 using stretched training utterances with various scaling factors

Stretch Training Set		1.25Train	1.43Train	1.67Train
LM1	%Correct	91.77	92.75	90.29
	Accuracy	91.34	92.19	89.23
LM2	%Correct	86.14	87.33	84.80
	Accuracy	85.43	86.70	83.81
LM3	%Correct	84.80	85.86	82.97
	Accuracy	83.81	84.24	81.28

Table 8. Recognition of shrinking FS3's utterances with various scaling factors

Shrinking Test Set		0.8Test	0.7Test	0.6Test
LM1	%Correct	92.12	92.89	92.26
	Accuracy	91.77	92.61	92.05
LM2	%Correct	85.38	86.42	84.38
	Accuracy	84.38	85.86	84.10
LM3	%Correct	83.95	83.81	83.53
	Accuracy	83.11	83.32	83.11

We examine the correctness and accuracy when the test utterances are shrunk with various scaling factors. The original training utterances are used for training our system. Similar to the case of stretching training utterances, shrinking utterances of FS3 to be 0.6, 0.7 and 0.8 times of the original, yields better recognition rates. Focusing on the most natural model LM2, the 0.7Test can achieve higher correctness and accuracy than the 0.8Test and 0.6Test. Shrinking the test utterance to be 0.7 times of the original duration can improve the recognition rate of 5.07% for correctness and 11.76% for accuracy, compared to the original test utterances.

5.5 Error Analysis

In the baseline experiment, as a consequence of setting the weight ratio between the acoustic model and the language model to be a low value, forcing the language model to be more important than the acoustic model, the insertion errors are explicitly reduced. At this point, the main errors in this task are substitution errors. Sets of alphabets that cause a lot of substitution errors are {'ฒ', 'ป', 'ม', 'พ', 'ษ', 'ฦ'}. For instance, the alphabet 'ฒ' is rather substituted by 'ป', 'ม', 'พ', 'ษ', or 'ฦ'. One potential reason is that these alphabets are pronounced with two syllables sharing the same vowel phone @@ in the first syllable and the phone aa in the second syllable.

Another substitution error is caused by the confusion of vowel pairs. Investigating recognition results of the baseline, we found out that the vowel alphabet 'อิ' (sound: /s-al//r-al//z-il/) is substituted by its long vowel pair 'อี' (sound: /s-al//r-al//z-ii0) as well as the vowel alphabet 'อุ' (sound: /s-al//r-al//z-ul/) is mostly substituted by 'อู' (sound: /s-al//r-al//z-uu0). After compensating for the duration difference between training and test utterances by stretching training utterances to be 1.25Train, these substitution errors are dominantly reduced.

6 Conclusions

We presented a general framework for Thai speech recognition enhanced with spelling recognition. Four styles in spelling Thai words were introduced and discussed. Without a spelling corpus, the spelling recognizer was constructed using a normal continuous speech corpus. To achieve higher correctness and accuracy,we adjusted the ratio of importance between the acoustic model and the language model, making the language models more important than the acoustic models. To compensate for   utterance speed among the training and test utterances, the training utterances were stretched and the experiments are performed on six subjects' test utterances. As a result, we gained correctness and accuracy. The experimental results for LM2 indicated a promising performance of 87.37% correctness and 87.18% recognition accuracy after this adjustment. To improve the recognition rate of the worst subject's test utterances, we experimented to find a good scaling factor of stretching the training utterances or shrinking the test utterances. As the result, the system achieved up to 12.60% accuracy improvement over the baseline. An analysis of recognition errors was also done. This work showed that applying a normal continuous speech corpus to train a spelling recognizer yield an acceptable performance. Our further works are (1) to construct a system that can recognize several kinds of spelling methods, and (2) to explore a way to incorporate spelling recognition to the conventional speech recognition system.

Acknowledgements

The authors would like to thank National Electronics and Computer Technology Center (NECTEC) for allowing us to use the NECTEC-ATR Thai Speech Corpus. We would like to thank Prof. Cercone for many useful comments on earlier draft of this paper. This work has partly been supported by NECTEC under project number NT-B-22-I5-38-47-04.

References

1. San-Segundo, R., Macias-Guarasa, J., Ferreiros, J., Martin, P., Pardo, J.M.: Detection of Recognition Errors and Out of the Spelling Dictionary Names in a Spelled Name Recognizer for Spanish. Proceedings of EUROSPEECH 2001. (2001)
2. San-Segundo, R., Colas, J., Cordoba, R., Pardo, J.M.: Spanish Recognizer of Continuously Spelled Names Over the Telephone. Journal of Speech Communication, Vol. 38. (2002) 287-303
3. Rodrigues, F., Rodrigues, R., Martins, C.: An Isolated Letter Recognizer for Proper Name Identification Over the Telephone. Proceedings of 9th Portuguese Conference on Pattern Recognition. (1997)
4. Mitchell, C.D., Setlur, A.R.: Improved Spelling Recognition using a Tree-based Fast Lexical Match. Proceedings of IEEE International Conference on Acoustics, Speech, and Signal Processing. 2(1999) 597-600
5. Bauer, J.G., Junkawitsch, J.: Accurate recognition of city names with spelling as a fall back strategy. Proceedings of EUROSPEECH 1999. (1999) 263-266
6. Pisarn, C., Theeramunkong, T.: Incorporating Tone Information to Improve Thai Continuous Speech Recognition. Proceedings of International Conference on Intelligent Technologies 2003. (2003)
7. Young, S., Evermann, G., Hain, T., Kershaw, D., Moore, G., Odell, J., Ollason, D., Povey, D., Valtchev, V., Woodland, P.: The HTK Book (for HTK Version 3.2.1). Cambridge University Engineering Department. (2002)
8. Pallone, G.: Time-stretching and pitch-shifting of audio signals: Application to cinema /video conversion. http://www.iua.upf.es/activitats/semirec/semi-pallone/index.htm
9. Verhelst, W., Roelands, M.: An overlap-add technique based on waveform similarity (wsola) for high quality time-scale modification of speech. Proceedings of IEEE International Conference on Acoustics, Speech, and Signal Processing, Vol 2. (1993) 554-557
10. Wikipedia: The free encyclopedia, Audio time stretching. http://www.ebroadcast.com.au/lookup/encyclopedia/au/Audio_time_stretching.html
11. Anastasakos, A., Schwartz, R., Shu, H.: Duration Modeling in Large Vocabulary Speech Recognition. Proceedings of IEEE International Conference on Acoustics, Speech, and Signal Processing. (1995) 628-631
12. Thubthong, N., Kijsirikul, B.: Tone Recognition of Continuous Thai Speech under Tonal Assimilation and Declination Effects using Half-Tone Model. Journal of International of Uncertainty, Fuzziness and Knowledge-Based System 9(6). (2001) 815-825

13. Betz, M., Hild, H.: Language Models for a Spelled Letter Recognizer. Proceedings of   IEEE International Conference on Acoustics, Speech and Signal Processing. (1995) 856-859
14. Jurafsky, D., Martin J.: Speech and Language Processing: An Introduction to Natural Language Processing, Computational Linguistics and Speech Recognition. Prentice Hall (2000)

Part-of-Speech Tagging
Without Training

Stéphane Bressan, and Lily Suryana Indradjaja

School of Computing, National University of Singapore
{go303015, steph}@nus.edu.sg

Abstract. The development of the Internet and the World Wide Web can be either a threat to the survival of indigenous languages or an opportunity for their development. The choice between cultural diversity and linguistic uniformity is in our hands and the outcome depends on our capability to devise, design and use tools and techniques for the processing of natural languages. Unfortunately natural language processing requires extensive expertise and large collections of reference data. Our research is concerned with the economical and therefore semi-automatic or automatic acquisition of such linguistic information necessary for the development of indigenous or multilingual information systems. In this paper, we propose new methods and variants of existing methods for part-of-speech tagging. We comparatively and empirically analyze the proposed methods and existing reference methods using the Brown English language corpus and we present some preliminary remarks on experiments with an Indonesian language Corpus.

1 Introduction

The development of the Internet and the World Wide Web can be either a threat to the survival of indigenous languages or an opportunity for their development. The choice between cultural diversity and linguistic uniformity is in our hands and the outcome depends on our capability to devise, design and use tools and techniques for the processing of natural languages. Unfortunately natural language processing requires extensive expertise and large collections of reference data. Our research is concerned with the economical and therefore semi-automatic or automatic acquisition of such linguistic information necessary for the development of other-than-English indigenous or multilingual information systems.

In this paper we are concerned with automatic part-of-speech tagging. Part-of-speech tagging is the task of assigning the correct class (part-of-speech) to each word in a sentence. A part-of-speech can be a noun, verb, adjective, adverb etc. It should not be confused with the role/position in a sentence, which includes subject, predicate and object. Different word classes may occupy the same position, and similarly, a part-of-speech can take on different roles in a sentence. Automatic part-of-speech tagging is therefore the assignment of a part-of-speech class (or tag) to terms in a document. In this paper, we present and evaluate several methods for the fully automatic acquisition of the knowledge necessary for part-of-speech tagging.

A. Aagesen et al. (Eds.): INTELLCOMM 2004, LNCS 3283, pp. 112–119, 2004.

We try and devise a method that relies on the general statistical properties that characterize languages yet that can be learned independently of particular knowledge about a particular language.

In the next section, we discuss the research efforts and results that represent the state of the art in the area of part-of-speech tagging. In section 3 we present the proposed methods and their detailed description. In section 4, we comparatively and empirically analyze the proposed methods and existing reference methods using the Brown English language corpus and we present some preliminary remarks on experiments with an Indonesian language Corpus. We conclude in section 5.

2 Related Work

The definition of part-of-speech and their association to words and units in a sentence or a text is an essential and possibly intrinsic component of a linguistic system. In information retrieval and computation linguistic, the applications of part-of-speech tagging are numerous and ubiquitous. Part-of-speech tagging can be a tool for tasks as various as word-sense disambiguation, indexing, stemming, and, of course, parsing.

The simplest part-of-speech taggers are based on n-gram (bigram or trigram) [5,4]. Taggers which implement n-gram models require a relatively large tagged training corpus. Transformation-based tagging as introduced by Brill in [3] also requires a tagged corpus for training. No pre-tagged corpus is necessary for Hidden Markov Models [12,6,14]. However, a lexicon that specifies the possible parts of speech for every word is still needed.

Several researchers have worked on learning grammatical properties of words. Elman (1990) trained a connectionist net to predict words, a process that generates internal representations that reflect grammatical categories. Brill et al. in [2] tried to infer grammatical category from bigram statistics. Finch and Chater in [9] and Finch in [10] used vector models in which words are clustered according to the similarity of their close neighbors in a corpus. Kneser and Ney in [13] presented a probabilistic model for entropy maximization that also relies on the immediate neighbors of words in a corpus. Biber in [1] applied factor analysis to collocations of two target words ("certain" and "right") with their immediate neighbors.

Schutze in [18] is the first to have presented an algorithm for tagging words whose part-of-speech properties are unknown. He hypothesized that syntactic behavior is reflected in co-occurrence patterns. The degree of similarity between two words is determined by the degree to which they share the same left and right neighbors as reflected by the cosine similarity in a vector space. The context vectors of all the words are then clustered using Buckshot clustering algorithm [7]. Schutze conducted two types of experiments: one that classifies word types, and one that categorizes individual word occurrences, i.e. different occurrences of the same word may be assigned different tags. We will subsequently refer to these two types of classification as *Schutze1* and *Schutze2*, respectively.

3 Proposed Methods

3.1 N-Gram Method and Sentence Splitting

The first method we propose is based on n-grams. It hypothesizes that the more examples of sentences or sequences of words that are identical but for a word in each sentence at the same position, the more these two words are likely to be of the same part-of-speech category. We consider all the sequences of n words (n-grams) that are identical in all but for one word. We then count the number of such occurrences in the whole corpus for each pair of words and form a similarity matrix. For example, if we have two trigrams (w1 w2 w3) and (w1 w4 w3), we increment by one the count in the entry (2, 4) of the matrix. We refer to such occurrence as the association between w2 and w4.

The sentence splitting approach tries and identifies words that frequently serve as pivots. Let us consider for instance two sentences that have three words (w1 w2 w3) and (w4 w2 w5). The method hypothesizes that the more such examples, the more likely w1 and w4, and similarly w3 and w5, are to be of the same part-of-speech category. The idea can be applied recursively by splitting sentences around pivots into sub-sentences until we find individual words. We then count such occurrences over the entire corpus and thus form a similarity matrix accordingly.

3.2 Clustering

After the similarity matrix in each of both the methods described above is formed we group the different words into classes using a clustering algorithm. The choice of clustering algorithm has a significant impact on the quality of the clustering results. In this paper, depending on its applicability to the different methods, we consider one of or both the Markov Clustering (MCL) algorithm and the k-means clustering algorithm. In the MCL algorithm, the words and their associations are viewed as the vertices and edges of a weighted graph, respectively. The algorithm partition the graph into connected regions, i.e. with many edges connecting vertices inside the partition and few connecting vertices inside the region with vertices outside the region. The number of edges connecting two vertices corresponds to the degree of similarity of the two vertices. By simulating flows (random walks) within this structure, it further strengthens the flow where the current (connection) is already strong, and weakens the flow where the current is weak, hence placing the vertices with higher degree of similarity in the same cluster and those with lower degree of similarity in different clusters. The K-means clustering algorithm, on the other hand, views the similarity between two words as the inverse of the distance of the two vectors representing the words. This algorithm first forms the desired number of clusters (k) and then proceeds by assigning components to the cluster to which their distance is the minimum.

3.3 Extended Schutze's Approach

Schutze in [18] measured the similarity between two words with respect to their syntactic behavior by the degree to which they share the same immediate neighbors on the left and right. The counts of neighbors are assembled into a vector, with one dimension for each neighbor. We refer to the vector of left neighbors of a word as its left context vector, and to the vector of right neighbors as its right context vector. For example, if w1 and w2 are the neighbors to be considered, the left and right context vectors of a word w – assuming that it only occurs in the phrase (w1 w w2) – are (1 0) and (0 1) respectively. Each of the context vectors in Schutze's approach consists of 250 entries, corresponding to the 250 most frequent words in the Brown corpus.

Schutze acknowledges in his paper that the decision to consider only immediate neighbors may lead to an error when two words of different classes are categorized into the same class because they share the same left and right neighbors. For example, the adverb "currently" in the sentence "Hester, currently Dean of ..." and the conjunction "if" in "to add that, if United States policies ..." have similar neighbors (comma, noun phrase). To address this problem, we extend Schutze's algorithm by considering a broader context. In addition to the left and right context vectors characterizing a word w, we form two more context vectors: one for the word preceding its immediate left neighbor one for the word following its immediate right neighbor. We will refer to these two additional context vectors as the secondary left and secondary right context vectors of w. Hence, the degree of similarity between two words is determined by the degree to which they share the same two neighbors on the left and right, respectively.

With each context vector consisting of 250 entries, each word in the extended Schutze's approach is characterized by a vector of 1,000 entries. We form a matrix of size n-by-250 for each type of context vector, where n is the number of words to be clustered. To allow us to work with smaller matrices, we reduce the dimensionality of the matrix by using the Singular Value Decomposition (see for instance [15]). Each of the matrices is reduced to its 50 main dimensions. We then concatenate the four reduced matrices to form a matrix of size n-by-200. The k-means clustering algorithm is used for clustering in the case of Schutze's method and its variants.

4 Experiments and Results

We evaluate the proposed methods using the Brown corpus [11] tagged by the Penn Treebank Project [16]. The Brown corpus consists of 500 texts in English, each consisting of just over 2,000 words. The texts were sampled from 15 different text categories, ranging from press editorials to fictions and humors. The corpus is made up of 52,108 sentences, constituting over 1 million words, with 47,649 of them being distinct. We form 16 classes of tags, with each tag associated with one or more tags from the Penn Treebank. We label each cluster found with the tag that occurs the most frequently in that cluster. We say a word is correctly tagged if it is in a cluster whose associated tag is the same as the one associated to that word in the tagged corpus. For each tag t from the Penn Treebank, we count the occurrences of t in the corpus, the number of correctly tagged words and the number of incorrectly tagged words. We use three performance metrics in the evaluation: the average precision of the 16 tags, the average recall, and the percentage of the number of words correctly clustered, i.e. the sum of the correct cases for all the 16 tags over the size of the corpus. The algorithms are implemented in Java. SVD is implemented using the JAMA package [17]. The k-means clustering algorithm implementation is our own, while the MCL algorithm is from [19].

4.1   Experiments on a Subset of the Brown Corpus

The first set of experiments comparatively evaluates the performance of the combination of the two trigram and sentence-splitting methods with the two clustering algorithms. We have randomly chosen a small subset of the Brown corpus, containing a total of 89,397 words with 12,664 of them being distinct in order to be able to obtain the clustering results in a reasonable time. With the k-means clustering algorithm, we present the best results obtained for k=200 clusters (recall from the previous section that MCL algorithm determines the number of optimal classes, so we do not need to specify the desired number of classes). Table1 summarizes the results of evaluating the sentence splitting and trigram approach on this corpus using both clustering algorithms.

Table 1. The results of clustering the words in a subset of the Brown corpus, using different combinations of sentence-splitting and trigram approaches with MCL and k-means clustering algorithms

Method	Clustering Algorithm	#Clusters	Average Precision	Average Recall	% Correct
Sentence splitting	MCL	498	0.74	0.43	52%
Sentence splitting	K-means	200	0.76	0.51	63%
Trigram	MCL	655	0.82	0.47	57%
Trigram	K-means	200	0.87	0.68	71%

We see that the trigram method consistently outperform the sentence-splitting methods in both recall and precision for both types of clustering. For an optimal value of k (=200) the best results in recall and precision are obtained by the k-mean algorithm for both methods. Yet the reader must remember that MCL does not require that the programmer anticipates the number of clusters. The reader notices that, in this context, the loss of performance of the trigram method with MCL over the trigram method with k-mean is mainly in precision.

4.2   Experiments on the Whole Brown Corpus

On the basis of the results obtained in the previous sub-section, we now compare the trigram and extended Schutze's methods. The two methods use the k-mean clustering. For the trigram method we reduce the matrix using the 300, 500, and 7000 most frequent words, successively. We use k=200. The experiments are run on the complete Brown corpus. The results for Schutze1 and Schutze2 are reported from [18] in which they have been described to be run with the same parameters on the same corpus. Table 2 shows the results obtained with these approaches. The extended Schutze's method, which we have proposed, consistently outperforms all other methods.

Table 2. Results of the trigram and extended Schutze's methods on the whole Brown corpus, using the k-means clustering algorithm. Words are classified into 200 clusters. The number in the brackets with the trigram approach indicates the number of most frequent words used for association

Method	Average Precision	Average Recall	% Correct
Trigram (300)	0.70	0.60	64%
Trigram (500)	0.74	0.62	66%
Trigram (700)	0.76	0.62	67%
Extended Schutze's	**0.90**	**0.72**	**81%**
Schutze1	0.53	0.52	65%
Schutze2	0.78	0.71	80%

The trigram method manages to find 31,838 words that are associated with at least one word in the corpus before the reduction to the 300, 500, and 700 most frequent words respectively. From the three sets of results, and as intuition suggests, we can anticipate that the gradient of improvement decreases as the number of the kept most frequent words increases. Recall from section 3 that the extended Schutze's approach counts the co-occurrence of words using four context vectors, each consisting of 250 entries corresponding to the 250 most frequent words in the corpus. With the extended Schutze's method and the 250 most frequent words use to compose the context vectors, we obtain 47,553 words that co-occur at least once with one of the 250 most frequent words. We observe from Table 3 that this method performs better (average precision/recall of 0.90/0.72) than the trigram approach. This is probably because with the trigram approach we only manage to associate 31,838 words with each other. The rest of the words not associated with any word in the corpus are characterized by a zero vector; hence we practically cluster only 31,838 words with the trigram approach, which is less than 70% of the number of words clustered with the extended Schutze's method. This extended method also performs better than the original Schutze's methods (Schutze1 and Schutze2, average precision/recall of 0.53/0.52 and 0.78/0.71 respectively). Recall from the end of section 2 that the method Schutze2 classifies individual word occurrences, i.e. different occurrences of the same word may be assigned different tags, while the extended Schutze's approach classifies word types only. While it seems that Schutze2 should be able to achieve higher precision in general, it is also possible that it assigns too many different tags to a word.

4.3   Experiments on the Indonesian Corpus

We applied the extended Schutze's method to a corpus of documents in the Indonesian language. Since no pre-tagged corpus is available for this language, we are not able to measure the precision and recall. Nevertheless, manual inspection of the clusters formed can show several interesting properties. In particular it shows that words with the same affixes tend to be in the same cluster. This is particularly interesting since the Indonesian language is a morphologically rich language with a predominant derivational morphology. Examples are given in table3. These observation suggest to use the methods proposed to guide and improve stemming algorithms for morphologically rich algorithms with a predominant derivational morphology or a inflectional morphology that differentiates parts-of-speech (and position in the sentence).

Table 3. Examples of clusters found from the Indonesian corpus with their associated affixes

Tag	Affix	Examples
Verb	me-i	menangani, mengatasi, mengulangi
Verb	di-kan	diperlukan, disiagakan, dipertemukan, disempurnakan
Noun	pe-	pengusaha, pejuang, pejabat, peneliti, pendiri
Noun	ke-an	keselamatan, kepentingan, keutuhan
Noun	-nya	kontraknya, strateginya, rambutnya

Finally, the methods achieve a finer granularity of clustering that suggest a semantic significance to the results beyond the part-of-speech tagging by grouping in clusters such as days, places, and people. This suggests that similar methods can also be used for name-entity recognition.

5 Conclusion

We have presented in this paper several effective methods for part-of-speech tagging in the absence of both a tagged corpus, a lexicon, and without a set of predefined tags. We evaluated the performance of the methods we proposed and their variants and compared them with the state of the art reference, the Schutze's methods (of which one of our methods is an extension). We showed that the extended Schutze's method that we have proposed yields a consistent improvement over all other methods with an average precision of 90%, and tagging correctly over 80% of the words in the corpus.

Further manual inspection of the clusters obtained during the experiments of various corpora suggested applications or combination of our approach to other domains such as stemming and name-entity recognition.

References

1. Biber, Douglas (1993). Co-occurrence Patterns among Collocations: A Tool for Corpus-based Lexical Knowledge Acquisition. Computational Linguistics, 19(3):531-538.
2. Brill, Eric; Magerman, David; Marcus, Mitch; and Santorini, Beatrice (1990). Deducing Linguistic Structure from the Statistics of Large Corpora. In Proceedings of the DARPA Speech and Natural Language Workshop, pages 275-282.

3. Brill, Eric (1993). Automatic Grammar Induction and Parsing Free Text: A Transformation-based Approach. In Proceedings of ACL 31. Columbus OH.

4. Charniak, Eugene; Hendrickson, Curtis; Jacobson, Neil; and Perkowitz, Mike (1993). Equations for Part-of-speech Tagging. In Proceedings of the Eleventh National Conference on Artificial Intelligence, pages 784-789.

5. Church, Kenneth W. (1989). A Stochastic Parts Program and Noun Phrase Parser for Unrestricted Text. In Proceedings of ICASSP-S9. Glasgow, Scotland.

6. Cutting, Doug; Kupiec, Julian; Pedersen, Jan; and Sibun, Penelope (1991). A Practical Part-of-Speech Tagger. In The 3rd Conference on Applied Natural Language Processing. Trento, Italy.

7. Cutting, Douglas R; Pedersen, Jan O; Karger, David; and Tukey, John W. (1992). Scatter/Gather: A Cluster-based Approach to Browsing Large Document Collections. In Proceedings of SIGIR 'g2, pages 318-329.

8. Elman, Jeffrey L. (1990). Finding Structure in Time. Cognitive Science, pages 179-211.

9. Finch, Steven and Chater, Nick (1992). Bootstrapping Syntactic Categories using Statistical Methods. In Walter Daelemans and David Powers, editors, Background and Experiments in Machine Learning of Natural Language, pages 229-235. Tilburg University. Institute for Language Technology and AI.

10. Finch, Steven (1993). Finding Structure in Language. Ph.D. Thesis, University of Edinburgh.Scotland.

11. Francis, W.N. and Kucera, F. (1982). Frequency Analysis of English Usage. Houghton Mifflin, Boston.

12. Jelinek, F (1985). Robust Part-of-speech Tagging using a Hidden Markov Model. Technical Report. IBM, T.J. Watson Research Center.

13. Kneser, Reinhard and Ney, Hermann (1993). Forming Word Classes by Statistical Clustering for Statistical Language Modelling. In Reinhard Kohler and Burghard B. Rieger, editors, Contributions to Quantitative Linguistics, pages 221-226. Dordrecht, The Netherlands.

14. Kupiec, Julian (1992). Robust Part-of-Speech Tagging using a Hidden Markov Model. Computer Speech and Language, 6:225-242.

15. Manning, C. D. and Schutze, Hinrich (1999). Foundations of Statistical Natural Language Processing. MIT Press, Cambridge, MA.

16. Marcus, M., Kim, G., Marcinkiewicz, M., MacIntyre, R., Bies, A., Ferguson, M., Katz, K., and Schasberger, B. (1994). The Penn Treebank: Annotating Predicate Argument Structure. In ARPA Human Language Technology Workshop.

17. Miller, Bruce (2000). http://math.nist.gov/javanumerics/jama/. National Institute of Standards and Technology.

18. Schutze, Hinrich (1999). Distributional Part-of-speech Tagging. In EACL7, pages 141-148.

19. van Dongen, Stijn (2000). Graph Clustering by Flow Simulation. Ph.D. Thesis, University of Utrecht. The Netherlands.

Context Adaptive Interaction with an Automatically Created Spoken Interface for Intelligent Environments

Germán Montoro, Pablo A. Haya, and Xavier Alamán

Universidad Autónoma de Madrid,
Departamento de Ingeniería Informática,
Ctra. de Colmenar Km. 15. Madrid 28049, Spain
{German.Montoro, Pablo.Haya, Xavier.Alaman}@uam.es

Abstract. In this paper we present the interpretation and generation processes of a spoken dialogue interface for intelligent environments. The interface is automatically created for each specific environment and the interpretation and generation vary depending on the environment and its context. These processes rely on a dialogue tree structure. Several modules process the tree structure and the environment context information to produce specific dialogues for the current environment state. Dialogues are provided with clarification, error recovering, anaphora resolution and other capabilities. The interface is implemented in a real intelligent environment laboratory.

1 Introduction

Intelligent environments have appeared as a new research field in the user interface scientific community. They interact with users in a natural way and support them in their everyday life. Computers and computational devices are hidden from the users, and these get services from the system, for instance, by means of context sensitive spoken natural language interfaces.

The appearance of these environments makes necessary to build new interfaces that allow to interact with the users in a natural way. These interfaces have to be able to carry on conversations regarding the environment, its elements and the services that may be offered to the user. Spoken dialogue interfaces have to adapt to these systems, so that they can cope with the new challenges proposed by the intelligent environments.

We present a Spanish spoken dialogue interface for intelligent environments that adapts to every domain environment. Dialogues are automatically created and they allow to interact with the environment and control its devices by means of spoken natural language interaction. The paper focuses on the interpretation and generation processes and it just briefly explains how the system builds the plug and play dialogues for any given environment, which is thoroughly described in [1].

To develop our research we have built a real intelligent environment. This consists of a laboratory furnished as a living room, provided of a range of devices. These are lighting controls, a door opening mechanism, a presence detector, smart-cards, speakers, microphones, a TV set, an IP video-camera, etc.

A. Aagesen et al. (Eds.): INTELLCOMM 2004, LNCS 3283, pp. 120–127, 2004.

2 Environment and Dialogue Representation

The environment representation is written in an XML document. At startup, the system reads the information from this XML document and automatically builds:

- A blackboard [2], which works as an interaction layer between the physical world and the spoken dialogue interface.
- A spoken dialogue interface which, employing the blackboard, works as an interaction layer between the users and the environment.

The blackboard holds a representation of multiple characteristics of the environment. This blackboard layer isolates the applications from the real world. The details of the physical world entities are hidden from the clients [3].

Entities from the blackboard are associated to a type of entity. All the entities of the same type inherit the same general properties. Some of these properties are employed to create the spoken dialogue interface by means of linguistic parts. This information is composed of a verb part (the actions that can be taken with the entity), an object part (the name that it receives), a location part (where it is in the environment), etc [1].

The dialogue structure is based on a linguistic tree. Every set of linguistic parts is transformed in a tree path, with a node for each part.

As an example, let us suppose that the entity *light_1* has the following two sets of linguistic parts: {"turn_off", "light", "", "ceiling above", ""} and {"turn_off", "fluorescent", "", "", ""}, which correspond with three possible ways of interacting with it. In this case, the word part "turn off" is at the same level in both sets of parts so that only one "turn off" node is created, and "light" and "fluorescent" both hang from it. If now we have a new entity called *radio_1*, with this linguistic set of parts: {"turn_off", "radio", "", "", ""}, the system only has to append the name of the entity *radio_1* to the "turn off" node. Next it adds a "radio" node as its child, at the same level as "light" and "fluorescent". Starting from an empty tree, the system would automatically create the linguistic tree showed in figure 1.

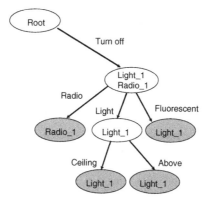

Fig. 1. Linguistic tree for light_1 and radio_1 entities

3 Interpretation and Generation

When the dialogue interface is created the system and the user may carry on conversations about the environment. The interface is managed by a dialogue supervisor, which is in charge of receiving the utterance from the speech recognizer, interpreting it and generating a result (a spoken answer or an action).

Initially, the system is asleep and does not recognize any utterance. If a user wants to initiate a conversation she has to wake it up by uttering the word *odyssey*. At that point, following the ideas defined by [4], the system considers that the goal of all the user utterances is to complete an action. If the user does not say anything in the next seven seconds (or seven seconds after the last dialogue interaction) the system returns to the sleeping mode.

3.1 Interpretation

When the system receives an interaction utterance from the recognizer the supervisor sends it to the utterance process module (UPM). The UPM checks for matches between the utterance and the children of the linguistic tree root (verb part nodes). If there is a match, the UPM goes down the tree to the matching node and checks for new matches with its children. This process continues until the UPM reaches an action node (the sentence was fully interpreted and the system may execute an action) or until there are not more matches (the system needs clarification).

Executing an Action. If the UPM reaches an action node it sends the node information to the node process module (NPM). The NPM gets the word related to the first node of the followed tree path (which corresponds with the verb part, that is, the action that the user has required to take). Then, the NPM orders the execution of the verb part by the action method associated to the reached action node. This execution usually implies a physical change in the environment, although it may also involve a system response. For instance, given the linguistic tree in figure 1, let us suppose that the user utters: *Please, could you turn off the ceiling light*. The UPM receives the sentence and checks for matches with the linguistic tree. *Turn off* matches with the "turn off" verb part node, *light* matches with the child of "turn off", and *ceiling* matches with the child of "light". The "ceiling" node is an action node. Then the NPM takes the control and gets that the action demanded by the user is *turn off*. As this node is associated to the *light_1* entity it executes the *light_1* action method, considering that the action requested by the user is *turn off*. Therefore, this action method can have two effects: it can turn off the *light_1* or it can inform the user about the fact that the *light_1* is already off. In any case, the UPM considers that the action was completed and goes back to its initial state, waiting for other utterances.

Clarification. If, after a user utterance the UPM does not reach an action node, somre clarification is needed. The NPM receives the node information from the UPM. This, again, gets the verb part (the action requested by the user) but does not execute any action. Now, the UPM sends the node information to the tree process module (TPM).

The TPM visits all the children of the current node, constructing an answer sentence to require more information from the user. This sentence is based on the visited nodes, always considering the environment context represented in the blackboard.

The TPM is based on a recursive depth-first tree search [5]. Its procedure is:

- It visits the first child of the node and checks if the action requested by the user is different to the current physical state of any of the entities associated to the node, employing the blackboard. If so, it stores the name of the entities with a different state and their tree level. Besides, it gets the word related to the node, to build the answer sentence.
- After that it recursively continues with the first child of this processed node, following the same steps.
- The recursive process with the first child of a node is repeated until the TPM reaches an action node or until the node does not have any entity with a physical different state. If the TPM reaches an action node, and it corresponds to an entity that has a different state to the user request, it increments by one the number of actions that can be offered to the user and stores the name of the entity that produces the action. In any case, it goes up to the parent node to continue the recursive tree inspection with the following child of the node.
- When the TPM visits a node which is not a first child (a second or following one), it makes sure that the entities that it contains are not the same as the entities of other processed nodes of the same level. This makes possible that synonyms can be represented in the tree, but only the right one is considered in the interpretation and generation processes.
- This algorithm is repeated until the TPM has inspected all the child nodes of the root and, if necessary, their subsequent children.

The facts of considering only those nodes which have entities with a different state to the state requested by the user and of processing only the first matching synonym make the tree search fully optimal. The TPM only has to follow the paths to the action nodes that can be processed in the current environment state, avoiding all the others.

Once the TPM has visited all the appropriate nodes, it has a full answer sentence (later explained in the generation section) and the number of actions that can be offered to the user. The UPM receives this information and, depending on the number of offered actions, it behaves as follows:

- If the number of actions is equal to zero, the UPM responds to the user that there is not any element in the environment that, in its current state, supports the requested action.
- If the number of actions is equal to one, the UPM directly executes the action method associated to the only entity that can produce an action. With this, we reduce the number of turns and assist the recognizer by employing the current environment context as one of the possible sources of information that improves the interpretation and understanding [6].
- If the number of actions is between one and three, the UPM utters the answer sentence built during the TPM tree search. This sentence presents all the possible entities that can perform the requested action, guiding the user through the dialogue [7].

− If the number of actions is higher than three, the UPM does not offer all the possible options. It utters a clarification question for the general user request. With this the system does not employ a sentence with too many options, which may be difficult to remember and tedious to hear, but still guides the user [8].

As we have seen, the interpretation varies depending on the current environment context. The same utterance may lead to different interpretations in different contexts. For dissimilar contexts the UPM can execute an action or consider that the user wants to interact with some environment entities.

As an example, let us suppose two different cases for the environment represented in the figure 1. They both share the same scenario, where the *light_1* and *radio_1* are both on:

1. In the first case the user utters *turn off the light*, so that the UPM stops at the "light" node. Then the NPM gets the requested action *turn off* and the TPM starts the clarification process. First, it goes down to the "ceiling" node and gets that the environment state of *light_1* (on) is different to the requested state (turn off), so it processes the node. Then, it adds the entity *light_1* to the list of entities visited under the "light" node, appends the word *ceiling* to the answer sentence and, given that it is an action node, increments the number of actions that can be offered and stores the name of the action entity *light_1*. After that it goes back to the "light" node and inspects the "above" node. Then it checks if the entities of this node are in the list of entities processed under the "light" node (this is, if it is a synonym of a previous processed node). As the "above" node belongs to the entity *light_1*, which is in the list of processed nodes for the "light" node, it does not process it. Finally it goes back to the original node, what concludes the tree search. The TPM returns the answer sentence, the number of offered actions and the list of action entities to the UPM. This verifies that there is only one possible action and executes it, that is, it turns off the ceiling light.

2. In the second case the user utters *turn off*, so that the UPM stops at the "turn off" node. Again, after the NPM gets that the requested action is *turn off* the TPM starts with the clarification procedure. First it gets that the state of *radio_1* is different to the requested state and that it is an action node. The TPM adds the entity *radio_1* to the list of processed entities under "turn off", increments the number of offered actions, appends the word *radio* to the answer sentence and adds the entity *radio_1* to the list of action entities. Next it goes back to the "turn off" node and after to the "light" node. Once there it works as explained in the previous case. Finally it goes back again to the "turn off" node and checks the "fluorescent" node. This node contains the same entity as a previously processed node under the "turn off" node (it is a synonym), so it is not considered. The UPM receives the answer sentence, the number of offered actions and the list of action entities. As the number of offered actions is equal to two it utters the clarification sentence: *do you want to turn off the radio or the ceiling light?* Notice that, as we have explained above, multiple synonyms are omitted in the clarification answer (this sentence only refers to the ceiling light and not to the fluorescent).

These very same sentences can produce different interpretations in a different context. Let us suppose a scenario where the *radio_1* is on and the *light_1* is off. If the user repeats the two previous sentences: (1) For the sentence *turn off the light*, now the UPM will inform the user that all the lights are off. (2) For the sentence *turn off*, now the UPM will turn off the *radio_1*, because it is the only action entity with a different state to the user requested state.

Another possible situation is produced when there is more than one entity of the same type in the environment (for instance, two or more lights). In this case for the user utterance *turn off the light* there can be three possible situations: (1) If all the lights are off the UPM will inform the user about that respect. (2) If only one light is on the UPM will turn off that light. (3) If more than one light is on the UPM will utter a clarification question. This clarification sentence will refer only to those lights that are on, omitting the lights that are already off.

As it has been illustrated in these examples, the interpretation varies depending on the current environment state and the active entities in the environment. New entities can appear or disappear, active entities can change their state or there can be multiple entities of the same type. The dialogue interface adapts to these situations, automatically altering its structure and behavior.

Finally, after a system clarification request the UPM interpretation process suffers a modification in the following interactions. As usually, it checks for matches with the linguistic tree nodes, starting from the root. Nevertheless, after a clarification request it also checks for matches starting from the node where it stopped in the previous interaction. From both tree searches, the UPM selects the node at a lower level or the node that corresponds with an action node. With this, the UPM allows either to continue with a previous interaction (after a clarification answer) or to initiate a new dialogue (leaving behind the clarification dialogue).

Error Recovering. The recognition, interpretation and clarification processes may lead, in some cases, to misrecognitions and misinterpretations. Additionally, users may not provide enough information to process an utterance. To recover of these problems, the system supports some specific features.

As we have seen above, after a clarification answer the UPM permits either to continue with a previous dialogue path or to initiate a new one. This was designed to allow to recover from system misinterpretations. If the clarification answer provided by the system does not correspond with one of the user goals he can start a new dialogue from the beginning, instead of continuing an erroneous dialogue path.

As an additional feature, the UPM does not only check the root of the linguistic tree and the node where it stopped in the previous interaction. If there is not any match for these two nodes, it will also check their children for matches. With this, the system may either recover from speech recognizer misrecognitions or accurately interpret sentences where the user only provided part of the information. For instance if for the scenario represented in the figure 1 the recognizer returns the sentence ...*the ceiling light* the UPM will not get any match for the root node. Then it checks the children of the root node, this is, the children of the "turn off" node, and so it gets a match for the "light" node and for its child, the "ceiling" node. It has recovered from recognition noise and thanks to the use of the environment context it may correctly interpret [9] that the original user utterance was *turn off the ceiling light*.

Anaphora Resolution. The spoken dialogue interface supports the resolution of pronominal anaphora to refer to the last mentioned entity.

To allow the use of anaphora the tree is modified to hold anaphora resolution nodes, one for each verb. These nodes are composed by a verb and a pronoun. Besides, after the UPM reaches an action node and executes its corresponding action, it stores the name of the referred object and the followed tree path.

When the UPM reaches an anaphora resolution node (the user has employed a pronoun to refer to an object) it goes to the tree node corresponding to that verb. Once there it goes down through the stored tree path until it reaches an action node and executes its associated action. Let us suppose that a user utters: *could you turn on the radio*. The UPM reaches the "radio" action node, turns the radio on and stores the full tree path of this action. Then the user utters *please, turn it down*. Now the UPM reaches the "turn it down" anaphora resolution node so it goes to the "turn down" tree node. Once there it follows the stored path, this is, it goes down to the "radio" node. As this is an action node, it turns the radio down.

3.2 Generation

As we have seen above, the generation process is carried out at the same time as the clarification process. The answer sentence is formed by words from nodes with entities that have a different state to the user request.

Initially the answer sentence is empty. Before the clarification process, it is filled with the question sentence *do you want to* and the words presented in the tree path that goes from the root node to the node where the UPM stopped. Words are added to the answer sentence by an addition word module (AWM). The AWM gets the number and gender of the word and appends its right form to the answer sentence, preceded by the appropriate article (in Spanish, nouns, adjectives and articles have number and gender). For instance, if in the figure 1 the UPM stops at the "turn off" node, the answer sentence will be initially formed by *do you want to turn off*. After that, the TPM appends the other appropriate tree words that it gets during the clarification process. Words are added as it was explained in the clarification section. Additionally, if a previous word at the same level was already added, before attaching the new word it appends the word *or*, in order to show alternatives. Furthermore, in Spanish it is necessary to append the preposition *from* before the modifier and location parts and the word *to* before the indirect object part. Following with the previous example, the TPM uses the AWM to append the words *the radio*. Next, given that "light" is at the same level as the "radio" node, it appends the word *or* and the words *the light*. After that, as *ceiling* is a location word, it appends the preposition *from* followed by the words *the ceiling*. The final answer sentence is (omitting some words, for a better translation to English): *do you want to turn off the radio or the ceiling light?*.

As it can be seen, the generation process also employs and adapts to the current environment context, automatically obtaining natural and suitable sentences for the given situation.

Additionally, the interface does not only generate answer sentences but also lightweight audio signs [10]. These audio signs are environmental sounds that try to provide information in a non-intrusive way, avoiding to disturb users if it is not necessary. Currently, environmental sounds are employed in two situations:

1. An audio sign (similar to a yawn) is reproduced when the recognizer returns to the sleeping state. If this happened because the user finished the interaction with the environment, it is not necessary to distract her by informing about this subject. If not, the user is still paying attention to the conversation, and an audio sign is enough to let her know about the new recognition state.

2. A different audio sign (similar to an interjection) is used when the UPM does not get any match at all. This sign is repeated in a next unsuccessful interpretation and only after a third consecutive failure, the system informs about the subject and requires the user to change his kind of sentence. We introduced this sign after checking with users that, in a few cases, the recognizer produced substitution or insertion errors, that is, it provided a different sentence to the uttered sentence or it interpreted noise (not an utterance) as a user sentence [11]. In the first case, we verified that it is faster and more efficient to reproduce an audio sign than to utter a whole sentence. In the second case, a recognizer error does not distract unnecessarily the user.

Acknowledgments

This work has been sponsored by the Spanish Ministry of Science and Education, project number TIN2004-03140.

References

1. Montoro, G., Alamán, X. and Haya, P.A. A plug and play spoken dialogue interface for smart environments. In Proceedings of CICLing'04. Seoul, Korea. February 15-21, 2004.
2. Engelmore, R. And Mogan, T. Blackboard Systems. Addison-Wesley, 1988.
3. Salber, D. and Abowd, G.D. The design and use of a generic context server. In Proceedings of Perceptual User Interfaces (PUI'98), 1998.
4. Searle, J. Speech Acts. Cambridge University Press. London, 1969.
5. Cormen, T.H., Leiserson, C. E., and Rivest, R. L.. Introduction to Algorithms. The MIT Press. Cambridge, Massachusetts. London, England. 2001.
6. Ward, K. and Novick, D.G. Integrating multiple cues for spoken language understanding. In Proceedings of CHI'95, Denver, May 7-11, 1995.
7. Yankelovich, N. "How do users know what to say?" ACM Interactions, 3, 6, December, 1996
8. Marx, M. and Schmandt, C. MailCall: Message presentation and navigation in a nonvisual environment. In Proceedings of CHI'96 (Vancouver, April 13-18), 1996.
9. Nagao, K. and Rekimoto J. Ubiquitous talker: Spoken language interaction with real world objects. In Proceedings of IJCAI-95, Vol. 2, 1284-1290, 1995.
10. Mynatt, E.D.; Back, M.; Want, R. and Frederick, R. Audio Aura: Light-weight audio augmented reality. In Proceedings of ACM UIST'97 (Banff, Canada), 211-212, 1997.
11. Schmandt, C. and Negroponte, N. Voice communication with computers: conversational systems. Van Nostrand Reinhold, New York. 1994.

Efficient Resource Allocation for IEEE 802.15.3(a) Ad Hoc Networks

Yi-Hsien Tseng[1], Hsiao-Kuang Wu[2], Kuen-Long Shieh[1], and Gen-Huey Chen[1]

[1] Department of Computer Science and Information Engineering,
National Taiwan University, Taipei, Taiwan
[2] Department of Computer Science and Information Engineering,
National Central University, Chung-Li, Taiwan

Abstract. IEEE 802.15.3(a) is working to design a higher speed PHY enhancement amendment to 802.15.3 such as ultra-wideband which can provide precise timing and location information. This paper proposes an effective resource allocation mechanism which can guarantee the QoS properties of multimedia traffics and provide higher channel utilization by the aid of location information. The proposed mechanism, which is executed by the piconet coordinator, consists of three components: grouping, call admission control, and best effort traffic maximization.

The grouping component groups non-interfering traffics together so that they are allowed to be transmitted simultaneously. The problem of grouping is shown equivalent to the graph coloring problem for which a lot of algorithms are available. The CAC component is responsible for QoS guarantee. The best effort traffic maximization component attempts to maximize the total throughput of best effort traffics. The maximization problem is formulated as a linear programming. Finally, simulation results verify the ability of QoS guarantee and higher channel utilization.

1 Introduction

IEEE 802.15.3 [1], which specified both the physical layer and MAC layer, was proposed for short range communication in wireless personal area networks (WPANs) with the advantages of low power consumption, low cost and low complexity. The physical layer can support data rate up to 55 Mbps. Then, for providing higher data rate, the IEEE 802.15 Task Group 3a (IEEE 802.15.3a) adopted ultra-wideband (UWB) technology and proposed new physical layer specifications whose data rate ranged from 110 Mbps to 480 Mbps. IEEE 802.15.3a could be used by the MAC layer of IEEE 802.15.3.

UWB technology [14] had been studied from the 1960's to the 1990's by the United States military for its use in modern RADAR. Later, the Federal Communications Commission (FCC) announced a Notice of Proposed Rule Making (NPRM) [2] to address rules for UWB emission. Furthermore, the FCC commissioners unanimously approved limited UWB uses in February 2002. UWB devices either had their fractional bandwidths greater than 0.25 or occupied 1.5 GHz or more of the spectrum. Instead of using the traditional RF carriers, UWB

A. Aagesen et al. (Eds.): INTELLCOMM 2004, LNCS 3283, pp. 128–142, 2004.

transmitters emitted a series of short pulses for data transmission. Each short pulse, also called a monocycle, is equivalent to a single sine wave. The duration of a UWB monocycle varies from 0.2 to 1.5 nanoseconds.

The IEEE 802.15.3 MAC protocol [1], which was designed for high data rate WPAN, can provide a reliable QoS supporting framework. The elementary topological unit for the IEEE 802.15.3 MAC layer is a piconet, which is a wireless ad hoc data communications system in essence. There are a number of independent data devices (DEVs) contained in a piconet that are allowed to exchange frames directly with each other. The master/slave relationship was adopted for these DEVs; a particular DEV, named piconet coordinator (PNC), acts as the master and the others are slaves.

Although the IEEE 802.15.3 MAC layer can provide a QoS supporting framework, it does not specify the functions of scheduling and admission control. So, an efficient scheduling method and a smart admission control strategy are still needed, in order to ensure smooth multi-service deliveries such as distinct bandwidth and delay requirements. They are intended to determine when a DEV can start transmission and decide which channel time requests are admitted.

With the location information provided by UWB technology and the transmission power control (TPC) supported by IEEE 802.15.3, a resource allocation mechanism for high-speed WPANs is proposed in this paper. This resource allocation mechanism contains an effective scheduling method and an effective admission control strategy. With this mechanism, the system throughput can be maximized and the channel utilization can be enhanced, while the QoS requirements are satisfied.

The rest of this paper is organized as follows. Related work is introduced in the next section. In Section 3, the IEEE 802.15.3 MAC protocol is briefly reviewed. The resource allocation mechanism is described in Section 4. Simulation and comparison results are shown in Section 5. Finally, this paper concludes with some remarks in Section 6.

2   Related Work

In this section, scheduling algorithms for both wireline and wireless networks are briefly reviewed. Basically, they are modifications or extensions of the well-known generalized processor sharing (GPS) [26]. GPS, which was originally proposed for wireline networks, is also known as weighted fair queueing (WFQ) model [11]. We note that GPS is an ideal fair scheduling model. In order for GPS to be implemented in a TDMA packet network, in which packets are not infinitely divisible and one session is served at a time, a practical packet-by-packet GPS (PGPS) was proposed in [26].

PGPS assigned each incoming packet a timestamp F_i^k which was computed by $F_i^k = S_i^k + L_i^k / R_i$ and $S_i^k = \max\{v(a_i^k), F_i^{k-1}\}$, where R_i is the transmission rate of session i and F_i^k, S_i^k, L_i^k, a_i^k are the virtual finish time, virtual start time, packet length and arrival time of the k-th packet of session i, respectively.

Besides, $v(t)$ is a virtual time function which was calculated according to $dv(t)/dt = C/(\sum_{i \in B(t)} R_i)$, where C is the fixed channel rate and $B(t)$ is the set of backlogged sessions at time t. Incoming packets were served in increasing order of their timestamps. There were other modified versions of GPS, i.e., worst-case fair weighted fair queueing (WF^{2}Q) [8], start-time fair queueing (STFQ) [15] and self-clocked fair queueing (SCFQ) [16]. More scheduling algorithms for wireline networks can be found in [29].

Since all GPS-based scheduling algorithms that were mentioned above assumed error-free channels, it is improper to implement them in wireless networks. Compared with wireline networks, wireless networks incline to a burst of location-dependent channel errors due to interference, fade and multipath effect. An additional compensation model should be added to these GPS-based scheduling algorithms, in order to deal with channel errors in wireless networks. The purpose of the compensation model is to enable lagging flows to reclaim services that were lost due to channel errors.

There were some scheduling algorithms proposed for wireless networks, e.g., channel state dependent packet scheduling algorithm (CSDPS) [7], idealized wireless fair queueing algorithm (IWFQ) [23], channel independent fair queueing algorithm (CIF-Q) [25], server based fairness algorithm (SBFA) [28] and wireless fair service algorithm (WFS) [23]. They all combined GPS-based scheduling algorithms with compensation models. GPS-based scheduling algorithms can guarantee QoS properties.

At the first glance, it seems possible to directly adapt GPS-based scheduling algorithms to the IEEE 802.15.3 MAC protocol. It was stated in [9] that when the network was at a high data rate, GPS-based scheduling algorithms might cause a bottleneck which was incurred by the heavy computation required for evaluating virtual time tags of packets and then sorting them. So, it is rather difficult to implement GPS- based scheduling algorithms in the IEEE 802.15.3 network, because DEVs have low computing power.

In this paper, a new scheduling algorithm for the IEEE 802.15.3 MAC protocol is proposed in which DEVs need not calculate virtual time tags. DEVs only have to inform the PNC of bandwidth requirements and delay limitations of pending traffics via request messages. With these information, the scheduling algorithm can guarantee QoS properties. These request messages do not involve heavy computation.

3   Review of IEEE 802.15.3 MAC Protocol

A piconet contains 236 DEVs at most. At the initialization of a piconet, one of the DEVs is elected to be the PNC. The PNC broadcasts the current status of DEVs periodically via beacons. DEVs are also aware of newly entering DEVs by beacons. When the PNC finds a more capable DEV, it hands over the control of the piconet to the DEV. That is, the old PNC is no longer the PNC and the DEV acts as the new PNC. Timing for a piconet is realized by superframes whose three parts are briefly described below (also refer to Figure 1).

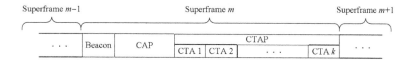

Fig. 1. A superframe and its three parts

- Beacon. It contains a beacon frame and announcement commands (see [1]) that are sent by the PNC as a beacon extension. Its purpose is to set timing allocations and to distribute management information over the piconet.
- CAP. It is optional. If existing, it allows the PNC and DEVs to change commands and/or asynchronous data in a contention manner (CSMA/CA).
- CTAP. It consists of some channel time allocations (CTAs), which are reserved for the PNC and DEVs to change commands, isochronous streams and asynchronous data in a non-contention manner (TDMA).

The durations of the CAP and the CTAP, which are determined by the PNC according to the channel time needs of current requests, may vary in different superframes. DEVs are allowed to change data during the CAP or the CTAP. The CAP is suitable for small and non time- critical data transmissions in a contention manner. On the other hand, the CTAP is suitable for data transmissions with QoS guaranteed. When a DEV intends to transmit data during the CTAP, it has to send a request message to the PNC first. The PNC then decides whether the request can be accepted or not according to the available time in the superframe. If accepted, the PNC will allocate enough CTAs for the DEV and announce this allocation in the next beacon.

The 802.15.3 MAC protocol provides a functionality of controlling transmitter power. The ability to control power enables DEVs to minimize the interference with other wireless networks that share the same channel and to decrease the power consumption. There are two methods for controlling transmitter power. One allows the PNC to set a maximum level of transmission power for the CAP and the beacon. The other, which is adopted by this paper, allows DEVs to enhance or reduce the transmission power.

4   A Resource Allocation Mechanism

In this section, an efficient resource allocation mechanism for IEEE 802.15.3(a) networks is proposed. We do not deal with any particular time-critical traffics (such as CBR and real-time VBR) and non-time-critical traffics (such as non-real-time VBR, UBR and ABR). Instead, we classify traffics into two categories: real-time traffics (RTs) and non- real-time traffics (NRTs). Using the method of [10] together with UWB technology, the PNC can compute relative positions of DEVs. They are also aware of the relative position of each other via beacons.

The IEEE 802.15.3 system architecture equipped with the proposed mechanism is shown in Figure 2. The proposed mechanism, which is implemented

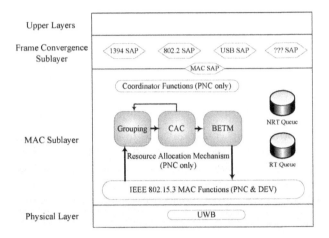

Fig. 2. The IEEE 802.15.3 system architecture with the proposed resource allocation mechanism

in the PNC only, contains three components: grouping, call admission control (CAC) and best effort traffic maximization (BETM). For each superframe, the grouping component determines the number of CTAs contained in it. The CAC component determines which traffic requests can be accepted. The BETM component determines the length of each CTA, the length of the superframe and the duration of each traffic request. The PNC informs all DEVs of these via beacons.

When a DEV wants to transmit data, it sends a request message to the PNC during the CAP. At the end of the CAP, the PNC may receive a number of request messages and the grouping component then forms these requests into groups so that non-interfering requests belong to the same group (one request may belong to more than one group). The number of distinct groups determines the number of CTAs required and traffics belonging to the same group can be transmitted simultaneously by dynamically adjusting transmission power. The problem of grouping is equivalent to the graph coloring problem [27].

The CAC component is responsible for checking whether there is enough time for transmitting RTs and whether their QoS requirements can be satisfied. If not, the CAC component will reject some RT requests and the grouping component will be invoked again with the rejected RT requests excluded. Otherwise, the BETM component then takes over whose objective is to maximize the total throughput of all NRTs subject to some constraints. At the same time, the length of each CTA can be determined and the channel utilization can be enhanced. The maximization problem can be formulated as a linear programming [20]. In the rest of this section, the three components are described in detail.

4.1   Grouping

The chief purpose of grouping is spatial reuse. Figure 3 further illustrates the concept. Since the transmission between a TV and a video device does not inter-

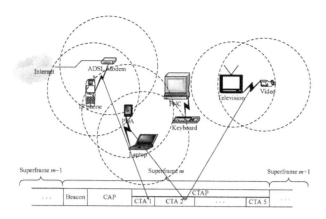

Fig. 3. The concept of grouping

ferewith the transmission between a PDA and a laptop, they can be scheduled in CTA 2. In this way, channel utilization is enhanced.

In traditional TDMA systems, one transmission was permitted at a time. That is, only one traffic request could be accepted for each CTA. By exploiting location information and transmission power control, which are supported by IEEE 802.15.3, more than one traffic request can be scheduled in a CTA. Now that every two neighboring DEVs can compute their distance, they can adopt minimal level of transmission power so that they can hear each other. Consequently, less interference occurs within a piconet, and more non-interfering traffics can be transmitted simultaneously.

In order for non-interfering traffics to be transmitted during the same time period, the PNC must be aware of all interference. DEVs having pending traffics are required to send request messages to the PNC during the CAP. Since these request messages contain the identifiers of source and destination DEVs, the PNC can easily determine if there is interference among these traffics by computing the distance of any two DEVs.

The grouping component attempts to schedule non-interfering traffic requests in the same CTA, with the objective of minimizing the number of CTAs in a superframe. With the same traffic requests, fewer CTAs are likely to have a better channel utilization. The problem of grouping can be formally described as follows.

The Problem of Grouping. Given a set $R = \{r_1, r_2, ..., r_n\}$ of traffic requests and a set $T = \{t_1, t_2, ..., t_k\}$ of CTAs, determine a mapping F from R to T so that $|F(R)|$ is minimized, subject to the constraint that $F(r_i) = F(r_j)$ implies no interference between r_i and r_j for all $1 \leq i \leq n$ and $1 \leq j \leq n$.

The following theorem shows that the problem of grouping is equivalent to the graph coloring problem as described below.

The Graph Coloring Problem. Given the vertex set $V = \{v_1, v_2, ..., v_n\}$ of a graph G and a set $C = \{c_1, c_2, ..., c_k\}$ of k distinct colors, determine a mapping H from

V to C so that $|H(V)|$ is minimized, subject to the constraint that $H(v_i) = H(v_j)$ implies that v_i and v_j are not adjacent in G for all $1 \leq i \leq n$ and $1 \leq j \leq n$. A feasible mapping H satisfying the constraint is called a $|H(V)|$-coloring of G.

Theorem 1. *The problem of grouping is equivalent to the graph coloring problem.*

Proof. We first show that each instance of the problem of grouping can be transformed into an instance of the graph coloring problem. Consider $R = \{r_1, r_2, ..., r_n\}$ and $T = \{t_1, t_2, ..., t_k\}$ an arbitrary instance, denoted by I, of the problem of grouping. Denote each r_i by a vertex v_i and each interference between r_i and r_j by an edge (v_i, v_j). The resulting graph is denoted by $G = (V, E)$, where $V = \{v_1, v_2, ..., v_n\}$.

Suppose that $F : R \rightarrow T$ is a feasible mapping for I, i.e., $F(r_i) = F(r_j)$ implies no interference between r_i and r_j. F has the following property for $G : F(v_i) = F(v_j)$ implies that v_i and v_j are not adjacent in G. Moreover, there exists a feasible F for I if and only if G has a $|F(R)|$-coloring, imaging that there is a one-to-one correspondence from $T = \{t_1, t_2, ..., t_k\}$ to $C = \{c_1, c_2, ..., c_k\}$. Hence, G is an instance of the graph coloring problem.

Similarly, each instance of the graph coloring problem can be transformed into an instance of the problem of grouping so that the former has a $|H(V)|$-coloring if and only if there exists a feasible mapping F with $|F(R)| = |H(V)|$ for the latter. □

With Theorem 1, both the problem of grouping and the graph coloring problem are referred to interchangeably from now on. The graph coloring problem is known to be NP-hard [22]. A graph G is k-colorable if there is a k-coloring of G. The minimum k so that G is k-colorable is called the *chromaticnumber* of G. There are some exact algorithms and approximation algorithms for the graph coloring problem. Most of exact algorithms are based on implicit enumeration. The well-known DSATUR algorithm [6] is one of them. Differently, Méndez Diaz and Zabala proposed an LP-based Branch-and- Cut algorithm in [24] for the graph coloring problem.

On the other hand, an approximation algorithm for coloring an n-vertex graph G were proposed in [5] [17] [19]. Interested readers may consult [24] [5] [19] for more solution methods, exact and approximate, to the graph coloring problem.

4.2   CAC

Since the length of a superframe is limited ($\leq 65535\mu s$), some requests should be rejected if the available channel time is insufficient. For example, when the total time required by the requests exceeds the maximally allowable length of CTAP, some requests should be rejected. The CAC component is responsible for resource management so that QoS properties can be guaranteed.

The CAC component deals with only RT requests because they are associated with delay limitations and bandwidth requirements. The PNC computes an upper bound on the length of a superframe and lower bounds on the lengths of CTAs for the purpose of admission control. If the summation of all lower bounds for CTAs is greater than the upper bound, the PNC will reject an RT request and then invoke the grouping component again. After regrouping, fewer CTAs may be used.

The upper bound is determined by two factors: the maximal length ($65535\mu s$) specified by the IEEE 802.15.3 standard and delay limitations associated with RT requests. The upper bound is computed as the minimum of the maximal length and those delay limitations. For example, the upper bound is 48 ms if there are three RT requests whose delay limitations are 78 ms, 65 ms and 48 ms, respectively. By keeping the length of the superframe below the upper bound, all delay requirements can be satisfied.

On the other hand, the lower bound for a CTA is computed as the maximal bandwidth requirement of the RT requests scheduled in it. If the CTA contains only NRT requests, the lower bound is set to zero. For example, refer to Figure 4 where there are three RT requests scheduled in CTA 1 and CTA 2. Since their bandwidths are 44 ms, 32 ms and 22 ms, the lower bounds for CTA 1 and CTA 2 are 44 ms and 22 ms, respectively. The lower bound for CTA k is zero because it contains no RT request.

Figure 4 also illustrates the concept of CAC. The upper bound represents the maximally allowable length of the superframe. If the summation of all lower bounds is greater than the upper bound, then the available channel time is insufficient for these RT requests and so an RT request should be rejected. The rejected RT request is the one interfering with the most RT requests. If there is more than one candidate, select the one with the smallest delay limitation. The grouping component is then invoked again with the rejected RT request excluded.

If the summation of all lower bounds is not greater than the upper bound, the BETM component then takes over, which is detailed below.

4.3   BETM

After the CAC component, the QoS requirements of all RTs are guaranteed. In this section, we intend to maximize the total throughput of all NRTs based on a reassignment of requests to CTAs. The maximization is subject to the

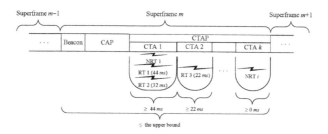

Fig. 4. The concept of CAC

constraints induced by the upper bound and lower bounds of Section 4.2. Recall that after the grouping component, each request, RT or NRT, is assigned to a unique CTA. Now a reassignment is to be made in order to increase the total throughput. Each NRT request in the reassignment may be assigned to extra CTAs, whereas each RT request remains the same assignment as before.

The reassignment is described as follows. Suppose that there are m NRT requests, denoted by $r_{\phi(1)}$, $r_{\phi(2)}$, ..., $r_{\phi(m)}$, and each $r_{\phi(i)}$ $(1 \leq i \leq m)$ interferes with $p_{\phi(i)}$ NRT requests. First, arrange these m NRT requests in a nondecreasing sequence of $p_{\phi(i)}$'s. Then, for each NRT request, say $r_{\phi(i)}$, in the sequence, sequentially perform the following: schedule $r_{\phi(i)}$ in a new CTA if it does not interfere with any (RT or NRT) request contained in the CTA.

Figure 5 shows an example. Suppose that there are two RT requests, denoted by RT 1 and RT 2, and three NRT requests, denoted by NRT 1, NRT 2 and NRT 3. The interference is expressed with a graph, as shown in Figure 5(a), whose vertices represent the requests and whose edges represent the interference among them. The assignment of the requests to CTAs after the grouping component is shown in Figure 5(b). The reassignment of NRT requests can be performed in the sequence of NRT 3, NRT 2 and NRT 1, and the result is shown in Figure 5(c). The reassignment schedules NRT 2 in CTA 3 and NRT 3 in CTA 1 and CTA 3, additionally. After the reassignment, the total throughput of all NRTs can be enhanced.

Let T_i be the set of CTAs where $r_{\phi(i)}$ is scheduled after the reassignment. For convenience, we use $|CTA\ j|$ to denote the time length of CTA j and $|r_{\phi(i)}|$ to denote the time length required by $r_{\phi(i)}$. Now that $r_{\phi(i)}$ is scheduled in the CTAs of T_i, $|r_{\phi(i)}|$ is distributed over them. We use $|r_{\phi(i)}|^{(q)}$ to denote the portion of $|r_{\phi(i)}|$ that is distributed in CTA q, where CTA $q \in T_i$. Clearly, the summation of all $|r_{\phi(i)}|^{(q)}$'s is equal to $|r_{\phi(i)}|$. For the example of Figure 5(c), consider $(r_{\phi(1)}, r_{\phi(2)}, r_{\phi(3)}) = $(NRT 1, NRT 2, NRT 3) and then $T_1 = \{CTA\ 3\}$, $T_2 = \{CTA1, CTA$

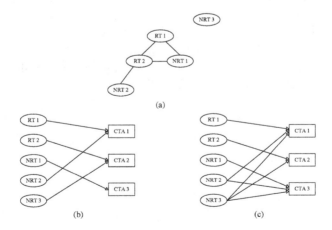

Fig. 5. An example.(a) The interference among requests.(b) The assignment after the grouping component.(c) The reassignment of NRT requests

3} and $T_3=\{$CTA 1, CTA 2, CTA 3$\}$. The distribution of |NRT 1|, |NRT 2| and |NRT 3| is illustrated in Figure 6.

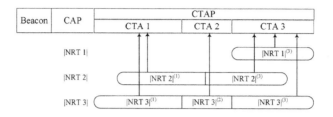

Fig. 6. The distribution of |NRT 1|, |NRT 2| and |NRT 3|

Suppose that k CTAs are used after the grouping component. We let U denote the upper bound and L_j denote the lower bound for CTA j, where $1 \leq j \leq k$. The goal of the BETM is to maximize $\sum_{i=1}^{m} |r_{\phi(i)}|$ subject to some constraints as follows. First, |CTA $j| \geq L_j$ assures that the bandwidth requirements for the RT requests that are scheduled in CTA j can be guaranteed. Second, $B +$ |CAP|$+\sum_{j=1}^{k}$|CTA $j| \leq U$ assures the maximal delay of any MAC frame is not greater than the maximally allowable length of the superframe, where B is the length of the beacon and |CAP| is the length of the CAP. In other words, the delay limitations of all RT requests are promised.

Third, $\sum_{\text{CTA } j \in T_i}$ |CTA $j| \geq |r_{\phi(i)}|$ and |CTA $j| \geq |r_{\phi(i)}|^{(j)}$ assure that the bandwidth requirement of $r_{\phi(i)}$ can be satisfied. Finally, $\sum_{\text{CTA } j \in T_i} |r_{\phi(i)}|^{(j)} = |r_{\phi(i)}|$, $|r_{\phi(i)}|^{(j)} \geq 0$ and $|r_{\phi(i)}| \geq 0$ are required. To sum up, the optimization problem can be expressed as a linear programming as follows.

$$\text{Maximize } \sum_{i=1}^{m} |r_{\phi(i)}|$$

subject to

$$|\text{CTA } j| \geq L_j \text{ for } 1 \leq j \leq k$$

$$B + |CAP| + \sum_{j=1}^{k} |\text{CTA } j| \leq U$$

$$\sum_{\text{CTA} j \in T_i} |\text{CTA } j| \geq |r_{\phi(i)}| \text{ for } 1 \leq i \leq m$$

$$|\text{CTA } j| \geq |r_{\phi(i)}|^{(j)} \quad \text{for } 1 \leq i \leq m \text{ and every CTA } j \in T_i$$

$$\sum_{\text{CTA} j \in T_i} |r_{\phi(i)}|^{(j)} = |r_{\phi(i)}| \quad \text{for } 1 \leq i \leq m$$

$$|r_{\phi(i)}|^{(j)} \geq 0 \quad \text{for } 1 \leq i \leq m \text{ and every CTA } j \in T_i$$

$$|r_{\phi(i)}| \geq 0 \quad \text{for } 1 \leq i \leq m$$

The optimization problem can be solved by several well-known methods, inclusive of the simplex method [12], the Karmarkar's interior point method [21], the ellipsoidal calculus method [18] and the Lagrange multiplier method [4]. They all can solve a linear programming efficiently.

5   Simulation Results

In this section, the performance of the proposed mechanism is evaluated by simulation. The Network Simulator (ns2) [3] are adopted for the simulation and the used IEEE 802.15.3 MAC functions are implemented by INTEL [13]. The simulation environment models a piconet which covers a 10m × 10m area, where the DEVs are randomly distributed. Each DEV is equipped with a radio transceiver that is capable of transmitting up to 10 meters over a wireless channel. Each DEV can adjust its transmitting power dynamically. Since the design purpose of IEEE 802.15.3 is for the use of a WPAN, it is assumed that every transmitting pair has a distance of no more than 1 meter. The transmission capability of each network interface is assumed 100 Mbps.

There are three CBR flows (a type of RTs) in the simulation scenario whose bandwidths are 32 Kbps, 1.5 Mbps and 15 Mbps, respectively, and whose delay limitations are set to 45 *ms*, 75 *ms* and 90 *ms*, respectively. In order to observe their QoS guarantee, up to ten FTP flows (a type of NRTs) are fed when the simulation proceeds. Since no scheduling method is specified in the IEEE 802.15.3 standard, first-come-first-served (FCFS) is implemented for comparison with the proposed mechanism. In the implementation, a traffic (RT or NRT) request will be rejected if it causes the total length of the beacon, the CAP and the CTAP exceeding 65535 *ms*.

As observed from Figure 7, each CBR flow has a smaller packet delay than the delay limitation. The reason is that a packet whose delay exceeds the delay limitation is dropped. The influence of FTP flows on the packet delay for the proposed mechanism is negligible, which is a consequence of an upper bound

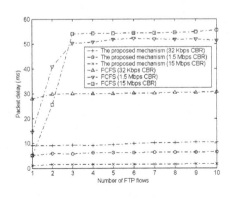

Fig. 7. Packet delay

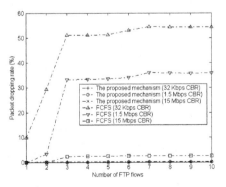

Fig. 8. Packet dropping rate

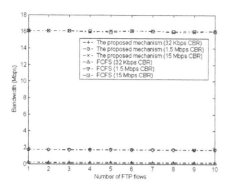

Fig. 9. Bandwidth

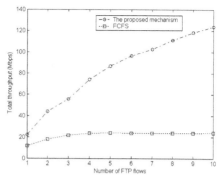

Fig. 10. Total throughput of NRTs

(obtained in Section 4) on the length of each superframe. The packet delay for FCFS is growing when the number of FTP flows is increasing until the bottleneck (three FTP flows in the simulation scenario) is reached.

Simulation results for packet dropping rate are shown in Figure 8. The packet dropping rate for the proposed mechanism approaches zero because the upper bound is not greater than the minimal delay limitation. All packets in the proposed mechanism are sent out before their delay limitations. Similar to Figure 7, the packet dropping rate for FCFS is growing when the number of FTP flows is increasing until the bottleneck is reached. Since the proposed mechanism results in a very low dropping rate, it can support multimedia traffics very well.

Simulation results for bandwidth are shown in Figure 9. Both the proposed mechanism and FCFS can guarantee the bandwidth requirement. Since IEEE 802.15.3 is TDMA based, it can guarantee the bandwidth requirement if there are enough CTAs for each RT. Both the proposed mechanism and FCFS can provide enough CTAs for each RT.

Simulation results for the total throughput of NRTs are shown in Figure 10, where each total throughput sums up the throughputs of all FTP flows. The total throughput for the proposed mechanism is much better than the total throughput for FCFS, which is a consequence of the grouping component and BETM component. After the grouping component, non-interfering FTP flows are allowed to be transmitted simultaneously, and after the BETM component, the total transmitting time of all FTP flows is maximized by applying any LP solution method. The total throughput for FCFS remains a constant when the number of FTP flows exceeds the bottleneck.

Finally, the numbers of accepted RTs for the proposed mechanism and FCFS are compared. Figure 11 shows the simulation results, where the bandwidth of the RTs is set to 15 Mbps. Since the proposed mechanism can transmit non-interfering RTs in parallel, it behaves better than FCFS.

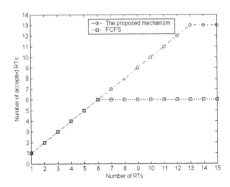

Fig. 11. Number of accepted RTs

6   Conclusion

In this paper, we have given an overview of the IEEE 802.15.3 MAC protocol and a description of UWB (IEEE 802.15.3a) technology. Both are greatly helpful to the future development of WPAN. An effective scheduling method is important for the IEEE 802.15.3 MAC to support novel applications in the future WPAN. Therefore, we proposed a resource allocation mechanism for the IEEE 802.15.3 MAC which contains a scheduling method. The effectiveness of the proposed mechanism was demonstrated by simulation. Since UWB technology can provide more accurate location information, it was used to improve the channel utilization.

The proposed mechanism comprises three components: grouping, CAC and BETM. The grouping component scheduled non-interfering traffics in the same CTA and attempted to minimize the number of CTAs used in the superframe. We proved that the problem of grouping is NP-hard, by showing that it is equivalent to the graph coloring problem. There are some existing algorithms, exact or approximate, for solving the graph coloring problem.

The CAC component performed admission control for QoS guarantee. The strategy is to compare the summation of all lower bounds for CTAs with the upper bound for the superframe. If the former exceeds the latter, it means that the available channel time is not adequate for RT requests and so the PNC has to reject an RT request. The BETM component scheduled NRTs so that their total throughput was maximized. To increase the total throughput, each NRT was scheduled to more CTAs as long as no interference occurred. The resulting optimization problem was formulated as an LP problem.

There are three advantages for the proposed mechanism. First, it can provide higher spatial reuse. By adjusting transmitting power, non-interfering traffics can be transmitted simultaneously. Second, it can guarantee the QoS properties of multimedia traffics. This was accomplished by the aid of lower bounds for all CTAs and the upper bound for the superframe, which were estimated according to the bandwidth requirements and delay limitations of RTs. Third, it can maximize the total throughput of NRTs. The maximization was based on a rescheduling of NRTs and an LP formulation.

Acknowledgment

This work was supported by the MediaTek Inc. under the project "Wireless Communication Systems". This work was also supported by National Science Council of Taiwan under the NSC93-2524-S-008-002 Integrated knowledge Management Project.

References

1. IEEE standard 802.15.3: Wireless Medium Access Control (MAC) and Physical Layer (PHY) Specifications for High Rate Wireless Personal Area Networks (WPANs), Inst. Elec. Electron. Eng., New York, USA, 2003.
2. FCC Notice of Proposed Rule Making, *Revision of Part 15 of the Commission's Regarding Ultra-wideband Transmission Systems*, ETDocket 98-153.
3. Ns2, the VINT project, http://www.isi.edu/nsnam/ns/.
4. G. Arfken, "Lagrange multipliers," in *Mathematical Methods for Physicists*, Academic Press, pp. 945-950, 1985.
5. A. BLUM, "New approximation algorithms for graph coloring," *Journal of the ACM*, vol. 41, pp. 470 -516, 1994.
6. D. Brélaz, "New methods to color the vertices of a graph," *Communications of the ACM*, vol. 22, pp. 251-256, 1979.
7. P. Bhagwat, P. Bhattacharya, A. Krishma and S. Tripathi, "Enhancing throughput over wireless LANs using channel state dependent packet scheduling," *Proceedings of IEEE INFOCOM*, vol. 3, pp. 1133-1140, 1996.
8. J. C. R. Bennett and H. Zhang, "WF2Q: worst-case fair weighted fair queueing," *Proceedings of IEEE INFOCOM*, vol. 1, pp. 120-128, 1996.
9. H. M. Chaskar and U. Madhow, "Fair scheduling with tunable latency: a round-robin approach," *IEEE/ACM Transactions on Networking*, vol. 11, pp. 592-601, 2003.
10. S. Capkun, M. Hamdi and J. P. Hubaux, "GPS-free positioning in mobile ad-hoc networks," *Proceedings of the 34th Annual Hawaii International Conference*, pp. 3481-3490, 2001.
11. A. Demers, S. Keshav, and S. Shenker, "Analysis and simulation of a fair queueing algorithm," *Proceedings of ACM SIGCOMM*, vol. 19, pp. 1-12, 1989.
12. G. B. Dantzig, "Programming of interdependent activities: II. mathematical model," *Econometrica*, vol. 17, pp. 200-211, 1949.
13. M. Demirhan, IEEE 802.15.3 MAC model for ns-2, http://www.winlab.rutgers.edu/~demirhan, Intel corporation.
14. J. Foerster, E. Green, S. Somayazulu and D. Leeper, "Ultra-wideband technology for short- or medium-range wireless communications," *Journal of Intel Technology*, 2nd quarter, 2001.
15. P. Goyal, H. Vin, and H. Cheng, "Start-time fair queueing: a scheduling algorithm for integrated services packet switching networks," *IEEE/ACM Transactions on Networking*, vol. 5, pp. 690-704, 1997.

16. S. Golestani, "A self-clocked fair queueing scheme for broadband applications," *Proceedings of IEEE INFOCOM*, vol. 2, pp. 636-646, 1994.
17. M. M. Hallórsson, "A still better performance guarantee for approximate graph coloring," *Information Processing Letters*, vol. 45, pp. 19 -23, 1993.
18. A. B. Kurzhanskiand and I. Vályi, *Ellipsoidal Calculus for Estimation and Control*, MA: Birkhäuser: Boston, 1996.
19. D. Karger, R. Motwani and M. Sudan, "Approximate graph coloring by semidefinite programming," *Journal of the ACM*, vol. 45, pp. 246-265, 1998.
20. H. Karloff, *Linear Programming*, Birkhauser: Boston, 1991.
21. N. Karmarkar, "A new polynomial-time algorithm for linear programming," *Combinatorica*, vol. 4, pp. 373-395, 1984.
22. R. M. Karp, "Reducibility among combinatorial problems," *Proceedings of a symposium on the Complexity of Computer Computations*, pp. 85-104, 1972.
23. S. Lu, T. Nandagopal and V. Bharghavan, "Fair scheduling in wireless packet networks," *Proceedings of ACM MOBICOM*, vol. 27, pp. 63-74, 1997.
24. I. Méndez Díaz and P. Zabala, "A Branch-and-Cut Algorithm for Graph Coloring," *proceedings of Computational Symposium on Graph Coloring and Generalizations*, 2002.
25. T.S. Ng, I. Stoica and H. Zhang, "Packet fair queueing algorithms for wireless networks with location-dependent errors," *Proceedings of IEEE INFOCOM*, vol 3, pp. 1103-1111, 1998.
26. A. Parekh and R. Gallager, "A generalized processor sharing approach to flow control in integrated services networks: the single node case," *IEEE/ACM Transactions on Networking*, vol. 1, pp. 344-357, 1993.
27. H. A. Peelle, "Graph coloring in J: an introduction," *Proceedings of ACM SIGAPL APL Quote Quad Conference*, vol. 31, pp77-82, 2000.
28. P. Ramanathan and P. Agrawal, "Adapting packet fair queueing algorithms to wireless networks," *Proceedings of ACM MOBICOM*, pp. 1-9, 1998.
29. H. Zhang, "Service Disciplines for Guaranteed Performance Service in Packet-switching Networks," *proceedings of the IEEE*, vol. 83, pp. 1374-1396, 1995.

Intelligent Features Within the J-Sim Simulation Environment

Nada Meskaoui[1,3], Dominique Gaiti[1,2], and Karim Kabalan[3]

[1] LIP6-Université de Paris 6, 8 rue du Capitaine Scott,
75015 Paris, France
[2] LM2S: Université de Technologie de Troyes, 12 rue Marie Curie,
10010 Troyes Cedex, France
[3] American University of Beirut,
Faculty of Engineering and Architecture, Lebanon

Abstract. This paper presents our approach integrating a high level of intelligence within telecommunication networks. Artificial intelligence has proved its efficiency in resolving complex issues in different fields like air traffic control, robotics, and medical diagnosis. However its usage in telecommunication networks is still very moderated. The main objectives of our framework is to encourage the deployment of techniques characterized by a high level of intelligence – inspired from the artificial intelligence domain in networking. For this reason, we build an extension, with intelligent capabilities, to the J-Sim simulation environment. This extension proposes an intelligent package having the essential entities required for simulating intelligent features. Using this intelligent package and the abstract node model (INET) proposed by J-Sim for network simulations, it will be possible to test the efficiency of integrating intelligent techniques in networking.

1 Introduction

The last few years have perceived great increase in the research efforts in different domains. In telecommunication, for example, the exponential evolution in the usage of the Internet and mobile networks along with the demands for better quality of treatments within the transit networks have encouraged the researchers to think about and propose new techniques and networking solutions to improve the network performance. Also, in the field of artificial intelligence, the needs for human like, dynamic and intelligent solutions has led to enforce the efforts in studying the efficiency of integrating intelligent features based on intelligent agents and multi-agent systems in different domains like the study of the consumer behavior in a competitive market or the assistance of the drivers in finding the best road to destination and data management and retrieval.

In networking, agents - especially mobile agents - were introduced to collect information, to discover the network topology and control the global functioning of the network. Therefore, solutions introducing a high level of reasoning in network management and control are not yet available. This paper proposes a framework for test-

A. Aagesen et al. (Eds.): INTELLCOMM 2004, LNCS 3283, pp. 143–150, 2004.

ing high level of intelligence within telecommunication networks, based on the J-Sim simulation environment [1].

2 J-Sim

J-Sim [1] is an open, component-based, compositional simulation environment, built entirely in Java upon the notion of the autonomous component architecture. It is a truly platform-neutral, extensible, and reusable environment as a system is composed of individual components able to be plugged into a software system, even during execution.

J-Sim proposes an implementation of an abstract network model (INET) on the top of the component-based architecture. This model defines the generic structure of a node and several generic network components with their associated contracts. INET proposes an internal node structure of the hosts and routers in two layers, which are the Upper Protocol Layer (UPL) that contains transport, routing, signaling, and application protocol modules and the Core Service Layer (CSL) that provides a set of well-defined services, which are common in most network architectures, to modules in the UPL.

The J-Sim working group has also proposed an implementation of some techniques like DiffServ and Intserv and recently an implementation of both MPLS and active networks were proposed.

3 Intelligent Features

Traditionally, intelligent features are inspired from the artificial intelligence domain and based on the concepts of intelligent agents and multi-agent systems. Agents and multi-agents systems (MAS) are two innovative and interesting concepts for a great number of researchers in different domains like road traffic control, biologic and social phenomena simulations, industrial applications, and others.

Agents are characterized by their autonomy, their ability to interact with other peers and devices. They can learn, plan future tasks and are able to react and to change their behavior according to the changes in their environment.

A multi-agent system is a group of agents able to interact and cooperate in order to reach a specific objective.

3.1 Agents

The concept of agents has occupied great importance in the domain of Artificial Intelligence (AI) where different interpretations and definitions were associated to the word "Agent". [2] considers that agents are intelligent entities that act according to their knowledge. [3] defines agents as high-level autonomous entities able to act in an environment where other agents and devices execute and [4] considers an agent as a person managing an agency or something that initiates a chemical reaction or an organism that causes a disease. Finally [6] considers that all these definitions confirm that the question "what is an agent?" is as embarrassing as the question "what is the intelligence?". It is so better not to confine to one definition and to define an agent according to its field of application.

Agents are characterized by their properties that determine their capabilities. Different properties are defined – like autonomy, proactive-ness, flexibility, adaptability, ability to collaborate and coordinate tasks and mobility. The agent according to its role within its environment acquires one or some of these properties.

Different types of agents can be defined like reactive, cognitive, mobile, hybrid, collaborative and others. Each of these types is characterized by some properties like for example autonomy, mobility, reactivity, pro-activeness, and collaboration.

3.2 Multi-agent Systems

A multi-agent system is a group of agents defined as "a loosely-coupled network of problem solvers that work together to solve that problems that are beyond their individual capabilities" [7]. These problem solvers are agents and are defined as autonomous entities able of acting in their environment. They are able to communicate directly with other agents, posses their own resources, perceive their environment (but to a limited extent), and have a behavior [5]. In the frame of this communication, agents cooperate in order to insure coherent behavior within the MAS. This cooperation, according to [8], lets the agent know the objectives of a peer and therefore adopt these objectives as its proper objectives in order to improve the global behavior of the MAS.

3.3 Agents in Telecommunication Networks

In the last few years, the research efforts was increased in the domain of telecommunication to study the ability of new techniques based on agents – especially mobile agents – and multi-agent systems in designing networks and network applications;

[9] presents a mobile-agents approach, highly distributed and decentralized with agents spread across the network working to accumulate connectivity information. The agents in this system move around the network, discover topology information, and carry with them the information they have gathered as they explore. Results prove that the cooperation between the agents and the diversity of behaviors between collaborating agents greatly improve the performance of the whole system.

Other researchers like [10] and [11], have borrowed metaphors from biological systems to develop higher-level network management frameworks. These frameworks rely on the ability of social insects to solve problems, sometimes-difficult problems, in a distributed way, without a central control, on the basis of local information. [10] and [11] used these abilities for network control in a telecommunication network, specifically to get dynamic update of the routing tables of the network nodes according to the different nodes' loads.

3.4 Platforms Simulating Intelligent Features

Agents and MAS oriented programming is an advanced software-modeling paradigm proposed by researches in the distributed artificial intelligence domain. It addresses the need for software systems to exhibit rational, human-like behavior in different domains.

MAS platforms are characterized by their architectures able to build systems that work on the full range of tasks expected from an intelligent agent, from highly routine to extremely difficult, open-ended problems. They have the ability to represent and use appropriate forms of knowledge and a full range of problem solving methods. These types of platforms are goal-oriented, based on states and operators. They continually try to select and apply operators to states until the achievement of a specific goal.

Different platforms were proposed for multi-agent systems simulation like JAFMAS, DECAF, JACK, DEMAS and others, each having its proper implementation and fields of application.

4   The Proposed Model

To introduce the concept of agents and multi-agent systems within the J-Sim node model, we propose to extend it with an intelligent package. This package represents the intelligent aspect of the whole system and implements the various classes that may serve as the building blocks for specifying and communicating agents. This means that all the entities required in a standard environment for multi-agent systems simulation should be implemented. These entities are: the communication between agents, the agent's resources, data base and rule base, the social model, and the linguistic features, as shows fig. 1.

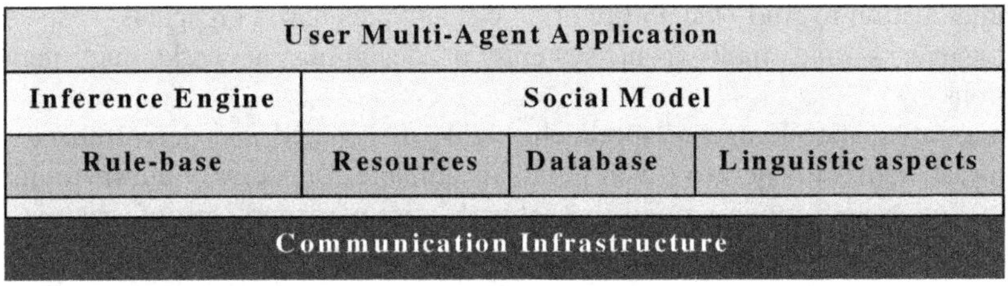

User Multi-Agent Application			
Inference Engine	Social Model		
Rule-base	Resources	Database	Linguistic aspects
Communication Infrastructure			

Fig. 1. Organization of the intelligent package

The user, according to its agents' type and behavior, defines the multi-agent system application. This application benefits from the services provided by the social model, which determines the way the agent communicates, cooperates and interacts with other agents of the system in order to bring about a coherent solution. During its communication, the agent exchanges messages using a common agent-independent language, defined by the Linguistic layer. In these messages, the agent exchanges resources and knowledge and then stores acquired data in the data model. To reason on this data, the agent implements a rule-base that contains the needed rules to decide about its future actions and invokes these rules using the inference engine.

Finally, we consider that the communication infrastructure is provided by the standard components proposed by J-Sim to connect and communicate different entities.

5   The Intelligent Package - Java Classes

We propose an implementation of the agent package in 18 main java classes that provide the essential elements and entities for the developers of intelligent applications within a telecommunication network. Five of these classes, related to the communication aspects, were originally taken from the multi-agent system platform JAFMAS, with some modifications to adapt them to our proposed model. The defined classes and the relationship between them are described in Fig. 2. It shows how the classes use each other's methods in order to build a coordinated framework.

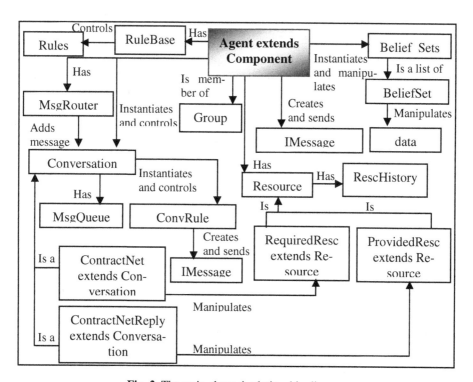

Fig. 2. The main classes' relationship diagram

The "Agent" class is implemented as an abstract component within J-Sim. This class provides the standard attributes and methods to be used by any agent type related to any possible application. It should be extended to define the agent related to a specific application. This agent requires interacting with different java classes in order to cooperate with other peers, to exchange messages and store data.

The social model is implemented in a list of java classes. The main are "Conversation" and "ConvRule". The linguistic aspect is mainly provided by the "IMessage" class that describes the format of the messages exchanged between the agents.

After the reception of a message, the agent treats it or directs it to its concerned conversation in case the message is sent in the context of a conversation between the agents. The "MsgRouter" java class is responsible of the routing of the received messages to their relative conversations. When the conversation receives a message, it stores it in its messages' queue using the "MsgQueue" class.

We consider that the agent may require communicating with other agents within the multi-agent system according to the Contract-Net protocol. For this reason, an implementation of this protocol was proposed in both the "ContractNet" and "ContractNetReply" classes.

The three java classes – "BeliefSet", "Belief_Sets" and "data" – are defined to manage and store data. An instance of the "Belief_Sets" class stores the different instances of a specific BeliefSet and provides methods to add, remove and query these instances and the data class defines the structure of an element of the BeliefSet.

The "Resources" class is an abstract java class that defines the common elements to the different types of resources. The "RequiredResc" and "ProvidedResc" classes that define respectively the elements and methods related to the required and provided resources extend this class and the user, to implement some methods according to the application requirements, should also extend the "RequiredResc" and "ProvidedResc" classes. The third class related to resources is the "RescHistory" class conceived to store the history of a resource.

The information concerning the different groups defined within the multi-agent system is stored in the "Group" class. This class extends the "Belief_Set" java class. Finally, the classes related to the representation and management of the production rules are "Rules" and "RuleBase".

6 Case Study

In this section we propose a case study integrating a multi-agent system within a transit network that provides different levels of treatments for different types of traffics, in the objective of preventing congestions.

In the following simulations we consider that two sources S1 and S2 send respectively to the destinations D1 and D2 traffics with two different levels of quality of services, where the traffic sent by S1 demands a higher level of quality of service than the traffic sent by S2. As both traffics transit the network (see Fig. 3), the S1 traffic is treated in priority to the S2 traffic in case of congestion. The implemented agent behavior tries to increase the S2 traffic throughput and to balance the traffic load within

Fig. 3. Global view of the network

the network, if congestions occur. The simulations' results show great increase in the throughput of the S2 traffic (see Fig. 5) if agents are integrated within the transit network.

In case agents are not integrated within the network, great loss of the S2 traffic is perceived as shows Fig. 4. Finally, Fig. 6 shows how the S1 traffic modifies its default road to destination due to a congested situation in one of the network's links. This behavior relieves the congestion and permits better use of the deployed resources within the network.

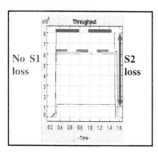

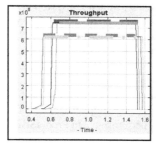

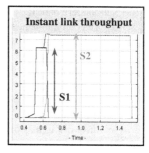

Fig. 4. Transit network without agent's integration

Fig. 5. The throughput of the S1 and S2 traffic after the agent's integration

Fig. 6. The throughput of the congested link. S1 is redirected to resolve the congestion

7   Conclusion

This paper presents our approach that builds an extension to the J-Sim simulation environment with intelligent capabilities. This extension provides an infrastructure for the validation of different techniques based on a high level of intelligence, in networking. Some applications integrating agents within different types of networks were tested using this extension [12], [13]. Simulations show great increase in the network performance after the integration of intelligent features. This means that our proposal could be considered as a first step towards both filling the gap between the artificial intelligence domain and networking and investigating intelligent capabilities in the world of telecommunications.

References

1. J-Sim team, Ohio State University, available at: www.J-Sim.org, updated 2004.
2. Demazeau Y. and Müller J.P.: Decentralized AI2. Editions North-Holland Elsevier Science B. V, 1991.
3. Shoham Y.: Agent Oriented Programming. Artificial Intelligence, 1993.
4. Minsky M., A conversation with Marvin Minsky, Communication of the ACM, 1994.
5. Ferber J.: Multi-Agent System: An Introduction to Distributed Artificial Intelligence. Harlow: Addison Wesley Longman, 1999.

6. Guessoum Z.: Un environnement opérationnel de conception et de réalisation de systèmes multi-agents. P.H.D. report, University of Paris VI, 1996.

7. Durfee E. H., Lesser V. and Corkill D. D.: Trends in cooperative distributed problem solving. IEEE transaction on knowledge and Data Engineering, vol. KDE-1, pp. 63-83, Mar 1989.

8. Gallier J.R.: Atheorical Framework for Computer Models of Cooperative Dialogue, Acknowledging Multi-Agent Conflict. P.H.D. report, Open University (UK), 1988.

9. Minar N., Kramer K and Maes P., "Cooperating Mobile Agents for Mapping Networks". In Proceedings of the First Hungarian National Conference on Agent Based Computing, May 24, 1998.

10. Schoonderwoerd R., Holland O., Bruten J. and Rothkrantz. L., "Ant-based Load Balancing in Telecommunications Networks. Adaptive Behavior", 5(2):169-207, available at: http://www-uk.hpl.hp.com/people/ruud/abc.html, 1997.

11. Bonabeau E., Henaux F., Guérin S., Snyers D., Kuntz P., and Theraulaz G., "Routing in Telecommunications Networks with "Smart" Ant-Like Agents". In Intelligent Agents for Telecommunications Applications'98, available at:
    http://www.santafe.edu/sfi/publications/Abstracts/98-01-003abs.html, 1998.

12. N. Meskaoui, D. Gaiti, K. Kabalan: Implementation of a multi-agent system within a Diffserv network to improve its performance. In Proc. ISE2003, Montreal, Canada July 2003.

13. N. Meskaoui,: A framework to model and simulate multi-agent systems within telecommunication networks: new environment, tools and behaviors. P.H.D. report, Paris 6 University, 2004. France.

Design Principles of a QoS-Oriented Transport Protocol

Ernesto Exposito[1], Michel Diaz[2], and Patrick Sénac[2,3]

[1] NICTA, NPC Program, Locked Bag 9013, Alexandria, NSW 1435, Australia
ernesto.exposito@nicta.com.au
[2] LAAS/CNRS, 7 avenue du Colonel Roche, 31077 Toulouse cedex 04. France
michel.diaz@laas.fr
[3] ENSICA, DMI 1 Place Emile Blouin 31056, Toulouse Cedex, France
patrick.senac@ensica.fr

Abstract. In this paper, the needs for specialized end-to-end communication services oriented to satisfy the QoS requirements of current and future multimedia applications are raised. Face to the complexity involved in the wide deployment of QoS guaranteed network services as well as the reduced set of services offered by traditional and recent transport protocols, a QoS-oriented transport protocol (QoSTP) is proposed as the adequate solution for common Internet users for next few years. The design of this QoSTP is based on a set of fundamental principles aimed at assuring the feasibly and efficient deployment of adequate mechanisms regarding the applications requirements. Experimental results demonstrate the feasibility and advantages of this proposal.

1 Introduction

Traditional and new generation of transport protocols have been designed taking into account only a subset of the QoS requirements of multimedia applications. Indeed, these protocols have been mainly focused to the implementation of congestion control mechanisms to save network resources (i.e. TCP, SCTP and DCCP) while providing full order and full reliability or non order and non reliability at all. Moreover, mechanisms intended to satisfy time constraints are not supported at the transport layer. A QoS oriented transport service based on the delay, jitter, throughput and synchronization constrains of multimedia applications and taking into account the partial order and partial reliability tolerance as well as the scalable characteristics of multimedia flows has not yet been provided. In addition, at the network layer, even if a lot of research aimed at the provision of end-to-end QoS guarantees has been carried out, today and for the next few years, the Best-Effort service will be the predominant and more accessible network service in Internet.

These are the reasons that led us to propose the design of a QoS-oriented transport protocol (QoSTP). This design has to be based on a set of fundamental principles aimed at assuring the feasibly and efficient deployment of adequate transport mechanisms regarding the applications requirements.

This paper is organized as follows. Next section introduces the design principles of this QoSTP. Sections 3 and 4 describe respectively the API and the mechanisms of

A. Aagesen et al. (Eds.): INTELLCOMM 2004, LNCS 3283, pp. 151–159, 2004.

QoSTP. Section 5 presents some experimental results. Finally, the conclusions and perspectives of this work are presented.

2 Design

The design of a QoSTP should answer the following fundamental questions:

- Application Programming Interface (API): how multimedia applications are going to communicate their QoS requirements to the transport protocol, minimizing application adaptation efforts?
- Mechanisms: which transport protocol mechanisms must be deployed to satisfy the application requirements taking into account the available resources and network services?

3 Transport Service API

The first design principle of a QoSTP is related to the facilities that have to be offered by its API to the multimedia applications. This API must offer enough expressiveness capabilities in order to allow new multimedia applications to explicitly specify their QoS requirements while preserving its backward compatibility with legacy applications. From the transport protocol point of view, the establishment/termination and transmission phases performed by the multimedia applications are translated in several transport services access points (TSAP): session control and media transmission.

- Session Control: Multimedia applications start establishing a session control connection. The messages exchanged over this connection can be very useful for the provision of QoS at the transport layer for the media flows participating in the session. For this reason, a QoSTP should provide session control service (i.e. fully ordered and fully reliable service), but in addition offering the possibility of mapping the application requirements to the adequate transport mechanisms. This connection allows preserving the backward compatibility with legacy multimedia applications which will use this service to establish, control and terminate multimedia sessions. Simultaneously, new multimedia applications could also use this connection to explicitly specify their QoS requirements. The preservation of compatibility with current applications and the offering of new specialized transport services could be assured using standard and opened specification techniques such as the XML-based language specifications [3, 4].
- Media Transmission: QoS Control and management mechanisms provided by the QoSTP will operate over the media flows exchanged by applications. These mechanisms require specific QoS information describing the packets composing the media flows (i.e. presentation time, importance degree, dependency, etc). In [2] some considerations for a new generation of protocols based on the Application Level Framing (ALF) concept have been presented. The ALF principle introduces the concept of "transfer syntax" as a mean to specify QoS-related information to every data packet to be transmitted. Currently, a description header preceding the payload of

every data packet is a usual way to convey this kind of QoS information between remote applications (i.e. multimedia applications implementing the RTP protocol).

4 Transport Mechanisms

Next paragraphs will present a detailed study related to the congestion control and the error control mechanisms intended to deduce the most adequate mechanisms to be provided by a QoSTP.

4.1 Congestion Control

The Internet protocol architecture is based on a connectionless end to end packet service using the IP protocol. These characteristics offer advantages in terms of flexibility and robustness, but a careful design is also required to provide good service under heavy load. In fact, lack of attention to the dynamics of packet forwarding can result in severe service degradation. This phenomenon is technically called congestion [8]. Network congestion is characterized by excessive delay and bursts of losses in delivering data packets. Congestion control mechanisms are intended to avoid network congestion and its consequences [7]. Some studies have been done in order to propose congestion control mechanisms adapted to the characteristics of multimedia applications [6]. One of these mechanisms is the TCP Friendly Rate Control or TFRC.

4.1.1 TCP Friendly Rate Control (TFRC)

TFRC is a source and model based congestion control mechanism that provides a TCP friendly sending rate while minimizing abrupt rate changes [9]. TFRC has been designed to be reasonably fair when competing for bandwidth with TCP flows. A flow is considered as being "reasonably fair" if its sending rate is generally within a factor of two of the sending rate of a TCP flow under the same conditions. Furthermore, TFRC has a much lower variation of throughput over time compared with TCP, which makes it more suitable for real-time multimedia applications. The sender sends a stream of data packets to the receiver at some rate. The receiver sends a feedback packet to the sender roughly once every round-trip time (RTT). Based on the information contained in the feedback packets, the sender adjusts its sending rate in accordance with the TCP throughput equation to maintain TCP-friendliness [8].

$$r = s / (R\ (2p/3)^{\wedge}(1/2) + 3RTO\ (3p/8)^{\wedge}(1/2)\ p\ (1+32p^{\wedge}2)\ )$$

Where r is the sending rate; s is the mean packet size; RTT is the round trip time; RTO is the retransmission timeout; and p is the loss event rate. If no feedback is received from the receiver in several RTTs, the sender halves its sending rate.

Currently, the TFRC can be considered as the most suitable congestion control mechanism to be implemented by a QoS oriented transport protocol. Indeed, the TCP model based characteristics, the minimization in the abrupt rate changes, as well as the error control independency are some of the required functionalities of a QoSTP. However, this mechanism uses a delaying policy to perform the rate control which could sometimes be non-compliant with delay-constrained multimedia applications (e.g. interactive applications). Next paragraphs introduce an enhancement to the TFRC congestion control mechanism.

4.1.2 QoS-Aware TFRC Congestion Control

The rate control mechanism of TFRC is based on a delaying policy aimed at adapting the flow to the allowed sending rate. This mechanism can penalize applications with strict delay constraints. Indeed, for these applications, received packet could be discarded if they arrive too late to be presented. An alternative to the delaying policy implemented by TFRC may be a quality adaptation policy. Quality adaptation mechanisms can be performed by applications (i.e. adaptive encoding, switching between multiple pre-encoded version, etc.). But usually these mechanisms are executed in long timescales. This proposal consists in performing quality adaptation at the transport level. This requires that QoS information describing the multimedia flows must be available at the transport layer. This information must include at least the time constraints associated to every ADU as well as specific QoS information aimed at performing the quality adaptation (i.e. ADU priorities, dependency, order, etc.). The delaying strategy of TFRC is based in the computation of the inter-packet interval time (IPIT) for every data packet to be transmitted. TFRC calculates this IPIT value as indicated in (1)

$$(1) \quad IPIT = s/r;$$
$$(2) \quad oneWayDelay = RTT/2$$
$$(3) \quad eDeliveryTimestamp = now + IPIT + oneWayDelay$$
$$(4) \quad eDeliveryTimestamp - timestamp > MAXDELAY$$

Where s is the packet size and r is the allowed sending rate. The IPIT value represents the time to be delayed the current data packet in order to respect the allowing sending rate. If the QoS information associated to data packets includes the delivery timestamp of every packet to the receiving application then the feasibility of this delaying strategy could be checked, taking into account the end-to-end delay of the applications. The one-way-delay must be known in order to perform this temporal validation. The one-way-delay can be estimated using the RTT as estimated in TFRC (2).

Using the oneWayDelay value, the delivery timestamp of the current data packet can be calculated as indicated in (3), where now is the current time. Data packet can be considered as obsolete by the receiving application if condition (4) is checked, where timestamp is the scheduled delivery timestamp and MAXDELAY expresses the delay tolerance of the application (i.e. 300 or 400 ms for interactive application).

These obsolete packets will be generally discarded by receiving applications. However, if the temporal validation is performed by the source, discarding could be anticipated in order to avoid the bandwidth being wasted. Nevertheless, this basic discarding policy could seriously affect the QoS perceived by the final user if important ADUs are discarded. For these reason, we propose the use of selective frame discarding methods based on ADU-related QoS information in order to optimize the QoS provided to the user while preserving network resources and respecting the application delay constraints. This selective frame discarding method can be applied if the medium has been encoded using specific compression and ADU segmentation techniques which facilitate the implementation of this method at the transport layer (i.e. ALF approach for the segmentation of flows such as MPEG, H.263, MJPEG, etc.).

The transport level quality adaptation strategy could be defined using the QoS description of the ADUs composing the multimedia flows. This information can be used to define a set of quality layers. For instance, for a MPEG flow composed by I, P and B images, 3 quality layers could be defined:

> Layer 2: I, P and B images
> Layer 1 only I and P images
> Layer 0: only I images

The definition of these different quality layers allow us to propose an enhancement to the TFRC algorithm intended provide a rate control compatible with the time constraints and the intrinsic characteristics of multimedia flows. Next algorithm describes this specialization of the TFRC mechanism:

```
currentLayer=0
join layer(currentLayer)
while (sessionIsActive) {
// When feedback received or noFeedBack timeout : estimate of TFRC parameters & compute r
// filtering
    If (currentPacket.layer>currentLayer) then currentPacket.discard=true
    else
      {
        IPIT = currentPacket.size / r; // inter-packets interval
        eDeliveryTimestamp  = (now + t_ipi + RTT/2 + delta) // estimation of time of data delivery
        eDelay = eDeliveryTimestamp  - currentPacket.timestamp // est. of presentation delay
        // quality adaptation action in response to the estimated delay
        if (eDelay <= MinDelayThreshold)  // i.e. 50 ms
            action=increase
      else (if eDelay >= MaxDelayThreshold)  // i.e. 400 ms
            action=decrease
        // quality adaption decrease action
        if (action==decrease)
            if (currentLayer==MIN_LAYER && eDelay <MinDELAY)
              { drop layer(currentLayer)
                STOP
              }
          else if (currentLayer> MIN_LAYER)
              {
                currentLayer=currentLayer-1;
                currentPacket.discard=true
              }
        // quality adaption increase action
        if (action==increase&&currentLayer< MAX_LAYER)
            currentLayer=currentLayer+1;
      }
    //scheduling of current packet transmission
    if not currentPacket.discard then  scheduleTransmission currentPacket,t_ipi
  }
```

Where now is the current time, RTT is the round trip time and delta is a tolerance constant including error in time estimations. In order to avoid abrupt changes in the QoS provided to the final user, quality layer increase and decrease actions have been proposed to be tailored by the MinDelayThreshold and MaxDelayThreshold obtained from the QoS requirements.

4.2 Error Control

Several multimedia applications present some preference for timeliness over order and reliability [12, 1, 11]. Actually, many of these applications do not require a fully ordered and fully reliable transport service when the delay incurred by this service is not compatible with their time constraints. For this reason, most of multimedia applications have been designed to use the UDP protocol without any guarantees of order and reliability. In some cases, these applications have to implement ad-hoc error control mechanisms to satisfy their requirements. In [5] different error control mechanisms based on the partial ordering and partial reliability constraints of multimedia flows and aimed at improving the QoS delivered to the multimedia applications have been proposed.

4.2.1 Partially Reliable, Differentiated and Time-Constrained ARQ

ARQ error control mechanisms work as follows: when a loss is detected, the receiver send a feedback message to ask the source to retransmit the message. This means that a retransmitted packet arrives at least three one-way trip times after the transmission of the original packet. Sometimes, this delay could exceed the delay constraints of the application. However, if the one-way trip time is short, this mechanism could be efficiently used to recover the losses. Time-constrained ARQ mechanisms can be implemented for unicast connections by source-based methods. This error control method is intended to avoid retransmissions of packets that will arrive too late to be presented. The retransmissions can be demanded by the receiver when losses are detected. The source will check the following condition before performing the retransmission:

If (now + RTT/2 < presentationTime) then Retransmission of packet

This mechanism can be easily implemented by the source if QoS information related to the time presentation is available at the transport layer. Indeed this method can be used to provide a differentiated and partially reliable service taking into account the notion of differentiated layers previously introduced. Furthermore, this mechanism could work in combination with the QoS-aware TFRC congestion control and a partially ordered mechanism controlled by the receiver to provide the specialized QoSTP services.

4.3 QoS Transport Mechanisms

This section has presented a proposal including a set of transport mechanisms to be implemented by a QoSTP (see figure 1).

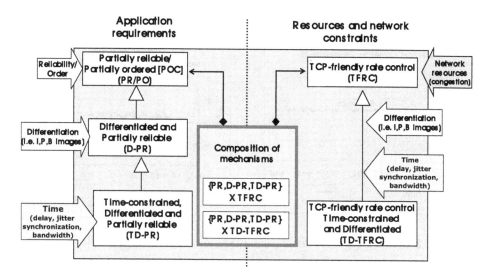

Fig. 1. Transport mechanisms to by provided by the QoSTP

These mechanisms include a congestion control mechanism intended to preserve the resources of networks providing a Best-Effort service. An error control mechanism intended to provide a partially ordered and partially reliable service explicitly or implicitly configured from the application requirements has also been presented. This error control mechanism has also been enhanced in order to provide a differentiated and partially reliable service. Both error and congestion control mechanisms have been enhanced to take into account intrinsic application time constraints. Furthermore, the composition of error and congestion control mechanisms provides a large set of transport services for different multimedia applications. Next section presents some experiments intended to evaluate the QoSTP services.

5 Experiments

In [5] several experiments involving interactive and Video on Demand (VoD) applications have been carried out to validate different transport service specifications and to evaluate the protocol performance. In this paper, the experiments intended to evaluate the congestion control mechanisms will be shown. These experiments have been carried out using streaming applications with specific time constrains and using a Java-based QoSTP implementation following the UML 2.0 specification presented in [5]. In these experiments, Best Effort network services have been emulated using the Dummynet emulator [10]. The emulation scenarios have been characterized by one-way delay of 50 ms and specific bandwidth limitations. This emulation based on bandwidth limitation is intended to create temporal network congestion (i.e. when application sending rate is higher than limited bandwidth).

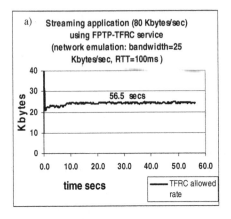
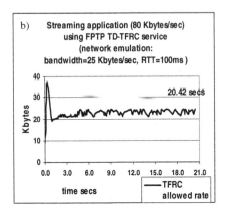

Fig. 2. TFRC vs TD-TFRC mechanisms with bandwidth limited to 25 Kbytes/sec

A first experiment involving a streaming application producing a multimedia flow of 80 Kbytes/sec (i.e. H.263 video flow composed by I and P pictures) during 20 seconds and with network bandwidth limited to 25 Kbytes/sec has been carried out. The conformance of the standard TFRC congestion control mechanisms implemented by QoSTP has been validated (i.e. sending rate according TFRC specification). However, the time required to complete the transmission under this emulated network scenario was of 56.5 seconds with an accumulated delay of 36.5 secs. (see figure 2.a). This delay is not admissible either for interactive or VoD time-constrained applications. In contrast, the time constrained and differentiated specialization of this mechanism (TD-TFRC) mechanism was able to adapt the video flow using the selective discarding policy (i.e. by taking advantage of partial reliability tolerance) in order to respect time constraints as shown in figure 2.b. These results show the advantages of providing adequate congestion control mechanisms for the transmission of scalable media flows with specific time constraints.

6 Conclusions and Perspectives

In this paper the main principles aimed at designing a QoSTP have been presented. The API of the QoSTP has been defined as an enhancement of standard BSD socket interface including session and media control connections. On one hand, the session control connection allows preserving the backward compatibility with legacy multimedia applications which will use this service to establish, control and terminate their multimedia sessions. Moreover, new multimedia applications could also use this connection to explicitly specify their QoS requirements related to the multimedia flows. On the other hand, media connections are intended to provide QoS Control and management mechanisms to operate over the media flows exchanged by applications.

The transport mechanisms to be implemented by a QoSTP have also been proposed. These mechanisms include standard congestion and error control mechanisms. Both mechanisms have been enhanced to take into account intrinsic media flow requirements and time constraints. Experimental results have demonstrated that a QoS oriented transport protocol implemented over a Best Effort network service can largely improve the QoS offered to multimedia applications. Future works to develop adequate mechanisms intended to take into account specialized communication services such as guaranteed network services should be done. Likewise, the specialization of current transport mechanisms in order to take into account specific network characteristics such as mobility, wireless and satellite networks will be carried out.

References

1. Amer, P., Chassot, C., Connolly, C., Conrad, P., Diaz, M.: Partial Order Transport Service for MM and other Appli. IEEE/ACM Trans. on Networking, vol.2, n5 (1994)
2. D. Clark and D. Tennenhouse, "Architectural considerations for a new generation of protocols", IEEE SIGCOMM'90, Sept. 1990
3. E. Exposito, M. Gineste, R. Peyrichou, P. Sénac, M. Diaz, S. Fdida, "XML QoS specification language for enhancing communication services", 15th International Conference on Computer Communication (ICCC'2002), Mumbai (India), August 2002
4. E. Exposito, M. Gineste, R. Peyrichou, P. Sénac, Michel Diaz, "XQOS: XML-based QoS specification language", MMM'03 The 9th International Conference on Multi-Media Modeling, January 7-10, 2003, Taiwan.
5. E. Exposito, "Specification and implementation of a QoS oriented transport protocol for multimedia applications", PhD dissertation, Institut National Polytechnique de Toulouse. December 2003, Toulouse, France.
6. S. Floyd and K. Fall, "Promoting the use of end-to-end congestion control in the Internet," IEEE/ACM Transactions on Networking, vol. 6, Aug. 1999
7. V. Jacobson, "Congestion avoidance and control", ACM SIGCOMM'88, pp. 314-329, Aug. 1988.
8. Floyd S., "Congestion Control Principles", IETF Request for Comments 2914, September 2000
9. Handley M. et al, "TCP Friendly Rate Control (TFRC): Protocol Specification", IETF RFC 3448, 2003
10. Rizzo L., "Dummynet: a simple approach to the evaluation of network protocols", ACM Computer Communication Review, Vol. 27, no. 1, January 1997
11. Luis Rojas-Cardenas, Emmanuel Chaput, Laurent Dairaine, Patrick Sénac, Michel Diaz, Video Transport Over Partial Order Connections,in Computer Networks and ISDN Systems, vol. 31, Issue 7, Elsevier, April, 1999, pp. 709-725
12. Sénac P., Exposito E., Diaz M., "Towards a New Generation of Generic Transport Protocols", Lecture Notes in Computer Science 2170, Springer, Eds. S.Palazzo, September 2001

Inferring Presence in a Context-Aware Instant Messaging System

Mikko Perttunen and Jukka Riekki

Department of Electrical and Information Engineering and Infotech Oulu,
P.O.BOX 4500, 90014 University of Oulu, Finland
{Mikko.Perttunen, Jukka.Riekki}@ee.oulu.fi

Abstract. The increasing volume of digital communication is raising new challenges in the management of the information flow. We discuss the usage of context to infer presence information automatically for instant messaging applications. This results in easy-to-use applications and more reliable presence information. We suggest a new model, context relation, for representing the contexts that are relevant for inferring presence. The key idea is to represent both the communication initiator's and the receiver's contexts. The model allows sophisticated control over presence information. We describe a fully functional prototype utilizing context relations.

1 Introduction

Instant messaging (IM) has proved its usefulness: its popularity is growing fast, and it has been introduced into corporate use as well. Due to the increasing importance of IM as a method of everyday interpersonal communication, the volume of messages and simultaneous messaging sessions will increase. This development may lead to excessive interruptions on the user's other tasks [1]. The problem can be solved by reducing the attention required from the user to manage the messaging.

IM has been described as "near-synchronous computer-based one-on-one communication" [2]. It is said to consist of two components: synchronicity and presence awareness. Synchronicity refers to real-time information transfer [3]. We define *presence* as the ability and willingness of a user to communicate with other users. This meaning has lately been designated as *availability* [4,5], but we prefer to speak about *presence* in a broad sense to cover the user's situation more extensively than just in terms of online status [6,7]. For example, presence information can define the user to be at her desk or to be currently typing a message [3]. Presence-awareness means that presence information is used to decide whether communication with a user can be initiated. This information can be used by the user about to initiate communication, or the IM application can deliver instant messages only to users with appropriate presence status.

In current IM applications, the users must update their presence information manually. For example, when a user enters a meeting room, she must remember to set her presence as *unavailable*. IM applications would be easier to use, if the updating of presence information were automatic. Such updating could be more reliable as well,

A. Aagesen et al. (Eds.): INTELLCOMM 2004, LNCS 3283, pp. 160–174, 2004.

since the users would not need to remember to manually set their presence. Further, more reliable presence information would eliminate unsuccessful attempts at communication, which unnecessarily interrupt the recipient and frustrate the initiator. Such automatic updating can be achieved by recognizing the user's context and inferring her presence from that. In the above example, a *meeting* context would be recognized, and presence would be automatically changed to *unavailable*.

This article shows how presence information can be updated automatically. Our main contribution is to use the contexts of both the recipient and the initiator in inferring the recipient's presence. In the work reported by others, only the context of the recipient has been used. We formalize the concept as a *context relation*. We describe a fully functional prototype IM system to demonstrate this approach.

We adopted the instant messaging terms presented in RFC 2778 [8]. In the general discussion, we map these terms in a simple IM system consisting of a separate IM application for each user and one server. *Presentity* (i.e. presence entity) and *watcher* are mapped into the IM application's roles. Hence, a presentity is an IM application providing its user's presence information to other IM applications. A watcher, in turn, is an IM application receiving other users' presence information. We postpone the discussion of the implementation of such functionality to the section presenting the prototype. Furthermore, the users are also called presentities and watchers according to their roles at the different phases of instant messaging.

The rest of the paper is organized as follows. In section 2 we list related work. In section 3 we describe context-aware instant messaging and the context relation. Section 4 presents our application prototype. It is followed by a discussion of the findings in section 5.

2   Related Work

In this chapter, we present the related work on IM and context. We adopted Dey's definitions of context and context-awareness [9]:

> *Context is any information that can be used to characterize the situation of an entity. An entity is a person, place, or object that is considered relevant to the interaction between a user and an application, including the user and applications themselves.*

> *A system is context-aware if it uses context to provide relevant information and/or services to the user, where relevancy depends on the user's task.*

Peddemors et al [7] presented a system which (among its other features) allows users to set rules that cause the system to update their presence to a certain value when they are at a certain location. They also state that presence can be interpreted as part of the context of a user. The statement is reasonable, because presence information indicates the user's current situation, sometimes also activity, which fits Dey's definition.

Ranganathan et al [10] developed ConChat, an IM system that automatically gives users cues about the context of their contacts. They also note the usability of context in avoiding semantic conflicts. ConChat, for example, automatically tags the currency of the sender's country when discussing money.

Tang and Begole [11] describe an IM system called Lilsys, which utilizes ambient sound, phone usage, and computer activity to infer the availability of a user. The Awarenex system [12] uses such parameters as location and current calendar events to give cues about a user's presence. Related to their work with the Awarenex prototype, the researchers also developed algorithms to detect and model patterns of availability and unavailability over time. They integrated the work with the Awarenex prototype and demonstrated that the system can predict, for example, the time when a person comes back from lunch [13].

When a user is typing on a computer, she may be performing some task requiring concentration. When she has not typed for a while, almost every instant messaging application updates the user's presence to *unavailable* by monitoring the keyboard and mouse activity. This is sometimes contradictory [11].

Voida et al identified contradictory user requirements in IM. For example, people want IM to be both asynchronous, in order to be able to be involved in many communication threads simultaneously, and synchronous, to get a prompt reply. Furthermore, they studied user expectations about context. They noticed, among other things, that the initiator of communication, despite the availability of the recipient, still wanted to query the recipient's context in the first message [14].

3   Improving Presence Inference with Context Relations

In IM, a message can be sent when the recipient is logged in to the system and her presence is *available*. This is interpreted by the sender as willingness of the recipient to receive messages and to respond to them in a timely manner. To avoid disturbance, a user can manually select to be *unavailable*. Because presence gives such an implication to the sender, it is important that the presence information provides maximally reliable information of the recipient's situation. The correctness of presence reduces unsuccessful communication attempts.

To be easy to use, the application should be able to update the presence of the user without the user's intervention. This also increases the reliability of the presence information, providing that the user might sometimes forget to update it. Presence updating should be based on automatic context recognition and function according to rules accepted by the user.

Automatic updating of presence can be achieved in two ways. First, only the context of the presentity can be used in inferring her presence to the watchers. In this case, the watcher's context has an effect only if it is part of the context of the presentity. The second way of inferring presence will be discussed in more detail later in this chapter.

The first way of inferring presence is illustrated in Figure 1. User B is the presentity and User A is the watcher. User A has subscribed User B's presence information. User B's context change triggers presence inference, and User A is notified of the new presence of User B. Inferring is done using User B's context-based presence rules.

Figure 2 shows how presence is inferred from user preferences and context information. Boxes denote data and circles functions. User preferences define the user's important locations, e.g. home and office. The context information used in the inference should be designed, as for any context-aware application, to best suit the needs in modeling the user's situations. Here, we use activity and place as examples in our illustrations. For example, the user might select a rule "When my activity is *conference*, I'm *unavailable*".

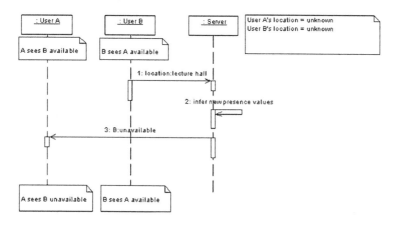

Fig. 1. Context-based inference of presence

Generally, the presence function in Figure 2 takes context as input and yields a presence value. Because both activity and place are derived from location, the rules may give conflicting values for presence. For example, a meeting could be scheduled to take place in the user's own office, in which case the activity could be *meeting* and the place *office*. This situation can be handled by defining activity as the higher-priority context. Thus, only when the user's activity is unknown is the place used to derive presence.

The above way of automatically updating presence easily leads to the following situation. User A and User B are both in the same lecture hall in a conference and find each other to be *unavailable*. However, for two friends, it would be natural be to be able to communicate and to exchange comments about the presentations. The desired scenario is illustrated in Figures 3 and 4: when User A enters the same lecture hall as User B, they are able to communicate. Such functionality can be achieved with the second way of inferring presence, context relation-based inference, which is discussed next.

In Figures 3 and 4, User A has User B on her contact list. User A has thus subscribed the presence changes of User B. Similarly, User B has User A on her contact list. At the beginning of the scenario illustrated in Figure 3, User B's context (location) changes, which causes the system to infer a new presence value for User B and to deliver it to the watcher, i.e. User A. This is straightforward for any context-aware IM system. The novelty of context relations suggested in this article is that the watcher's context has an effect on the presence of the presentity. Hence, a new presence value is inferred for User A as a reaction to the new context of User B. Figure 4 shows similar actions taken when User A's context changes. Consideration of the watcher's context enables the presence of User B to change when the context of User

A changes. At the end of the scenario shown in Figure 4, the users A and B see each other as *available* and are thus able to communicate.

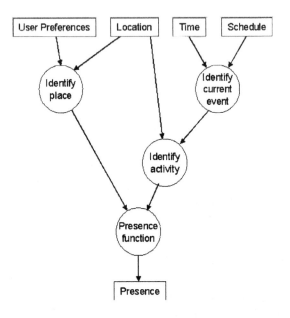

Fig. 2. Inferring presence from context and user preferences

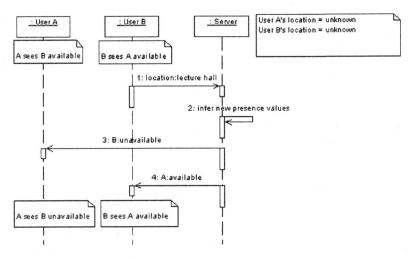

Fig. 3. Context relation-based inference of presence: User B goes into a lecture hall. User A sees User B as *unavailable* and User B sees User A as *available*

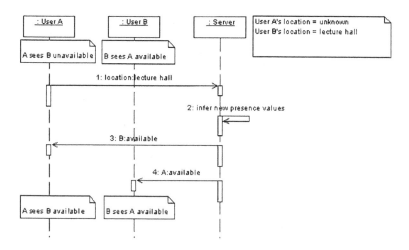

Fig. 4. Context relation-based inference of presence: User A goes into the same lecture hall where User B is already present. As a result, they see each other as *available*

We define the context pair (watcher, presentity) as a *context relation*. In IM, a context relation is established between two users when one adds the other on to her contact list. The contexts related by a context relation can be represented as:

$(context_w, context_p)$

where,

$context = context\ value,$
$p = presentity = user,$
$w = watcher = user\ or\ a\ group.$

In the above example, the user denotes an individual user of the IM system. The group denotes two or more users grouped together in the IM system. A wildcard *any* can be applied instead of a context value in the above expression. The number of context relations for a (watcher, presentity) pair is not constrained; there can be as many relations as are required to achieve the desired context-aware behavior. Furthermore, the watcher's context value refers to an individual user's context even when the watcher is a group. Groups are used to minimize the number of relations and rules needed to implement context-sensitive presence updating.

Context relations are used to form context relation-based rules that are controlled by the presentity. A rule for inferring presence from a context relation can be represented as:

$(context_w, context_p) \rightarrow presence_p.$

A wildcard *any* can be applied instead of a watcher or a context value in the above expression. A rule for *any* watcher is used when there are no specific rules for the watcher in question. Further, *any* context matches all contexts. It can be used, for example, to specify that, for a specific context of a presentity, a certain presence is to be inferred no matter what the watcher's context is.

The presence of a user is inferred separately for each watcher as follows: First, those rules for this (watcher, presentity) pair are triggered where the context values match the presentity's and the individual watcher's contexts. A rule for a watcher group is triggered if the individual watcher belongs to that group. Second, one rule of the triggered rules is selected (based on the rule priorities) and fired, resulting in a new presence value. The rules are owned by the presentities. Hence, the rules are used to control what presence the watchers see.

When the context of a presentity changes, the presence must be updated in two different ways:

1. *For each watcher, infer the new presence of the presentity according to the presentity's context relation rules.*
2. *For each contact, infer the new presence of the contact according to the contact's context relation rules.*

Context relations and rules can be illustrated by the example shown in Figure 5. James has the users Peter, Diana, and David on his contact list, which means that he is watching these three users. Sarah and Diana are watching James' presence (i.e. they have James on their contact lists). Now, James might have the following rules:

$$(office_{Sarah}, office_{James}) \rightarrow available_{James}$$

$$(any_{all}, office_{James}) \rightarrow unavailable_{James}$$

Let's assume that James' place changes to *office*. The system performs the steps 1 and 2 defined above. In step 1, James' rules are applied to infer James' presence for the watchers Diana and Sarah. For Sarah (assuming her context is *office*), both rules are triggered, but the first is fired as it has higher priority. There is no rule for Diana, so the rule for the group *all* is triggered and fired, because Diana is a member of this group. Further, the context *any* in the rule matches Diana's recognized context (even if the context is unknown). As a result, Sarah can communicate with James, but Diana cannot.

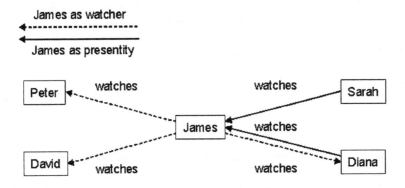

Fig. 5. Users as presentities and watchers

In step 2, we go through the contacts on James' contact list. Taking Peter as an example, the system would now find all the rules (not shown) for the presentity Peter. Then, a specific rule for the watcher James (or a group to which James belongs) would be searched and fired. This example illustrates how groups can be used to specify presence for the individual watchers that have no specific rules. The groups can be general, i.e. seen by many users, or a user can create groups for herself and specify the rules for those groups.

To further illustrate these issues, the steps 1 and 2 above are shown as a simple algorithm in Figure 6. In the figure, the watcher list is a list of watchers of a presentity. Furthermore, the Tables 1 and 2 show an example of how the contexts of a watcher and a presentity connected by a context relation can be represented. Each cell contains the resulting presence for a pair of context values (watcher, presentity), and each cell thus specifies a rule. The tables have a row for each context value of the watcher and a column for each context value of the presentity. Separate tables or rows are required for each separate watcher for which rules are defined.

Table 1. Presence rule table for context type activity for inferring presence from a context relation

		PRESENTITY'S ACTIVITY	
		CONFERENCE	UNKNOWN
WATCHER'S	CONFERENCE	AVAILABLE	AVAILABLE
ACTIVITY	UNKNOWN	UNAVAILABLE	AVAILABLE

Table 2. Presence rule table for context type place for inferring presence from a context relation

		PRESENTITY'S PLACE		
		OFFICE	HOME	UNKNOWN
	OFFICE	AVAILABLE	UNAVAILABLE	UNAVAILABLE
WATCHER'S	HOME	UNAVAILABLE	AVAILABLE	AVAILABLE
PLACE	UNKNOWN	AVAILABLE	AVAILABLE	AVAILABLE

In these tables, the value *unknown* may denote that the data is not available because of access control issues. It could also be interpreted as a place or activity that the system cannot recognize. The rules in Table 2 specify, for example, that when the user is at home, watchers at the office see her as *unavailable*, while watchers at home see her as *available*.

Although the context relation-based rules are applied automatically, the user can explicitly specify her presence (possibly for each watcher separately) at any given moment. The system may provide this option in two ways: First, the user can select her presence, as in an ordinary IM application, from a menu. Second, the user may be able to specify a rule "In the current context I'm *unavailable* for all users". This is semi-automatic context-based presence: the user manually selects the rule, and thus her presence, for the time being, but the presence is automatically updated according to changes in context. In the example, the user-defined rule determines the presence for the time the context remains the same. When the context changes, that rule is deactivated and automatic presence updating continues.

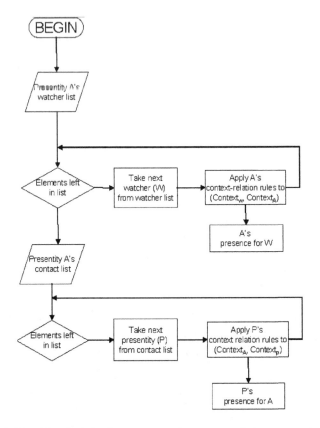

Fig. 6. Algorithm for inferring presence when a presentity's context changes

4 Application

4.1 Capnet System

The Capnet (Context-Aware and Pervasive Networks) program focuses on context-aware mobile technologies for ubiquitous computing. At the highest level, the Capnet architecture is decomposed into Capnet Engines, see Figure 7. Each device that belongs to the Capnet universe contains an engine. An engine may be in a powerful server without any user interface or in a mobile device with many application interfaces (UIs). As Capnet is a component-based software architecture, the basic building blocks of the engines are component instances, each specialized for producing the functionality of a certain domain area, such as service discovery, user interface, context recognition, media processing, connectivity management, component management, database access, or any service added to the system by developers. The Capnet universe is a distributed environment, which means that the engines can use component instances running on the local device as well as remote instances running in engines somewhere in the Capnet universe to provide the required functionality for the applications.

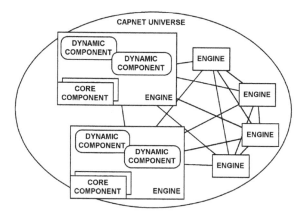

Fig. 7. Capnet universe

Considering the design of an IM system, the distribution shown in Figure 7 gives a natural starting point. As the users of IM are distributed in the network (using mobile devices or many different desktops), each engine in Figure 7 can be seen as a device hosting the IM application of a user. Considering the natural connectivity of the engines, the Capnet architecture seems well suited for developing an IM application.

The context components provide abstraction of context information for its consumers in the Capnet universe. Context components receive sensor data from a number of sensors and use the data to infer higher-level context information that is utilizable by the other Capnet components.

4.2 Design and Implementation

The context-aware instant messaging system was developed on the existing Capnet system. Below, we will describe the Capnet IM system briefly, without going into details of implementation.

The IM system is composed of the components shown in Figure 8. In Capnet, the schedule information comes from a calendar application, while the location information is provided by a location sensor component. The context components receive sensor data and infer contexts from it.

In our current implementation, automatic presence inference is performed by the IM component, which receives context information from the context component. In the next version, we plan to update the context component to provide presence information as well. The context types *activity* and *place*, as shown in the Tables 1 and 2, are used in inferring presence. The inference is done using hard-coded rules common for all users; explicit representation of these rules is one challenge for further research. There are rules for the groups *co-workers*, *family*, and *other*. The group used for presence inference is defined by the group of the watcher on the contact list of the presentity. If the watcher is not on the contact list of the presentity, then the group *other* is used for presence inference. A better way would be to show the watcher list for the presentity and to allow her to group the watchers.

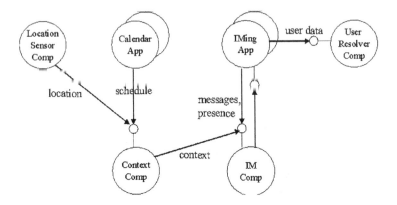

Fig. 8. Software components of the prototype IM system

If a user sets her presence manually, the application instance reports the value to the IM component, which delivers the information to the watchers. The messages travel through the IM component from application to application. The user resolver component is used to resolve users by their name and to fetch user data by the user ID. Unique email-like identifiers identify users, and an identity is associated with a user when she logs into the Capnet system.

Only the UI component is required to be executing in the thin terminal, e.g. a PDA, while the other component instances may be run on any device running a Capnet engine, i.e. on a network on some server.

4.3   Test Environment and Testing

The mobile device, Compaq iPAQ PDA, is equipped with WLAN cards and IBM's J9 virtual machine. All mobile device components are implemented according to the PersonalJava 1.2a specification. Devices are located with the Ekahau positioning engine that utilizes WLAN signal strengths measured in the devices. The university's premises covered by WLAN are used as the test environment. All inter-device communications utilize XML-RPC; the open-source Marquee XML-RPC library is used.

We demonstrated the system with two users according to the scenarios in the Figures 3 and 4. The users were using the PDAs described above. A smart living room environment was configured to be the home for the users, a meeting room to be the lecture hall in the scenarios and an office in our premises to be the office for the user. Also, we added an event occurring in the meeting room into the calendars of both users.

When a user entered the meeting room, the Capnet system recognized the context change, allowing the IM system to infer a new presence for the user. In the case of two co-workers present in the same meeting room, the system successfully utilized context relation to infer them as *available* for each other. Overall, the system functioned as shown in the scenario in Figures 3 and 4.

Below, we present two screen shots of the Pocket PC screen captured via Microsoft's Remote Display Control for Windows CE. Figure 9 shows the contact list view and a view of an ongoing chat of the IM application prototype. On the contact list, the user sees the presence of her contacts and the group that she has selected for each contact when entering it.

Fig. 9. Views from the IM application prototype. Left: Contact list view. Right: Chat view

From the screen shown on the left in Figure 9, one-to-one messaging can be started by selecting a user from the contact list and clicking the 'Chat' button. A single one-to-many message can be sent by selecting users from the contact list and clicking the 'Post' button. In both cases, the selected users must be *available*. In ongoing chats, the presence of the participants may change to *unavailable* at any time, but the communication can still continue. When inferring presence, the system also generates a textual description of the reason for resulting presence value specific to each context relation. Clicking the 'Show' button displays the description of the selected user.

5 Discussion

We introduced context relation as a new concept in context-aware instant messaging. The key idea is to utilize both the communication initiator's and the receiver's contexts in inferring presence. We presented an IM prototype that utilizes context relations to update users' presence information automatically. Automatic updating enables user-friendly IM applications with reliable presence updating. It reduces disruptions by minimizing the number of communication attempts by others when the user is not willing to communicate. Furthermore, utilization of context relations in automatic updating allows sophisticated control over the presence information delivered to others.

Being a new concept, context relation requires further research. Preliminary experiments show that the use of context relations in inferring presence may improve the user experience of IM applications, but this should be studied in more detail. Furthermore, a clear way to visualize the context relations and the rules would facilitate the creation and modification of personal relations and rules. Moreover, introducing more versatile contexts may require modifications of the context relation model we presented. Context relations could be used in other awareness applications as well, as awareness generally means knowing the activities of others [15].

Although we allow groups as watchers in the rules, the resulting context relations are one-to-one relations between two users. However, it would be possible to extend the relations to one-to-many. For example, the user could set a rule: "When my *co-workers* are having a *coffee break* and I am *working*, remind me about the coffee break". A separate threshold could specify the number of group members that are required to have a coffee break before the group context is set to *coffee break*. Similarly, we could allow presentity groups. For example, a system with the predefined groups *patients*, *nurses,* and *doctors* might set the presence of a nurse to *available* for patients when the nurse is at her desk and no doctor is near her (i.e. discussing with her). In this example, it is assumed that all patients and doctors are watchers of the nurses.

As automatic context recognition is such a challenging topic, systems providing automatic presence updating still need to support manual presence selection as well. Furthermore, the system could learn the manual selections – when a user selects the same presence in the same context repeatedly, the system could suggest automatic setting of presence. The routine learning methods presented in [16] could be used in learning the presence rules. It would be important that the user could control the learning, deciding which rules would be accepted and which rejected. Even when there is no learning, the user should be able to specify whether she wants to confirm the automatic presence changes, or if the new presence is applied without confirmation.

A context-aware instant messaging system should utilize the contexts of its users by all reasonable means. The other prototypes described in chapter 2 have demonstrated the feasibility of utilizing context in IM in various ways. The ConChat [10] prototype does well in enriching IM communication with context information. Awarenex provides awareness information on whether the contacts are having phone calls, are engaged in other IM discussions, or have a scheduled calendar event going on [12]. The Capnet IM system did not aim to enrich communications or to provide more awareness information, although we consider them equally important as reliable presence inferring for an IM system. As an addition to the features of Awarenex, Begole et al also demonstrated the prediction of availability from presence history data [13]. The routine learning methods discussed above could be used to predict presence as well. Predicted presence could be used in automatic presence inference when, for example, there is not enough information to infer presence from context.

Lilsys [11] infers user's availability from sensor data, such as sound, phone usage, and computer activity. Using inferred availability, the system gives cues to other users as 'neutral', 'possibly unavailable', or 'probably unavailable'. The system utilizes a wider range of sensor data than our prototype. The Capnet IM prototype aims for better presence inference by utilizing the context relation. The conceptual representation of the context relation enables the application of sophisticated rules to presence inference.

Dourish and Bellotti point out a problem in awareness: the appropriateness of information about a person's activity at a given time for a receiver depends on the receiver's needs [15]. This problem could be alleviated in a context-aware IM system by choosing the exposed context information about a user to a receiver based on the receiver's context. For example, more context information could be exposed about the users involved in the currently most active instant messaging session than about passive users on the contact list.

Although we did not discuss or implement any security or privacy issues, we want to mention that context relation also has implications for these design issues. Basically, the user must have control over who can access her presence, or context, information. Privacy in presence awareness systems has been studied widely, for example in [6].

In addition to security and privacy, instant messaging standards [17] need to be considered in future work. Another future topic might be representation of the context relation-based presence rules by RDF. As a conclusion, we have demonstrated the advantages of context relations and the rules applied to them. We will continue to develop the concept.

Acknowledgments

This work was funded by the National Technology Agency of Finland. The authors would like to thank all the personnel in the Capnet program, and the participating companies.

References

1. Cutrell E., Czerwinski M. and Horvitz E. (2001) Notification, disruption, and memory: Effects of messaging interruptions on memory and performance. INTERACT 2001 Conference Proceedings. IOS Press, IFIP, 263-269.
2. Nardi, B., Whittaker, S., & Bradner, E. (2000) Interaction and Outeraction: Instant messaging in action. Proceedings of the ACM Conference on Computer Supported Cooperative Work (CSCW 2000), New York, USA, 2000, 79-88.
3. Bradbury, D. (2001) Pigeon post for the 21st century. Computer Weekly, 2001 October 18, 1–6.
4. Fogarty, J., Lai, J., and Christensen, J. (in press) Presence versus Availability: The Design and Evaluation of a Context-Aware Communication Client. To appear in International Journal of Human-Computer Studies (IJHCS).
5. Greene, D., O'Mahony, D. (2004) Instant Messaging & Presence Management in Mobile Ad-Hoc Networks. In Proc. of the IEEE Annual Conference on Pervasive Computing and Communications Workshops (PERCOMW'04). Orlando, USA, March 14-17, 2004.
6. Godefroid, P., Herbsleb, J.D., Jagadeesan, L.J., Du Li. (2000) Ensuring Privacy in Presence Awareness Systems: An Automated Verification Approach. In Proc. of the ACM Conference on Computer Supported Cooperative Work (CSCW 2000). Philadelphia, USA, Dec. 2000, 59-68.

7. Peddemors, A.J.H., Lankhorst, M.M., de Heer, J. (2002) Combining presence, location and instant messaging in a context-aware mobile application framework. GigaMobile/D2.8 (TI/RS/2002/068) Telematica Instituut Enschede. https://doc.telin.nl/dscgi/ds.py/Get/File-21982/PLIM_d28.pdf

8. Day, M., Rosenberg, J., Sugano, H. (2000) A Model for Presence and Instant Messaging. RFC 2778, IETF.

9. Dey, A.K., Abowd, G.D. (1999) Towards a Better Understanding of Context and Context-Awareness, College of Computing, Georgia Institute of Technology, Atlanta GA USA, 1999, Technical Report GIT-GVU-99-22.

10. Ranganathan, A., Campbell, R.H., Ravi, A., Mahajan, A. (2002) ConChat: A Context-Aware Chat Program. IEEE Pervasive computing, Volume: 1 , Issue: 3.

11. Tang, J.C., Begole, J. (2003) Beyond Instant Messaging. ACM Queue 2003 November, Volume 1, Issue 8.

12. Tang, J., Yankelovich, N., Begole, J., Van Kleek, M., Li, F., Bhalodia, J. (2001) ConNexus to Awarenex: Extending awareness to mobile users. In Proc SIGCHI Conference on Human Factors in Computing Systems (CHI 2001). Seattle, USA, 2001, 221-228.

13. Begole, J. B., Tang, J. C. and Hill, R. (2003) Rhythm Modeling, Visualizations, and Applications. Proceedings of the ACM Symposium on User Interface Software and Technology (UIST 2003). Vancouver, Canada, 2003, 11-20.

14. Voida, A., Newstetter, W. C., Mynatt, E. D. (2002) When Conventions Collide: The Tensions of Instant Messaging Attributed. Proceedings of the SIGCHI Conference on Human Factors in Computing Systems (CHI 2002) Minneapolis, USA, 2002, 187-194.

15. Dourish, P. and Bellotti, V. (1992) Awareness and Coordination in Shared Workspaces. Proceedings of the ACM Conference on Computer Supported Cooperative Work (CSCW'92). Toronto, Ontario, Canada, 1992, 107-114.

16. Pirttikangas, S., Riekki, J., Porspakka, S., Röning, J. (2004) Know Your Whereabouts. 2004 Communication Networks and Distributed Systems Modeling and Simulation Conference (CNDS'04), San Diego, California, USA, 19-22 January 2004.

17. McCleaa, M., Yena, D.C., Huang, A. (in press). An analytical study towards the development of a standardized IM application. Computer Standards & Interfaces, Volume: 26, Issue: 4, August 2004, 343-355.

An Implementation of Indoor Location Detection Systems Based on Identifying Codes

Rachanee Ungrangsi[1], Ari Trachtenberg[2], and David Starobinski[2]

[1] Computer Science Program, Shinawatra University,
Pathumtani 12160, Thailand
rachanee@shinawatra.ac.th
[2] Electrical and Computer Engineering Department,
Boston University, MA 02215, USA
{trachten, staro}@bu.edu

Abstract. We present the design, implementation and evaluation of a location detection system built over a Radio Frequency network based on the IEEE 802.11 standard. Our system employs beacons to broadcast identifying packets from strategic positions within a building infrastructure in such a way that each resolvable position is covered by a unique collection of beacons; a user of such a system can thus determine his location by means of the beacon packets received. The locations from which beacons broadcast is determined from a formalization of the problem based on identifying codes over arbitrary graphs. We present experimental evidence that our location detecting system is practical and useful, and that it can achieve good accuracy even with a very small number of beacons.

1 Introduction

The theory of identifying codes was proposed in [4, 5] as a means of performing robust location detection in emergency sensor networks. That work was motivated by the emergence of wireless tiny sensors [1, 3] and the need for emergency personnel to identify the locations of personnel and trapped victims during emergency situations. The key to the approach involved positioning sensors in such a way that overlapping coverage regions are covered by a unique, and hence identifying, set of sensors. It turns out that determining an optimal placement of sensors is equivalent to constructing an optimal identifying code. The work in [4, 5] presented an algorithm ID-CODE for generating irreducible identifying codes over arbitrary topologies and proved various properties of this algorithm.

In this work, we describe the experimental design, implementation, and evaluation of the proposed location detection scheme, elaborating on a short summary that appeared in [5]. We provide a detailed description of our experimental framework and analyze various trade-offs associated with its design. Our testbed is implemented on the fourth floor of a nine-story building using wireless-equipped computer laptops. The testbed provides location detection capabilities for a portion of floor space, proving the feasibility of our system. We discuss and provide

A. Aagesen et al. (Eds.): INTELLCOMM 2004, LNCS 3283, pp. 175–189, 2004.

solutions for significant practical issues that arise in implementing such a system. Using extensive data collected for our testbed, we demonstrate the ability of the proposed system to detect user location, and we propose directions for enhancing the system's performance.

The main challenge in the system design is to construct a stable, distinguishable, underlying graph based on wireless connections in order to determine the beacon placement. Part of this challenge involves translating the soft information on node connectivity into a hard binary decision, for the purposes of generating an identifying graph. As part of experimentally determining how to produce this transformation, we have studied the effects of various design parameters, such as transmission power, data rate, packet size, and packet transmission rate. These experiments enabled us to set a packet reception rate threshold for making hard decisions on node connectivity. We present numerical results to illustrate the relationship between our design parameters and the rate of received packets.

The rest of this paper is organized as follows. Section 2 briefly explained related work in the fields of location detection technologies and identifying codes. In Section 3, we describe the outline of our proposed system, explaining the relationship between location detection in wireless networks and the construction of identifying codes for arbitrary graphs. The main theme of our paper is described in Sections 4- 7. The first two of these sections identify a number of design and implementation challenges for our work, and the last two sections describe our experimental wireless testbed, some decoding methods, and an analysis of our results. Finally, our conclusion summarizes the main findings of this work and presents plans for future research.

2   Related Work

Location detection systems have been proposed and implemented in the literature for a variety of applications. For outdoor applications, the satellite based *Global Positioning System* (GPS) is the most widely deployed scheme [6]. GPS relies on trilateration of position and time among four satellites, and can determine location in many cases within 1 to 5 meters when used in conjunction with a *Wide Area Augmentation System* (WAAS). However, signals from the GPS satellite system cannot always penetrate through walls and metallic structures, and therefore GPS reception is often intermittent in indoor settings. Alternative schemes must therefore be implemented for providing reliable location detection in indoor environments.

The *Active Badge* location system [7,8] was one of the first prototypes of indoor location detection systems. In this system, each user wears a badge that periodically emits a unique ID signal using infrared. This signal is typically received by one of the several receivers scattered throughout a building and forwarded to a central server. The identity of the receiver that overhears the user's signal determines the location of the user. This approach is referred to as *proximity-based* location detection, since the location of a user is resolved to be that of its nearest receiver.

The *Active Bat* [9] and MIT's *Cricket* [10] systems use ultrasound to provide location detection based on proximity. These systems measure the time-of-flight of ultrasound signals with respect to reference RF signals, thereby allowing a system to calculate the location of a user using a trilateration computation. Active Bat claims an accuracy within 9 cm for 95% of the measurements.

The main problem with infrared and ultrasound proximity-based schemes is that their coverage may be lost as soon as a path from a user to its nearby receiver becomes obstructed. This could be due to structural changes (e.g, the opening or closing of a door) or the presence of smoke in a building in fire.

Another powerful approach for indoor location detection is RF (Radio Frequency) because of its inherent ability to penetrate many types of surfaces, especially at lower frequencies. In addition, RF-based indoor location detection has significant cost and maintenance benefits, as it can be readily deployed over existing radio infrastructures, such as IEEE 802.11 wireless LANs. Several RF-based location detection systems have been proposed in the literature. In particular, the RADAR [12, 13] system is based on the construction of a Signal to Noise Ratio (SNR) map for a locatable area. The vector of signal strengths received at various base-stations is compared to this map to determine the position of a user. The Nibble system uses a similar approach but, to improve performance, also incorporates a Bayesian model for predicting the likely origin of a signal based on signal quality observed at access points [14].

In this work, we resort to RF to achieve spatial diversity. However, we do not rely on the knowledge of an SNR map, since in many applications, such as disaster recovery, it is impossible to determine an accurate signal map of the environment. Therefore our approach deliberately uses very limited knowledge of the signal landscape so as to be robust to changes. More specifically, its fundamental idea is to build redundancy into the system in such a way that each resolvable position is covered by a unique set of beacons which serve as a positional signature. This approach can be formalized using the theory of identifying codes [16, 17, 20], and its theoretical foundations are described in detail in [4, 5].

3   System Overview

In this section, we briefly review our location detection scheme based on the theory of identifying codes [4, 5]. Our proposed system divides the coverage area into locatable regions, and reports a point in this region as the location for a given target. The system is designed as follows:

- First, a set of points is selected for a given area.
- Then, based on the RF connectivity between the points, beacons are placed and activated on a subset of these points determined by a corresponding identifying code. This activation guarantees that each point is covered by a *unique* set of beacons.
- An observer can determine its location from the unique collection of ID packets that it receives.

The following example illustrates the approach. Let the selected points, on a given floor, be $P = \{a, b, c, d, e, f, g\}$, as illustrated in Step 1 in Figure 1(a), and let the RF-connectivity among these points be represented by the arrows in Step 2 Figure 1(b); in other words, there is an arrow between two positions if and only if RF communication is possible between these points. Using the ID-CODE algorithm described in [4, 5], we place four beacons at positions a, d, e and g. Each beacon periodically broadcasts a unique ID. The user stays for a (small) time T at its current position and collects the ID's from the packets it receives. For instance, in Step 3 Figure 1(c), an observer in the region of point b receives ID's from the beacons at position a and d. The set of ID's received at a given position x is called the *identifying set* of x and denoted $ID(x)$. Since the identifying set of each point in P is unique (see Figure 1(d)), the user can resolve its location unambiguously using a look-up table. A set of beacons that results into unique identifying sets is called an *identifying code*.

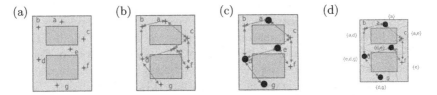

Fig. 1. Our location detection system. (a) Discrete locations. (b) Connectivity. (c) Beacon placements. (d)Covering regions of each discrete point and corresponding identifying sets

4   The Challenge: Constructing Underlying Graph Based on Wireless Connections

In our system, a graph representation of the network is essential to determine beacon placements. A node is represented by a circle, and a link between two nodes is usually represented by a line drawn between the nodes. Physically, the connectivity between two nodes implies a medium (such as air, wire, or fiber) that provides the communications system with a channel resource (such as bandwidth) and a system architecture that implements a channel signaling and modulation scheme using the channel resource available in the medium.

However, the wireless medium introduces difficulties for communication by virtue of its inherent nature. In following subsections, we discuss about several issues involving the graph construction in RF networks in detail. We will start with explaining why the connectivity between two nodes is not binary in nature for wireless networks.

4.1   Gray Zone

First let us consider radio propagation in free space [22, 23], in which the influence of obstacles is neglected. In this case, path loss becomes the most important parameter predicted by large-scale propagation models. We consider the model to be *isotropic*, where the transmitting antenna radiate power P_t uniformly in all directions. Examining path loss will indicate the amount of power available at the receiving antenna of area A_e at a distance r meters from the source. Using this model would allow us to easily determine the connectivity status (ON/OFF) between any two nodes. For a fixed distance r, if the power level at the receiver is greater than the power level threshold of the receiving antenna, which is prescribed by manufacturers, the connection is maintained. Otherwise both are disconnected.

To be more realistic, however, we have to consider the propagation in the presence of obstacles (such as ground, walls, or ceilings). There are three main propagation mechanisms that determine and describe path loss [22, 23] as follows: refection, diffraction, and diffusion. These three phenomenons introduce specific geographic location, called *gray zone*. In the gray zone, the power at the receiving antenna is very low and usually the antenna is not able to correctly detect any packets, but it may occasionally receives a few packets from a source due to multi-path propagation. This leads to a difficulty in making a hard decision about whether any two points in the space are connected. Furthermore, indoor radio propagation is much more variable than the outdoor propagation. The place where antennas are mounted also impacts packet reception. For example, antennas mounted at desk level in a room received vastly different signals from those mounted in the ground or on the ceiling.

4.2   Environmental Fluctuations

The channel *fading* [22, 23] occurs when the communicating device and/or components of its environment are in motion. These mobile objects introduce various distinct propagation paths, whose delay differences are very small compared to symbol intervals. The combination of these signals causes the fluctuation of the received signal with time. Furthermore, the speed of propagating waves depends on the temperature, because temperature affects the strength of particle interactions in air. This implies that the number of packets received between a pair of nodes also varies with time. As a result, RF connectivity is significantly impacted by changes in environment (such as movement of people and objects, changes in temperature, etc.) [24].

4.3   Orientation Issues

The radiation pattern of an antenna [25] plays an important role in packet transmission and reception, especially in a dense multi-path environment such as inside buildings. In general, an antenna can either be an omni-directional antenna, or a directional antenna. An *omni-directional* antenna can radiate or receive equally well in all directions, which implies that all packets are received equally well. On the other hand, a *directional* antenna can receive best from a specific direction. Thus if the radiation pattern of receiver antenna is directional, it is possible that two points may be connected if the receiver faces one direction, but may not be in other directions for the indoor environment. However, using omni-directional antennas may lead to indistinguishably graphs, so the directional antenna is useful for designing the desirable system in our scheme by adding or removing some links. Furthermore, the body of person carrying the receiver may absorb or block the packets in particular orientation, which introduces a systematic source of error.

4.4   Best Decision Formulation

Questions often arise concerning the meaning of there being a *connection* between any two points. Thus, making decisions about connectivity that minimize the probability of a wrong decision is very important in our location detection scheme. An usual strategy, such as Bayesian formulation [26], is not suitable because its decisions are based on the *ground truth*, which is inherently absent in our proposed system. The connection between any pair of nodes is not well defined for example, receiving one out of forty packets per second from a source may be considered "connected" in a system because the receiver can communicate to the source. On the other hand, one also can decide that it is "disconnected" because the receiver receives very small number of packets compare to the number of packets that actually are transmitted from the source. Therefore, finding a proper decision formulation to determine whether two nodes are connected is very important for improving the performance of the system.

5   Design Parameters

One important step prior to implementing our location detection system is to understand the relationship between the design parameters and the connectivity. Note that in our experiment, we used *packet reception rate* as a key metric for determining connections between any two points. We have built a small testbed to illustrate how to set the adjustable design parameters of the system in such a way that the connectivity between any two nodes can be clearly defined.

The testbed consists of five office rooms. Each room has a dimension of 9.5 feet × 18 feet. Rooms are separated by walls with an attenuation factor of 3 dB (measured at 1 mW transmitting power). We deployed two computer laptops serving as a transmitter and a receiver, both running Red Hat 8.0 and equipped with a Cisco 350 series wireless 802.11b adapter [27], operating at the 2.4 GHz band. During the experiment, we observed that the radiation pattern of this adapter is directional. Thus the orientation of the transmitter's antenna and the receiver's antenna are fixed throughout this experiment. The transmitter broadcasted user datagram protocol (UDP) [21] packets at a rate of 40 packets per second. We determine packet reception range by placing the transmitter in the leftmost room and closed to the leftmost wall, moving the receiver away from the transmitter and measuring the number of packet received for 5 minutes at position closest to the other wall. We increased number of walls and the distance between receiver and transmitter by moving receiver into the next room. Thus the packet reception range is represented by the minimum number of walls (or rooms) that makes the receiver disconnected from the transmitter. In our system, we are seeking for the setting such that the number of received packets in front of a wall and behind that wall are much different. In other words, the physical distance to transit from well connected state to disconnected state should be minimized. There are four parameters that we are interested in: data rates, transmitting power, packet size and packet arrival rate distribution.

- **Data Rates:** Cisco Aironet 350 Client Adapters support 1, 2, 5.5 and 11 Mbps data rates [27]. We chose to compare results between 1 Mbps and 11 Mbps and transmitted packets with length of 1000 bytes and transmitting power of 1 mW. Figure 2(a) illustrates that the packet reception range of a transmitter with 1Mbps data rate is larger than the range of transmitter with 11 Mbps. The number of packets received from the 1-Mbps transmitter gracefully decreases when the distance increases, which is undesirable for our proposed system. Thus high data rate can provide sharper range to determine whether two nodes are connected.
- **Transmitting Power:** Increasing transmitting power also increases transmission range. For a Cisco Aironet 350 Client Adapter, the transmission power is varied from 1 mW to 100 mW [27]. In our experiment, we wanted to compare between 1 mW and 100 mW transmitting power. The transmitter transmitted packets with length 1000 bytes at 11Mbps data rate. In

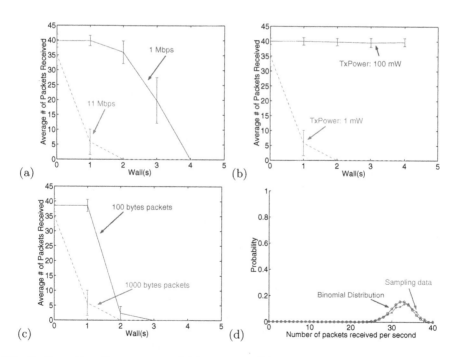

Fig. 2. Reception Range versus (a)data rates, (b)transmitting power, (c)packet size and (d)packet arrival rate distribution

Figure 2(b), packets transmitted with 1 mW power could not go through the second wall whereas packets of 100 mW were received well even in the fifth room. Therefore, the transmitting power can be used to control the coverage area of a transmitter.

- **Packet Size:** In the binary symmetric channel, each bit will be received correctly with probability (1-p) and incorrectly with probability p, where p is the probability of error due to noise in the channel. Intuitively, a larger packet has a higher probability of being corrupted. Thus the packet reception range of large packets should be small. In our experiment, we transmitted 100-byte packets and 1000-byte packets, respectively, at the data rate of 11 Mbps and 1 mW transmitting power. Figure 2(c) clearly depicts that transmitting larger packets provides a smaller range, as expected.

- **Packet Arrival Rate Distribution:** We also can model a packet as a symbol in the binary symmetric channel, where each packet will be correctly detected with probability (1-p). The connection between any two positions in the network can be represented by a value of p. Given a fixed packet transmission rate n, the reception of each packet has two possible outcome, "success" and "failure". All packets are independent, so the outcome of a packet has no effect on the outcome of another. The probability of success is (1-p). These indicate that the packet arrival rates should follows a binomial distribution. As expected, we empirically have found that the distribution of packet arrival rates are Binomially Distributed, as shown in Figure 2(d). Thus value of p for each connection can be observed based on the average number of packet received.

6   Experimental Testbed

6.1   Testbed Description

Our testbed was located on the 4th floor of the nine-story building. The floorplan is shown in Figure 6. There were 10 positions in the test-bed, which are to be located. Pentium-based laptop computers running Red Hat Linux 8.0 and equipped with an IEEE 802.11b standard compliant Cisco Aironet 350 series Client Adapter [27] were used in this experiment. As we discussed earlier in Section 5, we observed that transmitting packets at high data rates provided a sharp packet reception range. On the other hand, increasing transmit power increased the size of reception range. Furthermore, we also found that increasing packet size will decrease the size of the gray zone. Thus, in this testbed each transmitter transmits 40 UDP packets per second at a data rate of 5.5 Mbps and transmission power of 100 mW. Each packet is 1000-byte long including the transmitter's ID. This setting was obtained by measuring connectivity inside the testbed to obtain the stable distinguishable underlying graph.

The connectivity between every pair of positions was determined as follows: a transmitter was placed at one of the points and a receiver was placed at another point (as marked in Figure 6). Then, the transmitter was set to broadcast 40 packets per second, each containing the transmitter ID. If the receiver received at least 20 packets per second in average for five minutes each for all antenna orientations, the position were considered to be connected. This model of connectivity was used in this experiment for simplicity. The connectivity between the points is observed to be reliable with the setup used in this test-bed. The underlying graph was built using the connectivity information between every pair of points obtained as above. In our next step, we applied the ID-code algorithm to determine transmitter placements. The result from the algorithm suggested us to place four transmitters at position 0, position 1, position 2 and position 3 as indicated in Figure 6. The identifying set at each position is given in Figure 3.

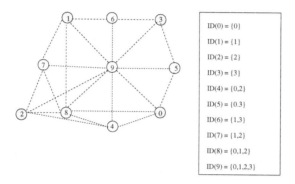

Fig. 3. The connectivity graph of the testbed and its identifying codes. The filled dots denote the positions that transmitters are placed

6.2   Data Collection and Processing

The data collection phase is an important step in our research methodology. We wrote a Java application to control the data collection process at the receiver. The packet arrival rate from all transmitters at each position was recorded. The information was collected during the day, when there are other possible sources of fluctuation such as moving people and objects. We observed that the packet arrival rate also varies with the receiver's orientation. Therefore, we also recorded the direction (North, South, East, West) that the wireless adapter is facing at the time of measurement.

The data collection phase is divided into 2 parts as follows:

- **Part I: The Distribution of Packet Arrival Rate.** In this test-bed, we are interested in determining the *correctness* of the system by measuring the probability of error in locating the region in which a stationary user is located. We have collected the data over extended periods (at least one hour per position) to observe the distribution of the packet arrival rate. For each orientation of each position, we recorded 1000 samples.
- **Part II: The Coverage Region.** Our location detection scheme discretizes the space. Therefore, one important characterization of the test-bed is the extent of the region around a reference position, where the receiver receives

the same code. For this purpose, the floor is divided into small grid points and the receiver is placed on one of the grid points for 60 samplings per orientation.

7   Experimental Results and Analysis

7.1   Packet Rate Distributions

In our testbed, we make use of packet arrival rates to determine the connectivity between any two points and then decode the position. To demonstrate that the packet arrival rate is a reasonable measure of connectivity, we show some examples of the probability distribution of the packet arrival rate for locations in our test-bed shown in Figure 4. The gap between codewords zero and one are sharply separated in almost all positions. This indicates that using packet arrival rates to infer location codewords is a promising approach for our scheme.

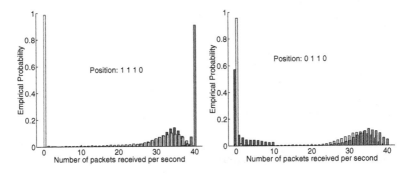

Fig. 4. The probability of packet arrival rate recorded at the five reference positions at transmission rate 40 packets/sec at position 1110 and 0110

7.2   Finding the Best Decoding Threshold

In our basic approach, given sample packet arrivals from each transmitter, called an observed packet vector (n_0, n_1, n_2, n_3), we determine the location that best matches this observation to a corresponding binary codeword in the lookup table. The lookup table is created when the system is setup and contains codewords corresponding to each location in the area. If a user obtains an unknown codeword, the system will choose the closest codeword as user's location. In our experiment, we use thresholding scheme, which is one of the simplest methods to decode an observed packet vector. If the sample interval exceeds a certain threshold θ, it will set to 1 s otherwise 0 s. To find the best threshold, the system needs to be trained by samples during the setup phase. This is a workable strategy, but it may not be optimal. You can find other possible decoding techniques in [2].

We use the empirical data obtained in the data collection and processing phase part I (see Section 6.2) to find the threshold that minimize probability of decoding errors. We characterize the performance of our estimate of a stationary user's location using probability of error to determine the region in which the user is located. In the analysis, we use all of the 5*4000 samples collected for all combinations of user locations and orientation (5 locations and 1,000 samples per location per orientation). For 1,000 iterations, we randomly chose 400 samples from each location regardless of the orientation as the training data set in the off-line phase and the remaining data is the testing data set in the on-line phase. In each iteration, we use the training data set to determine the best threshold that minimizes the overall probability of error for the whole system. We then apply this threshold to the testing data set, count the number of samples that are incorrectly decoded and compute probability of error. Finally we determine the average of the probabilities of error from all iterations to represent the performance of the single threshold method.

Figure 5 shows that 15 is the best empirical threshold of decoding for this testbed. Considering probability of error for varying threshold, we found that the threshold that gives the minimum probability of error is approximately between 10 and 20. We observe that increasing the training data set slightly improves the performance of the system [2].

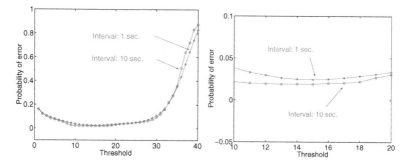

Fig. 5. The probability of error for varying threshold with Data Collecting Interval size of 1 sec and 10 sec

7.3 Data Collecting Interval

In wireless networks, changes in environment can cause fluctuation in the number of packets received. Collecting packets longer may help users to observe the real channel state and obtain the correct codeword. To analyze this, we compare the interval time to collect data per one decoding step between 1 second and 10 seconds. To decode the current position, we average all samples which are collected in the given interval. We then decode by the threshold and find the best matched location. Figure 5 explains the performance of the system when we increase the data collecting interval. As expected, most of thresholds show that the larger interval can reduce the probability of error in decoding step. However, when the threshold was set very high, the longer interval significantly degraded the performance of the system due to lost packets.

7.4   Impact of Packet Transmission Rate

Intuitively, transmitting packets at high packet rate can separate the packet arrival rate of *connected* transmitters and *disconnected* transmitters better than
the low packet rate. However, if the current location of a receiver is identified
by more than one transmitter, the number of packets received depends on the
current network traffic. To observe the impact of packet transmission rate, we
conducted our experiments at a position whose corresponding codeword is 110.
All three transmitters periodically emit ID packets with the same packet transmission rates (5, 10, 40, 60, and 70 packets/sec, respectively).

Figure 6(a) clearly shows that at the interested position , very low packet
transmission rate (such as 5 packets/sec and 10 packets/sec) cannot provide
clear separation between codeword one and codeword zero. Since packets were
periodically transmitted, low data rate creates large interval between two consecutive packets, which implies that at the receiver, the probability of packet
collisions occurring is low. The gap between the distribution of the third transmitter whose codeword is zero and the others (codeword one) increased when
the packet rate increased. With a higher data rate, the receiver can receive more
packets from transmitters who are connected to the position. The probability
of packet collisions is high enough to eliminate some spurious packets from the
third transmitter . However, when the packet transmission rate is greater than
60 packets/second, packet collisions result in less number of packets being received. Consequently, the difference between codeword one and codeword zero
based on the number of packets is decreased.

Furthermore, since we propose to use beacons for broadcasting identified
packets. Thus transmitting packets at very high rate creates high power consumption which is inefficient. In order to obtain the best performance, one needs
to find the optimal packets transmission rate that minimizes the probability of
error in a system.

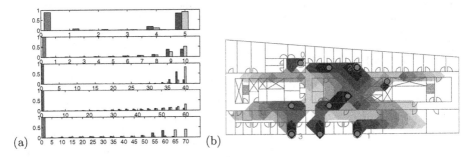

Fig. 6. (a) Setting a good packet transmission rate can improve the performance of
the system (b) A diagram demonstrates the range of each reference position with the
confident level of decoding at least 70%

7.5   Coverage Region

To evaluate the goodness of our system, another characteristic that we consider is the coverage region of the selected points, in other words, the resolution. Resolution is the distance between the actual user's location and the decoded location. The contour map in Figure 6(b) shows the resolution (0-70 feet) of the system with a 70% confidence level. Deploying four transmitters, the floor space can be divided into ten regions. These results show that an id code-based location detection system can achieve good accuracy with a very few number of beacons.

8   Conclusion

We have developed, analyzed, and refined a comprehensive set of techniques for indoor location detection systems based on the theory of identifying codes. In our scheme, based on the theory proposed in [4, 5], beacons are positioned in such a way that overlapping coverage regions are covered by a unique, and hence identifying, set of beacons.

The main contribution of our work is the development of a prototype location detection testbed in an office building using commodity Wi-Fi hardware. Our goal for this prototype was to provide reasonably accurate location detection capabilities for a portion of the floor-space of this building. Our experimental results show that our location detection scheme is feasible and useful. With four transmitters, our system can provide ten distinct locatable regions on the fourth floor of our chosen office building. Our system was able to identify a user's location region with a high degree of accuracy by using a simple thresholding scheme for determining RF connectivity.

Nevertheless, there remain a number of open issues. For one, it would be interesting to investigate whether signal attenuation and modulation can be exploited to enable more stable connections in an indoor environment. On the other hand, we plan to investigate the use of different carrier signals to avoid the absorption problems that are typical for the frequencies used by 802.11. Finally, the threshold decoder we used is very simple, and more sophisticated soft-decision decoders can very likely improve the performance of the system.

Acknowledgements

The authors would like to thank Dr. M. Karpovsky and Dr. L. Levitin for introducing them to identifying codes, S. Ray and F. De Pellegrini for fruitful discussions while developing the ID-CODE algorithm, Dr. J. Carruthers for his advice and C. Malladi for experiments on the testbed.

This work was supported in part by the US National Science Foundation under grants CAREER ANI-0132802, CAREER CCR-0133521, and ANI-0240333.

188   R. Ungrangsi, A. Trachtenberg, and D. Starobinski

References

1. S. E.-A. Hollar, "COTS dust," Master's thesis, University of California, Berkeley, 2000.
2. U. Rachanee, "Location Detection System in Emergency Sensor Networks Using Robust Identifying Codes ," Master's thesis, Boston University, Boston, 2003.
3. J. M. Kahn, R. H. Katz, and K. S. J. Pister, "Next century challenges: mobile networking for 'smart dust'," in *Proceedings of the fifth Annual ACM/IEEE international conference on Mobile computing and networking*, (Seattle, WA, United States), ACM, 1999.
4. S. Ray, R. Ungrangsi, F. De Pellegrini, A. Trachtenberg, and D. Starobinski, "Robust location detection in emergency sensor networks," in *IEEE INFOCOM 2003*, (San Francisco, CA), IEEE, 2003.
5. Saikat Ray, David Starobinski, Ari Trachtenberg and Rachanee Ungrangsi, "Robust Location Detection with Sensor Networks," IEEE JSAC (Special Issue on Fundamental Performance Limits of Wireless Sensor Networks), vol. 22, No.6, August 2004.
6. US Coast Guard Navigation Center, *Global Positioning System Signal Specigication*. 2nd edition ed., 1995.
7. R. Want, A. Hopper, V. Falcao, and J. Gibbons, "The active badge location system," *ACM Transactions on Information Systems*, vol. 10, pp. 91–102, January 1992.
8. R. Want, B. N. Schilit, N. I. Adams, R. Gold, K. Peterson, D. Goldberg, J. R. Ellis, and M. Weiser, "An overview of the PARCTAB ubiquitous computing experiment," *IEEE Personal Communications*, vol. 2, pp. 28–43, December 1995.
9. A. Harter, A. Hopper, P. Steggles, A. Ward, and P. Webster, "The anatomy of a context-aware application," in *MobiCom'99*, ACM, 8 1999.
10. N. B. Priyantha, A. Chakraborty, and H. Balakrishnan, "The cricket location-support system," in *6th ACM International Conference on Mobile Computing and Networking (ACM MOBICOM)*, (Boston, MA), ACM, 2000.
11. N. B. Priyantha, A. K. L. Miu, H. Balakrishnan, and S. Teller, "The cricket compass for contextaware mobile applications," in *7th ACM Conference on Mobile Computing and Networking (MOBICOM)*, (Rome, Italy), ACM, July 2001.
12. P. Bahl and V. N. Padmanabhan, "RADAR: An in-building RF-based user location and tracking system," in *IEEE INFOCOM 2000*, (Tel Aviv, Israel), IEEE, 2000.
13. P. Bahl, A. Balachandran, and V. Padmanabhan, "Enhancements to the RADAR User Location and Tracking System," Tech. Rep. MSR-TR-2000-12, Microsoft Research, February 2000.
14. P. Castro, P. Chiu, T. Kremenek, and R. R. Muntz, "A probabilistic room location service for wireless networked environments," in *Ubicomp*, (Atlanta, GA), ACM, 2001.
15. N. Bulusu, J. Heidemann, and D. Estrin, "GPS-less low cost outdoor localization for very small devices," in *Proceedings of IEEE Personal Communications*, pp. 28–34, IEEE, October 2000.
16. M. G. Karpovsky, K. Chakrabarty, and L. B. Levitin, "A new class of codes for identification of vertices in graphs," *IEEE Transactions on Information Theory*, vol. 44, pp. 599–611, March 1998.
17. I. Charon, O. Hudry, and A. Lobstein, "Identifying codes with small radius in some infinite regular graphs," *The Electronic Journal of Combinatorics*, vol. 9, 2002.

18. N. S. V. Rao, "Computational complexity issues in operative diagnosis of Graph-Based systems," *IEEE Transactions on Computers*, vol. 42, pp. 447–457, April 1993.
19. K. Chakrabarty, S. S. Iyengar, H. Qi, and E. Cho, "Grid coverage for surveillance and target location in distributed sensor networks," *IEEE Transactions on Computers*.
20. K. Chakrabarty, H. Qi, S. S. Iyengar, and E. Cho, "Coding theory framework for target location in distributed sensor networks," in *International Symposium on Information Technology: Coding and Computing*, pp. 130 –134, 2001.
21. L. L. Peterson and B. S. Davie, *Computer Networks: A systems approach*. Morgan Kaufmann, 2 ed., 2000.
22. Mark and Zhuang, *Wireless Communications and Networking*. Prentice Hall PTR, 2003.
23. T. S. Rappaport, *Wireless Communications: Principles and Practice*. Upper Saddle River NJ: Prentice Hall, 1996.
24. H. Hashemi, "The indoor radio propagation channel," in *Proceedings of the IEEE*, no. 7, pp. 943–968, July 1993.
25. J. C. Liberty, Jr. and T. S. Rappaport, *Smart Antennas for Wireless Communications: IS-95 and Third Generation CDMA Applications*. Prentice Hall PTR, 1999.
26. H. Chernoff and L. Moses, *Elementary Decision Theory*. Dover, 2 ed., 1986.
27. http://www.cisco.com/en/US/products/hw/wireless/ps4555/products_datasheet_09186a0080088828.html, "Cisco Aironet Wireless LAN Client Adapters Cisco Aironet 350 Series Client Adapters - Cisco Systems."

Just-in-Time Delivery of Events in Event Notification Service Systems for Mobile Users

Chit Htay Lwin[1], Hrushikesha Mohanty[1], and R. K. Ghosh[2]

[1] Department of CIS, University of Hyderabad, Hyderabad, India
{mc01pc08, hmcs}@uohyd.ernet.in
[2] Department of CSE, IIT Kanpur, Kanpur, India
rkg@cse.iitk.ac.in

Abstract. Advances in wireless network technology and the increasing number of handheld mobile devices enable service providers to offer several services to mobile users. Event notification service (ENS) system is a useful mean to push information to selective users and the same service can also be extended to mobile users. But mobility may cause delay in transferring subscriptions from the previous event server to the current event server and establishing new routes of notifications. This delay is not tolerable for many real-life applications, like stock exchanges, auction and traffic condition monitoring. In this paper, we propose an algorithm that ensures the timely delivery of published events to all interested mobile users with the help of regional route map which is a physical route map of a small neighborhood of the locations of mobile hosts.

1   Introduction

The development of portable computing devices such as notebook computers, personal digital assistants (PDAs) and 3G cellular phones along with wireless communication technology enable people to carry computational power with them while they are changing their physical locations in space. In an event notification service (ENS) system, producers publish events and consumers subscribe to them. If a consumer subscribes an event, an ENS system delivers all matched notifications that are published by any producer until the consumer cancels the respective subscription. An ENS system provides time decoupling and space decoupling [5]. The loose coupling of producers and consumers is the primary advantage of ENS systems. Although existing push-based technologies described in [7] and WAP push technology may enable mobile users to receive timely information, but they are not scalable as their services are centralized.

The event notification service approach can be used in many applications and many of them such as stock trading systems, auction systems, emergency notifications, banking, reservation systems and traffic condition monitoring systems need to manage deadline bound data items. Time bound applications require more functionality such as deadline constraints that enable scheduling of event delivery. A user may be willing to receive sports and news information with delay by a few minutes. But it may not tolerate delays or out of sequence in quotes for stock prices.

A. Aagesen et al. (Eds.): INTELLCOMM 2004, LNCS 3283, pp. 190–198, 2004.

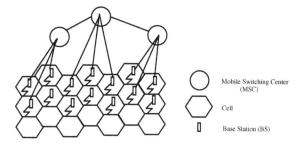

Fig. 1. A cellular mobile architecture

As an event notification service (ENS) system follows multicast communication protocol, it allows a producer to send the same event to many interested consumers with only one publishing operation. It can cope with dynamically changing operational environment where producers and consumers frequently disconnect and reconnect, as the system can operate with loose coupling of producers and consumers. Hence, an ENS system is a good candidate for a variety of e-commerce and m-commerce applications for mobile users. Huang [9] emphasizes on the issues that make an ENS system adaptable to dynamic changes occurring in a mobile computing environment. Several implementations of ENS systems (e.g. SIENA [1], JEDI [3], REBECA [6] and Elvin [12]) provide mobility support for delivery of events to the mobile users. Generally in these ENS systems, events notified to a consumer are stored at its event server (ES) located at the consumer's previous location during disconnection. On reconnection, the stored events are forwarded to the consumer's new location. Obviously mobile users expect uninterrupted service. In order to achieve it, users' subscriptions are not only to be registered at their new locations, but new routes need to be established at their new locations. This causes latency in delivery of events at new locations. In this paper we propose a solution that improves event delivery process for mobile users. The proposed solution ensures just-in-time event delivery i.e., a mobile user can receive notifications as soon as he/she reaches at new location. The rest of the paper is organized as follows. Section 2 describes the system model of mobile network for ENS systems, location management scheme, and, definitions and notations used in this paper. The proposed pre-handoff approach is presented in section 3. Section 4 describes the basic algorithm of location-based pre-handoff approach and section 5 concludes the paper.

2   System Model and Definition

2.1   System Model

We choose a model used in mobile cellular environment which is a collection of geometric areas called cells (Figure 1). Each cell is serviced by a base station (BS) located at its center [4]. Mobile terminals are connected to the network via the base stations. Cells can have different sizes: picocells are used in indoor environments; microcells and macrocells are used within cities and rural areas and highways [13].

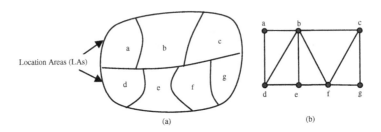

Location Areas (LAs)

(a)   (b)

Fig. 2. (a) Regional map with LAs (b) Graph model showing the interconnections of LAs

The network is assumed to be divided into a few big location areas (LA) as described in [8]. The graph model is used for representing interconnections of LAs as shown in Figure 2. Each LA, consisting of many cells (about 50 to 100), is served by a mobile switching center (MSC). An MSC acts as a gateway of the mobile network to the existing wired network. The base stations of a LA are connected to a MSC which stores the location and service information for each registered local mobile host. Tracking of the current location of a mobile host, involves two basic operations, terminal paging and location update and the network determines the mobile host's exact location within the cell granularity. This approach determines the mobile host's exact location within the cell granularity. Many works have been done on location management schemes [4]. But in ENS systems, the routing of events is dependent on event content rather than particular destination address. Hence location updates of mobile hosts only occur within a LA served by their event server.

Usually event servers (ESs) are implemented on separate servers. However, MSCs with enough computing resources can also be used as event servers. In the following sections, we use the term event server (ES) instead of MSC to be in tune with discussion concerning event notification service systems. We assume that all connections are bi-directional. Therefore, the abstract architectural model is an undirected graph.

2.2   Subscription and Notification

An ES checks an event against all subscriptions of its routing table to forward it to neighboring ESs or to deliver it to the local consumers. Registration of subscriptions by each consumer at every ES leads to explosion of information as well as traffic. This problem can be managed by using subscriptions covering test as described in [2, 11].

Each ES maintains a routing table (RT) for propagation of subscriptions and notifications. Routing table (RT) is a collection of tuples {<subscription>, <consumers>, <incoming servers>, <outgoing servers>};

i.e., RT := { < S, C_ID, IS, OS > }.

In RT, the consumers associated to a subscription S mean the local consumers who subscribe subscription S. Incoming servers of subscription S are the ESs from which subscription S is received, and outgoing servers of subscription S are the ESs to which S is forwarded to. As and when a mobile user ceases interest to an event, it can unsubscribe that event. If a notification N (an event) is received from a producer, local ES matches with all subscriptions stored in RT. The results are:

1. a set of consumers residing in the area covered by local event server, and,
2. a set of event servers to which N needs to be forwarded.

A notification N matches a subscription S if S covers N ($N \subseteq S$). If RT has subscription S matched with N (i.e. $\exists$ S in RT | $N \subseteq S$), the local ES delivers N to the consumers {(RT.S.C_ID)} and forwards N to event servers {(RT.S.IS)}.

2.3 Location Table and Border Cell Table

Each ES maintains mobile hosts location table (MLT), and local border cell table (BCT) besides the routing table (RT). A MLT is a collection of tuples {<mobile host ID>, <cell ID}. In an event notification service system, routing paths of events depend on content of events. Hence, location update occurs within a LA served by an ES and each ES updates its mobile host location table (MLT) every time a mobile host crosses the boundary of a cell.

Each ES also maintains a border cell table (BCT), a list of neighboring ESs relative to each border cell. Border cells mean the cells which are near the boundary of other regions. Hence, BCT is a collection of tuples {<border cell>, <neighboring event servers>}, i.e., BCT = {<CB>, <NES>}. By '·' extension convention, BCT·CB_k·NES, denotes the neighboring ESs with respect to the cell CB_k. The set of neighbouring cells adjacent to a border cell can be found statically from the regional route map described in subsection 2.1. We can use a pre-declared movement pattern of the mobile consumer; and employ certain heuristics [8] to predict the possible cells where a mobile consumer may show up from a border cell of a location area.

3 Pre-handoff Approach

The pre-handoff is a proactive strategy which initiates updates of routing and location tables (RT and MLT) of LAs to which a mobile host may visit during its travel. The main idea behind pre-handoff is to create virtual consumers at a set of expected locations of a mobile consumer in order to set up flow of notification before the mobile consumer reaches any of those locations. Loosely speaking, a virtual consumer is created on all ESs to which the mobile host is expected to connect in the "near" future. The set of virtual clients must change when the mobile host moves.

In an event notification service system, all the subscriptions of the users registered are recorded explicitly or implicitly at all ESs. Hence locations of event producers do not have any direct bearing in delivering of notifications and we do not take mobility of event producers in account. In the proposed approach, we assume that events are delivered in FIFO order with respect to the producer and that no events are duplicated and lost. To ensure ordering of events, [10] has proposed a causal ordering algorithm. Pre-handoff technique can successfully provide just-in-time service if and only if travel time of host from current border cell to that of new ES is more than equal the time for establishing paths of notifications at new ES.

3.1 Location-Based Pre-handoff

If an ES of a moving host executes pre-handoff at every neighboring ESs, it causes substantially unnecessary overheads. In order to avoid this problem, the proposed algorithm chooses ESs for pre-handoff based on locations of mobile hosts.

If a mobile consumer keeps moving in the interior cells of a LA, then the event server for the LA will be able to directly deliver the related notifications to the consumer. But if the consumer is moving around the border of a LA, it is likely that he/she may stray into a neighbouring LA. So we need to consider strategies to deliver the notifications related to the mobile consumer moving around the border cells of a LA should it ever stray into a cell under a neighbouring LA. It is done as follows. Each event server executes pre-handoff for mobile consumers which are moving in its border cells. As described in subsection 2.3, each event server maintains a local border cell table (BCT) that stores border cells and their adjacent LAs (i.e., neighboring ESs). So, an ES can use BCT in order to determine the neighboring ESs on which pre-handoff processes have to be executed on behalf of a moving consumer. The proposed mechanism creates virtual consumers (VC) and pre-subscribes at few ESs of possible future locations. When a mobile consumer (MH_s) gets connected to a new ES on which a VC is already running, it finds that its subscriptions exist and routing paths are already established. This ensures that MH_s can receive matched notifications immediately after connecting to the new ES.

Each ES needs to cancel pre-handoff processes of a mobile consumer MH_s in the following cases:

1. The MH_s is not in one of its border cells. It has to tackle two possible sub_cases:
   - MH_s moves from a border cell to a non-border cell within current LA.
   - MH_s moves to a border cell located within another LA.
2. The MH_s stops moving (i.e., it does not come out of a border cell) although the mobile is in a border cell.

In case 1, if MH_s has moved from a border cell to an interior cell under the current LA there is no need to execute a pre-handoff. Also if MH_s already move to a border cell under a new LA, unless pre-handoff is cancelled, it may lead to ping-pong situation. In case 2, the algorithm also needs to cancel pre-handoff processes. We can define time bound T to determine whether the host is moving or not. If a mobile host stays in a border cell greater than time T, the algorithm assumes that the mobile host is not moving (i.e., flag_mov(MH_s) = 0).

When a mobile consumer MH_s connects to a new ES, it must handle one of the following two cases.

1. The new event server has a virtual consumer of MH_s
2. The new event server does not have a virtual consumer of MH_s.

In case 1, the new event server need not execute normal handoff process which includes transferring subscriptions and re-subscribing and it can deliver matched notifications to MH_s immediately after connection. In case 2, the new event server did not create the virtual consumer of MH_s due to following reasons:

1. The mobile consumer MH_s was disconnected for long time and it reconnects to another event server. Hence, the new ES does not have a matching VC for MH_s.
2. The mobile consumer MH_s was in a border cell for long time (i.e., greater than T) and so the pre-handoff process was cancelled.

4 Algorithm

A host on reaching a cell belongs to a new LA registers at the ES of LA. Registration is triggered by a border cell of the LA from where MH_s has migrated after a pre-handoff, or it may be initiated by some cell in a new LA where MH_s pops up independently. In first case a surrogate of MH_s is already up under the new ES. So MH_s just needs to replace its surrogate. In the second case, a normal handoff should be initiated by the event server of LA where MH_s shows up.

Suppose a mobile consumer MH_s moves from the location area (LA) of ES_i to the LA of ES_j. Before the MH_s connects to ES_j, it must pass through a border cell CB_k of ES_i. When the border cell CB_k sends *register* (MH_s, ES_i, CB_k) to its event server ES_i, ES_i executes pre-handoff for MH_s. ES_i transfers all subscriptions of MH_s using *Preforward* (MH_s, ES_i, SSUBQ_MH$_s$) to a set of some neighboring ESs, $e \in E$, (i.e., E = BCT·CB$_k$·NES) including ES_j. Each of the ESs after receiving *Preforward* message creates a virtual consumer VC_MH$_s$ and forwards the subscriptions of MH_s to related ESs to establish a new route of notifications for MH_s. After sending *Preforward* (MH_s, ES_i, SSUBQ_MH$_s$) to e, ES_i needs to send *Pre_Subforward* (MH_s, ES_i, S) to e whenever it receives *Subscribe* (S, MH_s) from MH_s. On receiving *Pre_Subforward* (MH_s, ES_i, S), each ES forwards S to related neighboring ESs to update routing paths of notifications. For two cases that need to cancel pre-handoff, ES_i sends *Cancel_Preforward* to those ESs which have VC of MH_s. When MH_s connects to ES_j which already has VC_ MH$_s$, ES_j changes VC_ MH$_s$ as its local consumer and deliver notifications to MH_s without delay. If ES_j does not have VC_ MH$_s$, ES_j initiates normal handoff process as described in [10]. The basic location-based pre-handoff algorithm is described in Figure 3. The data structures used in the algorithm are as follows:

- $cell\_MH_s$ = current cell of mobile consumer MH_s.
- SSUBQ_MH$_s$ = queue to store subscriptions sent by local mobile consumer MH_s
- CB(ES_i) = {C_1, C_2, ..., C_k}= a set of all border cells of ES_i.
- flag_mov(MH_s) = 1 if mobile host MH_s is moving
- VC(ES_{ij}) = ES_i's awareness of virtual consumers created at ES_j for possible movements of hosts from ES_i to ES_j.
- VC(ES_i) = all virtual consumers located at a server ES_i.
- Local(ES_i) = a set of local mobile hosts at ES_i.

Let **MH**$_s$ moves from the LA of ES$_i$ to the LA of ES$_j$.

Algorithm A1:: Executed at event server ES$_i$ where MH$_s$ is residing.

On receiving **Register** *(MH$_s$, ES$_k$, cell_ MH$_s$)* /*ES$_k$ means the last connected ES */
    if (MH$_s \in$ Local(ES$_i$))
            if (*cell_MH$_s \in$* CB (ES$_i$) $\land$ flag_mov(MH$_s$) = 1)
                (a) E = BCT · *cell_ MH$_s$* ·NES
                    For all ES$_e \in$ E **do**
                        if (MH$_s \notin$ VC(ES$_{ie}$))
                            (1) Send **Pre_handoffRequest** *(ES$_i$, MH$_s$)* to ES$_e$;
                            (2) On receiving **Enable_prehandoff** *(ES$_e$, MH$_s$)*
                                Send **Preforward** *(MH$_s$, ES$_i$, SSUBQ_MH$_s$)* to ES$_e$;
                    endif
                endfor
                (b) On receiving **Subscribe** (S, MH$_s$) /*receiving S from MH$_s$*/
                      Send **Pre_Subforward** *(MH$_s$, ES$_i$, S)* to ES$_e$;
            else
                Send **Cancel_Preforward** *(MH$_s$, ES$_i$)* to ES$_e$; /*Cancel pre-handoff */
            endif
    else
            if (VC_ MH$_s \in$ VC(ES$_j$)) /*VC is already up for MH$_s$ */
                (1) Local(ES$_j$) = Local(ES$_j$) $\cup$ MH$_s$;
                (2) VC(ES$_j$) = VC(ES$_j$) – VC_MH$_s$;
            else
                Execute normal handoff process;
            endif
    endif

Algorithm A2:: Executed at event server ES$_j$.

    I.   On receiving **Pre_handoffRequest** *(ES$_i$, MH$_s$)*,
        (1) VC(ES$_j$) = VC(ES$_j$) $\cup$ VC_MH$_s$;
        (2) Send **Enable_prehandoff** *(ES$_j$, MH$_s$)* to ES$_i$;
    II. On receiving **Preforward** *(MH$_s$, ES$_i$, SSUBQ_MH$_s$)*,
        (1) Update routing table for all subscriptions S $\in$ SSUBQ_MH$_s$;.
    III. On receiving **Pre_Subforward** *(MH$_s$, ES$_i$, S)*,
        (1) Store S in SSUBQ_MH$_s$;
        (2) Forward S to neighboring event servers;
    IV. On receiving **Cancel_Preforward** *(MH$_s$, ES$_i$)*,
        (1) Unsubscribe each S $\in$ SSUBQ_MH$_s$;
        (2) VC(ES$_j$) = VC(ES$_j$) – VC_MH$_s$;

Fig. 3. Basic algorithm for location-based pre-handoff

5 Conclusion

Depending on the application domains, event notification service systems differ in architectures and in features they support. In this paper we have presented a pre-handoff approach for just-in-time delivery of events in an event notification service system for mobile environment. Handoff process may cause some delay in event notification when a mobile user change its location. This delay is due to transfer of subscriptions of the mobile consumer to the new ES and re-subscribing these subscriptions to establish new routes for notifications. The proposed algorithm is designed to reduce this delay by using pre-handoff by predicting a small set of probable destination locations of the mobile host. Currently, we are studying the performance of our algorithm in simulation environment.

In case of location based services (i.e., when notifications are sensitized to location properties), our approach cannot be applied directly because the same subscription may match different events in different locations. Hence, in pre handoff approach when an event server forwards location-based subscriptions of virtual consumers, it is necessary to qualify location attributes of these subscriptions with respect to possible destination locations.

In our approach, pre-handoff is executed only by event servers and event servers re-subscribe subscriptions on behalf of mobile consumers. Hence this approach is suitable for mobile environment with constraints such as low power consumption, low computing power of mobile devices, and low bandwidth of wireless links. The proposed algorithm can be extended to execute pre-handoff at an exact location area to which a mobile consumer will move by using the direction and speed of the moving mobile host or movement pattern of mobile hosts [8].

References

1. Caporuscio, M., Carzaniga, A., and Wolf, A. L.: An Experience in Evaluating Publish/Subscribe Services in a Wireless Network. In Proceedings of Third International Workshop on Software and Performance, Rome, Italy (July 2002)
2. Caarzaniga, A., Rosenblum, D. S., Wolf, A. L.: Design and Evaluation of a Wide-Area Event Notification Service. ACM Transactions on Computer Systems 19(3) (August 2001) 332-383
3. Cugola, G., Di Nitto, E., and Fuggetta, A.: The JEDI Event-based Infrastructure and Its Application to the Development of the OPSS WFMS. IEEE Transactions on Software Engineering 9(27) (September 2001) 827-850
4. DasBit, S. and Mitra, S.: Challenges of Computing in Mobile Cellular Environment-a Survey. Computer Communiations, Elseiver, 26(18) (December 2003) 2090-2105
5. Eugster, P. T., Guerraoui, R., and Damm, C. H.: On Objects and Events. In Proceedings of OOPSLA, Tampa Bay, USA (October 2001)
6. Fiege, L., Gärtner, F. C., Kasten, O., and Zeidler, A.: Supporting Mobility in Content-based Publish/Subscribe Middleware. In Proceedings of IFIP/ACM Middleware 2003 (June 2003)
7. Franklin, M., Zdonik, S.: Data in your face: push technology in perspective. In Proceedings of ACM SIGMOD International Conference on Management of Data, Seattle, WA, (1998)
8. Ghosh, R. K., Rayanchu, S. K., and Mohanty, H.: Location Management by Movement Prediction Using Mobility Patterns and Regional Route Maps. In Proceedings of IWDC'03, Vol. 2918, LNCS, Springer-Verlag, (2003) 153-162

9. Huang, Y., and Garcia-Molina, H.: Publish/Subscribe in a Mobile Environment. In Proceedings of the 2nd ACM International Workshop on Data Engineering for Wireless and Mobile Access, Santa Barbara, CA (May 2001)

10. Lwin, C., H., Mohanty, H., Ghosh, R. K.: Causal Ordering in Event Notification Service Systems for Mobile Users. In Proceedings of ITCC'04, IEEE, Las Vegas, USA (April 2004) 735-740

11. Muhl, G., Fiege, L., Buchmann, A.: Filter Similarities in Content-based Publish/Subscribe Systems. In Proceedings of ARCS'02, LNCS, Springer-Verlag, (2002)

12. Sutton, P., Arkins, R., and Segall, B.: Disconnectedness- Transparent Information Delivery for Mobile and Invisible Computing. In Proceedings of CCGrid'01, IEEE, (May 2001)

13. Wong, V. W.-S., and Leung, V. C. M.: Location Management for Next Generation Personal Communication Networks. IEEE Network, Special Issue on Next Generation Wireless Broadband Networks (2000)

Adapting Email Functionality for Mobile Terminals

Jon-Finngard Moe[1], Eivind Sivertsen[1], and Do van Thanh[2]

[1]Norwegian University of Science and Technology,
7491 Trondheim, Norway
{jonfinng, eivindsi}@stud.ntnu.no
[2]Telenor R&D,
1331 Fornebu, Norway
Thanh-van.Do@telenor.com

Abstract. There is an increasing need for mobile users to access email services anytime and anywhere. The solutions proposed so far, like Web/WAP [6] mail and VPN [7] tunneling are not ideal for mobile clients with limited resources. These solutions do not offer any new concepts to how the emails are transferred or the mail format itself. In this paper we present an XML Web Service [1] solution, which opens for new ways of providing email functionality to mobile as well as stationary systems. The paper starts with a brief summary of how email systems of today work. Ultimately, our solution based on XML Web Services and the proposed XMMAP (XML Mobile eMail Access Protocol) is explained thoroughly.

1 Introduction

So far, all attempts to find new killer applications for mobile phones after voice communication and SMS (Short Message Service) have not been very successful. However, there is strong indication that mobile email access may be a candidate. Indeed, for mobile professional users that have used data applications in their work for many years, it is valuable to be able to access their mails when being on the move.

Unfortunately, so far there is no satisfactory solution because of several issues. First, small displays and limited navigation capability are not suitable for displaying a large number of emails. Emails may also be unnecessary large in size due to excessive presentation formatting and large attachments.

Another difficulty is standardization of the user interface. The plurality and heterogeneity of mobile terminal types makes this a complex task.

2 Special Requirements for Mobile Terminals

Mobile terminals have many limitations compared to standard PCs that put new requirements on the application and service design for mobile terminals:

- Lower available bandwidth and transfer rate.
- Smaller screen size, less number of colors and resolution.
- Smaller Keyboard size and reduced control equipment.
- Lower processing capability.

A. Aagesen et al. (Eds.): INTELLCOMM 2004, LNCS 3283, pp. 199–206, 2004.

- Less support for application protocols.
- Less storage space on device.

3 Current Email Infrastructure

Current email communication systems consist of two main components, email Server and email Client. They are both compositions of several elements that are making use of multiple communication protocols, as well as internal service elements. Examples of protocols are SMTP [2] (Simple Mail Transfer Protocol), IMAP [3] (Internet Message Access Protocol), POP [4] (Post Office Protocol).

An SMTP mail object contains an envelope and content. In order to send and/or relay mail, we must follow the protocol described in RFC2821 [2].

Fig. 1 shows that a minimum of 11 message transfers is needed between the client and server in order to send a single email when using SMTP. Two extra transfers are introduced for every additional recipient. When using a mobile terminal with slow network connection, each message adds to the delay. It is therefore desirable to keep the number of message transfers to an absolute minimum.

SMTP - mailsending proceedure (SMTP Envelope)

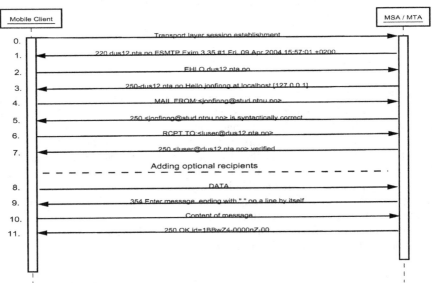

Fig. 1. SMTP message transfer

3.1 IMF and MIME

IMF and MIME [5] are standards used for representing the actual content of the email. IMF defines which headers are mandatory, and how a standard message should be organized. MIME is an extension to IMF, which defines how complex emails should be represented. These are typically emails that have file-attachments; multiple alternative representations formats or even enclosed sub-email-messages.

An email usually contains a lot of information enclosed in IMF headers. Most of this information is not relevant to the user, such as the list of mail servers the message has visited on it's way to its destination, and most "X-headers"[1]. This information is usually not presented in user-agents and introduces a significant amount of overhead[2].

MIME representations may become very complex, and may take time to process on terminals with limited processing capabilities. To view all parts a MIME encoded message, the end clients must have support for displaying the presentation formats and attachments sent. In cases when the clients lack this support, MIME body parts will end up as unnecessary overhead. Again, adaptations must be done for mobile terminals.

4 XML Web Service for Mobile Email Access

Mail servers normally reside inside the corporate network, protected from the Internet by a firewall. To enable email access from mobile phones, the XML Web Service concept is found most suitable due to the ubiquity of the World Wide Web and the ability to traverse firewalls using SOAP [8] (Simple Object Access Protocol). SOAP can run over HTTP and use port 80, which is open on many firewalls facing the Internet.

The most straightforward solution is to expose the whole SMTP and IMAP/POP as Web Services. Each SMTP and IMAP/POP command is mapped to a Web Service method. In effect, each SMTP or IMAP/POP command is encapsulated in a SOAP message and transported to the WS client.

Advantage in this solution compared to Web/WAP solutions is that there are no overhead data specifying the appearance of the content. Compared to VPN, this solution is more robust due to the use of SOAP. SOAP has a more relaxed way to handle sessions. This involves that sessions may survive even if the link is goes down for a period of time.

The disadvantage is the numerous functional requirements that are put on the mobile phone. To access and retrieve mails, the WS client must be capable of understanding *all* the SMTP/IMAP/POP commands and communicating properly with the email Server. It must therefore be equipped both with a MUA (Mail User Agent) with full SMTP support as well as an IMAP/POP client. This functionality is put on top of the SOAP engine.

Other disadvantages are the high number of interactions and also the high amount of downloaded data that are needed. Each SOAP message adds overhead themselves through their headers, making messages exchanges excessively verbose. This is definitely not suitable in a wireless network with limited bandwidth.

---

[1] "X-headers" are custom headers for providing extra information about the email. Typically added by clients, virus and spam-scanners.

[2] In an example email we were able to strip the header size of an email from 2351 to 323 bytes removing unnecessary header entries.

5 XMMAP Mail Web Service

To overcome the limitations and insufficiencies of the straightforward email XML Web service presented in the previous section and to solve the major problems related to email access from mobile terminals, we introduce a protocol called XML Mobile eMail Access Protocol (XMMAP).

As mentioned, a minimum of 11 SMTP messages is required between the client and server just in order to send an email. This is highly undesirable when using a mobile terminal. Additionally, every message transfer introduces unnecessary overhead from underlying protocols. On top of this we have the considerations regarding overhead from unnecessary headers and presentation information.

The major benefit when using XMMAP is that it both combines and simplifies the functionality and information given by both the MTA (SMTP), Access Agent (IMAP/POP) and the representation format (SMTP-IMF/XMTP[9]). This is achieved by mapping the information into an XML format and tying different parts of the format to specific requests and responses to SOAP – functions.

Like XMTP, XMMAP utilizes the strength of XML to simplify parsing of the received information. The terminal can use an XML-parser for retrieving the information from the XMMAP-message as well as constructing new XML documents. This makes implementation of an XMMAP-compatible mail client a very simple task compared to a full-scale email client.

XMMAP introduces a new concept of messaging. While traditional protocols rely on frequent message transfers with well-defined operations, XMMAP is more flexible, making it possible to do most operations in *one* message exchange. It is also possible to define some custom options within the scope of the format.

5.1 XMMAP Data Format

XMMAP is in its basic form a representation of an entire mail account, spanning everything from login credentials to flags in a specific message. This makes it possible to use sub-parts of the XMMAP-format for representing different parts of a mail account for different purposes. This is especially useful when utilizing XMMAP for invoking functions on the mail server. When invoking a function, only the relevant subparts of the formats are sent, thus avoiding unnecessary overhead. Here follows a standard email message represented in XMMAP:

```
<Message
  xmlns=''http://www.finngard.org/2004/03/xmmap/''
  xmlns:web=''http://www.w3.org/1999/02/22-rdf-syntax-ns#''
  web:about=''mid:1078406317002232@lycos-europe.com''>
  <BoxNumber mailbox=''INBOX''>12</BoxNumber>
  <Headers>
    <From>johndoe@telenor.com</From>
    <To>&lt;finngard@finngard.org&gt;</To>
    <Subject>XMMAP, suitable for PDA?</Subject>
    <Date>Fri, 2 Mar 2004 12:23:12 -0700</Date>
  </Headers>
  <Flags protocol=''imap''>
    <Seen>1</Seen>
    <Answered>0</Answered>
  </Flags>
  <Body charset=''ISO-8859-1''>
```

```
  Hi! Do you suggest using the XMMAP format for PDAs?
 </Body>
 <Attachments>
  <Attachment
    content-type=''application/x-ms-word''
    encoding=''base64''>
   <AttachmentNumber>1</AttachmentNumber>
    <Filename>pda_description.doc</Filename>
    <Size>1345</Size>
    <Content>/9j/4AAQSkZJRgABAQEAYABgAAD.. </Content>
  </Attachment>
 </Attachments>
</Message>
```

XMMAP maps perfectly into a standard SMTP-IMF message, with or without MIME extensions, and vice versa. In addition to this, an XMMAP-message may supply information given by both POP3 and IMAP mail access protocols.

In order to represent an entire account, some additional elements are needed. These are also defined within the XMMAP data format.[3]

5.2 XMMAP Message Transfer

The XMMAP data format is useful for representing an account in a minimalist way, and may also be well suited for storage purposes. On the other hand, the data format lacks the coupling to specific functions related to mobile mail access. This coupling is achieved by defining SOAP – methods which receives and responds with messages in XMMAP format. The following set of methods is implemented so far:

Table 1. SOAP/XMMAP methods

SOAP/XMMAP Methods	
LoginMobileTermXMMAP	setFlagXMMAP
LoginProfileXMMAP	getMessagesAsXMMAP
GetHeadersAsXMMAP	sendMailXMMAP
GetMailboxesXMMAP	deleteXMMAP
GetNewHeadersAsXMMAP	logoutXMMAP

Request message example:
```
<Account>
      <UserName>jon</UserName>
      <PassWord>secret</PassWord
>
      <Host>imap.ntnu.no</Host>
      <Protocol>IMAPS</Protocol>
      <Port>443</Port>
</Account>
```

Response message example:
```
<Mailboxes>
   <Mailbox>
      <BoxName>INBOX</BoxName>
      <Unread>2</Unread>
      <Total>23</Total>
   </MailBox>
</Mailboxes>
```

The methods listed in Table 1 are the most important methods that can be implemented by coupling SOAP and XMMAP for email access on mobile terminals.

---

[3] Due to space limitations, a complete description of each element in XMMAP is not given in this paper.

All these methods have well defined requests and responses, all in XMMAP format. Some of the methods have additional SOAP parameters for system specific purposes.

However, the XMMAP format is flexible, and can be extended by new elements in any part of the format if necessary. There is no fixed order in how the current messages are sent after the user has logged in. When defining new methods, this principle should be followed in order to keep every message independent from both previous and succeeding messages.

5.3   XMMAP Web Service Architecture

As shown in Figure 2, the mobile terminal needs support for SOAP and J2ME[10], and must have a Mail User Agent (MUA) capable of XML document creation and parsing. The MUA is used for sending and receiving XMMAP messages. No support for any other mail protocols is needed. This makes the client implementation much simpler compared to other solutions that require full SMTP and Access Agent support.

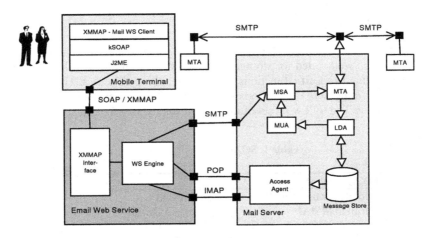

Fig. 2. Web Service Architecture

Figure 3 shows how the message exchanges are performed when sending a mail using the proposed architecture and XMMAP.

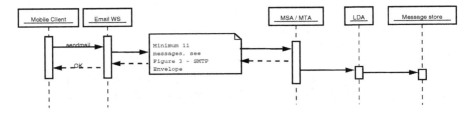

Fig. 3. Email messaging using XMMAP

5.4   Internal Web Service Functionality

As mentioned earlier, the XML Web Service will adapt the mail messages for mobile telephones and PDA's. In addition to removing unnecessary email headers, alternative representations of the same content (e.g. both plain text and HTML version of the message body) are reduced to one. Attachments are by default kept back until the user specifically asks to get them. These actions keep the amount of data transmitted on a minimum, which is important when having low bandwidth. A summary of the internal functionality offered of the XML Web Service (see Figure 2):

- SMTP-IMF to XMMAP gateway and vice versa.
- IMAP/POP to XMMAP gateway and vice versa.
- User authentication.
- User profile management.
- Session management for all interfaces and related active connections.
- Content adaptation. This includes everything from tag and attachment stripping to picture resizing.
- Optional: Local caching of messages and attachments.
- Provide necessary interfaces.

6   Conclusion

In this paper, we propose a solution that enables mail access from mobile terminals based on XML Web Service concept and a protocol called XMMAP (XML Mobile eMail Access Protocol). Such a solution has several advantages as follows:

- Our solution gives fewer message transfers between client and server, and less interaction gives better performance for low-bandwidth devices.
- Since only the message related information is delivered to the client, messages can be stored on the device. This cannot be done as easy and well arranged when accessing email accounts via e.g. webmail.
- The content is automatically adapted to fit the terminal by using information sent by the client software about display dimensions and color support etc. Unnecessary information is stripped away by the web service before replying to the client.
- Session timeout is a problem when working with services requiring authentication. Especially when accessing the Internet via a GPRS (General Packet Radio Service) network, the GPRS/Internet gateways tend to have short timeout periods. Reestablishment after a timeout often implies assignment of a different IP address, making all session on higher layers invalid. This problem is solved when using SOAP sessions, ensuring session mobility.
- Firewalls are no longer an issue, since all mail traffic can pass through SOAP messages.[4]

---

[4] This is of course only true if the corporate firewall allows global WWW access (when using HTTP as transport protocol).

The combined use of an XML web service and XMMAP makes a simple and flexible email solution for mobile users. XMMAP allows for a minimal client footprint and uses less bandwidth than other solutions.

References

1. XML Web Service. http://www.w3.org/2002/ws/
2. SMTP Simple Mail Transfer Protocol http://www.ietf.org/rfc/rfc2822.txt
3. IMAP Internet Mail Access Protocol http://www.ietf.org/rfc/rfc2060.txt
4. POP Post Office Protocol http://www.ietf.org/rfc/rfc1939.txt
5. MIME Multipurpose Internet Mail Extensions http://www.ietf.org/rfc/rfc1521.txt
6. WAP Specifications http://www.wapforum.org/what/technical.htm
7. VPN Virtual Private Networks Standards http://www.vpnc.org/vpn-standards.html
8. SOAP Specification. http://www.w3.org/TR/soap/
9. XMTP, XML MIME Transformation Protocol.
   http://www.openhealth.org/documents/xmtp.htm
10. J2ME Java 2 Micro Edition http://java.sun.com/j2me
11. Sivertsen, E., Moe, J-F., Søvik, A: Master Thesis, Institute of Telematics, Norwegian University of Science and Technology: "E-mail Access Using XML Web Services" (2004). http://xmmap.nta.no/report.pdf.

Design Architecture and Model of MDVM System

Susmit Bagchi

Department of Computer and Information Science,
Norwegian University of Science and Technology (NTNU)
Trondheim, Norway
susmit@idi.ntnu.no

Abstract. The realization of high-end mobile applications, such as virtual organization (VO), are becoming reality due to the enhanced wireless communication bandwidth, reliability and services offered by WWW. However, the general-purpose operating systems are not completely capable to handle the challenges of mobile computing paradigm. The novel concept of mobile distributed virtual memory (MDVM) extends the server CPU and memory resources to the mobile clients over the mobile communication interface in the VO framework. In this paper, the architecture and associated model of MDVM system are described.

Keywords: Mobile computing, Operating Systems, Virtual Memory, Distributed Computing.

1 Introduction

Mobile computing is becoming a reality due to the availability of portable computing devices having access to WWW [9]. The mobile computing paradigm has created a set of high-end mobile applications such as, m-commerce, SES [6] and virtual organization [7], which need the support of operating system to meet the challenges offered by mobile computing paradigm. Due to the limitation in battery power, mobile devices are limited in hardware resources [11] and operate in doze mode to reduce power requirement [2][10]. The existing wireless communication technology is restricted in terms of bandwidth and reliability [10]. Because of these restrictions, mobile computers limit the nature of user applications [2][10]. The existing operating systems offer very little support for managing and adapting to the mobile computation paradigm [1][3]. The trends in future technological advancements indicate that the wireless communication bandwidth and reliability will be enhanced [6]. Researchers argue that resource-thin mobile computers should utilize remote server based resources in order to support mobile applications [4][5]. It is reported that the remote memory on servers could be utilized in mobile computing system [8]. As a novel approach, the concept of mobile distributed virtual memory (MDVM) is introduced to enable mobile clients exploiting server resources using mobile communication network [13]. The MDVM system will reduce the resource constraints of mobile

A. Aagesen et al. (Eds.): INTELLCOMM 2004, LNCS 3283, pp. 207–219, 2004.

devices to a great extent, and will help to realize a set of mobile applications in virtual organization framework [13]. The MDVM system allows mobile clients to utilize server CPU and memory for data cache and process execution purposes [13]. In virtual organization architecture, mobile clients can utilize server memory as a large and reliable data cache. On the other hand, mobile clients can use server CPU, virtual memory and other devices by initiating remote processes on the server. The prior works on remote paging to realize distributed virtual memory (DVM) aim to utilize the high-speed network for paging rather than the local disk space assuming static network topology. Such assumptions are not applicable to MDVM system. Unlike the monolithic kernel-based MDVM system, the DVM system designs base on the user-space pager server of microkernel architecture. Researchers have directed to modify the kernel of operating system to handle the challenges of mobile computing in an efficient manner [12]. The MDVM design considers the monolithic kernel of a general-purpose operating system. The monolithic kernel architecture offers enhanced performance as compared to the microkernel by reducing context switch frequency, TLB misses and instruction count [15]. The inclusion of MDVM within the kernel offers the benefits of user transparency, performance, flexibility and greater control on system resources. This paper describes the architecture and an abstract model of MDVM system. We are currently designing and implementing the MDVM system in Linux kernel 2.4.22. The paper is organized as followings. The trends in future technological directions in mobile communication and devices along with their limitations are described in section 2. Section 3 introduces the MDVM system architecture. Section 4 describes the model of the MDVM system. Section 5 and 6 state the background work and conclusion respectively.

2   Technological Trends and Limits

The trend in the modern computer industry is to produce mobile computers [14]. Due to rapid development in hardware technology, the mobile computers are getting equipped with powerful microprocessors, high-speed network capabilities and other resources. The next generation mobile communication technology will be 3G and 4G as proposed in industry such as NTT DoCoMo [6]. The proposed capabilities of 3G and 4G mobile communication technologies are described in Table 1 [13]. The 3G and 4G mobile communication technology will offer significantly higher wireless communication bandwidth and reliability as compared to 2.5G [6]. A set of restrictions that would exist in future is: *(1) Limitation of computing time and peripheral devices due to power consumption [8], (2) Unavailability of secondary storage as a peripheral of mobile devices, (3) Performance limitation of FLASH memory, (4) Physical specifications of mobile devices are to be lightweight and small in size,* and *(5) The cost of wireless communication bandwidth is high.* The MDVM concept extends the server resources to mobile clients using mobile communication interface to reduce the resource constraints of mobile devices.

Table 1. 3G and 4G Mobile Communication Technology Capabilities

Technology	3rd Generation (3G)	4th Generation (4G)
Speed	384Kbps – 2Mbps	100Mbps
Applications	Voice, email, video-on-demand, multimedia	Voice, high-speed internet access, high-resolution video, IPv6

3   MDVM System Architecture

3.1   Dynamic Server-Group

The MDVM design concept considers a group of servers connected by high-speed wired network residing within the cells. The servers offer MDVM as services to mobile clients through the wireless network. The MDVM servers form a server-group (SG) as shown in Figure 1. Individual servers in a SG serve the mobile clients in the corresponding cell. The members of a SG elect a leader and co-leader to perform the periodic tasks in a SG. Such tasks are comprised of keeping the overall status of the SG-members, resource allocation history and to keep the replica of storage segments of MDVM located on other members of SG as a fault tolerance mechanism. The co-leader assumes the responsibility of the leader if the leader crashes. This eliminates the necessity of "*stop and leader-reelection*" in the system at any point of time due to leader crash. On the other hand, the co-leader shares the load on a leader eliminating the problem of central point of load concentration along with the saturation of network bandwidth around the leader. The members of a SG are required to handle the memory migration from another SG requiring inter-SG communication system. The 4G mobile networks standard supports protocol conversion techniques. This enables the two SGs to communicate using TCP/IP protocol stack over the high bandwidth wired link.

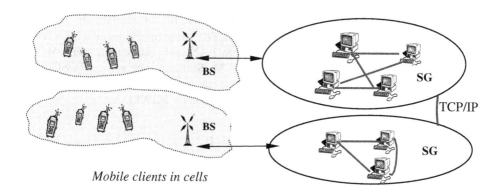

Mobile clients in cells

Fig. 1. The Server Groups and Mobile Clients

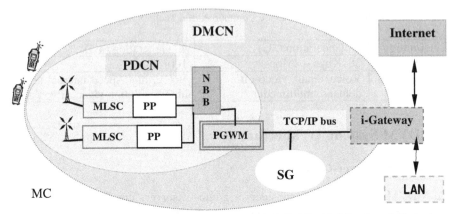

PDCN: *Packet Data Communication Network*, MLSC: *Mobile Local Switch Center*, PP: *Packet Processor*, NBB: *Network Backbone*, PGWM: *Packet Gateway Module*.

Fig. 2. The SG Embedded into Cellular Network

3.2 SG in Cellular Network

The architecture of mobile communication network containing MDVM servers is shown in Figure 2. The system architecture is consisting of mobile clients (MC) and stationary servers. The stationary servers of SG are placed in the Digital Mobile Communication Network (DMCN) on the TCP/IP bus. According to the IMT-2000 standard [6] the DMCN has capability to support TCP/IP network stack and protocol conversions. The servers in SG are interconnected by high-speed wired TCP/IP network and reside in between i-Gateway and PGWM. The PGWM interfaces TCP/IP bus and NBB. The job of NBB is to support the basic cellular communication system backbone. The data packet processing in the mobile communication system is handled by PP and MLSC. The BS in a cell is connected to NBB via MLSC. In 3G and higher mobile communication standard, the DMCN has capability to interface the Internet servers using special server i-Gateways using TCP/IP protocol. Hence, the MCs may communicate to the MDVM servers, corporate LAN and web servers via DMCN using the TCP/IP interface controlled by PGWM. Similarly, the servers in SG can reach corporate LAN and Internet via i-Gateway interface. The inter-SG communication is based on TCP/IP interface controlled by PGWM.

4 Placing MDVM in Monolithic Kernel

The MDVM is designed as a dynamically loadable kernel-module functioning as a kernel subsystem. No special hardware is involved with the design of MDVM system. MDVM device architecture creates the infrastructure within the monolithic kernel to exploit CPU and memory resources by offering them to the mobile clients. This indicates that MDVM, as a software subsystem, can be treated as a capability enhancement of a monolithic kernel to suit it in the mobile computing paradigm. The architecture of a typical monolithic kernel containing MDVM system is shown in Figure 3.

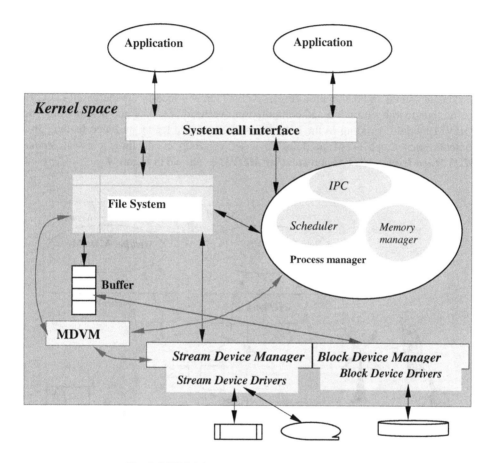

Fig. 3. MDVM System within a Monolithic Kernel

The mobile clients may need small amount of data access such as a byte or they may need to access larger chunk of data such as multiple pages. This requires MDVM system having capability of byte addressing and page addressing. A byte is considered as 8bit data and the memory page size is typically considered as 4KB. According to the concept of server-group, a set of resource-fat servers resides within each cell of mobile communication architecture connected by high-speed wired network supporting TCP/IP protocol stack. The MDVM system software module is placed within the kernel of all the servers offering MDVM services. The MDVM modules, as active entities in a cell, form the logical ring topology for communication and resource management purposes as shown in Figure 4. The mobile clients may reach the MDVM modules utilizing interface of protocol conversion supported by 3G and 4G communications standard. On the other hand, a MDVM module can communicate to other MDVM module using TCP/IP protocol over wired network. The messages among MDVM modules and mobile clients are mainly comprised of two types. These are the short message data packets and relatively large memory pages. The MDVM system servers consider the page size of 4KB. This is because the maximum transmission unit (MTU) of the packets over TCP/IP Ethernet link is in the order of 1.5KB. The larger the page size, the more are the fragmentation and joining of packets at source and destination respectively. This will lead to the increased network traffic, bandwidth saturation and computation overhead at source and destination. The MDVM modules residing in the kernel of servers elect a leader and a co-leader. This indicates that the MDVM modules in a server-group create three classes: *leader MDVM, co-leader MDVM* and *member MDVM* as shown in Figure 4.

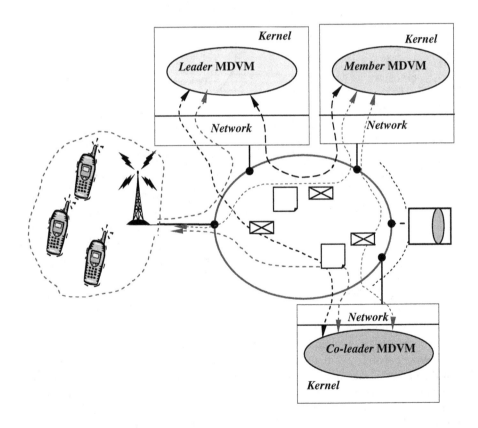

Fig. 4. MDVM System Network

The member MDVM modules offer the memory and CPU resources of the local servers to the mobile clients. The leader and co-leader MDVM modules maintain the replica of storage segment pages of MDVM offered by the member modules on the local disk. In addition, the leader module and co-leader module maintain the information about the operational status of the ring such as, number of active servers in a ring and the resource-loads on the servers. The update of such information is done periodically by *members-initiated* manner. The co-leader MDVM module of a ring automatically assumes the responsibility of the leader on the detection that the leader MDVM server is crashed. This will eliminate the necessity of complete system halt in order to elect a new leader in the ring on the face of leader failure. The election of the new co-leader will be started as soon as the former co-leader will assume the job of the leader. The election of a new co-leader can be done concurrently without halting all the members in the ring. In addition, the leader module diverts a part of the traffic to the co-leader if the load on the leader crosses a certain pre-computed threshold. This in a way increases the data cache availability due to the fact that the co-leaders also maintain a copy of the replica of cache pages handed over by the leader periodically. The communication paths involved in the MDVM system architecture can be between the two MDVM modules in the ring or between a module and the mobile clients as shown in Figure 4.

4.1 Required Kernel Subsystems

The MDVM system offers CPU and memory resources of the server to the mobile clients. In order to utilize memory efficiently, the MDVM system swaps cache pages to the local disk according to the page access patterns of mobile clients. It is better to swap the cache pages held in RAM on the local disk in order to free the page frames if the mobile clients holding such cache are inactive for sufficiently long time. The MDVM module uses RAM, CPU, network device and disk drive of a system in order to perform the required tasks. The kernel of the operating systems running on mobile devices map a part of the virtual memory as remote pages accessible through wireless communication network. The monolithic kernel of the server operating system can be subdivided in a number of subsystems: memory manager (MM), file system (FS), scheduler, process dispatcher (Exec), block device manager and stream device manager. The MDVM system module is placed within the kernel of the server operating system having interfaces to MM, FS, scheduler and network device. The access to the network device is designed by using the stream device manager interface because the network device is a class of stream device. The diagram showing interfaces between MDVM subsystem and the other subsystems of a monolithic kernel is depicted in Figure 5. The MDVM MM subsystem maintains the interface with the process scheduler in order to estimate CPU load, schedule a remote process execution and control or monitor the state of execution of remote processes started by mobile clients. The estimation of memory-load is done periodically. The interface with memory manager is used to allocate page frames to the mobile clients for the data cache. Because of the higher disk access latency, the cache pages of active clients will be prevented from being swapped out by the virtual memory manager of the kernel. The swapping of cache pages are done by the MDVM system based on the page access pattern of mobile clients. Hence, the interface to the local FS is required by the MDVM system in order to manage the swap space on local disk separately from that of the swap space managed by the virtual memory manager of kernel. The interface between the network device and MDVM will be required to maintain network communication activities using TCP/IP on wired network. The wired network to the wireless network protocol conversion is handled by the cellular communication infrastructure.

4.2 Modelling MDVM Architecture

The memory management system of the operating systems can be modelled with abstract and precise formalism in order to represent the design architecture [39][40]. The abstract modeling of the system architecture and memory management mechanisms allow the generalization of the concept and the easiness of understanding without tying up to a particular kind of implementation [38][39][40]. In this section, the abstract model of the MDVM system architecture is formulated. One of the main components of the MDVM system architecture is the server group (SG). Each server in a SG offers a set of pages from its virtual address space to the mobile clients in order to fulfil the storage and execution space needs of the clients. Let, the set of server groups in a MDVM system architecture is represented by S_g such that, $S_g = \{g_1, g_2, ...g_b\}$. There is no constraint on the $|g_i|$ meaning that $\forall g_i, g_j \in S_g$, either $|g_i| = |g_j|$ or $|g_i| \neq |g_j|$. Let z be a MDVM server and $z \in g_i$. Let $V_z = \langle 0, 1, 2, ...,G\text{-}1 \rangle$ is the set of virtual addresses available at z. The virtual address spaces can be segmented or paged. The MDVM system design model considers the paged virtual memory management system. A page p_z is consisting of a set of addresses $E_z = \{e_j \mid 0 \leq j < |p_z|\}$ residing at z such that $p_z \subset V_z$. Let n_z represents the total number of virtual memory pages available at z. The page frames of a system are generally numbered and indexed in the page frame table. If all the page frames of z are numbed by f then, $\forall e_j \in E_z$, $e_j = f. |p_z| + q$, $0 \leq q < |p_z|$ and $f = 0$, 1, 2, ..., h. Hence, a page p_z residing at z can be given by the ordered pair $\langle f, q \rangle$. The address map is the function to translate the virtual addresses into the physical memory addresses. Let β_t is such a function translating the memory addresses for the entire time space t. Then, β_t can be computed as, $\beta_t: v_z \rightarrow \langle f, q \rangle \cup \{\phi\}$ where $v_z \subseteq V_z$. The set of page frames residing at z can be given as, $P^z_M = \{p_w \mid 0 \leq w \leq m\text{-}1, m>0\}$. According to the definition of the virtual memory, the set of virtual address pages available at z can be computed as, $P^z_V = P^z_M \cup S_z$ and $|P^z_V| = n_z$. The set of pages $S_z = \{d_0, d_1, ...,d_{u-1}\}$ represents the swap space at MDVM server z, where $u = n_z - |P^z_M| + 1$. If the function $r(g_i)$ computes the total amount of virtual memory resource of the server group $g_i \in S_g$ then, $r(g_i) = \cup_{i=1, c} P^i_V$ such that $c = |g_i|$.

A MDVM server of a SG residing in a cell is capable to handle multiple mobile clients in the corresponding cell. Let C_z represents a set of mobile clients that are using MDVM at the server z and k is such a mobile client, $k \in C_z$. The MDVM request from k consists of process execution request and the request for data cache pages. The MDVM request from k is composed of $\langle \alpha^r_k, v^c_k \rangle$, where α^r_k is the set of virtual address spaces of the requested execution of the remote process r and v^c_k is the

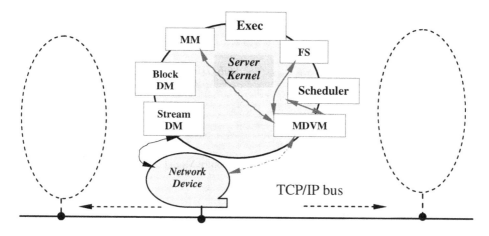

Fig. 5. Interfaces between MDVM Device and Monolithic Kernel Subsystems

set of requested virtual pages for data cache. The architecture of MDVM system is comprised of two components. These are a kernel-stub (D) and a kernel-server (T) as shown in Figure 6. The D and T have interface among each other and can avail services from kernel through the kernel interface. The MDVM system can be modelled as a list of mapping functions given by $\langle \delta_D, \{\delta^P_T, \delta^C_T\} \rangle$. The δ_D and δ^C_T map the data cache pages for a mobile client and the δ^P_T maps the virtual addresses for process execution on MDVM servers as requested by the client. The definitions of the δ_D and δ^P_T functions are given as, $\delta_D : P^z_V \rightarrow P^z_M$ and $\delta^P_T : P^z_V \rightarrow (\alpha^r_k \times P^z_V) \cup \{\phi\}$ such that, $\beta_t(\alpha \subseteq \alpha^r_k) \in p_z$ and $p_z \in P^z_M$. Let $B \in [0, 1]$ represents the state of the set of cache pages of k maintained at z. The values in B indicate whether the data cache pages are swappable or not. The values in B make it possible to either realize a binary logic or a multi-valued logic to recognize the state of the cache pages. Suppose, the function f^C_T is performed by T for the cache pages such that $f^C_T : v^c_k \rightarrow (\{\delta_D(v^c_k)\} \cup L) \times B$, where $L \subset P^z_M \cup \{\phi\}$. The symbol L signifies a set of page frames that are mapped by D but not used by T. Hence, L can be considered as a list of mapped free page frames. The list is maintained in order to enhance the memory utilization by keeping track of the previously mapped but unused page frames, if any. Suppose, at time instant t, $L \neq \phi$. This indicates that in the next time space t+, the memory map performed by δ_D and the residue in L cannot be overlapped, i.e. $\{\delta_D(v^c_k)\} \cap L = \phi$. Due to the mobility and limitation of battery power of clients or due to the change in the state of the wireless communication, a mobile client may go into doze mode or may get disconnected from the MDVM server z. Let H_z is the set of disk swap spaces at z maintained by T, $H_z \not\subset S_z$. Then, the function f^S_T is defined as, $f^S_T : P^z_M \times B \rightarrow H_z$. Thus, the cache page map of MDVM system, δ^C_T, can be realized as a composition of functions given by $(f^S_T \circ f^C_T)$. In the time space t, the virtual memory v^c_k may reside in page frames or in disk swap space depending on the state of the mobile client.

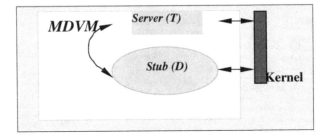

Fig. 6. MDVM Architecture Model

4.3 Memory Utilization Versus Page Fault Frequency

The page fault is a phenomenon that occurs when a process tries to access a page not resident in main memory. The mobile clients in C_z can request a set of pages for the data cache. Let, n is the number of pages requested by a mobile client. If n = 1, then a single page fault will be enough to allocate a page frame to the client. However, for n>1 there may exist two possible outcomes. Suppose, m = log₂n for some m∈ Z, m>0. In this case, mapping of n pages will incur n page faults if the memory manager allocates a single page frame at a time. However, the modern operating systems allow the buddy allocation algorithm where n number of such page frames would be allocated in a single page fault. On the other hand, if p = log₂n and m = $\lceil p \rceil$ where p∈ R⁺, then allocating n pages one by one will still incur n page faults. On the contrary, use of buddy algorithm will create the possibility of memory under-utilization as n<2ᵐ. The amount of under-utilization is (2ᵐ – n). The list L can hold (2ᵐ – n) pages for future use. The page fault frequency (PFF) is considered as the deterrent to the overall system performance. Hence, to reduce PFF to a lower level, δ_D may map 2ᵐ page frames, and T may maintain list L. The T may try to utilize the page frames from L in subsequent future requests until L = φ. It is interesting to note that if |L| becomes very large, then it may lead to considerable amount of the memory waste although the PFF will be reduced substantially. Hence, the memory management algorithm employed in MDVM system should try to balance the reduction of PFF and enhancement of the memory resource utilization by keeping |L| as much low as possible while reducing PFF.

5   Related Work

Prior works have addressed the issues in operating system related to mobility in the area of file systems [16][17][18], data management [19][11][20][21] and network-layer routing protocols addressing schemes and packet filtering [22][23][24]. Other works include issues related to caching and file system [16][18][25][26] and mobile communication system [27][28][29]. The existing DVM system [30] does not provide an easy way to dynamically use and share DVM resources preserving transparency, adaptability and extensibility [31]. The DVM system becomes non-scalable under the condition of mobility of clients. The DVM system design bases on the external pager-server in the microkernel. The remote paging concept employed in DVM assumes that network bandwidth is high and network topology is static and both the clients/servers are equipped with adequate RAM and disk drive. Such assumptions are not applicable in the MDVM system design. The bandwidth of existing disk drives is lower than that of high-speed network [14][32][33]. The aim of existing DVM system is to investigate the performance gain through remote paging over high-speed network. Hence, the performance of existing DVM systems is controlled by the network performance [32]. The majority of the remote memory paging system ([32][33][34][35]) and the DVM system ([30][31][37][34][36]) target to the stationary client-server architectures on wired LAN. However, the issues related to the location transparency of the remote memory under mobility, virtual memory management under dynamic memory-pressure and virtual memory migration among servers are not investigated. The concept of MDVM extending the server resources to the mobile clients did not get much attention. It is important to make operating system kernel "mobility aware" to tackle challenges of mobile computing. Unlike microkernel, the monolithic kernel offers enhanced overall system performance.

6 Conclusion

The MDVM system is intended to meet the resource constraints of the mobile devices by extending server resources to the mobile clients over wireless communication network. The system architecture, placing the MDVM servers in mobile communication framework, is outlined. The designing of MDVM in monolithic kernel will provide user transparency, performance, greater control on system resources and required system services. The required subsystems of a monolithic kernel in order to design MDVM as a software module are outlined. An abstract model of the MDVM system architecture is constructed. The Linux operating system is chosen for building experimental prototype of MDVM system because it is a monolithic kernel, free source and comparable to other commercial operating systems in terms of efficiency. We are currently implementing various building blocks of MDVM system in Linux kernel 2.4.22.

References

[1] Black A., Inouye J., System Support for Mobility, ACM SIGOPS, Ireland, 1996.
[2] Duchamp D., Issues in Wireless Mobile Computing, 3rd Workshop on Workstation OS, 1992.
[3] Bolosky W. et. al., OS Direction for the Next Millennium, Microsoft Research, Redmond.
[4] Forman G., Zahorjan J., The Challenges of Mobile Computing, UW CSE TR#93-11-03, 1994.
[5] Marsh B. et. al., Systems Issues in Mobile Computing, MITL-TR-50-93, Princeton, 1993.
[6] Nadia M., Kin Y., Designing Wireless Enterprise Applications on Mobile Devices, ICITA 2002.
[7] MOWAHS, IDI, NTNU, 2003, www.mowahs.com.

[8] Shigemori Y. et. al., A proposal of a Memory Management Architecture for Mobile Computing Environment, IEEE DEXA, 2000.

[9] Weiser M., Some Computer Issues in Ubiquitous Computing, ACM Communications, 1993.

[10] Pitoura E. et. al., Dealing with Mobility: Issues and Research Challenges, TR-CSD-93-070, 1993.

[11] Badrinath R. et. al., Impact of Mobility on Distributed Computations, ACM OS Review, 1993.

[12] Bender M. et. al., Unix for Nomads: Making Unix Support Mobile Computing, USENIX, Mobile & Location-Independent Computing Symposium, 1993.

[13] Susmit B., Mads N., On the Concept of Mobile Distributed Virtual Memory System, IEEE DSN, International Conference on Dependable Systems and Networks, Italy, 2004.

[14] Schilit B., Duchamp D., Adaptive Remote Paging for Mobile Computers, TR-CUCS-004-91, Columbia University, February 1991.

[15] Chen B., The Impact of Software Structure and Policy on CPU and Memory System Performance, PhD Thesis, CMU-CS-94-145, 1994.

[16] Tait D. et. al., Detection and Exploitation of File Working Sets, TR-CUCS-050-90, Columbia, 1990.

[17] Kistler J., Satyanarayanan M., Disconnected Operation in the Coda File System, ACM Transactions on Computer Systems, February, 1992.

[18] Tait D., Duchamp D., Service Interface and Replica Management Algorithm for Mobile File System Clients, 1st International Conference on Parallel and Distributed Information Systems, 1991.

[19] Badrinath R., Tomasz I., Replication and Mobility, In Proc. Of 2nd IEEE Workshop on Management of Replicated Data, November 1992, pp. 9-12.

[20] Alonso R., Korth H., Database System Issues in Nomadic Computing, MITL, December 1992.

[21] Tomasz I., Badrinath R., Querying in Highly Mobile Distributed Environments, In 8th International Conference on Very Large Databases, 1992, pp. 41-52.

[22] Ioannidis J., Duchamp D., Maguire G., IP-Based Protocols for Mobile Internetworking, ACM SIGCOMM, September 1991, pp. 235-245.

[23] Wada H. et. al., Mobile Computing Environment Based on Internet Packet Forwarding, In Winter USENIX, January, 1993.

[24] Zenel B., Duchamp D., Intelligent Communication Filtering for Limited Bandwidth Environments, IEEE 5th Workshop on HotOS-V, May 1995.

[25] Mummert L. et. al., Variable Granularity Cache Coherence, Operating Systems Review, 28(1), 1994, pp. 55-60.

[26] Mummert L., Exploiting Weak Connectivity in a Distributed File System, PhD Thesis, CMU, 1996.

[27] Lin C., An Architecture for a Campus-Sized Wireless Mobile Network, PhD Thesis, Purdue, 1996.

[28] Lee J., Routing and Multicasting Strategies in Wireless Mobile Ad Hoc Network, PhD thesis, California, 2000.

[29] Akyol B., An Architecture for a Future Wireless ATM Network, PhD Thesis, Stanford, June 1997.

[30] Khalidi Y. et. al., The Spring Virtual Memory System, Sun Microsystem Lab., TR-SMLI-93-9, February 1993.

[31] Ballesteros F. et. al., Adaptable and Extensible Distributed Virtual Memory in the Off Microkernel, TR-UC3M-CS-1997-02, Madrid, January 1997.

[32] Markatos E. et. al., Implementation of a Reliable Remote Memory Pager, In Proc. Of USENIX, San Diego, January, 1996.

[33] Liviu I. et. al., Memory Servers for Multicomputers, In Proc. Of 38th IEEE COMPCON, Spring 1993.

[34] Feeley M. et. al., Implementing Global Memory Management in a Workstation Cluster, 15th SOSP, 1995, pp. 130-146.

[35] McDonald I., Remote Paging in a Single Address Space Operating System Supporting Quality of Service, Technical Report, Glasgow, October 1999.

[36] McKusick M. et. al., A New Virtual Memory Implementation for Berkeley UNIX, Computer Systems Research Group, Univ. of California, Berkeley, 1986.

[37] Ballesteros J. et. al., An Adaptable and Extensible Framework for Distributed Object Management, In Proc. of ECOOP'96, Workshop on Mobility and Replication, Austria, 1996.

[38] Gary N., Operating Systems, 3rd Edition, Addison Wesley, 2004, pp. 152-154, 773.

[39] Liedtke J., On μ-kernel Construction, 15th ACM Symposium on Operating Systems Principles, SOSP, Colorado, December 1995.

[40] Greg M. et. al., Abstract Models of Memory Management, In the Proc. Of 7th International Conference on Functional Programming Languages and Computer Architecture, La Jolla, 1995.

About the Heterogeneity of Web Prefetching Performance Key Metrics[1]

Josep Domènech, Julio Sahuquillo, José A. Gil, and Ana Pont

Department of Computer Engineering (DISCA),
Polytechnic University of Valencia, Spain
jodode@doctor.upv.es, {jsahuqui, jagil,apont}@disca.upv.es

Abstract. Web prefetching techniques have pointed to be especially important to reduce web latencies and, consequently, an important set of works can be found in the open literature. But, in general, it is not possible to do a fair comparison among the proposed prefetching techniques due to three main reasons: i) the underlying baseline system where prefetching is applied differs widely among the studies; ii) the workload used in the presented experiments is not the same; iii) different performance key metrics are used to evaluate their benefits.

This paper focuses on the third reason. Our main concern is to identify which the main meaningful indexes are when studying the performance of different prefetching techniques. For this purpose, we propose a taxonomy based in three categories, which permits us to identify analogies and differences among the indexes commonly used. In order to check, in a more formal way, the relation between them, we run experiments and estimate statistically the correlation among a representative subset of those metrics. The statistical results help us to suggest which indexes should be selected when performing evaluation studies depending on the different elements in the considered web architecture.

The choice of the appropriate key metric is of paramount importance for a correct and representative study. As our experimental results show, depending on the metric used to check the system performance, results can not only widely vary but also reach opposite conclusions.

1 Introduction

The international and global nature of Internet makes arduous (or sometimes really impossible) to increase the system performance working in the networks and their interconnection elements because of the existing gap of time between technological advances in infrastructure and its use in the real life. As a consequence, research efforts have been concentrated on the web architecture and organization using and exporting techniques already learned and widely used in computer architecture to improve the performance.

Those techniques take advantage of the locality properties inherent to the web objects accesses. In the Web, the locality has three different characteristics: temporal, spatial and geographical, which permits to implement efficiently caching, prefetching

---

[1] This work has been supported by Spanish Government Grant TIC2001-1374-C03-02.

A. Aagesen et al. (Eds.): INTELLCOMM 2004, LNCS 3283, pp. 220–235, 2004.

and replication techniques in order to increase performance. As a result, many efforts (commercial and research) applying those techniques in the Web architecture have been carried out to increase performance.

In this paper we focus on prefetching techniques, although some of our studies and conclusions presented in this paper can also be extended to the general web performance analysis.

Many research studies concentrate on the proposals of new prefetching techniques. Performance comparison studies among them can not be fairly done because the proposed approaches are applied and tested in different baseline systems using also different workloads and conditions. In addition, the studies present different performance key metrics to evaluate their benefits.

In order to do fair performance comparison studies we need to tackle the mentioned drawbacks. To deal with the first drawback in a previous work we proposed [1] a general experimental framework which permits the implementation of prefetching techniques in a flexible and easy way, under the same platform and real workloads; therefore, the same experimental conditions can be considered.

In this paper, we address our work to tackle with the second drawback. To this end, we analyze a large subset of key metrics and propose a taxonomy based in three main categories, which permits us to identify analogies and differences among the metrics commonly used and check experimentally their relation.

The remainder of this paper is organized as follows. Section 2 describes a generic web prefetching system in order to set the basic glossary of terms that will be used in the remaining sections. Section 3 presents the proposed taxonomy for prefetching performance metrics. Section 4 illustrates the usefulness of the different metrics with some experimental examples and finally, section 5 includes some concluding remarks.

2 Generic Prefetch Architecture and Basic Glossary

We assume a generic web architecture composed by three main elements: clients, servers and proxies. Note that proxies act both as a client for the server and as a server for the client.

It is important to remark the difference between the user and the client. The user is the person in front of a computer (or a similar device) demanding information, whereas the client is the software (i.e., the browser) with which the user interacts, that manages the search and request of the demanded information to the appropriate server.

The main aim of prefetching techniques is to reduce the average latency perceived by the user. Several prefetching related techniques have been proposed focusing on different ideas to exploit the benefits of the prefetch; for instance: some research studies propose clients to download objects prior to be requested by the user [2],[3], [4],[5]; other studies propose to preprocess dynamic content [6]; some others concentrate on how to make pre-connections to server [7]; and so on. All prefetching related techniques start predicting or trying to guess the next objects the client will access to. This part of prefetch is usually referred as the prediction engine. Then, the prediction results are submitted to the prefetching engine, which decides whether to prefetch or not such results, depending on other parameters; e.g., available bandwidth or server load. Notice that both the prediction engine and the prefetching engine can be found in the same element (client, proxy or server). We define below some basic variables that will be used in section 3:

- *Predictions*: amount of predicted objects by the prediction engine.
- *Prefetchs*: amount of prefetched objects by the prefetching engine.
- *GoodPredictions*: amount of predicted objects that are subsequently demanded by the user.
- *BadPredictions*: those predictions that not result in good predictions.
- *PrefetchHits*: amount of the prefetched objects that are subsequently demanded by the user.
- *ObjectsNotUsed*: amount of prefetched objects never demanded by the user.
- *UserRequests*: amount of objects the user demands.

Analogously, we can define byte related variables ($Predictions_B$, $Prefetchs_B$, and so on) by replacing the objects by the corresponding size in bytes in their definition.

3   Web Performance Indexes Taxonomy

This section surveys the web performance indexes appeared in the open literature focusing on prefetch aspects. To the better understanding of the meaning of those indexes, we classify them into three main categories (see Figure 1), attending to the system feature they evaluate:

- Category 1: prediction related indexes.
- Category 2: resource usage indexes.
- Category 3: end-to-end perceived latencies indexes.

The first category is the main one when comparing prediction algorithms performance and includes those indexes which quantify both the efficiency and the efficacy of the algorithm (e.g., precision). The second category quantifies the additional cost that prefetching incurs (e.g., traffic increase or processor time). This cost may become really high; thus, it must be taken into account when comparing prefetching techniques, thus those indexes can be seen as complementary measures. Finally, the third category summarizes the performance achieved by the system from the user point of view. Notice that prefetching techniques must take care of the cost increase because they can negatively impact on the overall system performance (traffic increase, user perceived latencies). Therefore, the three categories are closely related since in order to achieve a good overall performance (category 3) prefetching systems must trade off the aggressiveness of the algorithm (category 1) and the cost increase due to prefetching (category 2).

Different definitions for the same index can be found in the literature (e.g., precision) and this fact increases the heterogeneity of the research efforts. In order to make more readable this survey, we only include the definition we consider more precise and appropriate for evaluation purposes. In the cases where several names match the same definition, we select the most appropriate index name our point of view. The goal of this section is not only to help the understanding of the indexes but also to discuss their usefulness, distinguishing those used for comparison purposes in any prefetching systems from those applicable to a particular prefetching technique (i.e. specific). Specific indexes are only found in the Category 1 (Prediction), as shown in Figure 1.

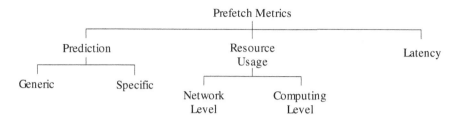

Fig. 1. Prefetching metrics taxonomy

3.1 Prediction Related Indexes

This group includes those indexes aimed at quantifying the performance that the prediction algorithm provides. Prediction performance can be measured at different moments, for instance when the algorithm makes the prediction and when prefetching is applied in the real system. Thus, each index in this category has a *dual* index; e.g., we can refer to precision of the algorithm and precision of prefetch. Notice that those indexes measured when the prediction list is given do not take into account system latencies because the prediction algorithm works independently of the underlying network and the user restrictions.

3.1.1 Generic Indexes

Precision (Pc). *Precision* measures the ratio of good predictions to the number of predictions [8],[9],[10],[11] (see equation 1). Precision, defined in this way, just evaluates the algorithm without considering physical system restrictions; e.g., cache, network or time restrictions; therefore, it can be seen as a theoretical index.

Other research studies refer to this index as *Accuracy* [4],[12],[13],[14],[15],[16], [17] while some others use a probabilistic notation; e.g., some Markov chains based models like [18] *Pr(hit|match)*.

Some research works measure the impact on performance of the precision [4],[14]. In these cases, the number of prefetched objects and prefetch hits are used instead of the number of predictions and good predictions respectively (see equation 2).

$$Pc = \frac{GoodPredictions}{Predictions} \qquad (1)$$

$$Pc = \frac{PrefetchHits}{Prefetchs} \qquad (2)$$

Recall (Rc). *Recall* measures the percentage of requested objects that were previously prefetched [9],[10],[11]. The *recall* quantifies the weight of the predicted (see equation 3) or prefetched objects (see equation 4) over the amount of objects requested by the user. Notice that this index only deals with the number of good predictions made but not with the total amount of predictions.

Some research works refer to this metric as *usefulness* [16],[17] or *hit ratio* [19]. *Predictability* has been employed in [6] to refer to the upper limit of the *recall*.

$$Rc = \frac{GoodPredictions}{UserRequests} \tag{3}$$

$$Rc = \frac{PrefetchHits}{UserRequests} \tag{4}$$

Applicability. Bonino et al [8] define *applicability* as the ratio of the number of predictions to the number of requests. This is the only research work using this index; nevertheless, authors fail when stating this index as synonymous of *recall*. Notice that this index can be obtained from the previous ones (i.e., dividing *recall* by *precision*); therefore no additional information is given. This is the main reason because no other works use this index.

$$Applicability = \frac{Predictions}{UserRequests} \tag{5}$$

Precision alone or together with *recall* has been the most widely used index to evaluate the goodness of prediction algorithms. Each response request time consists of four main time components; i.e., connection establishment, request submitting, request processing, and response transference. Both *precision* and *recall* are closely related on the three first components. Therefore, authors feel that a complete comparison study about prediction algorithms should also include byte related indexes to quantify the last component. In this sense, analogously to the web proxy caching indexes (e.g., the *byte hit ratio*) [20], we propose the use of *byte precision* and *byte recall* as indexes to estimate the impact of prefetching on the time that the user wastes when waiting for the bytes of the requested objects.

Byte Precision (Pc$_B$). *Byte precision* measures the percentage of prefetched bytes that are subsequently requested. It can be calculated by replacing the number of predicted objects by their size in bytes in equation 1.

Remark that, like *precision* does, *byte precision* quantifies how good the predictions are, but measured in bytes instead of objects. An earlier approach to this index is the *Miss rate ratio* [21], described below.

$$Pc_B = \frac{GoodPredictions_B}{Predictions_B} \tag{6}$$

Byte Recall (Rc$_B$). *Byte recall* measures the percentage of demanded bytes that were previously prefetched. As mentioned above, this index quantifies how many accurate predictions are made, measured in transferred bytes.

This index becomes more helpful than the previously mentioned *recall*, when the transfer time is an important component of the overall user perceived latency.

$$Rc_B = \frac{GoodPredictions_B}{UserRequests_B}$$ (7)

3.1.2 Specific Indexes

Request Savings. *Request savings* measures the number of times that a user request hits in the browser cache or the requested object is being prefetched, in percentage of the total number of user requests [2]. Furthermore, the request savings can be broken down into three groups depending on if they were previously prefetched; have been partially prefetched or cached as normal objects.

Notice that when prefetching is user-initiated the number of requests increases; therefore, this index makes sense when prefetching is proxy or server initiated. Fan *et al* use this index in a prefetch system where the proxy pushes objects to the client. Nevertheless, this index could be also used when prefetching pushes objects from the server to the proxy or from the server to the client (with no intermediate proxies).

Miss Rate Ratio. Bestavros defines the *miss rate ratio* [21] as the ratio between the byte miss rate when the prefetch is employed to the byte miss rate when the prefetch is not employed, where the byte miss rate for a given client is the ratio of bytes not found in the client's cache to the total number of bytes accessed by that client.

As one can see, this index quantifies in which percentage the miss rate in the client cache drops due to the prefetching system. This is a specific index since it is only applicable to those systems storing the prefetched objects in the client's cache.

Probability of Making a Prediction. Pitkow et al [18] quantify the probability that the last accesses match the pattern prediction; in such case the prefetch system computes the prediction outcomes. This index can be applied, for example, to those systems based in Markov models, but can not be applied to a large subset of prefetching systems; e.g., the top-10 approaches [19], so that it is classified as specific.

3.2 Resource Usage

The benefits of prefetching are achieved at the expense of using additional resources. This overhead, as mentioned above, must be quantified because they can negatively impact on performance.

Although some prediction algorithms may require huge memory or processor time (e.g., high order Markov models), it is not the current general trend, where the main prefetching bottleneck is the network traffic. Therefore, we break down indexes in this category into two subgroups: network level and computing level.

3.2.1 Network Level

Traffic Increase (ΔTr_B). *Traffic increase* quantifies the increase in traffic (in bytes) due to unsuccessfully prefetched documents [19]. It is also called *wasted bandwidth* [2], *extra bytes* [10], *network traffic* [17], and *bandwidth ratio* [21].

When using prefetch, network traffic usually increases due to two side-effects of the prefetch: bad predictions and overhead. Bad predictions waste network bandwidth because these objects are never requested by the user. On the other hand, the network traffic increases due to the prefetch related information interchange, called *Network overhead* by [4]).

Several research studies fail in not taking into account that overhead [16],[19],[22]; therefore, their results can not accurately estimate prefetching costs.

$$\Delta Tr_B = \frac{ObjectsNotUsed_B + NetworkOverhead_B + UserRequests_B}{UserRequests_B} \tag{8}$$

Object Traffic Increase (ΔTr_{ob})**.** *Object traffic increase* quantifies in which percentage increases the number of documents that clients get when using prefetching. Nanopoulus et al [16] refer to this index as *network traffic* and Rabinovich [10] as *extra requests*.

As equation 9 shows, this index estimates the ratio of prefetched objects never used with respect to the total user's requests. It is analogous to the *traffic increase*, but it measures the overhead in number of objects.

$$\Delta Tr_{ob} = \frac{BadPredictions + UserRequests}{UserRequests} \tag{9}$$

3.2.2 Computing Level

Server Load Ratio. *Server load ratio* is defined as the ratio between the number of requests for service when speculation is employed to the number of requests for service when speculation is not employed [21].

Space and Time Overhead. In addition to the server load, some research works discuss how the overhead impact on performance. For instance, Duchamp [4] discusses the memory and processor time the prefetch would need.

3.3 Latency Related Indexes

Indexes belonging to this category include those aimed at quantifying the end-to-end latencies; e.g., user or proxy related latencies. The main drawback of these indexes is that they include several time components, some of them difficult to quantify. Many times researchers do not detail what components their measures include, although they use a typical index name; e.g., latency. This situation is not the best for the research community, due to the fact that different proposals can not be fairly compared among them.

Through the different research works, latencies are measured both per page and per object. The *Latency per page* (L_p) is calculated by comparing the time between browser's initiation of an HTML page GET and browser's reception of the last byte of the last embedded image for that page [4]. Analogously, the *Latency per object* (L_{ob}) can be defined as the elapsed time since the browser requests an object until it receives the last byte of that object. In order to illustrate the benefits of prefetching, researchers calculate the ratio of the latency prefetching achieves (either per page [2],[4],[14] or per object [23]) to the latency with no prefetching.

Unfortunately, most proposals that use *latency* when measuring performance do not specify which latency they are referring to. This fact can be misleading because both indexes do not perform in the same way. In order to illustrate this fact we present the following example: a user requests an HTML object embedding two images (IMG1 and IMG2). As figure 2 shows, the transference of the HTML file starts at t_0 and ends in t_5. At times t_1 and t_3 the browser reads and processes the IMG tags of the embedded images then starts the transferences, which end at t_2 and t_5, respectively. In this case, the cumulative L_{ob} is the sum of the time taken by the three transferences ($L_{ob} = t_4\text{-}t_0 + t_2\text{-}t_1 + t_5\text{-}t_3$) where the *Latency per page* (L_p) is $t_5\text{-}t_0$. If it is assumed that IMG1 was previously prefetched, no waiting time for such object will be plotted; i.e. t_1 will match t_2, so it reduces L_{ob} but not L_p which will remain the same value.

To observe this feature into a real environment for a given client is necessary that the object retrieving times are each other independent. Nevertheless, although times are not independent, both indexes can measure different values, as experimental results will show.

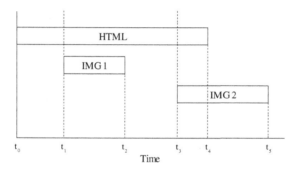

Fig. 2. Example where latency metrics behave different when the prefetch hits on one of the images

Furthermore, the *Latency per object* measured when an object is downloaded by the web browser has two main components: i) the queue time, since the browser has a limited number of connections, and ii) request time, including the time of connection establishment (if needed) and the object transference. The first component is often ignored whereas other research studies [5],[21] do not specify whether the latency measured includes queue time. The first component should not be ignored because prefetch hits do not compete for a free connection so the queue time of the remaining objects decreases and, consequently, their latency.

On the other hand, several names have been used instead of *latency*; for instance, *access time* [3], *service time* [21] and *responsiveness* [22],[24].

3.4 Summary: Synonymous and Experimental Index Category Used

Through the proposed taxonomy, we discussed the large variety of index names (synonymous) used to refer to the same metric. This heterogeneity can be observed through web performance studies appeared in the literature, adding extra difficulty to obtain a general view of the subject. Table 1 offers a scheme of the current situation. In addition, we also found that the same index name has been used when measuring different variables (e.g., *network traffic* appears both for *traffic increase* and for *object traffic increase*). As one can observe, the widest heterogeneity appears in the first category due to the large diversity of prediction algorithms appeared in the literature and its importance in the prefetching systems, which are the main focus of this work.

Table 2 relates the research works found in the open literature with the categories of indexes used in such works. As discussed above, a complete research work should include indexes belonging to the three categories. However, we only found this fact in 15% of the explored works, just three of twenty works (row 1).

Notice that the first column shows that 75% of the studied research works have considered at least one of the indexes belonging to the prediction category. Moreover, 40% of the studies only measure prediction metrics to evaluate the performance of the system. The second column shows that 60% of the papers do not measure resource usage metrics. Finally, in the third column we can observe that 55% of the research works do not quantify the end perceived latencies.

4   Experimental Examples

This section has three main goals. The first one is to illustrate the usefulness of the proposed indexes (i.e., *byte precision* and *byte recall*) as well as how they differ from the analogous classical ones. The second one is to study and show how indexes are related among them. Finally, the third goal is to identify the most meaningfulness indexes when evaluating the overall system performance.

In order to reach the second goal, we choose a subset of representative pairs of indexes that could be potentially related. Those pairs are selected from the most widely used indexes as discussed in Section 3: *precision, byte precision, recall, byte recall, traffic increase, object traffic increase, latency per page* and *latency per object*. A graphic is plotted for each pair in order to detect the possible relations. Then, in those graphics where some sign of linear relation appears, we quantify it statistically.

In order to obtain the experimental results presented in this section, we use the experimental framework described in [1]. To illustrate how the different indexes behave, we need both a prefetching system and a non-prefetching system. In order to provide a prefetching system, we implement the prefetching algorithm proposed by Padmanabhan and Mogul [3]. This algorithm uses a threshold value so that objects with less probability than such value to be requested in the following k accesses are not prefetched (in our experiments we take $k=4$). In order to observe how the indexes behave in a wide range of situations, the experiments were run ranging the threshold from 0.1 to 0.9.

Table 1. Relation between the selected index name in this paper and those appeared in the literature

| Category | Selected name | Literature | |
		Name	References
1. Prediction	Precision	Precision	[8],[9],[10],[11]
		Accuracy	[4],[12],[13],[14],[15],[16],[17]
		Pr(hit|match)	[18]
	Recall	Recall	[9],[10],[11]
		Usefulness	[16],[17]
		Hit Ratio	[19]
		Predictability	[6]
	Applicability	Applicability	[8]
2. Resource usage	Traffic increase	Traffic increase	[3],[4],[19]
		Wasted Bandwidth	[2]
		Bandwidth ratio	[21]
		Extra bytes	[10]
		Data transfer	[22]
		Network Traffic	[17]
	Object traffic increase	Network Traffic	[16]
		Extra requests	[10]
3. Latency	Latency per page	Latency	[2],[4],[14]
		Responsiveness	[22],[24]
	Latency per object	Latency	[5],[23]
		Access time	[3]
		Service time ratio	[21]

The system was configured to simulate users accessing to *Marca*, which is a Spanish popular news web server (www.marca.es). A trace collected during one week (about 145,000 accesses) was used to train the prediction engine while the logs of the following day (about 35,000 accesses) were used to obtain simulation results. Each simulation included about 250 clients. Plotted points in the figures that this section includes refer to the performance indexes measured for every client in each experiment (each plot consists of about 2,500 points). On the other hand, the measured values of the prediction indexes showed in this section refer to the prefetched objects, not to the predicted objects, as they are close to the real system performance. Available bandwidth per each simulated user was ranged from 48 kbps to 400 kbps but, due to space limitations, only 200 kbps users are presented and analyzed in this paper. In the whole set of experiments we saw that the correlation among the indexes increases as the available bandwidth does.

Table 2. Relation between research studies and indexes used grouped by category

References	Category			%
	1. Prediction	*2. Resource*	*3.Latency*	
[2],[4],[21]	X	X	X	15
[3],[22]		X	X	10
[14]	X		X	5
[5],[23],[24]			X	15
[16],[17],[19]	X	X		15
[6],[8],[9],[11],[12],[13],[15],[18]	X			40

Figure 3 plots the *Latency per object* ratio to the *Latency per page* ratio, both referring to different alternatives about how latency can be measured (as discussed in Section 3). Note that depending on the way the latency is measured, it is possible to reach not only different but also opposite conclusions. Suppose that we take a point in the upper left-side quarter and we consider the *Latency per object;* in such case, the prefetching system outperforms the non-prefetching system. However, if we consider the *Latency per page,* we would conclude the opposite. The correlation coefficient between both latency ratios corresponding to the points plotted in Figure 3 is 0.60, i.e., the indexes present a certain linear correlation but it is far from being strong; so that *Latency per object* and *Latency per page* ratios are not directly comparable.

Consequently, we suggest that studies should differentiate the use of both latency ratios because they are addressed to explore the performance from different points of view. The *Latency per page* ratio evaluates the system performance from the user's point of view (since it measures the latency as perceived by the user) while the *latency per object* ratio measures the performance from the http protocol point of view. Therefore, it should be used when the meaning of a page is not so clear; e.g. in a proxy.

Figure 4 presents an almost horizontal curve showing no apparent relation between precision and latency related indexes. The correlation coefficients showed in table 3 quantify this negligible linear correlation, which confirms the visual appreciation.

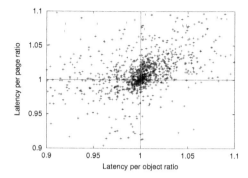

Fig. 3. *Latency per object* ratio as a function of *latency per page* ratio

Table 3. Linear correlation coefficient between prediction and latency indexes

Latency	Precision		Recall	
	Pc	Pc_B	Rc	Rc_B
L_p	-0.294	-0.403	-0.198	-0.526
L_{ob}	-0.291	-0.228	-0.625	-0.363

Figure 5 shows the relation between precision and traffic related indexes. One can appreciate that points define an area whose superior slope has certain resemblance to an inverse proportional function. The figure can be interpreted as the higher the (*byte*) *precision* is the lower probability of having high (*object*) *traffic increase*. The upper row (Figure 5.a, and Figure 5.b) shows that *precision* has better relation (defines better the inverse proportional area) to the *object traffic increase* than to the *traffic increase*, since points in this plot appear more widely dispersed. On the other hand, the right column (Figure 5.b, and Figure 5.d) shows the relation between *traffic increase* and both *precision* and *byte precision*. As expected, *byte precision* is closer related to *traffic increase* than *precision*. Despite this, to the best of our knowledge, no other research work has used *byte precision* as a performance index.

As the *traffic increase* can not be considered the main aim of the prefetching, precision indexes can not be used as main indexes to measure the system performance.

Figure 6 shows the relation between the *Recall* and both latency indexes. One can observe that there is a linear relation between the *recall* index and the *latency per object* ratio, but not to *latency per page* object. Due to fact that *recall* increases with the good predictions count, this index has a significant impact on the *latency per object*, but they are not directly comparable (the correlation coefficient is 0.62, as shown in table 3). Some extra elements not gathered by the *recall*, like queued time and object size heterogeneity justify why the relation is not stronger. On the other hand, the *latency per page* is not explained by the *recall* index since it involves more elements that affect it, like the simultaneous transference of objects (as explained in section 3.3). These results corroborate the differences between both latencies observed in the figure 3.

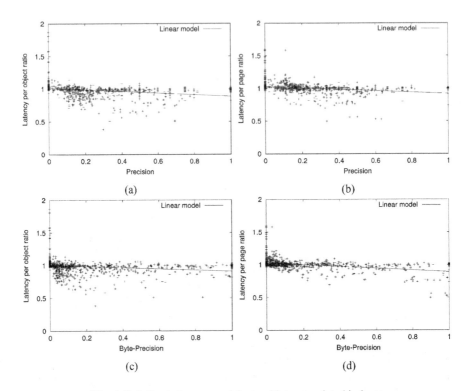

Fig. 4. Relation between precision and latency related indexes

5   Conclusions

A large variety of key metrics have appeared in the open literature in order to evaluate the performance of web prefetching systems. This paper has analyzed this wide heterogeneity trying i) to clarify both index definitions and how they are related, and ii) to help when deciding which metric or index should be selected to evaluate the system performance.

We have proposed a taxonomy, classifying the indexes related to prefetch in three main categories according to the part of the system they are addressed to evaluate: prediction, resource usage and latency. The goal of this taxonomy is not only to help the understanding of the indexes definition but also to analyze analogies and differences between them, in order to identify which the main useful metrics are when carrying out performance studies.

For each metric or index we have provided a definition (the one we considered more precise) among the large variety appeared in the literature. Then, looking for these definitions we observed certain analogies. To check possible relations among those indexes in a more formal way, we ran experiments and calculated the statistical correlation among a representative set of them. From these experiments we can extract the main following conclusions:

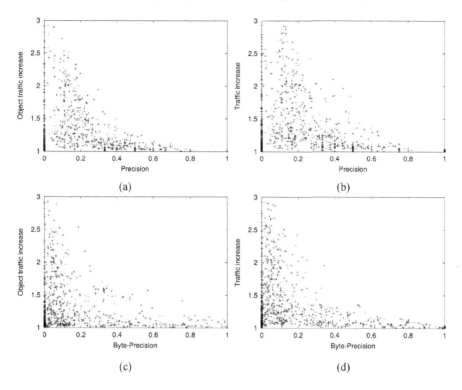

Fig. 5. Relation between precision and network level related indexes

- Performance studies should include at least latency related metrics. Depending on the goal of the performed study *latency per page* or *per object* is preferred. For instance, if the goal is to analyze the user's point of view, the latency per page must be included; whereas when evaluating from the point of view of a proxy server, the *latency per page* makes no sense due to the lack of page concept. Consequently, the *latency per object* can be the most useful metric.
- Latencies alone can not be used as metrics to check performance. Studies must analyze how the latencies reduction has been achieved for a given proposal. In this sense, resource usage indexes should be taken into account. *Traffic increase* is the one that provides more information; therefore, we suggest that performance studies should include at least this index.
- Our discussion has shown that is not recommendable to perform studies about the behavior of prefetching techniques just focusing on the algorithm point of view. Nevertheless, if some studies focus on this part, they should include *recall* and *byte recall* as performance metrics because they are the most correlated to the *latency per object* and *latency per page* respectively.

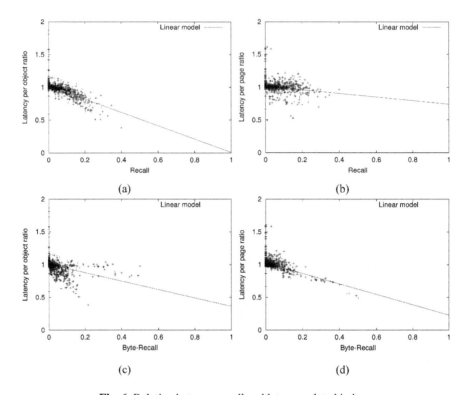

(a)   (b)

(c)   (d)

Fig. 6. Relation between recall and latency related indexes

References

1. Domènech, J., Pont, A., Sahuquillo, J., and Gil, J. A.: An experimental framework for testing web prefetching techniques. Proceedings of the 30th Euromicro Conference. Rennes, France (2004)
2. Fan, L., Cao, P., and Jacobson, Q.: Web prefetching between low-bandwidth clients and proxies: potential and performance. Proceedings of the ACM SIGMETRICS Conference on Measurement and Modeling of Computer Systems. Atlanta, USA (1999)
3. Padmanabhan, V., and J. C. Mogul.: Using predictive prefetching to improve World Wide Web latency. Proceedings of the ACM SIGCOMM '96 Conference. Palo Alto, USA (1996)
4. Duchamp, D.: Prefetching hyperlinks. Proceedings of the 2nd USENIX Symposium on Internet Technologies and Systems. Boulder, USA (1999)
5. Kokku, R., Yalagandula, P., Venkataramani, A., and Dahlin, M.: NPS: A non-interfering deployable web prefetching system. Proceedings of the USENIX Symposium on Internet Technologies and Systems. San Antonio, USA (2003)
6. Schechter, S., Krishnan, M., and Smith, M. D.: Using path profiles to predict HTTP requests. Proceedings of the 7th International World Wide Web Conference. Brisbane, Australia (1998)
7. Cohen, E., and Kaplan, H.: Prefetching the means for document transfer: A new approach for reducing web latency. Proceedings of the IEEE INFOCOM. Tel Aviv, Israel (2000)

8. Bonino, D., Corno, F., and Squillero, G.: A real-time evolutionary algorithm for web prediction. Proceedings of the International Conference on Web Intelligence. Halifax, Canada, (2003)

9. Albrecht, D., Zukerman, I., and Nicholson, A.: Pre-Sending documents on the WWW: A comparative study. Proceedings of the 16th International Joint Conference on Artificial Intelligence. Stockholm, Sweden (1999)

10. Rabinovich, M. and Spatscheck, O.: Web caching and replication. Addison-Wesley. Boston, USA (2002)

11. Cohen, E., Krishnamurthy, B., and Rexford, J.: Efficient algorithms for predicting requests to web servers. Proceedings of the Conference on Computer and Communications. New York, USA (1999)

12. Cunha, C. R., and Jaccoud, C. F. B.: Determining WWW user's next access and its applications to pre-fetching. Proceedings of the 2nd International Symposium on Computers and Communication. Alexandria, Egypt (1997)

13. Zukerman, I., Albrecht, D., and Nicholson, A.: Predicting users' requests on the WWW. Proceedings of the 7th International Conference on User Modeling. Banff, Canada (1999)

14. Loon, T. S., and Bharghavan, V.: Alleviating the latency and bandwidth problems in WWW browsing. Proceedings of the USENIX Symposium on Internet Technologies and Systems. Monterey, USA (1997)

15. Davison, B. D.: Predicting web actions from HTML content. Proceedings of the 13th ACM Conference on Hypertext and Hypermedia. College Park, USA (2002)

16. Nanopoulos, A., Katsaros, D., and Manopoulos, Y.: Effective prediction of web-user accesses: A data mining approach. Proceedings of Workshop on Mining Log Data across All Customer Touchpoints. San Francisco, USA (2001)

17. Palpanas, T., and Mendelzon, A.: Web prefetching using partial match prediction. Proceedings of the 4th International Web Caching Workshop. San Diego, USA (1999)

18. Pitkow, J. and Pirolli, P.: Mining longest repeating subsequences to predict World Wide Web surfing. Proceedings of the 2nd USENIX Symposium on Internet Technologies and Systems. Boulder, USA (1999)

19. Markatos, E. P., and Chronaki, C. E.: A top-10 approach to prefetching the web. Proceedings of the INET' 98. Geneva, Switzerland (1998)

20. Cherkasova, L., and Ciardo, G.: Characterizing temporal locality and its impact on web server performance. Proceedings of the 9th International Conference on Computer Communication and Networks. Las Vegas, USA (2000)

21. Bestavros, A.: Using speculation to reduce server load and service time on the WWW. Proceedings of the 4th ACM International Conference on Information and Knowledge Management. Baltimore, USA (1995)

22. Khan, J. I., and Tao, Q.: Exploiting webspace organization for accelerating web prefetching. Proceedings of the International Conference on Web Intelligence. Halifax, Canada (2003)

23. Kroeger, T. M., Long, D. D. E., and Mogul, J. C.: Exploring the bounds of web latency reduction from caching and prefetching. Proceedings of the USENIX Symposium on Internet Technologies and Systems. Monterey, USA (1997)

24. Tao, Q.: Impact of Webspace Organization and User Interaction Behavior on a Prefetching Proxy. Ph. D. Thesis. Kent State University, USA (2002)

A Semantic Service Orientated Architecture for the Telecommunications Industry

Alistair Duke, John Davies, Marc Richardson, and Nick Kings

BT Exact, Next Generation Web Research, Adastral Park, Martlesham Heath,
Ipswich IP5 3RE, United Kingdom
{alistair.duke, john.nj.davies, marc.richardson,
nick.kings}@bt.com

Abstract. A Service Orientated Architecture will allow organisations to enhance interoperability and encourage reuse of components and interfaces. In
this paper, the application of semantic descriptions to services is advocated
with the aim of further improving the SOA and enabling scalability. An
application of Semantic Web Services for the Telecommunications Industry is
described. It shows how services components forming part of a Service
Orientated Architecture can be described semantically in terms of shared data
and process ontologies. The potential benefits of this approach are explored. A
use case is presented that illustrates how the efficiency of a telecommunications
system designer can be improved with the use of Semantic Web Services.

1 Introduction

The Service Oriented Architecture (SOA) has emerged as a way in which organisations can enable interoperability and encourage reuse, thereby reducing cost. The
greater agility it affords will also allow organisations to respond to the needs of the
market more quickly and in ways that are more attractive to the customer. The SOA is
particularly applicable to the Telecommunications market where customer and operational support costs are high and customer satisfaction is a key differentiator. However, industries such as Telecommunications with complex internal organisations and
supply chains are finding that a scaleable SOA is not achievable without semantic
descriptions of services that can aid service discovery and integration.

The Telecommunications Industry is also seeking ways to encourage interopera-
bility at a business-to-business level. One such approach is the New Generation
Operations Systems and Software (NGOSS) initiative from the TeleManagement
Forum [1].

This paper examines an approach to combine the SOA with the models of the
NGOSS by creating semantic descriptions of services and system interfaces expressed
in terms of data and process ontologies derived from NGOSS. The intention is to
create explicit links between service components and a commonly understood view of
the industry allowing improved service discovery and service integration. A scenario
based around a solution designer carrying out a product assurance integration task is
presented. The paper examines how Semantic Web Services can be used to enhance

A. Aagesen et al. (Eds.): INTELLCOMM 2004, LNCS 3283, pp. 236–245, 2004.

the efficiency of the designer. Finally, an analysis of the approach is presented which examines the applicability of NGOSS as a domain ontology and the capabilities of existing Semantic Web Services initiatives for supporting a Service Oriented Architecture in the telecommunications industry.

2 Semantic Web Services for OSS

Standard information models are a key element of flexible and low cost integration of Operational Support Systems. Those developing and adopting these models will benefit from consideration of emerging semantic web standards which can make explicit the semantics of the data to aid integration and understanding. A common information model with explicit semantics is a key element to a Service Oriented Architecture, since only with semantic descriptions of services will a degree of automation be achievable for service discovery and composition.

This section will explain the proposed benefits of web services described semantically in the context of a common information model for the OSS domain. In order to do this, the limitations of current web services are first considered.

Web Services are generally described using XML-based standards namely WSDL [1] (which allows one to describe a web service in terms of what it does and what its inputs and outputs are), UDDI (which is a centralised registry allowing one to discover web services) and SOAP (which is a protocol allowing one to execute services). In addition to these low-level standards, work is on-going it create standards that allow services to be combined into a workflow e.g. WS-BPEL[2] (Web Services-Business Process Execution Language) and also to define permissible message exchange patterns and contents e.g. ebXML[3]. However, none of these standards provide a means to describe a web service in terms of explicit semantics. For a given service you might want to describe what kind of service it is, what inputs and outputs it requires and provides, what needs to be true for the service to execute (pre-conditions), what becomes true once the service has executed (post-conditions) and what effect the service has on the state of the world (and/or the data it consumes and provides).

The first of these requirements is partly addressed by UDDI in that a category and human readable description can be assigned to a web service in a registry to aid discovery. This provides only limited support for automated discovery since a computer will not understand the description or what the category means. The second and third of these requirements are partly addressed by WSDL in that XML tags can be attributed to inputs and outputs. A computer can easily match these but again has no notion of their meaning or relationship to other pieces of data.

Services can be described semantically by relating them to ontologies. The explicit relationship between services and ontologies is the key element for Semantic Web Services. It is envisaged that this will enable:

---

[1] http://www.w3.org/TR/wsdl

[2] http://www-106.ibm.com/developerworks/webservices/library/ws-bpel/

[3] http://www.ebxml.org/

- Improved Service Discovery

Semantic Web search technology allows users to search more precisely on ontological concepts or concept value rather than by keyword.

- Re-use of Service Interfaces in Different Products / Settings

Services that are described semantically can more easily be discovered, understood and applied thus reducing the need to create new services that serve the same purpose.

- Simpler Change Management

One example of how semantics can help here is when a proposed change is made to a data element, those services or interfaces that employ that data in some way can be dynamically discovered and appropriate action taken.

- A browseable, Searchable Knowledge Base for Developers (and Others)

This would allow developers and solution providers to perform queries relating to the data and processes they were concerned with, for example to determine the origin piece of data or its destination.Semi-automatic service composition

Given a high level goal which we wish a service or set of services to achieve, expressed in terms of an ontology, it should be possible to carry out decomposition into components parts and then match these components with appropriate services.

- Mediation between the data and process requirements of component services

Often there is need for two or more services to interact even though their communication requirements are semantically the same but syntactically different. In this case it should be possible to automatically construct a translation between message data elements that allows the services to communicate.

- Enterprise Information Integration

The Semantic Web should afford universal (or at least enterprise-wide) access to semantic descriptions of services (or information). One advantage of this is the ability to answer complex queries without having to consider how to access the various systems where the data required for the answer is held.

3 Use Case Scenario

The project scenario is based around a solution designer who, given a high-level requirement, wishes to compose a set of web services that will allow the requirement to be met. The scenario assumes that a set of services exist and that they are described semantically and related to a common information model. However, there is no clear approach for forming explicit links that will allow some degree of automation when moving from the model to the service description and vice-versa. Figure 1 illustrates how an explicit link can be created with the adoption of a set of technologies or approaches. These are now briefly described.

The work of the TeleManagement Forum in developing a framework for Next Generation OSS can be seen as ontology building in that NGOSS provides a level of shared understanding for a particular domain of interest. NGOSS [1] is available as a toolkit of industry-agreed specifications and guidelines that cover key business and technical areas including Business Process Automation delivered in the enhanced Telecom Operations Map (eTOM™) [2] and Systems Analysis & Design delivered in the Shared Information/Data Model (SID) [3].

The eTOM and SID have been considered in this work as ontologies in that they can provide a level of shared understanding for a particular domain of interest. The eTOM provides a framework that allows processes to be assigned to it. It describes all the enterprise processes required by a service provider. The SID provides a common vocabulary allowing these processes to communicate. It identifies the entities involved in OSS and the relationships between them. The SID can therefore be used to identify and describe the data that is consumed and produced by the processes.

Fig. 1. Semantic Service Descriptions create an explicit link

OWL-S is a OWL-based Web service ontology, which supplies Web service providers with a core set of mark-up language constructs for describing the properties and capabilities of their Web services in unambiguous, computer-interpretable form. OWL-S mark-up of Web services will facilitate the automation of Web service tasks, including automated Web service discovery, execution, composition and interoperation [4].

The OSS through Java (OSS/J) initiative provides a 'standard set of Java technology-based APIs to jump-start the implementation of end-to-end services on next-generation wireless networks, and leverage the convergence of telecommunications and Internet-based solutions' [5]. It is used here because it provides a set of telecommunications interfaces close to those that would be provided by services in a SOA.

The application area of the use case is trouble ticketing. The scenario is that given a service alarm, the service problem should be resolved while keeping the customer informed of progress. The goal is met by designing a composed service from a number of component services. In the scenario, these component services will first be discovered and then integrated in an appropriate manner according to their descriptions. The scenario will illustrate the benefits of ontological support by making use of process and data ontologies. In order to satisfy the goal it will be necessary to employ services that will create a trouble ticket to manage the resolution of the problem and create a task in a workforce management system to ensure that the problem is addressed. In the first part of the scenario consists of the following five steps:

1. A network problem results in an alarm being triggered. This is captured by the process manager.
2. The process manager reads the alarm to determine the affected resource. It then carries out a request to an inventory manager to determine the customer affected by the resource.
3. The inventory manager responds with details of the customer.

4. The process manager requests that the Trouble Ticket system creates a new trouble ticket and provides details of the problem.

5. The Trouble Ticket system creates a new ticket (and informs the customer of the problem) then responds to the Process Manager with an ID for the created ticket.

The scenario allows the services and the messages they require to be determined. For example the Inventory Manager might expose a service getCustomerID which requires and input message of a resourceID and provides an output message containing either a customerID or an error code.

4 Domain Ontologies

One of the aims of the use case is to make use of existing ontologies that exist for the telecommunication sector and understand how they can be used to enhance service descriptions. This section describes the modelling work of the TeleManagement Forum then illustrates how this can be converted to OWL for use in the case study.

In order to make use of the eTOM and SID within the project, it was necessary to express them in a formal ontology language i.e. OWL [6].

The eTOM and SID are subject to ongoing development by the TMF. The current version of the eTOM (3.6) is expressed in a set of documents although there are plans to provide a clickable HTML version (a previous version is already available in this form) and an XML version. The SID is also expressed in a set of documents but is also available as a set of UML class diagrams.

The eTOM can be regarded as a Business Process Framework, rather than a Business Process Model, since its aim is to categorise the process elements business activities so that these can then be combined in many different ways, to implement end-to-end business processes (e.g. billing) which deliver value for the customer and the service provider. [2]. The eTOM can be decomposed to lower level process categories e.g. 'Customer Relationship Management' is decomposed into a number of categories, one of which is 'Problem Handling'. This is then decomposed further into categories including 'Track and Manage Problem'. It is to these lower level categories that business specific processes can be mapped. Each category is attributed with metadata giving a name, a unique identifier, a brief and extended description and a set of known process linkages (i.e. links to other relevant categories).

The SID [3] is much more complex than the eTOM in both its aims and form. It provides a data model for a number of domains described by a collection of concepts known as Aggregate Business Entities. These use the eTOM as a focus to determine the appropriate information to be modelled. The SID models entities and the relationships between them. For example a 'customer' is defined as a subclass of 'role'. It contains attributes such as 'id' and 'name'. It is linked to other entities such as 'CustomerAccount' with an association 'customerPossesses'.

5 Semantic Service Descriptions

5.1 Service Grounding

The case study makes use of OSS/J interfaces. Although OSS/J has yet to be adopted commercially, extensive work by the OSS/J consortium has gone on to ensure that it meets the requirements of product vendors and consumers in delivering interfaces at the appropriate level. In order to make use of the interfaces in this case study, it was necessary to wrap them as WSDL web services since OWL-S only supports a grounding to WSDL.

In OWL-S, a service grounding creates a link between the semantic description of a service and the service itself which is described in WSDL. One aim of the use case is to illustrate discovery and composition at the level of WSDL operations e.g. get-CustomerID. For this reason, the decision has been made to model operations as OWL-S services. This is because a service has only one service profile, which is the means by which discovery is carried out. If a WSDL service had been modelled as an OWL-S service, then the profile would not allow advertisements of the operations within the service to be made.

5.2 Service Model

The Service Model describes what happens when the service is executed. The Process Model is a subclass of the Service Model and gives a detailed perspective of the service. The Process Model describes a service in terms of inputs, outputs, preconditions, effects, component sub-processes, and aims at enabling planning, composition and agent/service interoperation.

The service getCustomerID identified in section 3 is an example of an atomic service as it takes a number of inputs and returns a number of outputs. It maps directly to a WSDL description and can be invoked directly.

Inputs (e.g., resourceID), outputs (e.g., customerID), preconditions and effects are described separately. For brevity, inputs, outputs, preconditions and effects (iopes)

```
<process:AtomicProcess rdf:ID="getCustomerID">
  <process:hasInput rdf:resource="#resourceID"/>
  <process:hasOutput rdf:resource="#customerID"/>
</process:AtomicProcess>
```

In OWL-S, the service model allows inputs and outputs to be related to ontological concepts thus providing a frame of reference for the data requirements of the service.

Preconditions and conditional effects are described analogously to inputs and conditional outputs. Unfortunately, there is no standard way to express preconditions within OWL-S although placeholders for these have been provided in the OWL-S ontology. The proposed Semantic Web Rule Language[4] and related initiatives will provide such expressions.

---

[4] http://www.daml.org/2003/11/swrl/

In order to specify preconditions for the atomic services in the use case it is first necessary to consider the scenario in terms of the states that can exist between receiving a service alarm and closing a trouble ticket. These states can be characterised by the things that must be true for that state to exist. In the scenario, these things are embodied by the existence of data in variables or the value of those variables. Naturally, the variables are exactly the input and output data that is consumed and produced by the atomic processes. The conditions can be seen as postconditions of the preceding process and preconditions of the following process.

Where conditions are not provided, it is up to the designer to ensure that the correct input is provided to the generic WDSL operation. With Semantic Web Services it should be possible to specify the process to the extent that the designer no longer has the ability to add services to a composition in such a way that their preconditions or input requirements cannot be met.

Similarly, preconditions on the state of variables can be expressed. For example, in the scenario, it may be the case that the state of the trouble ticket can only be set to 'CLOSED' if the current status is 'CLEARED'. The following represents this requirement:

```
<process:AtomicProcess rdf:ID="closeTT_Process">
  <process:hasPrecondition rdf:resource=
    "#updateTroubleTicketStatusOutput_State_Out_CLEARED"/>
</process:AtomicProcess>
```

This requires the output from the previous process (which included an output State_Out) to be set to the required value.

In addition to preconditions, OWL-S has the notion of effects. These are the things that are true once a process has completed. For example, the effect of updating the trouble ticket once a job complete notice has been received is that the TTState is set to 'CLEARED'. That is of course if everything is correct with process e.g. that the trouble ticket ID sent is correct. The underlying WSDL operation contains an error flag that could be set if anything was wrong. Obviously, it would not be wise to set the TTState to 'CLEARED' under those circumstances. For this reason, the effects are conditional upon certain facts. In this case that the error flag is false.

The aim of the use case is to illustrate how a designer can compose services together to satisfy a high-level goal. The output of this activity will be a composed service. OWL-S allows atomic process to be composed together using a number of different constructs such as sequence, split-join, etc. The following example considers the composite process of following an alarm, collect details from the inventory manager then create a trouble ticket.

There are four possible states in this part of the process i.e. 'start', 'alarm received', 'got customer data' and 'trouble ticket queued'. The process is simplified in that it does not contain any error handling states. In the following example, if errors are received then there will be no state transition i.e. the process will return to the state that was current at the start of the attempted transition.

The following fragment shows the top level description of the composed process. The designer would name this and refer it to a service profile, allowing it to be advertised. The description also includes a pointer to the start state. All other states are encapsulated within the description of the start state so this is the only reference to the actual composition that is required.

```
<process:ProcessModel rdf:ID=
    "handleAlarmWithTroubleTicket_Process">
  <service:describes rdf:resource=
    "&service;#handleAlarmWithTroubleTicketService"/>
  <process:hasProcess rdf:resource="#StartState"/>
</process:ProcessModel>
```

The start state is described below as a composite process.

```
<process:CompositeProcess rdf:ID="StartState">
  <processComposedOf>
    <process:Sequence>
      <process:components rdf:parseType="Collection">
        <process:AtomicProcess rdf:about=
          "#getAlarmResource"/>
        <process:CompositeProcess rdf:about=
          "#AlarmReceivedState"/>
      </process:components>
    </process:Sequence>
  </processComposedOf>
</process:CompositeProcess>
```

The composition for this state is a simple sequence of two processes. The first is the atomic process 'getAlarmResource' which as described earlier takes the alarm as input and outputs the resource on which the alarm has occurred. The second process is the next state in the composition i.e. the 'AlarmReceivedState'. This is another composite process which includes a selection which determines the state transition based upon the output from the getCustomerID atomic process.

OWL-S provides the <process:sameValues> construct to allow the data flow to be constructed. This allows the output from one atomic process to be aligned to an input from another. For example the troubleTicketID which is an output of createTroubleTicket can be related to the corresponding input of populateTroubleTicket.

Although useful in this simple example, the construct is limited where more complex data flow is required such as when two outputs should be combined to form one input or where an output is a complex data type from which only a portion is required.

The output of the design process would be an OWL-S composed service along the lines of that described above. The composed service could then be advertised and discovered using its own process model without regard to the atomic processes that form it.

5.3 Service Profile

The service profile describes the service in terms of what it does. It is intended to advertise the capabilities of the service allowing it to be discovered. The profile includes non-functional and functional descriptions. Non-functional descriptions cover areas such as descriptions of the service provider, the quality rating of the service, etc. The most interesting non-functional description is classification of the service according to a domain ontology. This allows the services described in the case study to be classified according to the eTOM. The service profile exists as an instance of this class allowing it to be discovered by a matchmaking process that used the eTOM ontology.

Functional properties describe the service in terms of their iopes. These are intended to aid discovery by allowing goal services to be described in these terms. There are no encoded logical constraints between the inputs in the process model and the inputs in the profile model, therefore, at least in theory, the two sets may be totally unrelated. This is a major current deficiency of OWL-S since during matchmaking knowledge of how the iopes are used by the service would be of great benefit.

6 Conclusion

This document has considered the applicability of Semantic Web Technologies to OSS information modelling. It considers how Semantic Web Services can be applied to an OSS related scenario and which aims to create an explicit link between information models and low-level service / interface descriptions. These services have been described using WSDL wrapped OSS/J interfaces. Semantic annotations have been provided by OWL-S. Within these annotations, references are made to OWL ontologies which have been generated from the TMF's NGOSS models (eTOM & SID).

This process has allowed a number of observations to be made regarding the applicability of the Semantic Web in this field. The Web Ontology Language is in general flexible enough to capture the semantics of the TMF NGOSS models. Tool support for this process is poor. None of the major UML vendors support any Semantic Web languages.

The semantics of UML and OWL differ. One of the key barriers to the adoption of the Semantic Web is likely to be a shortage of skills. Database modellers and information architects could help solve this problem but in order to utilize them efficiently, methodologies for creating ontologies and a clear understanding of the differences between the closed world model and the open world model are required.

The TMF NGOSS initiative will provide process and data models for the Telecommunications industry. These are under development but it is clear that they are at a high level and require further modelling within a particular context if they are to perform as a domain ontology for Semantic Web Services. There is currently a mismatch between these model and underlying service components. Having said this, the eTOM provides a useful process framework for categorising processes or service functions. The SID provides a useful starting point when constructing a canonical data dictionary and/or exchange model for a particular environment.

OWL-S is an approach to allow the semantics of services to be expressed. It is currently the most concrete of the emerging initiatives in this area. OWL-S in its current form provides good support for mapping services and their data requirements (i.e. inputs and outputs) to ontological concepts. This can improve service discovery and promote a better understanding of the capabilities of a service within a wider domain. There are a number of outstanding issues with OWL-S. Firstly, support is required for expressing rules. This will allow the preconditions and effects of a service to be expressed. Secondly, the OWL-S' process model is too simple. The minimal set of control structures provided do not have formally specified semantics. Thirdly it does not distinguish between public and private processes. Fourthly, it only supports grounding to WSDL web services. Finally it has little in the way of tool support.

Alternative approaches are emerging that are attempting to overcome these shortfalls. The Semantic Web Services Initiative[5] (SWSI) is an ad hoc initiative of academic and industrial researchers. The Web Service Modelling Framework[6] (WSMF) is a major element of the EU-funded projects, SWWS[7] & DIP[8]. DIP will develop tools and trial WSMF on three major case studies within three years (one of which is based on B2B in the ICT sector). The coupling of OSS/J to web services promises a significant set of benefits for a telecom service provider, but the maturity of the underlying technologies are insufficient at this moment in time. Currently, there is no standardised mapping from OSS/J services to web services, which is crucial when inter working between two, or more, companies. Also, WSDL does not currently define a standardised, agreed way to describe and implement asynchronous services. Both of these features, however, are under development.

Much remains to be done but Semantic Web technologies have a key role to play in the development of efficient e-Business integration.

References

1. TeleManagement Forum, "NGOSS Overview Document". Available on the web at: http://www.tmforum.org/
2. TeleManagement Forum, "Enhanced Telecom Operations Map" (eTOM) data sheet. Available on the web at: http://www.tmforum.org/
3. TeleManagement Forum, "Shared Information/Data Model (SID)". Available on the web at: http://www.tmforum.org/
4. "OWL-S Technical Overview", http://www.daml.org/services/OWL-S/1.0/OWL-S.html
5. Sun Microsystems, Inc., "OSS through Java Initiative Overview", http://java.sun.com/products/oss/overview.html
6. D. L. McGuinness and F. van Harmelen (eds), "OWL Web Ontology Language Overview". Available on the web at: http://www.w3.org/TR/owl-features/

---

[5] http://www.swsi.org/
[6] http://www.wsmo.org/
[7] http://swws.semanticweb.org/
[8] http://dip.semanticweb.org/

On Using WS-Policy, Ontology, and Rule Reasoning to Discover Web Services

Natenapa Sriharee[1], Twittie Senivongse[2], Kunal Verma[3], and Amit Sheth[4]

[1, 2] Department of Computer Engineering, Chulalongkorn University,
Phyathai Road, Pathumwan, Bangkok 10330 Thailand
natenapa.s@student.chula.ac.th, twittie.s@chula.ac.th
[3, 4] Large Scale Distributed Information System (LSDIS) Laboratory,
Department of Computer Science, University of Georgia, Athens, GA 30602
{verma, amit}@cs.uga.edu

Abstract. This paper proposes an approach to behaviour-based discovery of Web Services by which business rules that govern service behaviour are described as a policy. The policy is represented in the form of ontological information and is based on actions relating to the service and conditions for performing them. The standard WS-Policy is used to associate such a policy to the Web Service. With a framework that extends standard discovery by UDDI, service consumers can query for Web Services by specifying business constraints. The policy of the Web Service will be evaluated against the consumer's query by using OWL ontology querying engine and a rule-based reasoning module. By considering business rules in addition to the conventional attribute-based search by UDDI, the approach will enable more satisfactory discovery results that better fit service consumers' requirements.

1 Introduction

Current standard UDDI registry for Web Services [1] defines fundamental attributes that characterise businesses and services they provide. Search with UDDI is hence restricted to matching of the attribute values in service consumers' queries to those published by service providers (e.g. search is by business name or business service category). This may give a not-so-accurate search result since search constraints cannot filter irrelevant information well and do not reflect semantics and behaviour of the businesses and their services. This paper proposes an approach to discover Web Services by using a policy that enforces service behaviour. The policy will describe rules that define choices of the behaviour of a Web Service. A retailer may, for instance, specify a policy on delivery time for the appliances, which are sold to the customers, based on the appliance types and areas of destination. Correspondingly, a customer may want to buy an appliance from a retailer that can deliver goods within a

---

[1] On visiting LSDIS Lab, The University of Georgia, Dec 2003–May 2004.

A. Aagesen et al. (Eds.): INTELLCOMM 2004, LNCS 3283, pp. 246–255, 2004.
© IFIP International Federation for Information Processing 2004

specified time. Therefore a mechanism to evaluate the retailer's policy against the customer's requirement will be provided.

The conditions under which the retailer's Web Service above provides its service can be defined using a policy in WS-Policy framework [2]. A policy consists of a collection of one or more policy assertions that can be bound to Web Services entities (e.g. operation, message, part) in order to enforce assertion rules on them. The framework allows policies to be created for various purposes (e.g. the currently available WS-Security policy standard [3]) and places no restriction on the language used to represent policy expressions. This paper introduces a business rules policy that is based on WS-Policy framework and concerns rules on business functions. The policy assertions will be modelled by the actions relating to the service and the conditions for performing them. An ontology language (OWL [4] in this case) is used to express the policy. To check the policy of a Web Service against a service consumer's request, an OWL ontology querying engine will be queried and a rule-based reasoning module will evaluate the policy assertions to determine actual service behaviour in response to the request.

The rest of this paper starts with Section 2 that discusses related work. Section 3 outlines the motivation for using policy for service discovery through a supply chain problem domain that will be discussed throughout the paper. Section 4 explains the ontology that conceptualises the business rules policy together with an example of an ontology-based policy. The policy is deployed onto UDDI in Section 5 and used in a discovery framework in Section 6. A discussion about our approach and a conclusion are in Section 7.

2   Related Work

Most of research work that uses policy for services focuses on administrative policies such as security and resource control policies. In [5], policy-based agent management is proposed for Grid services where policies for authorisation, encryption, and resource control are represented using DAML ontology language. In [6], authorisation and privacy for their Web Services are controlled by a language named Rei [7] which is based on RDF ontology language, and policy expressions in Rei will eventually be transformed to Prolog expression for reasoning. Their use of policy allows services to be described as requiring encrypted input or servicing with data privacy, and therefore service consumers can query for services that exhibit these policy-aware aspects. The work in [8] is closer to our work in that the policy will be defined using OWL and RuleML. Policy compatibility is considered in service composition but they do not consider deploying their mechanism onto standard UDDI or WS-policy framework. Our approach expresses rule-based policy from business functions aspect, and the rules will be used in service discovery to constrain the queries and be evaluated at query time. The policy will be deployed onto the standard UDDI and WS-Policy framework. To our knowledge, no other work has proposed a policy based on this framework to support service discovery.

3   Business Rules Policy for Supply Chain Domain

To demonstrate the need for involving business rules policies with the service selection process, a scenario of the parts-suppliers problem in a supply chain is as follows.

1. A retailer issues a purchase order for electronics parts to a distributor, specifying parts details including the number to order and the time duration for the parts to be delivered. For example, the order may specify 100 pieces of a particular part to be delivered within 5 days of purchase.
2. The distributor selects candidate suppliers from a UDDI service registry by considering some characteristics, e.g. the suppliers with whom the distributor has a contract or those who can supply the specified parts. In [9], the distributor has the parts from these candidate suppliers analysed to check if they are compatible.
3. The candidate suppliers may additionally publish a policy that relates to their business function. A candidate supplier may publish a policy as in Fig. 1 which specifies the action to be taken (i.e. either deliver parts or check inventory) based on the number of parts to be delivered. The service discovery framework hence should allow the distributor to check whether any candidate supplier has a delivery policy that satisfies the retailer's delivery time constraint based on the number of ordered parts given by the retailer. In this example, this candidate supplier will match by its first rule since 100 pieces of the part can be delivered within 3 days. The paper will focus in this step.
4. Finally, matched suppliers will be returned to the retailer.

```
Perform DeliverParts(days ≤  3)
        IF (numberOfParts  ≤ 100)
Perform DeliverParts(days ≤  10)
        IF (100  <  numberOfParts  ≤ 500)
Perform ContactInventoryBeforeConfirm
        IF (numberOfParts  > 500)
```

Fig. 1. Business rules policy for parts delivery

The business rules policy shown in Fig. 1 will be associated with a particular Web Service. Although many times business rules are tied to the level of business service, (i.e. group of related Web Services), rather than to the level of individual Web Services, it is out of scope of this paper. The focus here is on incorporating business rules policy for individual Web Services

4   Expressing Business Rules Policy by Ontology

We define common concepts as well as relations between those concepts to represent our business rules policy. A policy is specified as a collection of rules where each rule is an IF_conditions_THEN_action statement. If conditions are evaluated to True, the action is set or performed. The upper ontology for policy consists of the following classes of concepts (Fig. 2) which can be referred back to the example of the supply chain problem:

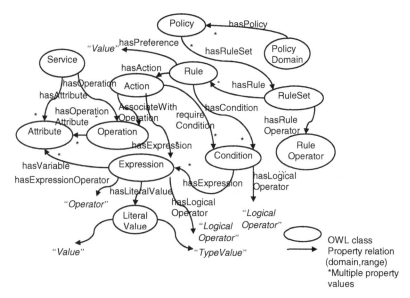

Fig. 2. Upper ontology for business rules policy

- Policy Domain is a service domain on which the policy is applied, e.g. the supply chain domain. A Policy Domain may have multiple Policies, e.g. the supply chain domain may have one policy about parts delivery and another one about payment.
- Policy defines constraints on a particular task within the service domain. A Policy may have multiple Rule Sets, e.g. the parts delivery policy may have one rule set about delivery time and another one about delivery means.
- Rule Set defines a set of Rules that relate to a particular aspect.
- Rule Operator is defined for a Rule Set to determine the level of rule enforcement within the Rule Set. Rule Operator can either be "All" to indicate that all of that all Rules within the Rule Set will apply, "ExactlyOne" to indicate that only one Rule will apply at a time, or "OneOrMore" to indicate that at least one Rule will apply. For the parts delivery policy in Fig. 1, "ExactlyOne" will apply.
- Rule is a conditions-and-action statement that says what action will be set when particular conditions are satisfied. In Fig. 1, three Rules are defined. A Rule may be tagged with a preference that indicates the degree of satisfaction when the Rule is matched. The preference can help in ranking the policies with matched rules.
- Action is an abstract term that may be associated with an Operation of a Service and Expressions that can be bound to logical operators. For example, the delivery parts action can be associated with the purchase parts operation of the parts supplier Web Service, and in the first Rule of Fig. 1., it is associated with the Expression (days ≤ 3).

- Condition is an abstract term that can be associated with Expressions that can be bound to logical operators.
- Expression specifies an expression that consists of Attribute, Expression Operator, and Literal Value. In the first Rule in Fig. 1, (numberOfParts ≤ 100) is an Expression for the condition of the rule where numberOfParts is Attribute, ≤ is Expression Operator, and 100 is Literal Value. Another Expression (days ≤ 3) in the first Rule is associated with the delivery parts action. An Expression Operator can either be relational operator or functional operator like min, max, and set (e.g. as in (numberOfParts min 100) for delivery parts action to perform, (numberOfParts max 1000) for credit purchase action to perform, or (cardholder(set{visa, amex, diners})) for credit purchase action to perform. A Literal Value consists of a value and the type of the value.

It is possible to use this upper ontology on its own, or as an enhancement to OWL-S service model [10] to allow rule-based policy evaluation for service composition. From the upper ontology, a domain expert may derive a domain-specific policy ontology that describes the vocabularies for policies, actions, conditions, attributes, and operations used commonly within the domain. Service providers in the domain can create their own policies by deriving from the domain-specific policy ontology, or simply by using a domain-specific policy template, filling in their own policy detail, and having an OWL-based policy specification automatically generated. Below is part of the policy specification called DeliverPartsToDistributorSupplierA of a supplier named supplierA. The information, represented in OWL, corresponds to the first rule in Fig. 1. Note that the upper ontology is referred to by the namespace po: and the domain-specific policy ontology by the namespace sp: .

```
xmlns:sp= "http://supplychain.com/policy.owl#"
xmlns:po= "http://samplepolicy.com/policy.owl#"
xmlns= "http://supplierA.com/policy.owl#

<!-----Policy -→
<sp:DeliverPartsToDistributorPolicy
            rdf:ID="DeliverPartsToDistributorSupplierA">
   <po:hasRuleSet rdf:ID="RuleSet1">
         <po:hasRuleOperator rdf:resource="po:ExactlyOne"/>
      <po:hasRule>
       <po:Rule rdf:ID="Rule1">
         <hasAction rdf:resource="#DeliverPartsRule1"/>
         <hasCondition rdf:resource="#CheckQuantity1"/>
       </po:Rule>
      </po:hasRule>
          …
   </po:hasRuleSet>
</sp:DeliverPartsToDistributorPolicy>

<sp:CheckQuantity rdf:ID="CheckQuantity1">
   <po:hasExpression>
    <po:Expression rdf:ID="ExpressionCondition1">
     <po:hasVariable>
       <po:Attribute rdf:resource="sp:NumberOfParts"/>
     </po:hasVariable>
     <po:hasExpressionOperator rdf:resource="po:isLessThanOrEqual"/>
     <po:hasLiteralValue>
       <po:LiteralValue rdf:ID="LiteralValue2">
```

```
           <po:hasValue
               rdf:datatype="http://www.w3.org/2001/XMLSchema#int">
                                              100</hasValue>
           <po:hasType rdf:resource="po:Integer"/>
        </po:LiteralValue>
      </po:hasLiteralValue>
    </po:Expression>
  </po:hasExpression>
</sp:CheckQuantity>

<sp:DeliverParts rdf:ID="DeliverPartsRule1">
  <po:associateWithOperation>
    <sp:PurchaseParts rdf:ID="PurchasePartsSupplierA"/>
  </po:associateWithOperation>
  <po:hasExpression rdf:ID="ExpressionAction1">
  <po:hasVariable>
    <po:Attribute rdf:ID="sp:DeliveryDay"/>
  </po:hasVariable>
  <po:hasExpressionOperator rdf:resource="po:isLessThanOrEqual"/>
  <po:hasLiteralValue rdf:ID="LiteralValue1">
        <po:hasValue
            rdf:datatype="http://www.w3.org/2001/XMLSchema#int"
                                          >3</po:hasValue>
        <po:hasType rdf:resource="po:Integer"/>
    </po:hasLiteralValue>
  </po:hasExpression>
  <po:requireCondition rdf:resource="#CheckQuantity1"/>
</sp:DeliverParts>
```

5 Deploying Business Rules Policy

A service provider can deploy an OWL-based business rules policy by attaching the policy to WSDL description of its Web Service [11]. Similarly to other kinds of policies that govern a Web Service, the business rules policy may be maintained separately or put into the all-policy specification together with other kinds of policies for easy management. Fig. 3 shows part of the all-policy specification file of supplierA's Web Service, say policy.xml, in which the new business rules policy Deliver-PartsToDistributorPolicy is added. This policy refers to the OWL-based DeliverPartsToDistributorSupplierA policy in Section 4.

```
base = "http://supplierA.com/policy.xml"
wspsp = "http://supplychainschema.com/policyspec"
…
<wsp:Policy Name="PurchasingProcess">
    <wsp:All>
        <wspsp:DeliverPartsToDistributorPolicy>
http://supplierA.com/policy.owl#DeliverPartsToDistributorSupplierA
        </wspsp:DeliverPartsToDistributorPolicy>

<!---Other policy for PurchasingProcess, e.g. WS-Security -→
…
    </wsp:All>
</wsp:Policy>
```

Fig. 3. Adding business rules policy to the all-policy specification of a Web Service

The policy.xml file will be associated with the Web Service by attaching it to WSDL [12]. In Fig. 4, the policy file is attached to the `PurchasePartsService` with `PurchasePartsPortType`, provided that the purchasing parts operation is defined in the port type. With this attachment, the policies in the file will be enforced on the Web Service instance.

```
base = "http://supplierA.com/purchaseparts.wsdl"
...
<wsp:PolicyAttachment>
  <wsp:AppliesTo>
    <wsp:EndpointReference>
      <wsp:ServiceName
            Name="PurchasePartsService"/>
          <wsp:PortType Name="PurchasePartsPortType/>
            <wsp:Address URI="http://supplierA.com/policy.xml" />
      </wsp:EndpointReference>
    </wsp:AppliesTo>
  <wsp:PolicyReference Ref="http://supplierA.com/policy.xml"/>
</wsp:PolicyAttachment>
```

Fig. 4. Attaching all-policy specification to WSDL of a Web Service

When the service provider publishes its Web Service with UDDI and specifies a tModel that references a corresponding WSDL file, the business rules policy is effectively published with UDDI via its attachment to that WSDL. In this way, candidate services can be discovered first by a typical query to standard UDDI (i.e. attribute values matching) or by other behaviour-based query such as the one in [9], [13]. The WSDL files of these candidate services will be retrieved and, as a result, the attached policy files can be referred to. The supporting discovery framework in Section 6 then can accommodate query based on business rules and can evaluate the policies by rule-based reasoning.

6   Policy-Based Discovery Framework

The discovery framework that supports policy-based service selection is depicted in Fig. 5. The main components that extend from standard UDDI are the Policy-Aware Discovery Proxy (or PADP) (a), Policy Server (b), Ontology Querying Module (c), and Rule Reasoning Module (d). PADP is a Web Service that interfaces with service consumers and is responsible for dispatching queries for evaluation and accumulating as well as ranking query results. Policy Server provides policy-defining templates that are associated with domain-specific ontologies. It generates OWL-based policies from the templates and also the corresponding rule-based specifications. It is a Web Service that works with Ontology Querying Module to evaluate semantic aspects of the policies and works with Rule Reasoning Module for rule-based evaluation.

Let us revisit to the parts-suppliers problem. The distributor is looking for suppliers that can deliver 100 pieces of the parts within 5 days. Part of the request that is related to the policy and submitted via a simple XML template (Fig. 6) is invoked on PADP (1).

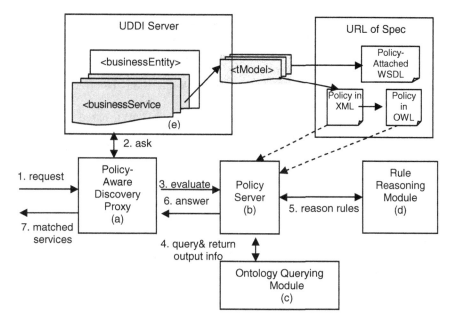

Fig. 5. Policy-based discovery framework

```
<findPolicy>
      <domain>SupplyChain</domain>
      <policy>DeliverPartsToDistributorPolicy</Policy>
      <action name="DeliverParts">
            <expression attribute="DeliveryDay">
                  <Value>5</Value>
                  <expressionOperator>isLessThanOrEqual
                                    </expressionOperator>
            </expression>
      </action>
      <condition name="CheckPartsQuantity">
            <expression attribute="NumberOfParts">
                  <Value>100</Value>
                  <expressionOperator>isEqual</expressionOperator>
            </expresion>
      </condition>
</findPolicy>
```

Fig. 6. Policy-based request in XML template

Assume that some candidate services that satisfy some characteristics of the request are already obtained by the method discussed at the end of Section 5. PADP
will consult UDDI server for the tModels that refer to WSDL files of all candidate
services (2). From WSDL, PADP can get the reference to the all-policy file for each
Web Service and sends the reference to the file to the Policy Server (3). On receiving
the reference, the Policy Server then loads the corresponding all-policy file, extracts
the reference to the OWL-based file, and at the end retrieve the OWL-based business
rules policy. The Policy Server will interact with the Ontology Querying Module to

match ontological concepts of the policy specification and the request (4) such as matching of domain and policy. The Policy Server further parses the OWL-based policy into a rule-based specification and contacts the Rule Reasoning Module to evaluate the specification (5). Finally, the Policy Server reports matched results back to PADP (6) which may in turn rank the results before returning to the distributor (7).

On technical details, we use StAX [14] to generate OWL-based policy and the corresponding rule-based specification in ABLE Rule Language [15]. SNoBASE [16] is used as the ontology querying tool and ABLE [17] is the rule reasoning engine.

7 Conclusion

In this paper we have proposed a new approach to defining business rules policies for Web Services and using such policies in Web Services discovery. An OWL ontology language is used to represent rules for business functions while rule-based reasoning is used for evaluation of rules in service matching. The deployment of the policies is adhered to the standard WS-Policy framework.

By the definition of policy as a set of rules, it is obvious that the effective way to represent a policy is by using a rule-based language since it is the most convenient for policy evaluation with a rule-based engine.   Nevertheless, we take the overheads of representing the policy with an ontology language and later transforming it into a rule-based representation.   This is due to the added benefit that policy evaluation would gain from ontological inference. For example, a supplier may have a policy `Perform OrderAndDeliverParts(days ≤ 2)` which means the supplier will order parts from another supplier first before making a delivery and all this is done within 2 days. If the distributor is looking for a supplier who can deliver parts within 3 days and there is an ontology that declares `OrderAndDeliverParts` as a subclass of `DeliverParts`, then this supplier will match the requirement.

This paper is merely an initial attempt to integrate the benefit from the world of ontology with the benefit of rule-based reasoning through the use of business rules policies. We plan to explore such integration further and consider the mechanism to determine policy compatibility, the degree of matching, and policy conflict. We also see the possibility to unify the policy ontology in this paper with the behavioural ontology in our previous work [13], which models a Web Service in terms of its operation, input, output, precondition, and effect, so that the behaviour of Web Services is better modelled.

Acknowledgements

This work is partly supported by Thailand-Japan Technology Transfer Project and Chulalongkorn University-Industry Linkage Research Grant Year 2004.

References

1. uddi.org: UDDI: Universal Description, Discovery and Integration of Web Services Version 3 (online). (2002) http://www.uddi.org
2. Box, D. et al.: Web Services Policy Framework (WS-Policy) (online). (2003). http://www-106.ibm.com/developerworks/library/ws-polfram/
3. Della-Libera, G. et al.: Web Services Security Policy (online). (2002) http://www-106.ibm.com/developerworks/webservices/library/ws-secpol/
4. w3.org: OWL Web Ontology Language Overview (online). (2004) http://www.w3.org /TR/2004/REC-owl-features-20040210/
5. Uszok, A. et al.: KAoS Policy and Domain Services: Toward a Description-Logic Approach to Policy Representation, Deconfliction, and Enforcement. In: Proceedings of Policy Workshop, Italy (2003) 93-98
6. Kagal, L., Paolucci, M., Srinivasan, N., Denker, G., Finin, T., Sycara, K.: Authorization and Privacy for Semantic Web Services. In: Proceedings of AAAI 2004 Spring Symposium on Semantic Web Services (2004)
7. Kagal, L.: Rei: A Policy Language for the Me-Centric Project. HP Labs : Tech Report: HPL-2002-270 (2002)
8. Chun, S. A et al.: Policy-Based Web Service Composition. In: Proceedings of 14th International Workshop on Research Issues on Data Engineering: Web Services for E-Commerce and E-Government Applications (RIDE'04) (2004)
9. Verma, K. et al.: On Accommodating Inter Service Dependencies in Web Process Flow Composition. In: Proceedings of 1st International Semantic Web Services Symposium (2004)
10. DAML: OWL-S: Semantic Markup for Web Services (online). (2004) http://www.daml.org/ services/owl-s/1.0/
11. w3.org: Web Services Description Language (WSDL) 1.1 (online). (2001) http://www.w3.org/TR/wsdl
12. Box, D. et al.: Web Service Policy Attachment (WS-PolicyAttachment) (online). (2003) http://www-106.ibm.com/developerworks/library/ws-polatt/
13. Sriharee, N., Senivongse, T.: Discovering Web Services by Using Behavioural Constraints and Ontology. In Stefani, J-B., Demeure, I., Hagimont, D. (eds.): Proceedings of 4th IFIP International Conference on Distributed Applications and Interoperable Systems (DAIS 2003). Lecture Notes in Computer Science, Vol. 2893. Springer-Verlag (2003) 248-259
14. StAX: Streaming API for XML Version 1.0 (online). (2003) http://dev2dev.bea.com /technologies/stax/index.jsp
15. ABLE Rule Language User's Guide and Reference, Version 2.0.1 (online). (2003) http://www.alphaworks.ibm.com/tech/able
16. Lee, J., Goodwin, R.T., Akkiraju, R., Doshi, P., Ye, Y.: SNoBASE: A Semantic Network-Based Ontology Management (online). (2003) http://alphaWorks.ibm.com/tech/snobase
17. ABLE: Agent Building and Learning Environment (online). (2003) http://www.alpha works.ibm.com/tech/able

Preserving Referential Constraints in XML Document Association Relationship Update

Eric Pardede[1], J. Wenny Rahayu[1], and David Taniar[2]

[1] Department of Computer Science and Computer Engineering,
La Trobe University, Bundoora VIC 3083, Australia
{ekpardede, wenny}@cs.latrobe.edu.au}
[2] School of Business System,
Monash University, Clayton VIC 3800, Australia
David.Taniar@infotech.monash.edu.au

Abstract. In this paper we propose the usage of W3C-standardized query language, XQuery, to accommodate XML Update. Our main aim is to enable the update without violating the semantic constraint of the documents. The focus of the update is on the association relationship. Therefore, we distinguish the relationship type based on the number of participants, cardinality, and adhesion. We also propose the mapping of the association relationship in the conceptual level to the XML Schema. We use XML Schema for structure validation, even though the algorithm can be used by any schema languages.

1 Introduction

In the last few years the interest in storing XML Documents in the native XML Databases (NXD) has emerged rapidly. The main idea is to store the documents in their natural tree form. However, it is well-known that many users still prefer to use DBMS that are based on established data models such as Relational Model for their document storage. One reason is the incompleteness of NXD query language. Many proprietary XML query languages and even W3C-standardized languages still have limitations compared to the Relational Model SQL. One of the most important limitations is the lack of the update operations support [8].

Different NXD applies different strategies for XML updates. Very frequently after update operations, the XML document contains many dangling references, loses the key attribute, has unnecessary duplications, and many other problems that indicate very low database integrity. To our best knowledge, there is no XML query language that has considered the integrity issues that emerge from the update operations. We suggest this as an important issue to raise and to investigate further.

This paper proposes the XQuery [6][11] for update operations. It is based on the basic operations firstly mentioned in [9]. Our main contribution is that we have included semantic constraints in the operations. It focuses on the update for association relationship, which can be defined as a "reference" relationship between one to another node/document in an XML tree. We will distinguish different association type

A. Aagesen et al. (Eds.): INTELLCOMM 2004, LNCS 3283, pp. 256–263, 2004.

based on the number of participants and on the cardinality. The XQuery update considers different target contents whether it is a key node or a key reference node. By doing this, we remove the possibilities of low integrity data after each update operation.

For XML update we need structure validation and we propose the use of XML Schema [10]. Thus, a part of the paper is allocated to developing a transformation on the association relationship into XML Schema, in a way that suits our proposed XQuery.

2 XML Document Update: An Overview

There are several strategies for updating XML documents in NXDs [1][8]. At the time of writing, there are three main strategies: (i) use **proprietary update language** that will allow updating within the server [3][7], (ii) use **XUpdate**, the standard proposed by XML DB initiative for updating a distinct part of a document [5][12], and (iii) use **XML API** after retrieving the document out of the database [4]. It is important to mention that none of these are concerned with the semantic constraint of the updated XML document.

Different strategies have limited the database interchangeability. To unite these different strategies, [9] has tried to propose the update processes for XML Documents into an XML language. These processes are embedded into XQuery and thus, can be used for any NXD that has supported this language.

In [9] the update is embedded in the XQuery FLOWR expression. Note the difference between the original XQuery (Fig.1) and its extension [(Fig. 2). The UPDATE clause specifies the node targets that will be updated. Inside the UPDATE clause, we determine the operation types.

```
FOR $binding1 IN path
    expression…
LET $binding := path
    expression…
    WHERE predicate, …
    ORDER BY predicate, …
        RETURN results
```

```
FOR. . .LET. . .WHERE. . .
UPDATE $target{
    DELETE $child|
    INSERT content
        [BEFORE|AFTER $child]|
    REPLACE $child WITH $content|
    {,subOp}*
    }
```

Fig. 1. XQuery FLOWR Expressions   **Fig. 2.** XQuery UPDATE Extensions

Nonetheless, even with this proposal there is a basic question to answer. We do not know how the update operations can affect the semantic correctness of the updated XML Documents. Specifically for the association relationship, this proposal does not maintain the referential constraint between the associated nodes/documents. This fact has motivated us to take the topic a step further.

3 Association Relationships in XML Document

Association relationship is a "reference" relationship between one object with another object in a system. For an XML document, the object is a node or a document. Semantically, this relationship type can be distinguished by some constraints such as *number of participant type*, *cardinality*, and *adhesion*. These constraints can be easily identified in XML Data Model such as in Semantic Network Diagram [2]. We will show a running example describing different association relationship constraints (see Fig. 3).

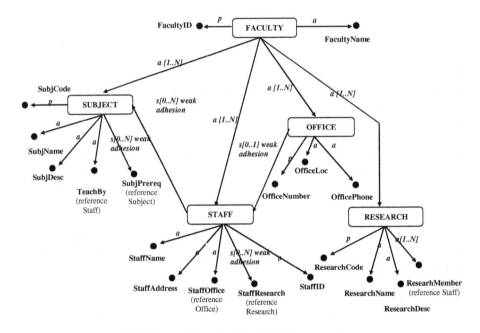

Fig. 3. Association Types in XML Document Tree

The number of participants can be distinguished into unary and binary. In the former, an object refers to another object of the same type. For example, there is one unary relationship, where node *SubjPrereq* in a subject document refers to another subject. In the binary relationship, the participants come from different types. In our example above, there are: Subject:Staff, Staff:Office, and Staff:Research.

Association cardinality identifies the number of objects of the same type to which a single object can relate to. For example, a staff can teach no subject at all to many subjects [0..N]. In the diagram the default cardinality is [1..1].

Finally, association adhesion identifies whether the associated objects must or must not coexist and adhere to each other. In the diagram, the default adhesion is a strong adhesion. For example, Staff has weak adhesion association to Subject, which means that the former does not require the latter to exist.

4   Mapping Association Relationship to XML Schema

XQuery update will require a schema to validate the document structure. We select XML Schema because as well as its precision in defining the data type, XML Schema has an effective ability to define the semantic constraints of a document. It includes the cardinality, adhesion, and referential integrity constraint depicted in Fig. 3.

First, the cardinality constraint is very straightforward and well-known. We can determine the "minoccurs" and "maxoccurs" after an element declaration. It is a general practice that these constraints are not used for attribute. A particular attribute will appear, at most, once in an object/instance.

Second, the adhesion constraint can easily be indicated by the "use" constraint. A strong adhesion has use "required" and a weak adhesion has use "optional". However, in practice the "use" constraint can only be attached in attribute. We will find a problem if, for example, the adhesion constraint is applied to an element. Fortunately, we can utilize the cardinality constraint to define the adhesion constraint as well. Cardinality [0..1] or [0..N] indicates a weak adhesion, while [1..1] or [1..N] indicates a strong adhesion.

For a consensus we provide a table combining the two constraints that can be very useful for the next section.

Table 1. Adhesion and Cardinality Constraints in XML Schema

Adhesion	Cardinality	What to Use
Strong	1:1	Attribute (use = "required")
	1:N	Element (minoccurs="1" maxoccurs="unbounded")
	N:N	Element(minoccurs="<2.. >" maxoccurs="unbounded")
Weak	0:1	Attribute (use = "optional")
	0:N	Element (minoccurs="0" maxoccurs="unbounded")

Third, for the referential integrity constraint, XML Schema provides two options ID/IDREF and key/keyref. We have chosen to use the latter for several reasons: (i) key has no restriction on the lexical space [10], (ii) key cannot be duplicated and thus facilitate the unique semantic of a key node, and (iii) key/keyref can be defined in a specific element and, thereby, helping the implementer to maintain the reference.

For our design, we propose to create a specific element under the root element called "GroupKey" to store all keys and keyrefs. It is required to track the path of the associated elements once an update is performed. We cannot just declare the key/keyref inside the element where they are appeared. We will experience problems in tracking an associated element since keyref can only trace the key declared in the same element or in its direct predecessor. For example, if we declare the keyref *TeachBy* inside subject element and key *StaffID* inside staff element, the keyref cannot trace the key and thus, if we update a staff, there is no checking done to ensure the subject refers to the particular staff.

In a unary relationship, the key and keyref attribute/element is located under one element. In a binary relationship we have to determine the location of the keyref attribute/element. The adhesion constraint is used for this purpose. Locate the keyref attribute/element under the associated element that has strong adhesion towards the other. In the case where both associated elements are in strong adhesion, the keyref attribute/element will be added in both elements. For example (see Fig.3), in the relationship between staff and research, we add reference *ResearchMember* inside research element that refers to *StaffID*, and reference *StaffResearch* inside research element that refers to *ResearchCode*.

5   Proposed XQuery Update

Now we have shown how to map the conceptual model into logical XML Schema, we can begin to propose the XQuery for Update processes. The update can be differentiated into three main parts: deletion, insertion, and replacement.

5.1 XQuery for Delete Operation

Deletion is the simplest update operation, especially if we want to delete an attribute/element that contains simple data. In this case we only require the binding to the parent and the child. We do not need to perform predicate checking on instances. However, if the attribute and element also have roles as key/keyref the checking on instances is required to maintain the referential integrity constraint.

For our proposed XQuery, we differentiate the operation for key and keyref since we put focus on the association relationship. For deletion however, there is no constraint checking required for keyref node since it is treated like simple data content.

The following XQuery shows functions used for predicates in key deletion. Function *checkKeyRefNode* checks whether the target key node has keyref node referred to it. This function highlights one reason why we select key/keyref instead of ID/IDREF. Now the implementer can check only the path where the keyref is defined. Since we have grouped all key and keyref declarations in the "GroupKey" element, we only need to check the "GroupKey" element.

Under a condition (see the function), the *checkKeyRefNode* function proceeds to function *checkKeyRefInstance*. This function checks that there is no instance that has keyref attribute/element referring to the target key content. This is the reason we also need to pass the content of the target key node. If the function returns false, we cannot perform the deletion.

```
FUNCTION checkKeyRefNode($gKBindingPath, $keyName, $keyContent) RETURN
BOOLEAN {
    LET $gkRef := $gKBindingPath/keyref/[@refer]
    RETURN
        IF $gkRef = $keyName
            THEN getKeyRefInstance($gKBindingPath, $keyName, $keyContent)
            ELSE TRUE}

FUNCTION checkKeyRefInstance($gKBindingPath, $keyName, $keyContent)
RETURN BOOLEAN
```

```
{
FOR $keyRefBinding IN $gKBindingPath/keyref[@refer=$keyname]
LET $keyRefName:=$gKBindingPath/keyref/@name
    $keyRefPath:=$keyRefBinding/selector/xpath
    $keyRefInstance:=$keyRefPath[@$keyRefName, "$keyContent"]
RETURN
    IF exists ($keyRefInstance)
        THEN FALSE
        ELSE TRUE}

Example:
FOR $g IN document("Faculty.xml")/Faculty/GroupKey
    $p IN document("Faculty.xml")/Faculty/Subject(@SubjCode = "ADB41")
    $c IN $p/SubjCode
LET $cContent := "ADB41"
UPDATE $p{
WHERE checkKeyRef($g, "SubjCode", $cContent)
        UPDATE $p{
                DELETE $p (:delete the key and the siblings:)
                        }}}
```

The example following the functions shows the key deletion *SubjCode* in document "Faculty.xml" of instance with *SubjCode* equals to "ADB41". We know that there is a node *SubjPrereq* that refers to *SubjCode*. Thus, if there is any instance where *SubjPrereq* value refers to *SubjCode* "ADB41", the deletion should be restricted.

Note that if the *checkKeyRef* function returns TRUE, we will delete whole elements and not only the key *SubjCode*. This is because we do not have trigger-based delete, which will delete the whole element if the key is deleted.

5.2 XQuery for Insert Operation

Unlike deletion, insertion requires the constructor of a new attribute or new element. Beside the XQuery for key insertion, we have to propose insertion for keyref as well, to make sure that the new keyref actually refers to an existent key.

Function *checkKeyDuplicate* returns TRUE if the target is not duplicating an existing instance. The example following the function shows the checking if we want to insert a *SubjCode* with content "ADB41".

```
FUNCTION checkKeyDuplicate($bindingPath) RETURN BOOLEAN
{
RETURN
    IF EXISTS($bindingPath)
        THEN FALSE
        ELSE TRUE}

Example:
FOR $g IN document("Faculty.xml")/Faculty(@FacID = "FSTE")
    $p IN $g/Subject(@SubjCode="ADB41")
LET $c:= SubjCode
    $cContent:="ADB41"
UPDATE $p{
WHERE checkKeyDuplicate($p)
        UPDATE $p{
                INSERT new_att($c, $cContent)
                        }}
```

For keyref insertion, we propose three additional functions. The first is for the referential integrity constraint and the following two are for the cardinality constraint. The cardinality is required since a keyref can actually refer to more than one key instance.

Function *checkKeyInstance* passes the keyref name and content, and then checks the key being referred. Function *getMaxOccurs* and *checkMaxOccurs* are used to calculate the maxoccurs constraint of a keyref node. If the particular instance has the maximum number of keyref, we will disable the insertion of another keyref content.

```
FUNCTION checkKeyInstance($gKBindingPath, $keyRefName, $keyRefContent)
RETURN BOOLEAN
{
FOR $keyRefBinding IN $gKBindingPath/keyref[@name = $keyRefName],
LET $keyName:=$gkeyRefBinding/@refer,
    $keyPath:=$gKeyRefBinding/selector/xpath,
    $keyInstance:=$keyPath[@$keyName, "$keyRefContent")
RETURN
   IF EXISTS($KeyInstance)
      THEN TRUE}

FUNCTION getMaxOccurs($xsName, $parentName, $childName) RETURN INTEGER
{
FOR $pDef IN document($xsName)//xs:element[@name=$parentName],
    $cDef IN $pDef/xs:element[@name=$childName],
LET $cMaxOccurs:=$cDef/maxoccurs,
RETURN $cMaxOccurs}

FUNCTION checkMaxOccurs($bindingPath, $cMaxOccurs) RETURN BOOLEAN
{
LET $instanceOccurs:=count($bindingPath)
RETURN
    IF $cMaxOccurs >= $instanceOccurs + 1
       THEN FALSE
       ELSE TRUE}
```

5.3 XQuery for Replace Operation

Since replacement can be seen as a combination of deletion and insertion, we can reuse the functions we have already described in the last two sub-sections. In fact, we do not need the functions for cardinality constraints during keyref replacement as well.

For replacement of a key, we have to check whether the new key content does not duplicate any existing instance. For replacement of a keyref, we just need to check whether the new keyref content refers to a valid instance. No cardinality checking is required since to accommodate a new keyref, we must have deleted another keyref. XQuery below shows the example of replacement for keyref *TeachBy* element.

```
FOR $g IN document("Faculty.xml")/Faculty/GroupKey
    $p IN document("Faculty.xml")/Faculty/Subject(@SubjCode = "ADB41")
    $c IN $p/TeachBy
LET $cName := TeachBy
    $cContent := "WR01"
UPDATE $p{
WHERE checkKeyInstance($g, $cName, $cContent)
       UPDATE $p{
              REPLACE $c WITH <TeachBy>WR01</TeachBy>
                      }}
```

6   Conclusion

In this paper, we propose extending XQuery to preserve semantic constraints during an XML update. The update operations are divided into deletion, insertion, and replacement. The focus in the paper is on the association relationship type, thus each operation considers the key and key reference target node. By doing this, we can avoid database anomalies that might occur using conventional XQuery.

Since Update requires a document structure validation, we also propose the transformation of the relationship into XML Schema. The constraints captured are cardinality, adhesion, and referential integrity constraint.

With this extension, XML query languages (in the form of XQuery) are becoming more powerful. Concurrently, it can increase the potential of using tree-form XML repository such as Native XML Database.

References

1. Bourett, R.: XML and Databases. http://www.rpbourret.com/xml/XMLAndDatabases.htm, (2003)
2. Feng, L., Chang, E., Dillon, T.S.: A Semantic Network-Based Design Methodology for XML Documents. ACM Trans. Information System, Vol. 20, No. 4. (2002) 390-421
3. Ipedo.: Ipedo XML Database, http://www.ipedo.com/html/products.html, (2004)
4. Jagadish, H. V., Al-Khalifa, S., Chapman, A., Lakhsmanan, L. V. S., Nierman, A., Paprizos, S., Patel, J. M., Srivastava, D., Wiwattana, N., Wu, Y., Yu, C.: TIMBER: A native XML database. VLDB Journal, Vol. 11, No. 4. (2002) 279-291
5. Meier, W.M.: eXist Native XML Database. In Chaduri, A.B., Rawais, A., Zicari, R. (eds): XML Data Management: Native XML and XML-Enabled Database System. Addison Wesley (2003) 43-68
6. Robie, J.: XQuery: A Guided Tour. In Kattz, H. (ed.): XQuery from the Experts. Addison Wesley (2004) 3-78
7. SODA Technology.: SODA. http://www.sodatech.com/products.html, (2004)
8. Staken, K.: Introduction to Native XML Databases. http://www.xml.com/pub/a/2001/10/31/nativexmldb.html, (2001)
9. Tatarinov, I., Ives, Z.G., Halevy, A. Y., Weld, D. S.: Updating XML. ACM SIGMOD (2001) 413-424
10. Vlist, E. V-D.: XML Schema, O'Reilly, Sebastopol (2002)
11. W3C: XQuery 1.0: An XML Query Language. http://www.w3.org/TR/xquery, (2001)
12. XML DB: XUpdate – XML Update Language, http://www.xmldb.org/xupdate/, (2004)

ASMA: An Active Architecture for Dynamic Service Deployment

Habib Bakour and Nadia Boukhatem

Computer Science and Network Department,
Ecole Nationale Supérieure des Télécommunications,
46, Rue Barrault – 75013 Paris – France
{bakour, boukhatem}@infres.enst.fr

Abstract. The deregulated telecommunication market tends to force network operators to open their infrastructure to third party service providers to offer a large variety of services. This trend is already appearing, particularly in the mobile environment, and it is widely admitted that this situation will not take a long time to be applied to the information technology (IT) communications, thereby creating a strong competition between the different network actors. In this context, one of the major stakes for both operators and service providers is to be capable of quickly providing new and attractive services. For instance, on-demand service creation and deployment will enable the diversification of the service offerings and will provide more business opportunities. This article presents an approach for a dynamic service deployment based on the virtual active networks (VAN) concept. In particular, we present the ASMA (Active Service Management Architecture) platform which we developed to provide an environment allowing flexible service deployment and management.

1 Introduction

Until recently, the deployment of new services within the network operator infrastructure could only be achieved with the commitment of manufacturers, due to the closed nature of network equipments. Any modification in network equipment functionalities would usually be expensive and require a long time before being operational, due to standardization and development processes.

Active networks provide programmability to enable third parties (end-users, application and service providers) to run their own services within a network. By *programmability* we mean that active nodes are able to execute code injected by the third parties to create the desired functionality at run-time. This provides an open environment allowing new services to be deployed more or less on-demand.

While facilitating the introduction of new services within the network, active networks make the management even more complex, in particular resource management. Indeed, several services belonging to different customers can be executed within the same active node and thus can share the same processing and network resources. The network provider must implement an efficient resource management scheme in order to avoid a specific service to monopolize the resources, thus penalizing and affecting other services.

A. Aagesen et al. (Eds.): INTELLCOMM 2004, LNCS 3283, pp. 264–272, 2004.

To better manage network resources, we use the VAN (Virtual Active Network) concept. As traditional virtual networks, a VAN is a logical network intended to organize network resources and to reduce the complexity of resource management.

Some recent works [1][2][3] have used the concept of VAN, however each of them has its own motivation and interpretation. The Genesis project [1] introduced the notion of "spawning networks", where a child network can be dynamically created, and inherit parts of the resources and functionality of the parent network. The specification of a child network is produced manually by a network architect. The VAN project [2] is mainly focused on the definition of abstractions through which applications can specify a VAN. The VAN [3] project achieved within ETH-Zurich focuses on the implementation of a service management toolkit that facilitates designing and managing services. Our aim is to define and implement a whole platform based on the VAN concept allowing a dynamic service deployment.

In this paper, we present ASMA (Active Service Management Architecture) platform which on the one hand, allows the implementation of the VAN concept and its management and, on the other hand, provides functionality allowing a dynamic and flexible service management, within a VAN.

This paper is organized as follows. In section 2, we give an overview on ASMA platform and present its interfaces and their functionalities. Section 3 is devoted to service management. In section 4, we provide details about the ASMA prototype. Finally, we conclude with a summary of this contribution and give some remarks.

2 The ASMA Architecture

In the ASMA platform, a VAN is considered as a service abstraction offered by a provider to its customers. We assume that the provider infrastructure is based on active networking technology.

For the provider, the VAN represents the means to partition the network resources and isolate the customers from one another in virtual environments. For the customer, the VAN represents the environment in which it can install, configure and run its own services without further interaction with the provider. A customer can be an end-user, a service provider or another network provider. The network provider is the entity that owns the network resources. The customer buys the resources from the provider in form of a VAN to install and run its own services.

At the lowest level, a VAN can be described as a graph of virtual active nodes interconnected by virtual links. Virtual active nodes provide active packet processing functionality inside the network. They constitute execution environments (EE) having their own resources (memory, CPU...). A virtual link is built on top of physical links connecting two virtual nodes (a virtual link can cross several physical links). Each virtual link has an amount of bandwidth allocated to it.

When a customer requests the creation of a VAN with specified needs (topology, memory, CPU, bandwidth, etc.), an EE is created on the active node. The VAN's needs are translated within an EE in term of allocation of virtual memory and virtual processing capacities. The creation of several VANs involves the creation of several independent EEs running on the same active node.

At the higher level, the ASMA platform allows the customer and the network provider to communicate through specific interfaces (see figure 1).

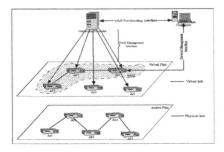

Fig. 1. ASMA Interfaces

The first interface (*VAN provisioning Interface*) gives the customer the ability to request a VAN from the network provider. The communication between the customer and the provider is achieved through a dynamic negotiation protocol which enables the customer to specify his needs (topology, resources...).

The second interface (*VAN Management Interface*) offers to the provider an environment for managing the VANs of his domain. Through this interface, the provider can create, modify, remove and supervise the VANs running within his management domain.

The third interface (*Service Management Interface*) is related to service deployment and management. As stated previously, a VAN constitutes an environment in which the customer can install, manage and run active services in an independent manner. The service management interface provides the customer with a means to manage and control his own services within his own VAN.

2.1 VAN Negotiation Protocol

The VAN creation requests are taken in charge by the network provider through the *"VAN Provisioning Interface"*. This interface is modeled as a dynamic negotiation protocol allowing the customers to request the creation of a VAN according to a defined VAN level specification. It allows also the customers to renegotiate this service level on-demand.

A VAN can be seen as a specific service which has particular requirements. To specify a VAN, we define the following parameters (VAN-Spec): Resource requirements and VAN Topology. Resource requirements specify the amount of resources needed by the customer (Memory, Bandwidth, Disk and CPU). VAN topology specifies the topology features of the VAN. This concerns the number of links, the number of nodes, and the way they are interconnected (chain, ring, star, etc.). When the SM receives a VAN creation request, it maps the virtual VAN topology onto a physical topology through a proposed mapping algorithm [4].

To request a VAN installation, the customer sends a REQUEST message to the SM with the desired VAN level specification. The SM replies with a RESPONSE message indicating if it accepts or rejects the VAN request. In case of rejection, the SM proposes another VAN specification. In both cases, the customer sends a REPORT message either to confirm the acceptance or rejection of the proposed VAN specification. The exchanged messages between the customer and the SM are depicted in figure 2.

During the VAN lifetime, the customer has the possibility of modifying his VAN-Spec. He can add/remove nodes or reconsider the reserved resources. For this purpose, he has to renegotiate his VAN-Spec. The renegotiation proceeds in the same manner as the negotiation, except that the customer has to specify the VAN identifier (VANId) in the REQUEST message.

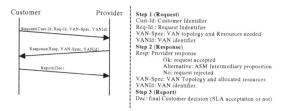

Fig. 2. Dynamic VAN negotiation protocol

2.1 VAN Management

The ASMA architecture consists of several functional components. The main component is the SM (System Manager, see figure 3) which resides in a node within the provider domain and is responsible for domain-wide VAN management.

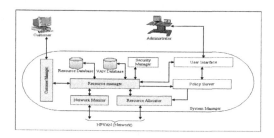

Fig. 3. SM Components

When the SM receives VAN creation requests through the Customer Manager (CM) it contacts the resource manager (RM) which determines if sufficient resources are available to meet that new demand. This decision is based on measurement state information which is maintained by the RM.

The network information is stored in two databases: resource database (RDB) and VAN database (VANDB). The RDB stores information concerning the available resources within a domain. This database is updated by the Network Monitor which receives the network information from the monitoring agents installed in the NPVAN nodes. The VANDB contains the information related to the VANs topology and VANs allocated resources. This database is updated at each VAN creation, modification or removal.

In case of a successful negotiation, the resource manager sends the VAN specification (topology, resources...) to the policy server. The policy server builds policies – according to the VAN specification –, and sends them to the Resource Allocator (RA), which installs these policies in the corresponding nodes.

The security manager deals with the access control and enables to authenticate customers. Only authorized customers will access their corresponding VANs.

2.2.1 Resource Management

Active services require access to diverse system resources, such as forwarding network bandwidth, router CPU cycles, state-store capacity and memory capacity. The resource management is one important issue in our platform. The latter should provide capabilities to isolate the VANs owing to different customers. To each VAN a specific amount of resources, as specified in the VAN-Spec, should be allocated. In addition, services running in the same VAN should also be controlled.

Our ASMA architecture defines a resource model [5] consisting of three functions: admission control, resource allocation, and resource consumption and access control. These functions are ensured mainly by the Resource Manager. The resource consumption and access control are related to service execution and will be presented in 3.

The resource database (RDB), presented above, constitutes the basis for the resource admission control. Indeed, when a new VAN creation demand is received, the VAN manager uses this database and the VAN-Spec to determine if the new demand can be satisfied. This database is updated using network-monitoring agents, which are installed in all NPVAN nodes (i.e. all the active nodes of the domain).

It exists several EEs running in each active node. Each EE corresponds to a VAN. In particular, the NPVAN_EE corresponds to the NPVAN.

Each EE contains an agent which monitors the state of its resource consumption (CPU, Memory, Disk, bandwidth_out and bandwidth_in) through the NodeOS primitives.

The NPVAN_EE contains a monitoring agent which collects the monitoring information of the other agents and updates its local resource database (LRB). The LRB contains information related to the resource state in the active node.

The resource allocation is insured by the RA through the policy installation. Once the RM has decided to allocate resources to a VAN, it informs the policy server which instantiates policies using the VAN-Spec values. Then, the RA forwards these policies and installs them in the appropriate nodes through the NPVAN. In an active node, the policies are stored in the policy base in order to be used to control the resource consumption.

3 Service Management

The processing of packets inside traditional networks is limited to operations on packet headers which are mainly used for routing purposes. Active networks allow more efficient processing by allowing the active nodes to perform customized computations.

Active processing gives customers ability to dynamically deploy their services. As mentioned above, in an active node, an execution environment (EE) is associated with a VAN (e.g. the NPVAN_EE is associated with the NPVAN). The creation of several VANs within an active node implies the creation of several independent EEs running in this active node. In order to differentiate between different VANs, each active packet contains an identifier to specify the VAN and so, the EE that will process it. The active node integrates a demultiplexer, which forwards the packets to the corresponding EEs for processing. The architecture of an active node is presented in figure 4.

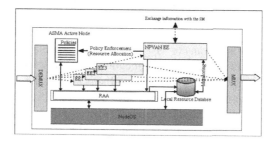

Fig. 4. Active Node Architecture

In ASMA, each service is characterized by: its *owner*, its *execution place*, and its *control* and *behavior* applications. The *owner* corresponds to the customer who owns the service. The *execution place* represents the list of nodes where the service will be executed. This place can contain a part of the VAN or all the nodes of the VAN.

The *control application* is the program that enables a customer to control his services. Through this application, the customer can install, activate/deactivate, update, delete his services. The *behavior application* is the program that defines the service behavior in the active node.

Once the service is activated, arriving packets to the active node are processed by the corresponding *behavior application* at the corresponding EE (each packet contains the identifier of the service which will process it). If the EE does not find a corresponding *behavior application* (when the service is deactivated, for example), then the active packet will be forwarded to the next node (following the routing table).

The execution of an active service implies the consumption of active node resources. The resource consumption and access control is ensured by an agent, called RAA (Resource Access Agent), which is located between the NodeOS and the different EEs (figure 4). The RAA authorizes resource access according to the installed policies, and sends a warning message to the SM server and to the service owner in case the service exceeds its limits.

To guarantee a safe execution of the services, the RAA uses a virtual resource control mechanism. This consists in the definition of resource objects (ROs), where each RO corresponds to a resource category (Process, Storage, Network). When an active service wants to access a physical resource, it invokes the corresponding RAA access function.

4 Implementation and Experiments

In this section, we present an experiment illustrating the feasibility of a VAN-based platform allowing a flexible active services deployment. This experiment is based on a scenario that presents an example of a service deployment. In particular, we developed an active multimedia streaming control service. This active service is used in the case of a video on demand allowing video clients to request video movies from a multimedia server.

The ASMA platform is deployed over PC/Linux using the Java NodeOS [6] and ANTS (Active Network Transfer System) [7] as execution environment. In this prototype, we distinguish two main applications: the System Manager Application, which is responsible for managing VANs and supervising the network behavior, and the Customer application which allows the customer to request a VAN from the System Manager, install services and manage them.

Different packages are developed, and integrated to the ANTS environment. These packages concern particularly the RAA agent and the monitoring services.

A graphical interface was developed. It enables the administrator to browse the SM information databases of system resources and installed VAN information.

In our scenario, an active video control service is deployed on a VAN which has the characteristics depicted in figure 5.

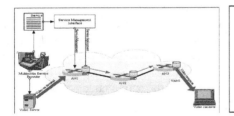

Characteristics of VAN1 :

- VANId: VAN1
- VAN Topology: Chain
- Number of nodes: 3 (AN1, AN2, AN3)
- Maximum Bandwidth: 40 kbytes/s
- Maximum Disk Consumption: 20 Mbytes
- Maximum CPU usage: 30 % of the CPU time

Fig. 5. Example of a video service deployment

The developed service consists in an MPEG-4 [8] video streaming control mechanism. We remind that in the MPEG compression algorithm, the MPEG encoder generates three types of compressed frames: Intra-coded (I), Predictive (P), and Bi-directional (B) frames. The different parts of the video data stream have not the same importance for the quality of the decoded video. The damages caused by some data loss in a reference picture (I-Frame or P-Frame) will affect subsequent picture(s) due to inter-frame predictions. Subsequently, I-Frame must be protected more than P-Frame and P-Frame more than B-Frame [9].

The video streaming control mechanism developed in our experiments is based on the Video Group of Picture Level Discard algorithm. This algorithm enables maintaining the state of a whole Group of Pictures (GoP). Thus, when the I-Frame is dropped, all the corresponding P-Frame and B-Frame are also dropped. To identify a Frame, the active program should be aware about the video structure.

For our experiments, the MPEG-4 presentation was obtained by using a set of multimedia components. We used the video components of the MPEG-4 coded Jurassic Park movie as an example of a medium video activity traffic. This trace file of this movie is freely available at [10].

Figure 6 shows the traffic entering at the active node AN1. This figure shows that the bandwidth never exceeds the level of 40 kbytes/s. This is due to the strict control performed by the RAA agent over the VAN1 (Max bandwidth = 40 kbytes/s), in particular at the entrance of the AN1 node.

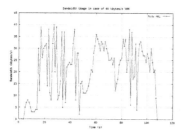
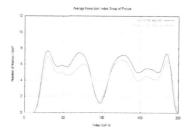

Fig. 6. Bandwidth usage at AN1   **Fig. 7.** Frame loss per GoP

When our service is activated, the active node drops randomly the video packets but when I-Frame is dropped, all the corresponding P-Frame, and B-Frame are also dropped.

The experiment is performed twice: before service control installation, and after its installation. Figure 7 shows the average of frame loss (due to frame drop or unusable frames) per GoP.

This figure shows that if the service control is activated, the video destination will receive more usable frames. This means that the installation of a video control service enables enhancement of video quality. In fact, dropping unusable frames (when the I-Frame is missing) guarantees delivery of only usable frames, and therefore frees network resources to guarantee transfer of a maximum of usable GoP.

We notice that, the nodes AN2 and AN3 do not make significant treatment on the service traffic, since the latter is regulated at the network access, e.g. at AN1 level. This is due to the nature of the implemented service itself.

5 Conclusion

Rapid deployment of new services based on an efficient resource control has motivated us to design and implement ASMA platform.

ASMA allows the customer to request VAN through a dynamic negotiation protocol, to manage his VANs and to deploy freely his active services. Moreover, the ASMA platform allows the provider to manage and supervise all VANs created in his domain.

A resource management model is proposed. The resource admission control function is used to determine if a new VAN can be created on not, according to the resource availability. Once a VAN is installed, the resource allocation is materialized by the installation of policies according to the negotiated VAN-spec. The execution of a service is subjected to a strict resource consumption and access control performed by the RAA.

An ASMA prototype is developed using the Janos operating system. Some experiments have been presented to show that a strict control is applied if the installed services exceed the negotiated limits.

We aimed through this work to show that the network virtualization allows the active networks technology to find in dynamic service deployment an extremely promising applicability.

References

1. M. Kounavis et al.: "The Genesis Kernel: A Programming System for Spawning Network Architectures" – IEEE Journal on Selected Areas in Communications (JSAC), Special Issue on Active and Programmable Networks, Vol. 19, No.3, pp. 49-73, March 2001.
2. G. Su, Y. Yemini: "Virtual Active Networks: Towards Multi-Edged Network Computing"- Computer Networks, pp. 153-168, July 2001
3. M. Brunner, R. Stadler : "Virtual Active Networks – Safe and Flexible Environment for Customer-managed Services" – DSOM'99, Zurich, October 1999
4. Habib Bakour, Nadia Boukhatem: "ASMA: Active Service Management Architecture" Technical report – ENST Paris, March 2003
5. Habib Bakour, Nadia Boukhatem: "Dynamic service management in active networks" – IEEE SoftCOM 2003, Italy/Croatia, October 2003
6. P. Tullman et al: "Janos: A Java-oriented OS for Active Networks" – IEEE Journal on selected Areas of Communication. Volume 19, Number 3, March 2001
7. D. Wetherall, J. V. Guttag and D. L. Tennenhouse: "ANTS: A Toolkit for Building and Dnamically Deploying Network Protocols", IEEE Openarch, April 1998 http://www.cs.utah.edu/flux/janos/ants.html
8. ISO/IEC 14496-1 "Coding of audio-visual objects: Systems -final committee draft.", may 1998
9. T. Ahmed et al.: "Encapsulation and Marking of MPEG-4 Video over IP Differentiated Services", IEEE ISCC'2001, Tunisia, July 2001
10. http://www-tkn.ee.tu-berlin.de/~fitzek/TRACE/ltvt.html

An XML-Based Framework for Dynamic Service Management

Mazen Malek Shiaa, Shanshan Jiang, Paramai Supadulchai,
and Joan J. Vila-Armenegol

Department of Telematics,
Norwegian University of Science and Technology (NTNU),
N-7491 Trondheim, Norway
{malek, ssjiang, paramai}@item.ntnu.no, vilaarme@stud.ntnu.no

Abstract. Service systems are likely to be highly dynamic in terms of changing resources and configurations. On the one hand, resources are increasingly configurable, extendable, and replaceable. On the other hand, their availability is also varying. For this reason, the handling of these changes is crucial to achieve efficiency. To accomplish this objective, a framework for dynamic service management with respect to service specification and adaptation is proposed.

1 Introduction

A service system, in general, is viewed as a composition of service components. In the lifecycle of service systems (or service components) there are two main phases: the service specification and the service execution phases. The first handles the way services being specified, while the second comprises all the tasks related to service instantiation, operation and maintenance. Historically, service management as a concept has always been discussed and disputed within the second phase only, i.e. independently from the *Service Specification*. Manual modification of the service specification and thereafter configuration and reconfiguration are therefore needed. The concept of *Dynamic Service Management* will take a different approach to service management. It will propose procedures that will make services adaptable to the dynamic changes in their execution environment, based on modifiable and selectable service specifications.

In this paper, we propose a framework for Dynamic Service Management, which addresses two key issues; *Service Specification* and *Service Adaptation*. The main idea is to use behavior specifications with generalized action types as the service specifications. The actual executing code, or the action libraries that include routines specific to the execution environment, is determined during run-time. The system resources are represented by the so-called *Capability* and *Status* of the system, which characterize all the information related to resources, functions and data inherent to a particular node and may be used by a service component to achieve its functionality. *Service Adaptation* is achieved by allowing the service components to dynamically modify their functionality by requesting changes to their service specification. The framework uses web services to manage the availability and communication of service components.

A. Aagesen et al. (Eds.): INTELLCOMM 2004, LNCS 3283, pp. 273–280, 2004.

2 Related Work

Service management, and dynamic service management, has been dealt with in a number of papers, e.g. in active networks [1], replacement of software modules in [2]. In general, the principles discussed in [3] are considered to serve as a basis for any dynamic change management, which are also followed in this paper. Another approach, sharing our view of *Capability* availability, can be found in [4]. It addresses the problem of providing information access to mobile computers using the principle of adjusting the data according to the environment status. Each application is responsible for deciding how to exploit available resources by selecting the fidelity level of the transmitted data. The adaptation is based on choosing between different versions of the data (fidelity levels) in order to match the resource availability. Our work targets the adaptation of any kind of behavior, instead of the adaptation of data itself. It requires that the behavior is rich in its processing possibilities. In this regard, the support platform (that executes in the nodes) is responsible for monitoring resource availability, notifying applications of relevant changes to those resources and enforcing resources allocation decisions. Each application is responsible for deciding how best to exploit available resources.

3 Service Specification

As a basic assumption in the framework, a service is viewed as a composition of one or more service components (we also consider a service as a *play* consisting of different *roles*.) Each Service Component is realized or carried out by one or more Role-Figure (being an entity in the architecture that is capable of representing some well-defined functionality). A Role-Figure is realized by a software component (or a collaboration of software components, e.g. multi-threaded processes) executing in a node. However, throughout this paper, and as an abstraction from the implementation domain, Role-Figure will be the constituent of the architecture that is used to provide a basis for service specification and instantiation. In this regard, a Role-Figure specification is the service (or part of a service) specification, which gives a service behavior description. The most intuitive way to model such a specification is by a State Machine model (one well-known and applied model is the Extended Finite State Machine, EFSM, that is considered here.) [5]. Fig. 1 shows the EFSM data structure for the Role-Figure specification. The behavior description defined in the Role-Figure specification consists of *states*, *data* and *variables*, *inputs*, *outputs*, and different *actions*. Actions are functions and tasks performed by the Role-Figure during a specific state. They may include calculations on local data, method calls, time measurements, etc. The *<Action>* list in the Role-Figure specifications specifies only the action type, i.e. the method name, and parameters for the action. Each action type belongs to some Action Group according to the nature of action.

Declaring Actions by their general types and classifying them into Actions Groups (e.g. *G1*: Node Computation Capability, *G2*: Communication model, *G3*: Graphics, *G4*: I/O interaction) is a technique used to tackle the problem of platform and implementation independence, as well as achieving a better flexibility and reusability in service and application design. Using Action Types and Action Groups in the service specification keeps the specification short, clean and abstract from how it would eventually be implemented in different end-user devices, operating policies, and executing environments. For instance, actions such as terminate, exit, error handling, etc. can be classified in *"G100: Control Functions"*. Consequently, the action *terminate* would be used in a specification as: <actionType>*terminate*</actionType> <actionGroup>*G100*</actionGroup>.

The *Capability* concept abstracts all the information related to functions, resources and data required by the Role-Figures to achieve their functionality. Examples of such capabilities can be: software/hardware components, such as units of processing, storage, communication, system data, etc. Role-Figures achieve tasks by performing or executing actions. Such actions would naturally consume or require resources, or capabilities. A Role-Figure specification explicitly specifies what sorts of capabilities are required. Occasionally, the execution of the Role-Figure halts if certain capabilities are not available. *Status* comprises observable counting measures to reflect the resulting state of the system.

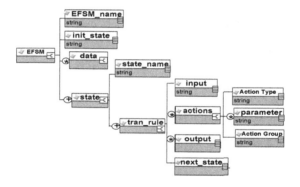

Fig. 1. EFSM model data structure

As have been indicated previously, Action Types, and eventually their classes or Action Groups, are not *"executables"* that may be run in a specific environment or device. Therefore, service designers should map their actions to executable routines provided by device manufacturers (Usually using built-in function calls, with explicit and proper parameter values, through the device's Application Programming Interface, or API.) In this regard, these executable routines should also be classified, to indicate what operating circumstances and capability requirements, they are working within and demanding for. We refer to this classification as *Capability Categories,* so that each category represents a capability set. Examples of Capability Categories can be: *C1*: Powerful PDA, *C2*: Basic PDA, *C10*: Bluetooth, *C11*: WLAN, *C100*: Default CC for G100. A mapping is therefore required to link the action definitions in the service specification to the executable routines stored in Action Libraries.

4 Dynamic Service Management Framework

The Framework presented here considers three distinct forms of Role-Figure specification. Firstly, Role-Figure specification exists as a static representation of the behavior of the Role-Figure functionality. Secondly, Role-Figure specification would exist as an instantiated code or class instances, with all the necessary mappings to their executing environment, which is "*instantiated Role-Figure specification.*" However, a third form may exist between these two forms. Once the capability category is determined, it is important to extend and convert certain actions into corresponding sets of actions, e.g. providing extra security and authentication checks. This form we refer to as "*calculated Role-Figure specification.*"

The framework for Dynamic Service Management is illustrated in Fig. 2. The components of the framework are:

1. *Play Repository:* a data base that contains the service definitions and includes:
   - *Role-Figure Specifications*: provide behavior definitions for each Role-Figure, including the Action Types to be performed and their corresponding Action Groups.
   - *Selection Rules*: provide information for dynamically selecting the proper Role-Figure Specification, if it has several corresponding specifications.
   - *Mapping Rules:* specify the mapping between capabilities and capability categories.

2. *Capability and Status Repository (CSRep):* is a database that provides a snapshot of the resources of the system. It maintains information on all capability and status data in all system nodes.

3. *Action Library:* is a database that contains codes for the state machine-based actions. These codes are implemented according to the capability category they require.

4. *Service Manager (SM):* is responsible for the handling of *Initial Service requests* (to instantiate a Role-Figure), *Role-Figure move* (to move an already instantiated Role-Figure from one node to another), and *Function Update requests* (to change the functionality of an already instantiated Role-Figure). It, first, selects a specific Role-Figure specification based on the *Selection Rules.* Secondly, it calculates the offered Capability Category according to the *Mapping Rules,* which is denoted as *Mapping table.* Then it generates the *calculated Role Figure Specification* by adding the corresponding Capability Category information and the substructures that can be used for decision-making when capability changes occur. This *calculated Role Figure Specification* and the *Mapping table* are then sent to the proper *State Machine Interpreter* for execution.

5. *Requests:* supply, on the one hand, the identification of the Role-Figure to be instantiated or modified. On the other hand, they provide the information to be taken into consideration during the calculation of the Capability Category. Three types of service requests may be handled by the SM:
   - *Initial Service Request* indicates a role to be executed in a node.
   - *Role-Figure Move* is issued when there is a severe deterioration in certain capabilities availability or the Role-Figure is requested to move to achieve a mobility task for instance. [6] gives an overview of the mobility management of Role-Figures.
   - *Function Update Request* is issued to update a functionality due to capability change.

6. *Results:* are the outcomes of the calculations performed by SM, which contains the following:

- *Calculated Role-Figure Specification* indicates a changed Role-Figure specification.
- *Mapping Table* is the result of calculating and matching of Capability Categories based on the given instantaneous capability situation, Mapping rules, and incoming request and its parameters.

7. *State Machine Interpreter (SMI)*: is a State Machine execution support [5]. This is the primary entity in the framework responsible for the execution of Role-Figures according to the *instantiated Role-Figure Specification*. The framework allows for a decentralized computation. The dotted-arrow connecting the *Play Repository* and the SMI allows for the calculation of the Role-Figure Specification to be conducted in the node where it will execute, i.e. by the SMI instead of the SM that is, in most cases, would exist at a remote location. This option can solve problems related to over-loaded SM, congested network, time-critical applications, etc.

The next specification is of a *clientMultimediaPlayer* Role-Figure that runs on a Laptop, with both the capability of WLAN (default) and Bluetooth (used when WLAN is unavailable).

```
<state name="stMediaPlay">
  <actionType>MediaPlay</actionType>
  <actionGroup>G2</actionGroup>
  <CapCategory>C10</CapCategory>
  <CapCategory>C11</CapCategory>
  <Config>
    <defaultCC>C10</defaultCC>
    <ProblemType>
      <List>out of coverage</List>
      <List>congestion</List>
    </ProblemType>
    <choice>
      <check>Check Bluetooth neighbourhood</check>
      <substate name="Bluetooth">
        <condition value="available">
          <output>
            <msg type="FunctionUpdate">
              <param>
                <name>manuscript</name>
                <value>SchoolClient</value>
              </param>
              <param>
                <name>C10</name>
                <value>out of coverage</value>
              </param>
              <param>
                <name>Wireless Communication</name>
                <value>unavailable</value>
              </param>
              <dest>ServiceManager</dest>
            </msg>
          </output>
          <nextState>stWaitForManuscript</nextState>
        </substate>
        <substate name="NoBluetooth">
          <condition value="unavailable" offline="No">
            <actionType>Terminate</actionType>
            <actionGroup>G100</actionGroup>
            <CapCategory>C100</CapCategory>
            <nextState>stTerminate</nextState>
        </substate>
        <substate name="Offline">
          <condition value="unavailable" offline="Yes">
            <actionType>ChangeToOffline</actionType>
            <actionGroup>G100</actionGroup>
            <CapCategory>C100</CapCategory>
            <nextState>stWaitUserInput</nextState>
        </substate>
      </choice>
    </Config>
    <nextState>stWaitUserInput</nextState>
</state>
```

Part of a calculated specification for a *clientMediaPlayer* Role-Figure, in which an action of simple communication has been converted into a structure of additional actions and substates.

5 Implementation Issues

The framework has been developed and implemented as part of the TAPAS architecture, see [6,7,8] and the URL: http://tapas.item.ntnu.no/. The implementation of the framework is built around the support functionality of the TAPAS core platform. Java Web Services Developer Pack (Java WSDP) [9] was applied to develop the main communication parts of the framework, while Apache Axis [10] was used as a SOAP server. In this regard, nodes running the platform will have an entity that supports Web Services requests and replies. Fig. 3 shows a possible

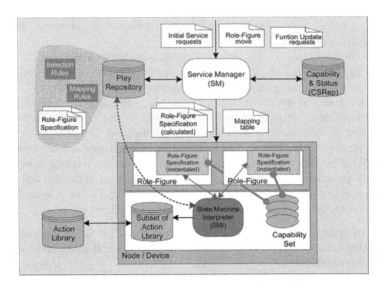

Fig. 2. Dynamic Service Management Framework

implementation of the framework, in which a configuration of two nodes running two and three distinct Role-Figures is applied, beside a node running the SM and a web server containing the repository data. The TAPAS Core Platform has been extended with Web-services communication routines, node registry capabilities, and extended configuration data reflecting the reachability of SM. In the figure a connection is highlighted between the CSRep and the nodes participating in the execution of these

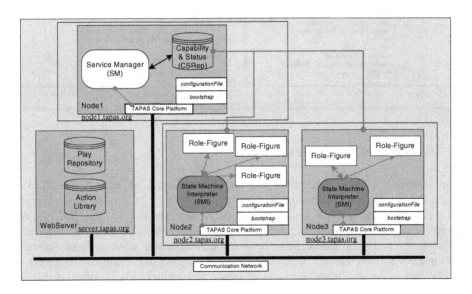

Fig. 3. An implementation of the Dynamic Service Framework within the TAPAS platform

Role-Figures. Although it has not been fully implemented, a capability registration and update mechanism is considered, which keeps the CSRep updated in terms of any capability change in the nodes. Throughout the experimentation process such update has been conducted manually in order to simplify the overall processing.

6   Experimentation Scenarios

Several scenarios have been proposed to demonstrate the applicability and foremost features of the framework. During the experimentation, simple application scenarios have been used. The application used was the Teleschool, which is an application facilitating distance-learning, allowing students and teachers to participate in virtual class activities in real-time or off-line modes, using multimedia capabilities on various types of terminals and devices. The est scenarios were limited to run and execute the client Role-Figures, and examine their proper functionality. Here we instantiate *SchoolClient* Role-Figure on a node featuring a Bluetooth and WLAN communications. Below we show an example of a *Role-Figure move* request to initiate a move functionality of a Role-Figure from a node to another one.

```
<RoleFigureMoveRequest>
  <sender><oNode>http://Node2.tapas.org</oNode>
  </sender>
  <dateTime />
  <serviceType>Teleschool</serviceType>
  <roleRequesting>SchoolClient</roleRequesting>
  <RFSUsed>SchoolClient_Advanced</RFSUsed>
  <preferredConfiguration>
    <nodeInstalling>
      http://Node3.tapas.org
    </nodeInstalling>
  </preferredConfiguration>
  <contextInfo>
    <connectionUsed>LAN</connectionUsed>
      <userSubscription>Advanced</userSubscription>
      <MMSupport>VideoPlayer</MMSupport>
    </contextInfo>
    <stateInfo>
      <currentState>stInitUserInterface
      </currentState>
      <variables>
        <variable>
          <name>v_server</name>
          <value>aaaaaa</value>
        </variable>
      </variables>
    </stateInfo>
</RoleFigureMoveRequest>
```

An example *Role-Figure move* request used to move a Role-Figure from Node2 to Node3

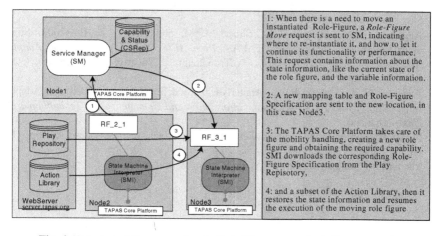

1: When there is a need to move an instantiated Role-Figure, a *Role-Figure Move* request is sent to SM, indicating where to re-instantiate it, and how to let it continue its functionality or performance. This request contains information about the state information, like the current state of the role figure, and the variable information.

2: A new mapping table and Role-Figure Specification are sent to the new location, in this case Node3.

3: The TAPAS Core Platform takes care of the mobility handling, creating a new role figure and obtaining the required capability. SMI downloads the corresponding Role-Figure Specification from the Play Repisotory,

4: and a subset of the Action Library, then it restores the state information and resumes the execution of the moving role figure

Fig. 4. Experimentation scenario of a Role-Figure move including two nodes

7 Conclusion

In this paper some challenges of the Dynamic Service Management have been discussed, and a framework has been proposed to tackle them. In a highly dynamic system, components composing the system come and go, as well as the system resources that are allocated for them vary and change all the time. The demonstrated framework provides a way of enabling the dynamic service management based on specifications that can be selected, their behavior be computed, and their handling of system resources are all based on the available capabilities in the execution environment. Specifications contain only Action Types and Action Groups, while the executable code or Action Libraries are available on a different database. This distinction is mainly to achieve flexibility. Capability Categories classify these executables based on the capability information in the system.

References

1. M. Brunner and R. Stadler, Service Management in Multiparty Active Networks, *IEEE Communications Magazine*, Vol. 38, No. 3, pp. 144-151, March 2000.
2. Christine R. Hofmeister and James M.Purtilo. Dynamic reconfiguration in distributed systems: Adapting software modules for replacement. *In Proceedings of the 13th International Conference on Distributed Computing Systems, IEEE Computer Society Press,* May 1993.
3. Jeff Kramer and Jeff Magee. The Evolving Philosophers Problem: Dynamic Change Management. *IEEE Transactions on Software Engineering,* 16(11):1293-1306, Nov. 1990.
4. B.D. Noble and M. Satyanarayanan. Experience with adaptive mobile applications in Odyssey (1999). *Mobile Networks and Applications*, 4, 1999.
5. Jiang, S. and Aagesen, F. A. (2003) XML-based Dynamic Service Behaviour Representation. *NIK'2003*. Oslo, Norway, November 2003. [http://tapas.item.ntnu.no]
6. Shiaa M. M and Aagesen. F. A. (2002) Architectural Considerations for Personal Mobility in the Wireless Internet, *Proc. IFIP TC/6 Personal Wireless Communications (PWC'2002),* Singapore, Kluwer Academic Publishers, October 2002. [http://tapas.item.ntnu.no]
7. Aagesen, F. A., Anutariya, C., Shiaa, M. M. and Helvik, B. E. (2002) Support Specification and Selection in TAPAS. *Proc. IFIP WG6.7 Workshop on Adaptable Networks and Teleservices,* Trondheim Norway, September 2002. [http://tapas.item.ntnu.no]
8. Aagesen, F. A., Helvik, B. E., Anutariya, C., and Shiaa M. M. (2003) On Adaptable Networking, *Proc. 2003 Int'l Conf. Information and Communication Technologies (ICT 2003),* Thailand.
9. SUN Microsystems, the Web services Homepage, Java Web Services Developer Pack (WSDP) documentation, http://java.sun.com/webservices/index.jsp
10. The Apache homepage, Apache Axis 1_1, http://ws.apache.org/axis

Flexible Middleware Support for Future Mobile Services and Their Context-Aware Adaptation

Marcin Solarski[1], Linda Strick[1], Kiminori Motonaga[2], Chie Noda[3], and Wolfgang Kellerer[3]

[1] Fraunhofer FOKUS, Kaiserin-Augusta-Allee 31a,
10589 Berlin, Germany
{solarski, strick}@fokus.fraunhofer.de
[2] NTT DATA, Kayabacho Tower Bldg, 21-1 Shinkawa 1-chome Chuo-ku, Tokyo
motonagak@nttdata.co.jp
[3] DoCoMo Communications Laboratories Europe GmbH, Landsberger Strasse 312,80687
Munich, Germany
{noda, kellerer}@docomolab-euro.com

Abstract. This paper presents a flexible peer-to-peer-based middleware for future user-centric mobile telecommunication services, which supports key functionalities needed to address personalization, adaptation and coordination of services running on top of it. The underlying communication pattern is based on dynamic negotiation that enables interworking of autonomous decentralized entities in a rapidly changing and open environment. This paper focuses on the middleware's support for context-aware adaptation of a multimedia service for mobile users. Service adaptation takes into account both user preferences and contextual changes to modify the service behavior and contents. The middleware implementation is based on JXTA extended by a mobile agent platform and is deployable on a range of mobile devices including mobile phones and PDAs.

1 Introduction

With the recent developments in 4G mobile environments (heterogeneous access networks, 4G radio access, ad-hoc sensor networks) and the large availability of any kind of mobile computing devices such as Personal Digital Assistants, mobile smart phones, we are experiencing the availability of an increasingly powerful mobile computing environment, which is exposed to high dynamicity.

In a future mobile environment, the emergence of ubiquitous computing is envisioned [1]. Heterogeneous devices, ranging from low-end devices (e.g., tiny sensor devices) to high-end devices (e.g., a 3D video streaming terminal), are surrounding humans. Heterogeneity of radio access networks (e.g., 3G/4G radio access and ad-hoc sensor network) is another attribute of future mobile services [2]. Thus particular users' environments, including devices, networks and, services have to be adapted and configured according to user's changing environment, context, status, and preferences, i.e. *context awareness*. To enable access to services from hetero-

A. Aagesen et al. (Eds.): INTELLCOMM 2004, LNCS 3283, pp. 281–292, 2004.

geneous devices through heterogeneous access networks, *context-aware adaptation* is one of the fundamental requirements of a middleware for future mobile services.

Furthermore, there is no centralized gateway to that all available services are registered or that acts as an intermediary component to support their adaptation to the environmental contexts such as network bandwidth and terminal capabilities. These requirements lead us to design a novel middleware platform, called Mercury which is an acronym for *MiddlEware aRChitecture for User centRic sYstem*, which supports context-aware adaptation of mobile services and is based on a peer-to-peer and asynchronous interaction paradigm.

The structure of this paper is as follows; Section 1 gives a short introduction to future mobile services and the Mercury architecture. In Section 2, the overview of the Mercury middleware is given and the communication pattern called Dynamic Service Delivery Pattern in presented briefly. Related work and the advantages of our approach are described in Section 3. In Section 4, we discuss our design of context-aware adaptation and related subsystems realized in the Mercury middleware. Section 5 discusses an application scenario, along a video-on demand service, to show how context-aware adaptation works by utilizing the middleware subsystems. Section 6 summarizes the approach towards a flexible middleware support for context-aware service adaptation.

2 Mercury Overview

Mercury is a service middleware for user-centric service provisioning in mobile environments driven by the demands and the behavior of users. There are two fundamental requirements for a middleware platform for mobile services.

One is to support asynchronous communication, since wireless access can be disconnected when mobile devices are out of the coverage area, or due to data rate variation, since the downlink data transmission rate is usually much faster than uplink. Another requirement is the distribution of middleware components to resource-constrained devices, in terms of low performance, limited memory, and low power consumption. These requirements heavily influence the decision on the selection of enabling technologies to build our middleware platform.

A dynamic service delivery pattern, which enables to publish/subscribe advertisement of services, to negotiate interactively between peers, and aggregate for service execution, is introduced in Section 2.2.

2.1 Design Overview

In the Mercury middleware, the complex functionality needed to match the above requirements on future mobile services is divided into a number of subsystems, which are then grouped into three layers for the sake of modularity and reusability[7,8]. In this way we introduce an additional user support layer on top of a service support and traditional network layer. The user support layer includes subsystems for *Adaptation*, *Community*, and *Coordination*. The introduction of this layer reduces unnecessary user interactions with the system and enables the provision of user-centric services. Furthermore, the user support layer allows the establishment and maintenance of virtual ad-hoc communities, and their coordination toward a common guidance for service usage.

The service support layer contains most functionality of traditional middleware, such as *Discovery & Advertisement* for getting establishing entity communication, *Authentication & Authorization* for secure communication and *Contract Notary* used for managing service agreements. These subsystems are used by the *Dynamic Service Delivery Pattern*, which is the basic interaction paradigm between the Mercury entities (see Section 2.2). This paper focuses on the other subsystems in this layer, namely *Transformation*, *Context Management* and *Profiling*, used for context-aware adaptation (i.e. used by *Adaptation* subsystem); these are presented in more detail in Section 4. Finally, the network support layer provides connectivity in IP-based networks, including *Mobility management*, *Call & Session management*, and *QoS management* subsystems.

The above-mentioned requirements of asynchronous communications and resource-constrained devices support lead us to build our middleware on a mobile agent platform, enago Mobile [9] in our current prototype. Mobile agents support asynchronous communications and can autonomously work temporarily disconnected from other facilities. Connectivity is only required for the period for migration, but not for service execution. They also solve the problem of resource-constrained devices by allowing on-demand and flexible deploying code to both mobile devices and the infrastructure.

2.2 Dynamic Service Delivery – Underlying Interaction Pattern

The Dynamic Service Delivery Pattern describes the process of (1) agreeing on entity interaction behavior, called negotiation scheme, leading to a service agreement, (2) establishing the concrete service agreement itself, which determines the conditions of

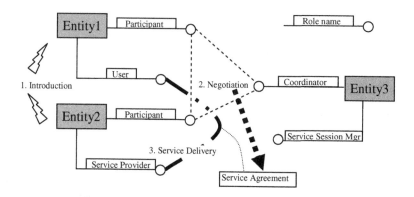

Fig. 1. Example entities participating in the Dynamic Service Delivery Pattern

the service delivery and, finally, (3) managing the service delivery phase using the notion of a service session. A Mercury entity is any piece of software which can play one or more roles, including the predefined ones: Participant, Coordinator (negotiation-related roles), User and Service Provider (service delivery-related roles). Optionally authentication and authorization mechanisms can be used, which are defined in separate middleware subsystems. The dynamic service delivery pattern is used for every communication between any Mercury entity, including the middleware subsystems.

The dynamic service delivery pattern contains three subsequent phases:

1. *Introduction Phase* – entities are introduced to each other by using the publish/subscribe interface for service discovery and advertisement.
2. *Negotiation Phase* – entities interact in a negotiation dialog, playing the role of *Participant* or *Coordinator*. The negotiation handles negotiation schemes, credentials, proposals and agreements in order to reach a service agreement.
3. *Service Delivery Phase* - entities, in the role of *Service Provider* and *User*, interact to fulfill the terms of the negotiated contract. The service delivery phase is organized as service session, which is managed by an entity playing role *Service Session Manager*.

Figure 1 depicts example entities participating in the negotiation phase of the Dynamic Service Delivery Pattern. It is assumed that `Entity1` and `Entity2` have been introduced to each other using the *Discovery and Advertisement* system and that there is an entity which they both trust so that it can coordinate the negotiation process. The negotiation is then started by agreeing on the negotiation scheme, followed by the actual negotiation interaction, which is coordinated by `Entity3`, playing the role of the coordinator. As a result of the negotiation process, a service agreement is established which is then distributed to all the participants before the service delivery phase starts, i.e. the service session is started by the Service Session Manager (in the example `Entity3`). A more detailed description of the Dynamic Service Delivery Pattern can be found in [7].

3 Related Works

There have been quite a lot of research efforts for adaptation of services and context-aware adaptation. [3] proposes a framework for multimedia applications adaptation, by utilizing differentiation within IP session(s) based on proprietary of packets indicated by QoS-aware applications. [4], a middleware platform for context aware services is built on active networks and mobile agent technologies, where active networks is used as communication channels for mobile agents, i.e. mobile agents migrate to other nodes are realized by an active packet containing data and program in active networks. In [5], the tasks for adaptation of multimedia applications are divided into two: selection of the most applicable adapted output format in accordance with the information form the Composite Capability/Preference Profiles (CC/PP) [6], and adaptation execution by using different adaptation agents. Context-aware adaptation of web-line service content has been a hot topic in the literature [10,11]. In [10], the author present a proxy-based (centralized) content adaptation architecture and an adaptation mechanism based on content semantics analysis and a device-independent model for content description. In their implementation, they apply CC/PP-based Universal Profiling Schema to define both different type of user context, including device profiles and XQuery for extracting contextual information relevant to the content adaptation process. The approach presented in [11] presents an adaptation engine which automates selection of content transcoding mechanisms considering user preferences, device capabilities, networking parameters as well as content metadata so that the content presentation quality is optimal. The selection is determined user-given weighted quantification of content quality along various quality axes. Previous work [12], focused on application-aware adaptation, which proposes building underlying systems to discover the context and notify the application to take the adaptive actions. Such applications become complex as they have to handle the adaptation by themselves. Mercury follows systems which advise hiding the adaptation complexity into the underlying system layers.

In our approach, we design a flexible middleware for context-aware adaptation by introducing a dynamic service delivery pattern as a generic negotiation framework between peers, which can be applications, devices, or even subsystems in the middleware. The negotiation scheme defines the negotiation protocols [13], which are used to automatically exchange and align contracts. Compared to other approaches to context aware service adaptation, Mercury has the following advantages:

a) *Adaptation as an aggregated service.* The adaptation subsystem is designed so that it combines a number of adaptation strategies specialized for different services to adapt. A most suitable strategy is automatically chosen at the moment of negotiation the usage of the adaptation; the selection is done by evaluating the meta information of the service to adapt as well as the auxiliary resources and services that may be used.

b) *Adaptation dynamics.* On one hand, adaptation offers adapted version of some existing services, on the other, it uses other services, including context providers, profile managers and transformers when needed. Like other Mercury entities, the adaptation subsystem follows the Dynamic Service Delivery Pattern both to provide its functionality and to use other services and resources it needs. Thus, the actual adaptation functionality is created dynamically and may include interactions to spontaneously discovered services needed to achieve the adaptation objective.

c) *Functionality decoupling and modularization.* The Mercury middleware defines two key subsystems needed for service adaptation: adaptation and transformation subsystems. Whereas the first defines so called adaptation strategies, which realize the autonomous functionality and logic determining the conditions when some and what adaptive actions are to be taken, the transformation subsystem maintains concrete adaptation mechanisms, called transformers, which are used by the adaptation strategies. Additionally, the context-related and profile-related functionality is defined in separate middleware subsystems.

4 Service Adaptation Support in the Mercury Middleware

The complex tasks needed to perform user-centric service adaptation is divided into four subsystems in the Mercury middleware, as mentioned in section 2. These are the two key subsystems, adaptation and transformation, and two supplementary subsystems, context management and profiling. The Adaptation subsystem implements the adaptation logic specifying how to change the target service and the related resources under certain conditions on the service context, the Context Management and Profiling subsystems are used by the adaptation to (1) acquire needed information on the service context and relevant preferences, and the Transformation subsystem to (2) carry out the service adaptation and other resource usage adjustment.

The interrelations of the subsystems are shown in a UML class diagram in Figure 2.

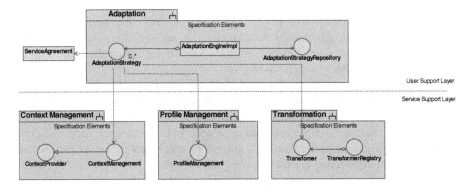

Fig. 2. An design overview of the interrelationships between Adaptation subsystem and other Mercury middleware subsystems involved in service adaptation

The application of each subsystem is illustrated with an example used in our application scenario described in Section 5.

4.1 Adaptation

The Adaptation subsystem is designed to support any type of service adaptation by (1) personalization the service to user profiles (e.g., preferences) and (2) modifying the service considering the user contexts (e.g., user environmental capabilities and available resources). The adaptation subsystem is implemented as a Mercury service. Its adaptation strategies handle adaptation specialized with regard to the service type and available resources are maintained in a repository. In this sense, the adaptation subsystem can be seen as an aggregation of specialized adaptation services. Whenever service adaptation is requested, the requestor has to provide some information on the service itself and the resources, including other services, which have to be used. The adaptation service checks the availability of adaptation strategies suitable to handle the given service during the negotiation process. If a matching strategy is registered within the subsystem, the service adaptation is possible and a service agreement may be established only if the negotiating parties agree on the non-technical factors as well. This behavior is facilitated by implementing a specialized negotiation template which allows for checking the demands on the registered adaptation strategies.

The framework for defining concrete adaptation strategies allows for flexible adaptation to specific services. Strategies compliant to that framework may be inserted into the system on demand and are provided by the adaptation service. An adaptation strategy in the model represents a process of service adaptation which is expressed by transforming the service to the required quality, as specified in the service agreement. The service agreement includes information on the constraints on the quality of service as well as on available resources and auxiliary services to use for adaptation of the given service. Each concrete adaptation strategy defines the relevant context information needed to react to and retrieves it in a preferred way by using one or many context providers, or context managers, from the management system.

An example adaptation strategy has been implemented for the use in the Video Service scenario described in Section 5.

4.2 Context Management

Context-aware services are those that make use of the context information for their purposes. In particular, adaptation strategies in the adaptation subsystem belong to this class of services.

Context is a set of environmental states that either determines an application's behaviour or in which an application event occurs. Contexts can be classified in the following four categories: *user context* (e.g., the user's location, and the current social situation), *time context*, *physical context* (e.g., lighting, traffic condition, temperature), and *computing context* (e.g. communication bandwidth, available memory and processing power, and battery status). The Context Management subsystem offers a means to provide context information in either a push or pull mode. Moreover, the context information can be pushed either if the required context matched the given criteria or at regular time intervals. The subsystem has also a mechanism to manage access to the so called *Context Providers*, which are the entities that actually sense and retrieve some specific context, e.g., via sensors. Figure 3 presents the relation between context provider, context management subsystem and context-aware services. Even though *ContextProviders* may also be directly used by context-aware services, The Context management system provides additional functionality to aggregate and filter context of several context providers.

4.3 Profiling

Profiles are collections of data that may be used to adapt services to a user's specific environment and preferences. Profiles can be classified to the following categories: *user profile, service profile, terminal profile,* and *network profile.* This subsystem supports management of profiles, by offering a means to select, retrieve, store and update profiles to users. A user may have more than one profile and select the most appropriate one, or it may be chosen automatically upon other criteria. Additionally, each profile include access right information: two access rights are distinguished, profile read and write, which can be granted to different entities or entity groups. The profile manager is the component responsible for giving access to the managed profiles according to the access rights. As profiles may include references to other profiles, possibly managed by other profile managers, the profile manager may optionally access other profile managers.

```
[CCPP:component]
  ┌ RDF:ResourceDescription ->
  │    mercury:ReadACL -> ["All"]
  │    mercury:WriteACL -> ["ResourceOwnerID"]
  │    mercury:ProviderUuid -> "uuid1"
  │    mercury:ResourceUuid -> "uuid2"
  │    mercury:ResourceType -> "VideoDisplay"
  │
  └ RDF:TerminalPlatform ->
       mercury:ReadACL -> ["All"]
       mercury:WriteACL -> ["ResourceOwnerID"]
       [CCPP:HardwarePlatform] - CCPP:BitsPerPixel- > 16
       [CCPP:HardwarePlatform] - CCPP:ScreenResolutionX ->240
       [CCPP:HardwarePlatform] - CCPP:ScreenResolutionY ->320
       [CCPP:HardwarePlatform] - CCPP:NetworkAdapter ->802.1b
```

Fig. 4. An example of a CC/PP –based device profile in the graphical notation

In the Mercury prototype, the profiles are represented as XML documents compliant to the W3C CC/PP standard [6]. Each profile includes a part on the resource description and additional resource-specific parts called CC/PP components which correspond to different aspects of the resource the profile describes. An example profile, presented in Figure 4 in a semi-graphical notation proposed in the W3C documents on CC/PP, of a graphical display device contains an additional component describing the hardware-specific parameters of the terminal (TerminalPlatform in the example), which includes another component HardwarePlatform with its ScreenResolutionX and ScreenResolutionY. The example also contains some statements determining access rights to the associated components: the part on resource description can be accessed by all, whereas it can be modified only by the resource owner having the ResourceOwnerID identifier.

4.4 Transformation

The transformation system defines a framework for handling software components, called transformers, processing some service data, typically stream-oriented contents, for the purpose of service adaptation. Transformers are defined as components implementing a process of changing the input data to some other data produced at the transformer output. It is assumed that the data to transform come from a number of *sources* that the *Transformer* may retrieve by itself or it is notified of the data availability. The transformed data at the transformer's output may be propagated to a number of *sinks,* which may be possibly other transformers. Thus, transformers may be chained to perform data in a more advanced or to reuse the existing transformers performing parts of the needed transformations. There are several aspects of the service contents that can be transformed: *format and encod-*

ing (e.g. H.263 or MPEG1 streaming formats in case of the video contents), *type* (e.g. video, audio and text), and *structure* (e.g. XML and HTML).

The transformation framework is extendable so that it allows for inserting new transformers that perform some specific data transformation. An example transformer that was developed for the purposes of the application presented in Section 5 is concerned with processing video streams. This transformer is responsible for (1) on-the-fly redirecting the video contents ordered by the user to a given display and (2) modifying the stream quality of service parameters. The redirection of the video stream is done out-of-bound so that the transformer does not have to be deployed on one of the intermediate nodes between the video server and video player; instead the transformer uses a control protocol to make the server send the video to the given receiver. The display is assumed to be capable of receiving video streams and playing them back so that the play back can be remotely controlled. With regard to the other transformer functionality, the video stream QoS is modified so that the video stream can be optimized to match the hardware constraints of the target display, like the maximum screen resolution or supported number of colors in bits per pixel, and the video processing capabilities of the software controlling the display.

5 Example Application Scenario

The text below describes the application scenario developed using the Mercury middleware. The core of the application is a video-on-demand service that is leveraged by the context-aware adaptation supported by the underlying middleware.

A passenger enters an airport lounge before boarding a flight. Attracted by personal video booths in the lounge, she decides to watch her favorite movie in one of them. Unfortunately, all of booths are occupied and she decides to start watching the movie on her mobile device until a booth is available to her. After accessing the video streaming service in the lounge service menu and choosing the movies she likes, the system offers to reserve a booth for her to watch the movie in a more comfortable environment. A video player appears on the display of her mobile device and she starts watching the video. A notification about an available booth draws her attention while watching the video, and so she suspends the video and gets into the booth. After she makes herself comfortable in the booth, she resumes the video on her mobile device. Now the video is projected onto the big display in the booth and the movie sound comes out of the hi-fi sound boxes that are automatically selected by the context-aware system according to her preferences. The passenger may continue watching the movie until a notification pops up to remind her that boarding gate closes soon. She suspends the video again and proceeds to a boarding gate.

5.1 Events Occurring in Application Scenario

Figure 5 shows an overview of major events occurring in the middleware. Resources and services are detected considering user's context or preferences. The detected services are negotiated between the user and their providers through the intermediation of a coordinator agent. After reaching agreement, resources are adapted or personalized according to the service agreement, user's context or preferences.

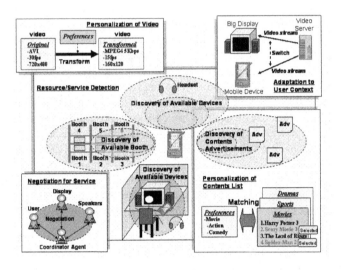

Fig. 5. An overview of the events occurring in the application scenario

5.1.1 Negotiation for Services

In the scenario presented above, a passenger wants to watch some video content. In order to watch the movie, user and provider need to negotiate about the usage of the content service according to the Dynamic Service Delivery Pattern as introduced in Section 2.2.

1. A video content provider issues an advertisement of the video contents, i.e. the movies, he offers. The advertisement includes the video content description, the proposed video cost as well as some information on how to contact the provider for further negotiation. On the other hand, the software acting on behalf the passenger, the user agent, looks for video with some characteristics determined by the user preferences (e.g. movie genre, favorite actor) and possibly discovers a matching advertisement sent by one of the video content providers. If there are many different contents available and matching the user criteria, the passenger chooses one and a negotiation with corresponding video providers may start.

2. The user agent and the video providers, in the role of participants, interact in a negotiation dialog, exchanging negotiation schemes, credentials, proposals according to the agreed negotiation scheme until the negotiation is complete (the participant agree on proposals of others) and a service agreements can be established. Compared to the information in the initial advertisement, the proposals add some details on the quality of the contents to provide (in this case the maximal video size, language variant) or just modify the initial values of the data, e.g. the final price for the movie. The resulting service agreement includes some information needed to start and use the service, like the access data to the movie.

3. When the service delivery starts (here requested by the passenger), all the participants are requested to be ready. In case of the video provider, it means that the content in question has to be made accessible to the user according to the terms in the service agreement.

5.1.2 Adaptation to User Context

In the application, the user wants to watch the movie at the best possible quality, which means here using the best available display and with best quality supported by this display. The adaptation subsystem includes a strategy which allows to detect available displays around the user and to redirect the video stream so that it is displayed at the currently best display with a video quality optimized to that display. This strategy is used in this scenario so that it subscribes for the availability information of device nearby (context information) and it installs the specialized video transformer on the PDA used by the user. To perform the latter, the user has to provide some execution resources on the PDA so that the transformer code can be deployed there; this resource is one of the requirements of the adaptation strategy announced in the negotiation process. The transformer allows for controlling the local display on the PDA or any other intelligent display that can be controlled remotely using an RTSP-like protocol. It is deployed on the user's PDA to efficiently intercept the control commands for the player coming from the GUI operated by the user on the PDA. Whenever the adaptation detects a better device, the transformer is reconfigured to redirect the video stream and modify the quality of video.

6 Conclusions

In future, mobile service provisioning will include not only services that are offered by a central server system but also services that have to work in the current users' environment, independent from the facilities available in the infrastructure. Furthermore, future mobile environments will be characterized by co-existence of heterogeneity of devices and networks, including also resource constrained and intermittently connected devices and by rapidly changing context. To deal with such ubiquitous services, designing of a flexible and smart support for service adaptation is a major challenge.

The Mercury middleware proposes some solutions to this challenge. Its design benefits from the peer-to-peer communication paradigm and autonomously interacting software agents, which address the issues of decentralization, loose-coupling and making use of intermittent connectivity. These features are complemented with a flexible interaction paradigm, called Dynamic Service Delivery Pattern, which allows for secure and dynamic interworking of 3rd party software components. The Mercury prototype has been implemented on top of a mobile agent platform extended by peer-to-peer communication mechanisms of JXTA.

Furthermore, the Mercury middleware provides strong user support for personalized, context aware service provisioning. In a heterogeneous mobile environment adaptability is a key feature for the success of such system. A flexible service adaptation is achieved by using specialized subsystems dealing with adaptation logic, context management, user profiling, and transformation mechanisms as illustrated in this paper.

292 M. Solarski et al.

We believe that the Mercury middleware system is an essential contribution to next generation mobile service provisioning, since it addresses the needs for advanced personalization and the identified requirements on service provisioning in a ubiquitous mobile environment.

References

1. M. Weiser: The Computer for the 21st Century. Scientific American, September 1991, pp. 94-104
2. H. Yumiba, K.Imai, M.Yabusaki: IP-Based IMT Network Platform. IEEE Personal Communications Magazine, October, 2001
3. H. Shao, W. Zhu, Y. Zhang: A New Framework for Adaptive Multimedia over the Next Generation Internet
4. I. Sygkouna, S. Vrontis, M. Chantzara, M. Anagnostou, E. Sylas: Context-Aware Service Provisioning on Top of Active Technologies. Mobile Agents for Telecommunication Applications (MATA), Marakech, Morocco, October 2003
5. M. Metso, J. Sauvola: The Media Wrapper in the Adaptation of Multimedia Content for Mobile Environments. Proceedings SPIE Vol. 4209, Multimedia Systems and Applications III, 132-139, Boston, MA
6. W3C: Composite Capabilities/Preference Profiles: Structure and Vocabularies 1.0. http://www.w3.org/TR/2004/REC-CCPP-struct-vocab-20040115/
7. C. Noda, A. Tarlano, L. Strick, M. Solarski, S. Rehfeldt, H. Honjo, K. Motonaga and I.Tanaka: Distributed Middleware for User Centric System. WWRF#9 conference, Zurich, July 2003
8. WWRF, Wireless World Research Forum WG2, Service Infrastructure of the Wireless World. http://www.wireless-world-research.org/
9. IKV++ Technologies AG: enago Mobile Agent Platform. http://www.ikv.de/content/Produkte/enago_mobile.htm
10. T. Lemlouma, N.Layaïda: Context-Aware Adaptation for Mobile Devices, IEEE International Conference on Mobile Data Management, Berkeley, CA, USA, January 2004, pp. 106-111
11. Wai Yip Lum and Francis C.M. Lau: A Context-Aware Decision Engine for Content Adaptation, IEEE Pervasive Computing, July-Sept. 2002, p.41-49.
12. Brian D. Noble, M. Satyanarayanan, Dushyanth Narayanan, James Eric Tilton, Jason Flinn, Kevin R. Walker: Agile Application-Aware Adaptation for Mobility, Sixteen ACM Symposium on Operating Systems Principles, 1997
13. C. Bartolini, C. Preist, N.Jennings: A Genric Softwrae Framework for Automated Negotiation, AAMAS'02, Bologna, Italy, July 2002

A Breadth-First Algorithm for Mining Frequent Patterns from Event Logs*

Risto Vaarandi

Department of Computer Engineering, Tallinn University of Technology, Estonia
risto.vaarandi@eyp.ee

Abstract. Today, event logs contain vast amounts of data that can easily overwhelm a human. Therefore, the mining of frequent patterns from event logs is an important system and network management task. This paper discusses the properties of event log data, analyses the suitability of popular mining algorithms for processing event log data, and proposes an efficient algorithm for mining frequent patterns from event logs.

1 Introduction

Event logging and log files are playing an increasingly important role in system and network administration (e.g., see [1]), and the mining of frequent patterns from event logs is an important system and network management task [2][3][4][5][6][7]. Recently proposed mining algorithms have often been variants of the Apriori algorithm [2][3][4][7], and they have been mainly designed for detecting frequent event type patterns [2][3][4][5][7]. The algorithms assume that each event from the event log has two attributes – time of event occurrence and event type. There are several ways for defining the *frequent event type pattern*, with two definitions being most common. In the case of the first definition (e.g., see [7]), the algorithm views the event log as a set of overlapping *windows*, where each window contains events from a time frame of t seconds (the *window size t* is given by the user). A certain combination of event types is considered a frequent pattern if this combination is present at least in s windows, where the threshold s is specified by the user. In the case of the second definition (e.g., see [5]), the algorithm assumes that the event log has been divided into non-overlapping slices according to some criteria (e.g., events from the same slice were all issued by the same host). A certain combination of event types is considered a frequent pattern if this combination is present at least in s slices (the threshold s is given by the user). Although the use of this definition requires more elaborate pre-processing of the event log, it also eliminates the noise that could appear when events from different slices are mixed. In the rest of this paper, we will employ the second approach for defining the frequent event type pattern.

---

* This work is supported by the Union Bank of Estonia and partly sponsored by the Estonian Science Foundation under the grant 5766.

A. Aagesen et al. (Eds.): INTELLCOMM 2004, LNCS 3283, pp. 293–308, 2004.

Events in windows or slices are usually ordered in occurrence time ascending order. The order of events in windows or slices is often taken into account during the mining, since this could reveal causal relations between event types – e.g., instead of an unordered set {*DeviceDown*, *FanFailure*} the algorithm outputs a sequence *FanFailure* → *DeviceDown*. However, as pointed out in [7], the mining of unordered frequent event type sets is equally important. Due to network latencies, events from remote nodes might arrive and be written to the log in the order that differs from their actual occurrence order. Even if events are timestamped by the sender, system clocks of network nodes are not always synchronized, making it impossible to restore the original order of events. Also, in many cases the occurrence order of events from the same window or slice is not pre-determined (e.g., since events are not causally related). In the remainder of this paper, we will not consider the order of events in a slice important.

Note that it is often difficult to mine patterns of event types from raw event logs, since messages in raw event logs rarely contain explicit event type codes (e.g., see [1]). Fortunately, it is possible to derive event types from event log lines, since very often the events of the same type correspond to a certain line pattern. For example, the lines *Router myrouter1 interface 192.168.13.1 down*, *Router myrouter2 interface 10.10.10.12 down*, and *Router myrouter5 interface 192.168.22.5 down* represent the event type "Router interface down", and correspond to the line pattern *Router * interface * down*. Thus, the mining of frequent line patterns is an important preprocessing technique, but can be very useful for other purposes as well, e.g., for building event log models [8].

Let $I = \{i_1, ..., i_n\}$ be a set of items. If $X \subseteq I$, X is called an *itemset*, and if $|X| = k$, X is also called a *k-itemset*. A *transaction* is a tuple $T = (tid, X)$ where *tid* is a transaction identifier and X is an itemset. A *transaction database* D is a set of transactions, and the *cover* of an itemset X is the set of identifiers of transactions that contain X: $cover(X) = \{tid \mid (tid, Y) \in D, X \subseteq Y\}$. The *support* of an itemset X is defined as the number of elements in its cover: $supp(X) = |cover(X)|$. The task of *mining frequent itemsets* is formulated as follows – given the transaction database D and the *support threshold* s, find all itemsets with the support s or higher (each such set is called a *frequent itemset*).

When the event log has been divided into m slices (numbered from 1 to m), then we can view the set of all possible event types as the set of items I, and each slice can be considered a transaction with its *tid* between 1 and m. If the *i*th slice is $S_i = \{E_1, ..., E_k\}$, where $E_j = (t_j, e_j)$ is an event from S_i, e_j is the type of E_j, and t_j is the occurrence time of E_j, then the transaction corresponding to S_i is $(i, \cup_{j=1}^{k}\{e_j\})$. When we inspect a raw event log at the word level, each line pattern consists of fixed words and wildcards, e.g., *Router * interface * down*. Note that instead of considering entire such pattern we can just consider the fixed words together with their positions, e.g., {(*Router*, 1), (*interface*, 3), (*down*, 5)} [8]. Similarly, if the *i*th line from a raw event log has k words, it can be viewed as a transaction with identifier i and k word-position pairs as items.

If we view event logs as transaction databases in the ways described above, we can formulate the task of mining frequent event type patterns or frequent line

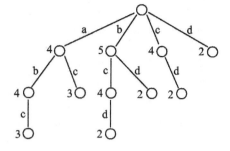

Transaction ID	Itemset
1	abcde
2	abc
3	bcd
4	abc
5	ab

Fig. 1. A sample transaction database and an itemset trie

patterns as the task of mining frequent itemsets. We will use this formulation in the rest of this paper, and also use the term *pattern* to denote an itemset.

In this paper, we propose an efficient algorithm for mining frequent patterns from event logs that can be employed for mining line and event type patterns. The rest of the paper is organized as follows: section 2 discusses related work on frequent itemset mining, section 3 presents the properties of event log data and the analysis of existing mining algorithms, section 4 describes a novel algorithm for mining frequent patterns from event logs, section 5 discusses the performance and implementation of the algorithm, and section 6 concludes the paper.

2   Frequent Itemset Mining

The frequent itemset mining problem has received a lot of attention during the past decade, and a number of mining algorithms have been developed. For the sake of efficient implementation, most algorithms order the items according to certain criteria, and use this ordering for representing itemsets. In the rest of this paper, we assume that if $X = \{x_1, ..., x_k\}$ is an itemset, then $x_1 < ... < x_k$.

The first algorithm developed for mining frequent itemsets was Apriori [9] which works in a breadth-first manner – discovered frequent k-itemsets are used to form candidate $k+1$-itemsets, and frequent $k+1$-itemsets are found from the set of candidates. Recently, an efficient *trie* (prefix tree) data structure has been proposed for the candidate support counting [10][11]. Each edge in the *itemset trie* is labeled with the name of a certain item, and when the Apriori algorithm terminates, non-root nodes of the trie represent all frequent itemsets. If the path from the root node to a non-root node N is $x_1, ..., x_k$, N identifies the frequent itemset $X = \{x_1, ..., x_k\}$ and contains a counter that equals to $supp(X)$. In the remainder of this paper, we will use notations $node(x_1, ..., x_k)$ and $node(X)$ for N, and also, we will always use the term *path* to denote a path that starts from the root node. Figure 1 depicts a sample transaction database and an itemset trie (the support threshold is 2 and items are ordered in lexicographic order).

As its first step, the Apriori algorithm detects frequent 1-itemsets and creates nodes for them. Since every subset of a frequent itemset must also be frequent, the nodes for candidate $k+1$-itemsets are generated as follows – for each node $node(x_1, ..., x_k)$ at depth k all its siblings will be inspected. If $x_k < y_k$ for the sibling $node(x_1, ..., x_{k-1}, y_k)$, then the candidate node $node(x_1, ..., x_k, y_k)$ will be inserted into the trie with its counter set to zero. In order to find frequent $k+1$-itemsets, the algorithm traverses the itemset trie for each transaction $(tid, Y) \in D$, and increments the counter in $node(X)$ if $X \subseteq Y, |X| = k + 1$. After the database pass, the algorithm removes nodes for infrequent candidate itemsets.

Although the Apriori algorithm works well when frequent itemsets contain relatively few items (e.g., 4–5), its performance starts to deteriorate when the size of frequent itemsets increases [12][13]. In order to produce a frequent itemset $\{x_1, ..., x_k\}$, the algorithm must first produce its $2^k - 2$ subsets that are also frequent, and when the database contains frequent k-itemsets for larger values of k (e.g., 30–40), the number of nodes in the itemset trie could be very large. As a result, the runtime cost of the repeated traversal of the trie will be prohibitive, and the trie will consume large amounts of memory.

In recent past, several algorithms have been proposed that explore the search space in a depth-first manner, and that are reportedly by an order of a magnitude faster than Apriori. The most prominent depth-first algorithms for mining frequent itemsets are Eclat [12] and FP-growth [13]. An important assumption made by Eclat and FP-growth is that the transaction database fits into main memory. At each step of the depth-first search, the algorithms are looking for frequent k-itemsets $\{p_1, ..., p_{k-1}, x\}$, where the prefix $P = \{p_1, ..., p_{k-1}\}$ is a previously detected frequent k-1-itemset. When looking for these itemsets, the algorithms extract from the database the data describing transactions that contain the itemset P, and search only this part of the database. If frequent k-itemsets were found, one such itemset is chosen for the prefix of the next step, otherwise the new prefix is found by backtracking. Since the database is kept in main memory using data structures that facilitate the fast extraction of data, Eclat and FP-growth can explore the search space faster than Apriori.

The main difference between the Eclat and FP-growth algorithm is how the transaction database is stored in memory. Eclat keeps item covers in memory, while FP-growth saves all transactions into *FP-tree* which is a tree-like data structure. Each non-root node of the FP-tree contains a counter and is labeled with the name of a certain frequent item (frequent 1-itemset). In order to build the FP-tree, the FP-growth algorithm first detects frequent items and orders them in support ascending order. Frequent items of each transaction are then saved into FP-tree in *reverse* order as a path, by incrementing counters in existing nodes of the path and creating missing nodes with counters set to 1. In that way, nodes closer to the root node correspond to more frequent items, and are more likely to be shared by many transactions, yielding a smaller FP-tree [13].

Unfortunately, Eclat and FP-growth can't be employed for larger transaction databases which don't fit into main memory. Although some techniques have been proposed for solving this problem (e.g., the partitioning of the database), these techniques are often infeasible [14]. In the next section we will show that this problem is also relevant for event log data sets.

3   The Properties of Event Log Data

The nature of data in the transaction database plays an important role when designing an efficient mining algorithm. When conducting experiments with event log data sets, we discovered that they have several important properties. Table 1 presents eight sample data sets that we used during our experiments. The first five data sets (named *openview, mailserver, fileserver, webserver*, and *ibankserver*, respectively) are raw event logs from different domains: HP OpenView event log file, mail server log file, file and print server log file, web server log file, and Internet banking server log file. We used these event logs for frequent line pattern mining experiments. The rest of the data sets (named *websess, ibanksess*, and *snort*) were obtained from raw event logs by arranging events into slices, and we used them during our experiments of mining frequent event type patterns. In *websess* data set each slice reflects a user visit to the web server, with event types corresponding to accessed URLs. In *ibanksess* data set a slice corresponds to a user session in the Internet bank, where each event type is a certain banking transaction type. The *snort* data set was obtained from the Snort IDS alert log, and each slice reflects an attack from a certain IP address against a certain server, with event types corresponding to Snort rule IDs.

Table 1. The properties of event log data

Data set name	# of transactions	# of items	Items that occur ten times or less	Items that occur at least once per 1,000 transactions	Max. frequent itemset size (supp. 0.1%)
openview	1,835,679	1,739,185	1,582,970	1,242	65
mailserver	7,657,148	1,700,840	1,472,296	627	15
fileserver	7,935,958	11,893,846	11,716,395	817	118
webserver	16,252,925	4,273,082	3,421,834	396	24
ibankserver	14,733,696	2,008,418	1,419,138	304	11
websess	217,027	22,544	17,673	341	21
ibanksess	689,885	454	140	110	12
snort	95,044	554	476	45	7

Firstly, it is evident from Table 1 that the number of items in the transaction database can be quite large, especially when we mine frequent line patterns from raw event logs. However, only few items are relatively frequent (occur at least once per 1,000 transactions), and also, most items appear only few times in the data set. Secondly, Table 1 also indicates that frequent itemsets may contain many items (the table presents figures for the support threshold of 0.1%), which means that Apriori is not always adequate for processing event log data.

The third important property of event log data is that there are often strong correlations between frequent items in transactions. If items are event types, such strong correlations often exist because of causal relations between event types (e.g., when the *PortScan* event appears, the *TrafficAnomaly* event also appears), or because of distinct patterns in the user behavior (e.g., if the web page A is accessed, the web page B is also accessed). In the case of raw event logs where items are word-position pairs, this effect is usually caused by the message formatting with a certain format string before the message is logged, e.g., *sprintf(message, "Connection from %s port %d", ip, port)*. When events of the same type are logged many times, constant parts of the format string will become frequent items which occur together many times in the data set. There could also be strong correlations between items corresponding to variable parts of the format string, e.g., between user names and workstation IP addresses.

In order to assess how well the Apriori, Eclat, and FP-growth algorithms are suited for mining frequent patterns from event logs, we conducted several experiments on data sets from Table 1 with support thresholds of 1% and 0.1% (during all our experiments presented in this paper, we used Apriori, Eclat, and FP-growth implementations by Bart Goethals [15]). In order to reduce the memory consumption of the algorithms, we removed very infrequent items (with the support below 0.01%) from all data sets, and as a result, the number of items was below 7,000 in all cases. A Linux workstation with 1.5 GHz Pentium 4 processor, 512 MB of main memory, and 1 GB of swap space was used during the experiments. Our experiments revealed that when the transaction database is larger, depth-first algorithms could face difficulties when they attempt to load it into main memory (see Table 2).

Table 2 suggests that Eclat is unsuitable for mining frequent patterns from larger event logs, even when infrequent items have been filtered out previously and the algorithm has to load only few thousand item covers into memory. With *fileserver* and *ibankserver* data sets the Eclat algorithm did run out ofphysical memory, and was able to continue only because of sufficient swap space;

Table 2. The size of the memory-resident database

Data set name	Eclat 1%	FP-growth 1%	Eclat 0.1%	FP-growth 0.1%
openview	359.2 MB	2.8 MB	370.7 MB	5.7 MB
mailserver	263.3 MB	2.9 MB	280.5 MB	10.8 MB
fileserver	1009.1 MB	4.0 MB	1024.4 MB	8.6 MB
webserver	Out of VM	64.0 MB	Out of VM	249.9 MB
ibankserver	657.5 MB	37.2 MB	678.0 MB	77.5 MB
websess	5.7 MB	2.4 MB	6.0 MB	9.8 MB
ibanksess	17.5 MB	3.3 MB	17.6 MB	10.6 MB
snort	2.9 MB	2.2 MB	2.9 MB	2.2 MB

with *webserver* data set, the algorithm terminated abnormally after consuming all available virtual memory. Based on these findings, we removed Eclat from further testing. Table 2 also suggests that the FP-growth algorithm is more convenient in terms of memory consumption. The reason for this is that the FP-tree data structure is efficient for storing transactions when strong correlations exist between frequent items in transactions. If many such correlations exist, the number of different frequent item combinations in transactions is generally quite small, and consequently relatively few different paths will be saved to FP-tree. However, it should be noted that for larger data sets the FP-tree could nevertheless be rather large, especially when the support threshold is lower (e.g., for the *webserver* data set the FP-tree consumed about 250 MB of memory when the support threshold was set to 0.1%).

We also tested the Apriori algorithm and verified that in terms of performance it is inferior to FP-growth – for example, when the support threshold was set to 1%, Apriori was 11.5 times slower on *mailserver* data set, and 9.5 times slower on *ibankserver* data set. However, on *openview* and *fileserver* data sets (which contain frequent itemsets with a large number of items) both algorithms performed poorly, and were unable to complete within 24 hours.

The experiment results indicate that all tested algorithms are not entirely suitable for mining frequent patterns from event logs. In the next section we will present an efficient mining algorithm that attempts to address the shortcomings of existing algorithms.

4   A Frequent Pattern Mining Algorithm for Event Logs

In this section we will present an efficient algorithm for mining frequent patterns from event logs. It combines the features of previously discussed algorithms, taking also into account the properties of event log data. Since depth-first Eclat and FP-growth algorithms are inherently dependent on the amount of main memory, our algorithm works in a breadth-first manner and employs the itemset trie data structure (see section 2). In order to avoid inherent weaknesses of Apriori, the algorithm uses several techniques for speeding up its work and reducing its memory consumption. These techniques are described in the following subsections.

4.1   Mining Frequent Items

The mining of frequent items is the first step of any breadth-first algorithm which creates a base for further mining. In order to detect frequent items, the algorithm must make a pass over the data set and count how many times each item occurs in the data set, keeping item counters in main memory. Unfortunately, because the number of items can be very large (see section 3), the memory cost of the item counting is often quite high [8].

In order to solve this problem, our algorithm first estimates which items *need not* to be counted. Before the counting, the algorithm makes an extra pass over the data set and builds the *item summary vector*. The item summary vector is made up of m counters (numbered from 0 to m-1) with each counter initialized to zero. During the pass over the data set, a fast hashing function is applied to each item. The function returns integer values from 0 to m-1, and each time the value i is calculated for an item, the ith counter in the vector will be incremented. Since efficient hashing functions are uniform [16], each counter in the vector will correspond roughly to n/m items, where n is the number of different items in the data set. If items $i_1, ..., i_k$ are all items that hash to the value i, and the items $i_1, ..., i_k$ occur $t_1, ..., t_k$ times, respectively, then the value of the ith counter in the vector equals to the sum $\sum_{j=1}^{k} t_j$.

After the summary vector has been constructed, the algorithm starts counting the items, ignoring the items for which counter values in the summary vector are below the support threshold (no such item can be frequent, since its support does not exceed its counter value). Since most items appear only few times in the data set (see section 3), many counter values will never cross the support threshold. Experiment results presented in [8] indicate that even the use of a relatively small vector (e.g., 100 KB) dramatically reduces the memory cost of the item counting.

4.2   Cache Tree

Eclat and FP-growth algorithms are fast not only because of their depth-first search strategy, but also because they load the transaction database from disk (or other secondary storage device) into main memory. In addition, the algorithms don't attempt to store each transaction as a separate record in memory, but rather employ efficient data structures that facilitate data compression (e.g., the FP-tree). As a result, the memory-resident database is much smaller than the original database, and a scan of the database will take much less time.

Although recent Apriori implementations have employed a prefix tree for keeping the database in memory [10][11], this technique can't be used for data sets which don't fit into main memory. As a solution, we propose to store most frequently used transaction data in the *cache tree*. Let D be the transaction database and F the set of all frequent items. We say that a set of frequent items $X \subseteq F$ *corresponds to m transactions* if $|\{(tid, Y) \mid (tid, Y) \in D, Y \cap F = X\}| = m$. Cache tree is a memory-resident tree data structure which is guaranteed to contain all sets of frequent items that correspond to c or more transactions, where the value of c is given by the user. Each edge in the cache tree is labeled with the name of a certain frequent item, and each node contains a counter. If the set of frequent items $X = \{x_1, ..., x_k\}$ corresponds to m transactions and is stored to the cache tree, it will be saved as a path $x_1, ..., x_k$, and the counter in the tree node $node(x_1, ..., x_k)$ will be set to m. This representation of data allows the algorithm to speed up its work by a considerable margin, since instead of processing m transactions from disk (or other secondary storage device), it has to process just one memory-resident itemset X that does not contain infrequent (and thus irrelevant) items.

In order to create the cache tree, the algorithm has to detect which sets of frequent items correspond to at least c transactions. Note that if the algorithm simply counts the occurrence times of sets, all sets would end up being in main memory together with their occurrence counters (as if $c = 0$). For solving this problem, the algorithm uses the summary vector technique presented in section 4.1 – for each transaction $(tid, Y) \in D$ it finds the set $X = Y \cap F$, hashes X to an integer value, and increments the corresponding counter in the *transaction summary vector*. After the summary vector has been constructed, the algorithm makes another pass over the data, finds the set X for each transaction, and calculates the hash value for it. If the hash value is i and the ith counter in the vector is smaller than c, the itemset X is saved to the *out-of-cache* file as a separate record, otherwise the itemset X is saved into the cache tree (the counter in $node(X)$ is incremented, or set to 1 if the node didn't exist previously).

In that way, the transaction data that would be most frequently used during the mining are guaranteed to be in main memory, and the representation of this data allows the algorithm to further speed up its work. On the other hand, the algorithm does not depend on the amount of main memory available, since the amount of data stored in the cache tree is controlled by the user.

4.3   Reducing the Size of the Itemset Trie

As discussed in section 2, the Apriori algorithm is not well suited for processing data sets which contain frequent k-itemsets for larger values of k, since the itemset trie could become very large, making the runtime and memory cost of the algorithm prohibitive. In order to narrow the search space of mining algorithms, several recent papers have proposed the mining of closed frequent itemsets only. An itemset X is *closed* if X has no superset with the same support. Although it is possible to derive all frequent itemsets from closed frequent itemsets, this task has a quadratic time complexity.

In this subsection, we will present a technique for reducing the size of the itemset trie, so that the trie would still represent all frequent itemsets. When there are many strong correlations between frequent items in transactions, many parts of the Apriori itemset trie are likely to contain information that is already present in other parts. The proposed reduction technique will enable the algorithm to develop only those trie branches that contain unique information.

Let $F = \{f_1, ..., f_n\}$ be the set of all frequent items. We call the set $dep(f_i) = \{f_j \mid f_i \neq f_j, cover(\{f_i\}) \subseteq cover(\{f_j\})\}$ the *dependency set* of f_i, and say that an item f_i *has m dependencies* if $|dep(f_i)| = m$. A *dependency prefix* of the item f_i is the set $pr(f_i) = \{f_j \mid f_j \in dep(f_i), f_j < f_i\}$. A *dependency prefix* of the itemset $\{f_{i_1}, ..., f_{i_k}\}$ is the set $pr(\{f_{i_1}, ..., f_{i_k}\}) = \cup_{j=1}^{k} pr(f_{i_j})$.

Note that the dependency prefix of the itemset has two important properties:

(1) if $pr(\{f_{i_1}, ..., f_{i_k}\}) \subseteq \{f_{i_1}, ..., f_{i_k}\}$, then $pr(\{f_{i_1}, ..., f_{i_{k-1}}\}) \subseteq \{f_{i_1}, ..., f_{i_{k-1}}\}$,
(2) if $pr(X) \subseteq X$, then $supp(X \setminus pr(X)) = supp(X)$ (this follows from the transitivity property – if $a, b, c \in F$, $a \in pr(b)$, and $b \in pr(c)$, then $a \in pr(c)$).

The technique for reducing the size of the itemset trie can be summarized as follows – *if the itemset does not contain its dependency prefix, don't create a node in the trie for that itemset*. As its first step, the algorithm creates the root node, detects frequent items, and finds their dependency sets. If no frequent items were found, the algorithm terminates. Otherwise, it creates nodes only for these frequent items which have empty dependency prefixes, attaching the nodes to the root node. From then on, the algorithm will build the trie layer by layer. If the current depth of the trie is k, the next layer of nodes is created by processing the itemsets previously saved to the cache tree and the out-of-cache file. If the itemset $\{x_1, ..., x_m\}$ was read from the cache tree, i is set to the counter value from the cache tree node $node(\{x_1, ..., x_m\})$, otherwise i is set to 1. Then the itemset is processed by traversing the itemset trie recursively, starting from the root node (in the rest of this paper, this procedure is called *ProcItemset*):

1. If the current node is at depth d, $d < k$, let $l := k + 1 - d$. If $m < l$, return; otherwise, if there is an edge with the label x_1 from the current node, follow that edge and process the itemset $\{x_2, ..., x_m\}$ recursively for the new node.
2. If the current node is at depth k, the path leading to the current node is $y_1, ..., y_k$, and $pr(x_1) \subseteq \{y_1, ..., y_k\}$, check whether there is an edge with the label x_1 from the current node to a candidate node. If the edge exists, add i to the counter in the candidate node; if the edge does not exist, create the candidate node $node(y_1, ..., y_k, x_1)$ in the trie with the counter value i.
3. If $m > 1$, process the itemset $\{x_2, ..., x_m\}$ recursively for the current node.

After the data pass, the algorithm removes candidate nodes with counter values below the support threshold, and terminates if all candidate nodes were removed.

When the algorithm has completed its work, each non-root node in the trie represents a frequent itemset which contains its dependency prefix, and also, if X is a frequent itemset which contains its dependency prefix, the node $node(X)$ is present in the trie (this follows from the first property of the itemset dependency prefix). Although the trie is often much smaller than the Apriori itemset trie, all frequent itemsets can be easily derived from its nodes. For $node(X)$ that represents the frequent itemset X, derived itemsets are $\{X \setminus Y \mid Y \subseteq pr(X)\}$, with each itemset having the same support as X (this follows from the second property of the itemset dependency prefix). Also, if V is a frequent itemset, there exists a unique node $node(W)$ in the trie for deriving V, where $W = V \cup pr(V)$.

The algorithm can be optimized in several ways. The first optimization concerns the frequent item ordering. For the Apriori algorithm, a popular choice has been to order items in support ascending order [10][11]. We propose to order frequent items in dependency ascending order, i.e., in the order that satisfies the following condition – if $f_i < f_j$, then $|dep(\{f_i\})| \leq |dep(\{f_j\})|$. This ordering increases the likelihood that the dependency prefix of an item contains all elements from the dependency set of the item, and thus increases the effectiveness of the trie reduction technique. The second optimization comes from the observation that when frequent items have very few dependencies, our algorithm could produce much more candidate nodes than Apriori. Fortunately, candidates can still be generated within our framework in Apriori fashion – if the trie reduction technique was not applied at node N for reducing the number of its child nodes, and node M is a child of N, then the siblings of M contain all necessary nodes for the creation of candidate child nodes for M. After we have augmented our algorithm with the Apriori-like candidate generation, its final version can be summarized as follows:

1. Make a pass over the database, detect frequent items, and order them in lexicographic order (if the number of items is very large, an optional pass described in section 4.1 can be made for filtering out irrelevant items). If no frequent items were found, terminate.
2. Make a pass over the database, in order to calculate dependency sets for frequent items and to build the transaction summary vector.
3. Reorder frequent items in dependency ascending order and find their dependency prefixes.
4. Make a pass over the database, in order to create the cache tree and the out-of-cache file.
5. Create the root node of the itemset trie and attach nodes for frequent items with empty dependency prefixes to the root node. If all frequent items have empty dependency prefixes, set the APR-flag in the root node.
6. Let $k := 1$.
7. Check all nodes in the trie at depth k. If the parent of a node N has the APR-flag set, generate candidate child nodes for the node N in Apriori fashion (node counters are set to zero), and set the APR-flag in the node N.
8. Build the next layer of nodes in the trie using the *ProcItemset* procedure with the following modification – if the APR-flag is set in a node at depth k, don't attach any additional candidate nodes to that node.
9. Remove the candidate nodes (nodes at depth $k+1$) with counter values below the support threshold. If all candidate nodes were removed, output frequent itemsets and terminate.
10. Find the nodes at depth k for which the trie reduction technique was not applied during step 8 (during calls to the *ProcItemset* procedure) for reducing the number of their child nodes, and set the APR-flag in these nodes. Then let $k := k + 1$ and go to step 7.

It is easy to see that the Apriori algorithm is a special case of our algorithm – if frequent items have no dependencies at all, our algorithm is identical to Apriori. Otherwise, the algorithm will employ the trie reduction technique as much as possible, avoiding to develop trie branches that would contain redundant information. If the trie reduction technique is not applicable for certain branches any more, the algorithm will switch to Apriori-like behavior for these branches.

Figure 2 depicts a sample reduced itemset trie for the same transaction database as presented in Fig. 1 (the support threshold is 2). The reduced itemset trie in Fig. 2 is obtained as follows – first the set of frequent items is found, yielding $F = \{a, b, c, d\}$. Then dependency sets are calculated for frequent items: $dep(d) = \{b, c\}, dep(c) = dep(a) = \{b\}, dep(b) = \emptyset$. After ordering frequent items in dependency ascending order $b < c < a < d$, their dependency prefixes are: $pr(b) = \emptyset, pr(c) = pr(a) = \{b\}, pr(d) = \{b, c\}$. Only the node $node(b)$ can be attached to the root node, since b is the only item with an empty dependency prefix. Also, although the itemset $\{b, d\}$ is frequent, the node $node(b, d)$ will not

Transaction ID	Itemset
1	*abcde*
2	*abc*
3	*bcd*
4	*abc*
5	*ab*

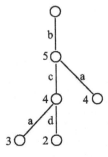

Fig. 2. A sample transaction database and a reduced itemset trie

be inserted into the trie, since the set $\{b\}$ does not contain the item c from the dependency prefix of d. Altogether, there are 11 frequent itemsets – the node $node(b)$ represents one itemset $\{b\}$ with support 5, the node $node(b, c)$ represents two itemsets $\{b, c\}$ and $\{c\}$ with support 4, the node $node(b, c, a)$ represents two itemsets $\{b, c, a\}$ and $\{c, a\}$ with support 3 (but does not represent $\{a\}$, since $\{b, c, a\} \setminus pr(\{b, c, a\}) = \{c, a\}!$), the node $node(b, c, d)$ represents four itemsets $\{b, c, d\}$, $\{b, d\}$, $\{c, d\}$, and $\{d\}$ with support 2, and the node $node(b, a)$ represents two itemsets $\{b, a\}$ and $\{a\}$ with support 4.

In the next section we will discuss the performance and implementation issues of our algorithm.

5   Performance and Implementation

In order to measure the performance of our algorithm, we decided to compare it with the FP-growth algorithm, because experiment results presented in section 3 suggest that FP-growth is much better suited for mining patterns from event logs than Eclat and Apriori. Also, we wanted to verify whether our algorithm that uses the breadth-first approach is able to compete with a fast depth-first algorithm. We conducted our experiments on a Linux workstation with 1.5 GHz Pentium 4 processor and 512 MB of memory. For the sake of fair performance comparison, we configured our algorithm to load the entire transaction database into main memory for all data sets. The results of our experiments are presented in Table 3, Table 4, and Table 5.

First, the experiment results indicate that the trie reduction technique is rather effective for event log data sets, and often significantly smaller itemset trie is produced than in the case of Apriori (if there are m frequent itemsets, the number of nodes in the Apriori itemset trie is $m+1$). As a result, the algorithm consumes much less memory and is much faster than Apriori, since the repeated traversal of a smaller trie takes much less time. The results also indicate that our algorithm performs quite well when compared to FP-growth, and outperforms it in several cases. The only exceptions are *webserver* data set, and *websess* data

Table 3. The performance comparison of algorithms for the 1% support threshold

Data set name	# of frequent itemsets	# of nodes in the reduced trie	Max. size of freq. itemset	Runtime of our algorithm	Runtime of FP-growth
openview	$> 2^{64}$	2,257,548	65	469 s	> 24 hours
mailserver	11,359	559	13	113 s	165 s
fileserver	$\approx 2^{57}$	135,721	57	449 s	> 24 hours
webserver	14,083,903	39,816	20	1286 s	845 s
ibankserver	18,403	4,499	10	289 s	455 s
websess	80	81	6	3 s	2 s
ibanksess	3,181	1,186	10	10 s	10 s
snort	33	34	4	2 s	1 s

Table 4. The performance comparison of algorithms for the 0.5% support threshold

Data set name	# of frequent itemsets	# of nodes in the reduced trie	Max. size of freq. itemset	Runtime of our algorithm	Runtime of FP-growth
openview	$> 2^{64}$	3,161,081	65	601 s	> 24 hours
mailserver	50,863	1,927	14	113 s	174 s
fileserver	$> 2^{64}$	275,525	87	489 s	> 24 hours
webserver	38,735,679	84,679	21	2229 s	855 s
ibankserver	53,105	11,430	11	307 s	495 s
websess	280	281	6	3 s	3 s
ibanksess	6,279	2,229	10	10 s	10 s
snort	42	43	4	2 s	1 s

Table 5. The performance comparison of algorithms for the 0.1% support threshold

Data set name	# of frequent itemsets	# of nodes in the reduced trie	Max. size of freq. itemset	Runtime of our algorithm	Runtime of FP-growth
openview	$> 2^{64}$	7,897,598	65	3395 s	> 24 hours
mailserver	302,505	8,997	15	117 s	192 s
fileserver	$> 2^{64}$	2,235,271	118	834 s	> 24 hours
webserver	319,646,847	443,625	24	8738 s	949 s
ibankserver	328,391	71,229	11	375 s	518 s
websess	2,346,654	1,076,663	21	329 s	17 s
ibanksess	41,103	12,826	12	15 s	12 s
snort	214	121	7	2 s	1 s

set for the 0.1% support threshold. When we investigated these cases in more detail, we discovered that with a lower support threshold there are quite many different combinations of frequent items present in the transactions of these data sets, and therefore our algorithm will also generate many candidate nodes, most of which corresponding to infrequent itemsets.

On the other hand, the results suggest that our algorithm is superior to FP-growth when the data set contains frequent itemsets with a large number of items and frequent items have many dependencies – for example, on *openview* and *fileserver* data sets our algorithm is much faster. The reason for the poor performance of FP-growth is as follows – when the data set contains many frequent k-itemsets for larger values of k, the total number of frequent itemsets is very large, and since FP-growth must visit each frequent itemset during its work, its runtime cost is simply too high. This raises an interesting question – can the FP-growth algorithm be augmented with the same technique that our algorithm uses, i.e., if the frequent itemset P does not contain its dependency prefix, the algorithm will not search for frequent itemsets that begin with P. Unfortunately, when frequent items are ordered in dependency ascending order, frequent items of transactions will be saved to FP-tree in dependency descending (reverse) order, because the FP-growth algorithm processes the FP-tree in a bottom-up manner [13]. Since items with more dependencies tend to be less frequent, the FP-tree nodes closer to the root node are less likely to be shared by many transactions, and the resulting FP-tree is highly inefficient in terms of memory consumption. When conducting experiments with data sets from Table 1, we found that the FP-tree did not fit into main memory in several cases.

We have developed a mining tool called LogHound that implements our algorithm. The tool can be employed for mining frequent line patterns from raw event logs, but also for mining frequent event type patterns. LogHound has several options for preprocessing input data with the help of regular expressions. In order to limit the number of patterns reported to the end user, it has also an option to output only those patterns that correspond to closed frequent itemsets. Figure 3 depicts some sample patterns that have been discovered with LogHound.

```
Dec 18 * myhost * connect from
Dec 18 * myhost * log: Connection from * port
Dec 18 * myhost * fatal: Did not receive ident string.
Dec 18 * myhost * log: * authentication for * accepted.
Dec 18 * myhost * fatal: Connection closed by remote host.
```

(a) Sample frequent line patterns

```
[1:1256:7] [1:1002:5] [119:2:1] [1:1945:1]

[1:1256:7] - WEB-IIS CodeRed v2 root.exe access
[1:1002:5] - WEB-IIS cmd.exe access
[119:2:1]  - HTTP DOUBLE DECODING ATTACK
[1:1945:1] - WEB-IIS unicode directory traversal attempt
```

(b) Sample frequent event type pattern
    (the CodeRed worm footprint that was detected from the Snort IDS log)

Fig. 3. Sample frequent patterns detected with LogHound

LogHound is written is C, and has been tested on Linux and Solaris platforms. It is distributed under the terms of GNU GPL, and is available at http://kodu.neti.ee/~risto/loghound/.

6   Conclusion

In this paper, we presented an efficient breadth-first frequent itemset mining algorithm for mining frequent patterns from event logs. The algorithm combines the features of well-known breadth-first and depth-first algorithms, and also takes into account the special properties of event log data. The experiment results indicate that our algorithm is suitable for processing event log data, and is in many occasions more efficient than well-known depth-first algorithms.

References

1. C. Lonvick: The BSD syslog Protocol. RFC3164 (2001)
2. H. Mannila, H. Toivonen, and A. I. Verkamo: Discovery of frequent episodes in event sequences. Data Mining and Knowledge Discovery $1(3)$ (1997) 259-289
3. Qingguo Zheng, Ke Xu, Weifeng Lv, and Shilong Ma: Intelligent Search of Correlated Alarms from Database Containing Noise Data. Proceedings of the 8th IEEE/IFIP Network Operations and Management Symposium (2002) 405-419
4. Sheng Ma and Joseph L. Hellerstein: Mining Partially Periodic Event Patterns with Unknown Periods. Proceedings of the 16th International Conference on Data Engineering (2000) 205-214
5. Jian Pei, Jiawei Han, Behzad Mortazavi-asl, and Hua Zhu: Mining Access Patterns Efficiently from Web Logs. Proceedings of the 4th Pacific-Asia Conference on Knowledge Discovery and Data Mining (2000) 396-407
6. Jaideep Srivastava, Robert Cooley, Mukund Deshpande, and Pang-Ning Tan: Web Usage Mining: Discovery and Applications of Usage Patterns from Web Data. ACM SIGKDD Explorations $1(2)$ (2000) 12-23
7. Mika Klemettinen: A Knowledge Discovery Methodology for Telecommunication Network Alarm Databases. PhD thesis, University of Helsinki (1999)
8. Risto Vaarandi: A Data Clustering Algorithm for Mining Patterns From Event Logs. Proceedings of the 2003 IEEE Workshop on IP Operations and Management (2003) 119-126
9. Rakesh Agrawal and Ramakrishnan Srikant: Fast Algorithms for Mining Association Rules. Proceedings of the 20th International Conference on Very Large Data Bases (1994) 478-499
10. Ferenc Bodon: A fast APRIORI implementation. Proceedings of the IEEE ICDM Workshop on Frequent Itemset Mining Implementations (2003)
11. Christian Borgelt: Efficient Implementations of Apriori and Eclat. Proceedings of the IEEE ICDM Workshop on Frequent Itemset Mining Implementations (2003)
12. Mohammed J. Zaki: Scalable Algorithms for Association Mining. IEEE Transactions on Knowledge and Data Engineering $12(3)$ (2000) 372-390
13. Jiawei Han, Jian Pei, and Yiwen Yin: Mining Frequent Patterns without Candidate Generation. Proceedings of the 2000 ACM SIGMOD International Conference on Management of Data (2000) 1-12

14. Bart Goethals: Memory issues in frequent itemset mining. Proceedings of the 2004 ACM Symposium on Applied Computing (2004) 530-534
15. http://www.cs.helsinki.fi/u/goethals/software/index.html
16. M. V. Ramakrishna and Justin Zobel: Performance in Practice of String Hashing Functions. Proceedings of the 5th International Conference on Database Systems for Advanced Applications (1997) 215-224

Management Information and Model of GSMP Network Open Interface

YoungWook Cha[1], TaeHyun Kwon[1], ChoonHee Kim[2], and JunKyun Choi[3]

[1] Andong National University, Korea
{ywcha, taehyun}@andong.ac.kr
[2] Daegu Cyber University, Korea
chkim@dcu.ac.kr
[3] Information and Communications University, Korea
jkchoi@icu.ac.kr

Abstract. General switch management protocol (GSMP) is a network open interface between a label switch and a controller, and it provides connection, configuration, event, performance management and synchronization. There will be two considerations for network management services in GSMP interfaces. The first one is what kind of management information base will be used for network management services in GSMP interface. The second consideration is where network management functions for network management services will be located in GSMP interface. We guided the usage of management information base for each network management service. We proposed the network management model, in which management functions are distributed in a controller and a label switch according to network management services.

1 Introduction

Network technology is moving form monoliths to component-based network elements. In the environment of component-based network elements, the open interface allows the technologies of forwarding and control to evolve independently from each other [1-2]. General switch management protocol (GSMP) provides a network open interface that can be used to separate the data forwarder from the routing and other control plane protocols [3]. GSMP has been considered to be an open interface in several organizations such as a multi-service switching forum, IEEE programmable interface network, and automatic switched optical network in ITU-T [1].

Figure 1 shows the GSMP interface between a controller and a label switch. GSMP protocol is asymmetric, the controller being the master and the switch being the slave. This means that the controller makes decisions to establish connection and routing, and that the switch merely responds to the commands from the controller. GSMP allows a controller to establish connections across the label switch, manage switch ports, request configuration information, reserve switch resources, and gather statistics. It also allows the label switch to inform the controller of asynchronous events such as a link going down [3].

A. Aagesen et al. (Eds.): INTELLCOMM 2004, LNCS 3283, pp. 309–318, 2004.

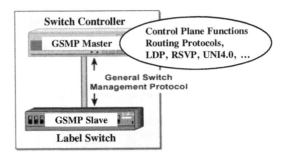

Fig. 1. GSMP Interface

Traditionally, network management (NM) services are classified into five categories: configuration, performance, fault, accounting, and security management services. Network management functions for these services can be located in either a controller or a label switch. There had been no considerations for NM services in GSMP interface before the draft document [4].

There are two considerations for network management services in GSMP interfaces. The first one is what kind of management information base (MIB) will be used for network management services in GSMP interface. GSMP protocol MIB of RFC 3295 [5] is just a protocol MIB, which cannot support traditional network management services. We guided the usage of MIBs for each network management service in the GSMP interface. The second consideration is where network management functions for network management services will be located in the GSMP interface. We proposed the network management model, in which management functions are distributed in the controller and the label switch according to network management services.

The remainder of this paper is organized as follows. In section 2, we described each network management service and its related managed objects in the GSMP interface. We discussed the locations of network management functions according to network management services in section 3. Finally, section 4 presented concluding remarks with some issues for further research.

2   Managed Objects for Network Management Services

2.1   Approaches to Selection of Managed Objects

There have been two studies of managed objects (MOs) in the GSMP interface: GSMP protocol MIB of RFC 3295 [5] and GSMP NM service MIB [6]. The managed objects of RFC 3295 are only defined to configure, monitor and maintain GSMP protocol entity. GSMP protocol MIB cannot support traditional network management services such as fault, configuration, accounting, performance, and security management services. GSMP NM service MIB includes managed objects to support network management services in the GSMP interface. Managed objects of this MIB are based on information elements of GSMP messages. GSMP NM service MIB is classified into the configuration group, the connection group and the performance group.

For NM services in the GSMP interface, there will be two approaches to choosing the relevant MIBs. The one approach is using the existing managed objects, which are defined in ATM-MIB [7] or MPLS-MIB [8]. In this approach, new managed objects will be defined if the existing managed objects could not be used for supporting a specific network management service. The advantage of this approach is that new definitions of managed objects will be minimized. The other approach is to use GSMP NM service MIB [6]. In this approach, network management functions will be simply mapped with the GSMP functions, because GSMP NM service MIB was defined to accommodate the information elements of GSMP messages.

2.2 Configuration Management

GSMP configuration messages permit the controller to discover the capabilities of the switch. Three configuration request messages have been defined in the GSMP: Switch, Port, and Service messages [3]. In the existing MIBs [7-8], there are no managed objects or tables, which are mapped with the GSMP configuration messages. To support switch and service configuration in the GSMP interface, it is required to define new configuration tables. Table 1 shows GSMP configuration messages and their related management tables in GSMP NM service MIB [6]. The columnar objects of these table entries are based on the information elements of the GSMP configuration messages.

Table 1. Configuration Tables of GSMP NM Service MIB

GSMP Messages	Configuration Tables
Switch Configuration	gsmpSwitchConfTable
Port Configuration	gsmpInterfaceConfTable
	gsmpPortServiceMapTable
Service Configuration	gsmpServiceConfTable

The entry of interface configuration table represents the configuration information of a single switch port. The entries of service configuration table are the service lists of the switch, which are characterized by traffic and quality of service (QoS) parameters. The entries in the service mapping table of a port are service lists supported by the specific port. Figure 2 shows the relationship among interface configuration table, service configuration table and service mapping table of a port.

InterfaceConfIndex

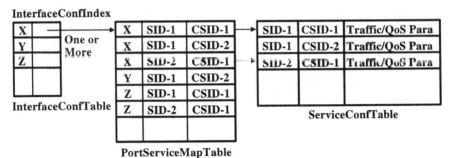

PortServiceMapTable

SID : Service ID CSID : Capability Set ID

Fig. 2. Relationship among Configuration Tables

2.3 Connection Management

For connection management service, we can use traffic parameter, in-segment, out-segment, and cross-connect tables of the existing MIB [7-8] or the GSMP service MIB [6]. Figure 3 shows the relationship among the interface configuration table and the connection related tables. A connection is modeled as a cross-connect consisting of in-segment and out-segment at a switch. These segments are related to input and output interfaces, and their characteristics are defined by the entries of the traffic parameter table. The interconnection of the in-segment and out-segment is accomplished by creating a cross-connect entry.

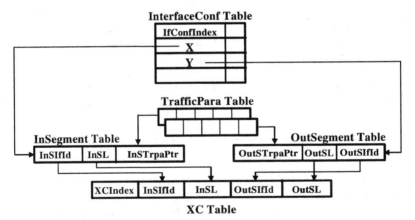

If : Interface , Conf : Configuration , S : Segment , L : Label , Id : Index , TrpaPtr : Traffic Parameter Row Pointer , XC : Cross-Connect

Fig. 3. Relationship among Connection Management Tables

2.4 Performance Management

The performance messages of GSMP permit the controller to request the values of various hardware counters associated with the connections, input and output ports [3]. For connection performance management, we can use segment performance tables of the existing MIB or the GSMP NM Service MIB. Each entry of the interface performance table in the existing MIB or the GSMP NM Service MIB will be used for a port performance management. However, the columnar objects of existing table entries cannot be exactly mapped with the GSMP performance counters. The GSMP NM service MIB has interface and label performance tables, which are designed to be fully mapped with the GSMP performance messages.

2.5 Event Management

GSMP allows the switch to inform the controller of asynchronous events. The event messages defined in GSMP are Port Up, Port Down, Invalid Label, New Port, Dead Port and Adjacency Update messages [3]. GSMP protocol MIB [5] defines notifications, which are mapped with the GSMP event messages. Table 2 shows GSMP events and their related notifications in the GSMP protocol MIB.

Table 2. GSMP Event and Notification

Events	Notifications
Port Up	gsmpPortUpEvent
Port Down	gsmpPortDownEvent
Invalid Label	gsmpInvalidLabelEvnet
New Port	gsmpNewPortEvent
Dead Port	gsmpDeadPortEvent
Adjacency Update	gsmpAdjacencyUpdateEvent

3 Distribution of Network Management Functions

Network management functions can be located either in the controller or the label switch, but the location has not been clearly defined for the GSMP interface. We will discuss the locations of NM functions according to network management services.

3.1 NM Function for Connection Management

Connections are usually classified into two types: a dynamic connection is established by the signaling protocol, and a provisioned connection is configured by the network management function. In the GSMP interface, switch resources for dynamic connections are managed by the controller, which admits a new dynamic connection, and commands the label switch to setup the admitted connection. The switch merely establishes the requested connection and responds to the controller [9].

Switch resources for provisioned connections will be managed by the controller or the label switch according to the location of connection management function. If the switch has connection management function, then it manages its resources for provisioned connections. This means that switch resources are managed by the controller or the label switch according to connection types. This separated management of switch resources will cause resource reallocation or inefficient resource usage. On the other hand, if the controller has connection management function, it will manage all switch resources for the dynamic and provisioned connection, so inefficient resource usage or resource reallocation problem can be dissolved [10].

Figure 4 shows the reservation and establishment procedures for a provisioned connection in the GSMP interface, where connection management function is located in the controller.

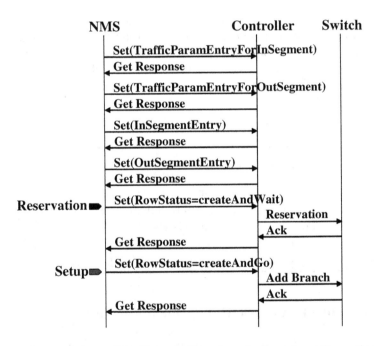

Fig. 4. Reservation and Establishment Procedures for Provisioned Connection

Network management station (NMS) first sets segment entries and their associated traffic parameter entries. After the segments are successfully created, the manager will request the controller to create a cross-connect entry. If the row status of the cross-connect entry is "createAndWait", then the controller commands the label switch to reserve the provisioned connection by sending GSMP Reservation message. After the controller receives the acknowledgement, it will complete the reservation of the provisioned connection by returning simple network management protocol (SNMP) Get Response message to the manager.

NMS will activate the reserved connection by setting "createAndGo" in the row status of cross-connect entry. Then, the controller commands the label switch to establish the provisioned connection by sending GSMP Add Branch message. The manager deletes the provisioned connection by setting the row status of the cross-connect entry as destroy. Then, the controller requests the switch to delete the provisioned connection by sending GSMP Delete Tree message.

3.2 NM Function for Performance Management

Figure 5 shows information flows according to the locations of performance NM function.

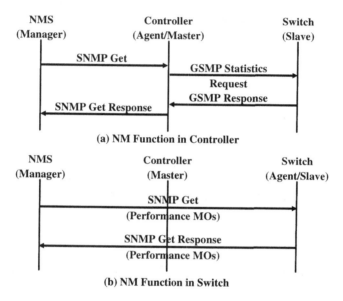

Fig. 5. Information Flows for Performance Management

If performance management function is located in the controller as shown in Fig. 5(a), the NMS issues SNMP Get message with performance related MOs to the controller. Then, the controller commands the label switch to collect performance information by sending GSMP Statistics message [3]. The controller returns SNMP Get Response message to the manager, when it receives the response from the switch. These information flows require mapping procedures between NM functions and GSMP functions, because NM functions are only in the controller.

If the switch has performance management function (see Fig. 5(b)), then the NMS could directly query the label switch about the performance information without mapping overhead in the controller. This direct interaction is feasible because performance information is actually collected and maintained by the switch.

3.3   NM Function for Fault Management

Figure 6 shows information flows according to the locations of event NM function.

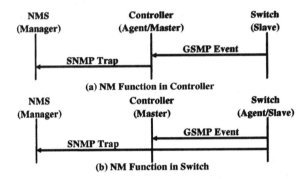

Fig. 6. Information Flows for Event Management

If fault management function is located in the controller as shown in Fig. 6(a), the controller maps the received GSMP event [3] into the SNMP Trap message to be transferred to the manager. This mapping overhead will cause a barrier for rapid fault management. If the switch has fault management function (see Fig. 6(b)), then the switch would inform the event to the controller and manager simultaneously. This direct notification is feasible, because event detection can be accomplished by the switch itself.

3.4   Locations of NM Functions

Figure 7 is our proposed NM model in the GSMP interface, which has distributed NM functions in the controller and the label switch according to NM services.

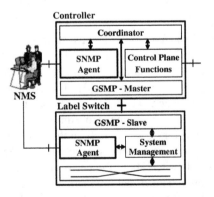

Fig. 7. Distributed NM Model in GSMP Interface

In the GSMP interface, the controller implements control plane functions, which are supported by signaling and routing protocols [9]. This means that the controller completely makes decisions of connection and routing, and that the label switch merely responds to the commands from the controller. We put connection and configuration management functions in the controller, because connection admission control and service configuration are performed by the controller. On the other hand, we put NM functions for performance and fault management services in the switch, because the maintenance of performance information and event detection can be accomplished by the switch itself.

4 Conclusion

GSMP provides an open interface used to separate the data plane from the control plane. We guided the usage of MIB for each network management service in the GSMP interface. For GSMP connection and performance management functions, GSMP NM service MIB or existing MIB can be used. It is required to use configuration tables in GSMP NM service MIB, because existing MIB has no managed objects or tables, which can configure switch and service in the GSMP interface. Notifications in GSMP protocol MIB can be used for event management.

We proposed the network management model in the GSMP interface, which has distributed management functions in the controller and the label switch according to network management services. Our distributed NM model is based on which node controls connection resources, configures service and switch, collects performance data and detects events in the GSMP interface.

As the next step of our studies, we will extend and generalize the network management model of the GSMP interface and apply the generalized model to other open interfaces.

Acknowledgement

This work was supported in part by the Korea Science and Engineering Foundation (KOSEF) through OIRC project, and by a grant from 2004 Research Fund of Andong National University.

References

1. Nils Bjorkman et al., "The Movement from Monoliths to Component-Based Network Elements," IEEE Communications Magazine, January 2001.
2. Thomas M. Chen, "Evolution to the Programmable Internet," IEEE Communications Magazine, March 2000.
3. A. Doria, et al., "General Switch Management Protocol," RFC 3292, June 2002.
4. YW Cha et al., "Network Management for GSMP Interface," Internet draft, <draft-cha-gsmp-management-01.txt>, November 2002.

5. H. Sjostrand et al., "Definitions of Managed Objects for the General Switch Management Protocol," RFC 3295, June 2002.
6. YW Cha et al., "Definitions of Managed Objects for Network Management Services in General Switch Management Protocol (GSMP) Interface," Internet draft, <draft-cha-gsmp-service-mib-00.txt>, November 2002.
7. K. Tesink et al., "Definitions of Managed Objects for ATM Management," RFC 2515, February 1999.
8. Cheenu Srinivasan et al., "MPLS Label Switch Router Management Information Base Using SMIv2," Internet draft, <draft-ietf-mpls-lsr-mib-09.txt>, October 2002.
9. A. Doria, et al., "General Switch Management Protocol Applicability," RFC 3294, June 2002.
10. YW Cha et al., "Network Management Services in GSMP Open Interface," International Human.Society@Internet Conference, June 2003.

Towards Service Continuity for Generic Mobile Services

Ivar Jørstad[1], Do van Thanh[2], and Schahram Dustdar[3]

[1] Norwegian University of Science and Technology, Dept. of Telematics,
O.S. Bragstads plass 2E, N-7491 Trondheim, Norway
ivar@ongx.org
[2] Telenor R&D, Snarøyveien 30 N-1331 Fornebu, Norway
thanh-van.do@telenor.com
http://www.item.ntnu.no/~thanhvan
[3] Vienna University of Technology, Distributed Systems Group (DSG),
Information Systems Institute A-1040 Wien, Argentinierstrasse 8/184-1, Austria
dustdar@infosys.tuwien.ac.at
http://www.infosys.tuwien.ac.at/Staff/sd/

Abstract. This paper discusses models of generic mobile services. The goal is to gain understanding of the challenges in designing, developing and deploying advanced mobile data services. First, a composition model describing the components of a generic mobile service and the components relationships is given. Second, distribution models describing the distributions of the components in the former model across hosts, networks and domains are presented. After presenting these generic models, a brief mobility analysis is carried out, followed by a discussion of mobility and service continuity dependency on the service distribution. The functions necessary to provide service continuity are identified and incorporated in a service continuity layer.

1 Introduction

Till now, the focus in mobile communications has been on providing service continuity of communication services when a mobile terminal is roaming between networks, i.e. avoiding abruption of access. The underlying mechanism for achieving service continuity is called handover or handoff. With the increasing number of devices that users have at their disposition, it is quite relevant to provide service continuity across heterogeneous devices. For example, a user, when arriving at the office, may want to transfer the conversation session from the mobile phone to the multimedia PC acting as an IP phone. The goal of this paper is to examine how service continuity can be provided. The paper adopts a formal and analytical approach. It starts with an analysis of current services and derives the functions and capabilities that are necessary to achieve service continuity.

2 Modeling Mobile Services

It is possible to model mobile services according to their *composition* or their *distribution*. Whereas the composition model is concerned with the division of a service

A. Aagesen et al. (Eds.): INTELLCOMM 2004, LNCS 3283, pp. 319–326, 2004.

into discrete components according to their nature and role, the distribution model is concerned with the distribution of components of a service across devices, networks and domains.

2.1 Composition Model

Fig. 1 displays a UML (Unified Modeling Language [1]) Class Diagram showing the composition of a mobile service. *Service logic* is the program code that constitutes the dynamic behavior and provides the functions of a service. Usually, this does not only consist of one autonomous unit, but in this model the service logic represents the collection of program code units for a given service.

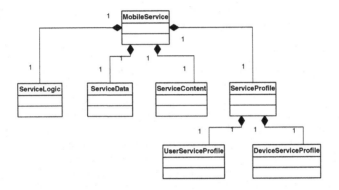

Fig. 1. Composition model of Mobile Service

Service State contains data used in the execution of the service logic and reflects the state of it. They are for example variable values, temporal parameters, register values, stack values, counting parameters, etc. In order to provide service continuity and personalisation we propose to introduce two additional service components; *Service content* and *Service profile*.

Service Content refers to data that are the product of service usage. For example it can be a document written in a word processor or the entries in a calendar. Service content can be produced or consumed by the user.

A *Service Profile* contains the service settings that are related to the user or/and the accessing device. A service profile can further be divided into a *User Service Profile* and a *Device Service Profile*.

All of the components of a mobile service as defined above can be subject to various distributions, as in other distributed systems [2].

2.2 Distribution Model

According to the Distributed Computing paradigm, the distribution of a service/application should be hidden and the mechanisms to support distribution are incorporated in the Distributed Computing middleware such that the developer can concentrate on the core functions of the application [3][4]. However, for mobile services, distribution plays a crucial role that must be considered at service design. Indeed, when the user is moving and is accessing services from different places, the location of a service and its components relative to the user's location will have great influence on its availability, quality, service continuity and personalization offerings.

In order to model the distribution, we introduce the notions that are depicted in Fig 2. A user can be at one location at a time but one location may be visited by zero or more users. A location may have zero or more hosts. One or more locations belong to a domain. A domain is defined as a set of locations containing a number of hosts that are controlled by an actor. The access to and from the domain is controlled by this actor, e.g. enterprise, home user, telecom operator, etc.

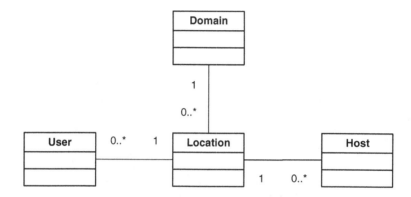

Fig. 2. Relationship between notions used in the distribution models

2.2.1 Monolithic Services

The first distribution model is a system where all components of the mobile service, i.e ServiceLogic, ServiceData, ServiceProfile and ServiceContent are installed in the same host which is located at the same location as the end-user. Such services can be called *monolithic*, as they constitute a single, autonomous unit. Examples of this service type are word processors, spreadsheets, stand-alone games, calculator, etc. With such a service, if the user is at the same location as the host containing all the service components, he will have access to the service.

2.2.2 Thin-Client/Server Services

The previous model is very restricted. This is partly remedied by the second model (Fig. 3) which splits the service logic into two parts; one generic part (GenericServiceLogic) and one specialized part (ServiceLogic). Service content, data and profiles are all co-located with the specialized part. The generic part is a thin-client presentation layer. Typical examples of the GenericServiceLogic are Telnet or rlogin.

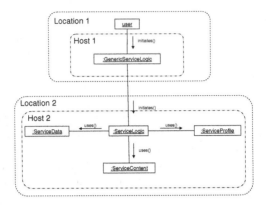

Fig. 3. Distribution model for thin-client/server mobile services

2.2.3 Client/Server Services

In the third model (Fig. 4), a model similar to the previous is defined. The difference is that while in the previous model, the client application (GenericServiceLogic) was generic and used for a lot of different services. In the client/server model, Service-Logic1 is a client application specialized for a particular service.

Both components have their own service data, and ServiceLogic2 has access to a service profile and the service content as well. As an option, ServiceLogic1 can also keep its own service profile and service content. A refinement of this model is the multi-component service. In addition to employing a client/server distribution, the server is then further divided into two or more components.

It is worth emphasizing that a service type is characterized by both the service composition and the service distribution.

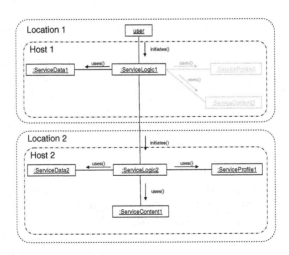

Fig. 4. Distribution model for client-server mobile services

2.3 Mobility Analysis

All the presented models are static and represent common views of distributed systems that do not regard user mobility as an issue. It is thus important to add and discuss the notion of movement of the user between different Locations, and to consider what effects these movements have on services of various types. For clarity, we introduce the following axiom:

Axiom 1: *"Mobility does not have any impact on service availability and continuity as long as the user moves together with all discrete components of the service."*

From this axiom, it follows that: *"Only changes in relative Location between user and parts of, or all discrete components of a service have impact on service continuity in that particular service."*

Movements of the user will have different impact on each service type due to their distribution. Whereas concepts like personal mobility and device mobility is usually concerned with the communication service at network layer (OSI layer 3), service continuity is a concept that supports generic, data based services. The service continuity concept can be broken into two types; seamless service continuity and non-seamless service continuity.

We define seamless service continuity as: *"...the ability to pick up a service at a new Location, where service disruption is bounded by the time it takes the user to move between the two Locations."*

Non-seamless service continuity is defined as: *"...the ability to pick up a service at a new Location, where service usage can proceed from the 'point'/state where it were left at the previous Location, but where additional disruption is introduced due to a required reorganization of the service composition."*

Additional disruption in the second definition can be due to necessary user interaction (e.g. installation of required client software).

2.3.1 The Notion of Movement in UML

The basis for the notation used in the following analysis is UML collaboration diagrams. However, UML does not define a notion for movement, which is one of the most critical aspects in this analysis. The notion of movement is thus introduced using the stereotype <<moves>> along with a unidirectional association defining the direction of movement.

2.3.2 Service Type Specific Analysis

The remainder of this section describes a usage scenario for a specific service type.

Based on this analysis, the next section will provide an initial framework for improved service continuity support in generic mobile services. Due to space limitation, only the client/server service type defined in Fig. 4 is considered. Mobile agents and mobile code [5] are technologies that earlier have been suggested as solutions to some of the challenges with service continuity.

Consider a scenario where UserX is accessing a service S1 in Location1 through Host1, using ServiceLogic1A. At one point, UserX moves from Location1 to Location2. The question is then how to ensure service continuity. There are two alternatives:

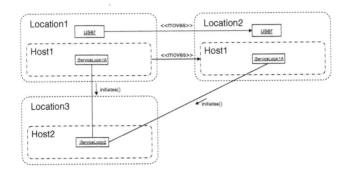

Fig. 5. User moves together with Host to a new Location

1. If Host1 moves together with the user, as depicted in Fig.5, there is no relative movement between the user and the service components that he is directly accessing. Service continuity is obtained by ensuring the continuity of communication between ServiceLogic1A and ServiceLogic2. This is the familiar case of the terminal handover that mobile communications have focused on. In these figures, other components of the service than service logic are excluded to ensure clarity and avoid cluttering. It is implicit that all the other components of the service are coexisting with the service logic as earlier described.
2. If Host1 is not moving together with the user, it will not always be possible to realize seamless service continuity, but often only non-seamless service continuity. For seamless service continuity, a copy or an instance of the ServiceLogic1A must already exist at the new Host, such that the user can continue the service. For non-seamless service continuity, this service logic must be installed at the new Host. In both cases, it must be possible to reinitiate the communication towards ServiceLogic2. Typical example of such a case is a web browser, e.g. Internet Explorer, of which two instances are installed on two PCs.

3 Support for Service Continuity: Service Continuity Layer

The service continuity layer can be seen as a management layer with support functions for realizing maximum service continuity and availability of generic services due to user movement relative to service components. Service continuity should be supported by appropriate middleware. Others have argued that the application layer is suitable for providing flexible solutions to handling service continuity and mobility issues [6].

A service continuity layer needs to have access to relevant information from the application layer (e.g. current state of service), but also from the lower layers (e.g. to infer decisions about network resources). The elements of the service continuity layer are 1) a monitor, 2) a handover manager, 3) an interoperability evaluator, 4) a service composition module and 5) an input/output redirector.

First, there is a need for a *monitor* which keeps a resource map and includes mechanisms and methodologies for describing surroundings of a host more detailed than only nodes in the current network (e.g. WLAN zone), which can be deduced from ARP requests on an Ethernet (i.e., neighbour discovery). There is a need for describing network boundaries, domain boundaries, restrictive elements (middleboxes [7]) etc. These must be known by the service continuity layer so that possible re-distributions of a service, to provide service continuity, can be identified.

Second, a *handover manager* is needed. High-level service handover has earlier been considered in [8]. Handover between cells in mobile telecom systems (GSM) is based on measurements of the surroundings (e.g. of received signal strength level) for the system to be able to act proactively as handover becomes necessary to provide a sustained service. Although a soft handover is not necessarily required for service continuity in data based services, the idea of monitoring surroundings could be applied here also, and performed by the service continuity layer, thereby increasing the user experience of mobile services. The monitor together with the handover manager can instruct the service composition module to design and implement a new service composition of an existing service as soon as it is recognized that a handover will be necessary, thus decreasing the disruption time in service usage.

The third required element is an *interoperability evaluator*. If a service is to be re-organized based on decisions by the monitor, a new service will be composed using either a replication of or an equivalent of each of the current components of the service. To ensure sustained service access, it must be ascertained that potential components for the new composition are interoperable with, and provide a satisfactorily equivalent interface as, the current components. The task of the interoperability evaluator is thus to match compatible components based on both their *interfaces* (syntax) and their *behavior* (semantics).

A fourth element is the *service composition* element. Based on what the Service Continuity Layer knows about the systems and the restrictions, it can dynamically compose a new service by using only components that have been validated by the interoperability evaluator. In general, and as specified for XML Web Services, service composition can be either choreographed or orchestrated [9]. Orchestration seems to be the most feasible for the service continuity layer considered in this paper.

The fifth and last element is an input/output redirector. Input/Output (I/O) redirection can be used between service logic components in a mobile service to avoid moving entire components around, when requirements otherwise would suggest this as a solution. A mechanism for performing the actual redirection must exist, and in addition, a generic way of representing I/O for transport between services must be defined to simplify the interfaces between service components.

4   Conclusion

This paper initially describes the composition of generic mobile services and then provides an overview of possible distribution models for such services. The paper proceeds with a user-movement based analysis of one of the models. For the model chosen, it is suggested that service continuity can be assured if either a) a new instance of the initial service logic is available in the new location or b) a re-implementation of the initial service logic is available in the new location, and c) the communication between ServiceLogic1A and/or B and ServiceLogic2 can be reinitiated.

The analysis culminates with required functionalities included in a Service Continuity Layer which consists of a) resource map of surroundings, b) high level service handover functionality, c) interoperability evaluation and compatibility matching, d) service composition and e) generic i/o redirection between service components (service logic).

As part of future work, the user-movement based analysis will be extended and UML modeling of concepts discussed will be carried out.

References

1. Martin Fowler, UML Distilled: A brief guide to the standard object modeling language, 3rd Edition, ISBN 0-321-19368-7, 2004
2. George Coulouris et. al, Distributed Systems: Concepts and Design, 3rd Edition, ISBN 0-201-619-180, Addison-Wesley, Pearson Education, 2001
3. ITU-T X.901 I ISO/IEC 10746-{1,2,3,4}, Open Distributed Processing Reference Model Part 1,2,3 AND 4
4. Kerry Raymond, Reference Model of Open Distributed Processing (RM-ODP): Introduction - kerry@dstc.edu.au - CRC for Distributed Systems Technology -Centre for Information Technology Research - University of Queensland Brisbane 4072 Australia
5. Stefano Camapdello & Kimmo Raatikainen, Agents in Personal Mobility, Proceedings of the First International Workshop on Mobile Agents for Telecommunication Application (MATA'99). Ottawa Canada October 6-8 1999. World Scientific, pp. 359-374
6. Proceedings of the Italian Workshop "From Objects to Agents: Intelligent Systems and Pervasive Computing" (WOA'03), Italy, ISBN 88-371-1413-3, September 10-11, 2003
7. IETF, RFC 3303: Middlebox communication architecture and framework, August 2002
8. Thomas Strang, Claudia Linnhoff-Popien, Matthias Roeckl, Highlevel Service Handover through a Contextual Framework, MoMuC 2003, 8th International Workshop on Mobile Multimedia Communications, Munich/Germany, October 2003
9. Chris Peltz, Web Services Orchestration: A review of emerging technologies, tools, and standards, Hewlett Packard, Co., January 2003

Author Index

Lecture Notes in Computer Science

For information about Vols. 1–3216

please contact your bookseller or Springer

Vol. 3266: J. Solé-Pareta, M. Smirnov, P.V. Mieghem, J. Domingo-Pascual, E. Monteiro, P. Reichl, B. Stiller, R.J. Gibbens (Eds.), Quality of Service in the Emerging Networking Panorama. XVI, 390 pages. 2004.

Vol. 3265: R.E. Frederking, K.B. Taylor (Eds.), Machine Translation: From Real Users to Research. XI, 392 pages. 2004. (Subseries LNAI).

Vol. 3264: G. Paliouras, Y. Sakakibara (Eds.), Grammatical Inference: Algorithms and Applications. XI, 291 pages. 2004. (Subseries LNAI).

Vol. 3263: M. Weske, P. Liggesmeyer (Eds.), Object-Oriented and Internet-Based Technologies. XII, 239 pages. 2004.

Vol. 3262: M.M. Freire, P. Chemouil, P. Lorenz, A. Gravey (Eds.), Universal Multiservice Networks. XIII, 556 pages. 2004.

Vol. 3261: T. Yakhno (Ed.), Advances in Information Systems. XIV, 617 pages. 2004.

Vol. 3260: I.G.M.M. Niemegeers, S.H. de Groot (Eds.), Personal Wireless Communications. XIV, 478 pages. 2004.

Vol. 3258: M. Wallace (Ed.), Principles and Practice of Constraint Programming – CP 2004. XVII, 822 pages. 2004.

Vol. 3257: E. Motta, N.R. Shadbolt, A. Stutt, N. Gibbins (Eds.), Engineering Knowledge in the Age of the Semantic Web. XVII, 517 pages. 2004. (Subseries LNAI).

Vol. 3256: H. Ehrig, G. Engels, F. Parisi-Presicce, G. Rozenberg (Eds.), Graph Transformations. XII, 451 pages. 2004.

Vol. 3255: A. Benczúr, J. Demetrovics, G. Gottlob (Eds.), Advances in Databases and Information Systems. XI, 423 pages. 2004.

Vol. 3254: E. Macii, V. Paliouras, O. Koufopavlou (Eds.), Integrated Circuit and System Design. XVI, 910 pages. 2004.

Vol. 3253: Y. Lakhnech, S. Yovine (Eds.), Formal Techniques, Modelling and Analysis of Timed and Fault-Tolerant Systems. X, 397 pages. 2004.

Vol. 3252: H. Jin, Y. Pan, N. Xiao, J. Sun (Eds.), Grid and Cooperative Computing - GCC 2004 Workshops. XVIII, 785 pages. 2004.

Vol. 3251: H. Jin, Y. Pan, N. Xiao, J. Sun (Eds.), Grid and Cooperative Computing - GCC 2004. XXII, 1025 pages. 2004.

Vol. 3250: L.-J. (LJ) Zhang, M. Jeckle (Eds.), Web Services. X, 301 pages. 2004.

Vol. 3249: B. Buchberger, J.A. Campbell (Eds.), Artificial Intelligence and Symbolic Computation. X, 285 pages. 2004. (Subseries LNAI).

Vol. 3246: A. Apostolico, M. Melucci (Eds.), String Processing and Information Retrieval. XIV, 332 pages. 2004.

Vol. 3245: E. Suzuki, S. Arikawa (Eds.), Discovery Science. XIV, 430 pages. 2004. (Subseries LNAI).

Vol. 3244: S. Ben-David, J. Case, A. Maruoka (Eds.), Algorithmic Learning Theory. XIV, 505 pages. 2004. (Subseries LNAI).

Vol. 3243: S. Leonardi (Ed.), Algorithms and Models for the Web-Graph. VIII, 189 pages. 2004.

Vol. 3242: X. Yao, E. Burke, J.A. Lozano, J. Smith, J.J. Merelo-Guervós, J.A. Bullinaria, J. Rowe, P. Tiño, A. Kabán, H.-P. Schwefel (Eds.), Parallel Problem Solving from Nature - PPSN VIII. XX, 1185 pages. 2004.

Vol. 3241: D. Kranzlmüller, P. Kacsuk, J.J. Dongarra (Eds.), Recent Advances in Parallel Virtual Machine and Message Passing Interface. XIII, 452 pages. 2004.

Vol. 3240: I. Jonassen, J. Kim (Eds.), Algorithms in Bioinformatics. IX, 476 pages. 2004. (Subseries LNBI).

Vol. 3239: G. Nicosia, V. Cutello, P.J. Bentley, J. Timmis (Eds.), Artificial Immune Systems. XII, 444 pages. 2004.

Vol. 3238: S. Biundo, T. Frühwirth, G. Palm (Eds.), KI 2004: Advances in Artificial Intelligence. XI, 467 pages. 2004. (Subseries LNAI).

Vol. 3236: M. Núñez, Z. Maamar, F.L. Pelayo, K. Pousttchi, F. Rubio (Eds.), Applying Formal Methods: Testing, Performance, and M/E-Commerce. XI, 381 pages. 2004.

Vol. 3235: D. de Frutos-Escrig, M. Nunez (Eds.), Formal Techniques for Networked and Distributed Systems – FORTE 2004. X, 377 pages. 2004.

Vol. 3234: M.J. Egenhofer, C. Freksa, H.J. Miller (Eds.), Geographic Information Science. VIII, 345 pages. 2004.

Vol. 3233: K. Futatsugi, F. Mizoguchi, N. Yonezaki (Eds.), Software Security - Theories and Systems. X, 345 pages. 2004.

Vol. 3232: R. Heery, L. Lyon (Eds.), Research and Advanced Technology for Digital Libraries. XV, 528 pages. 2004.

Vol. 3231: H.-A. Jacobsen (Ed.), Middleware 2004. XV, 514 pages. 2004.

Vol. 3230: J.L. Vicedo, P. Martínez-Barco, R. Muñoz, M. Saiz Noeda (Eds.), Advances in Natural Language Processing. XII, 488 pages. 2004. (Subseries LNAI).

Vol. 3229: J.J. Alferes, J. Leite (Eds.), Logics in Artificial Intelligence. XIV, 744 pages. 2004. (Subseries LNAI).

Vol. 3226: M. Bouzeghoub, C. Goble, V. Kashyap, S. Spaccapietra (Eds.), Semantics of a Networked World. XIII, 326 pages. 2004.

Vol. 3225: K. Zhang, Y. Zheng (Eds.), Information Security. XII, 442 pages. 2004.

Vol. 3224: E. Jonsson, A. Valdes, M. Almgren (Eds.), Recent Advances in Intrusion Detection. XII, 315 pages. 2004.

Vol. 3223: K. Slind, A. Bunker, G. Gopalakrishnan (Eds.), Theorem Proving in Higher Order Logics. VIII, 337 pages. 2004.

Vol. 3222: H. Jin, G.R. Gao, Z. Xu, H. Chen (Eds.), Network and Parallel Computing. XX, 694 pages. 2004.

Vol. 3221: S. Albers, T. Radzik (Eds.), Algorithms – ESA 2004. XVIII, 836 pages. 2004.

Vol. 3220: J.C. Lester, R.M. Vicari, F. Paraguaçu (Eds.), Intelligent Tutoring Systems. XXI, 920 pages. 2004.

Vol. 3219: M. Heisel, P. Liggesmeyer, S. Wittmann (Eds.), Computer Safety, Reliability, and Security. XI, 339 pages. 2004.

Vol. 3217: C. Barillot, D.R. Haynor, P. Hellier (Eds.), Medical Image Computing and Computer-Assisted Intervention – MICCAI 2004, Part II. XXXVIII, 1114 pages. 2004.